PARTNERS
IN CRIME

PARTNERS IN CRIME

THE CLINTONS' SCHEME TO MONETIZE
THE WHITE HOUSE FOR PERSONAL PROFIT

JEROME R. CORSI, PH.D.

 WND Books

PARTNERS IN CRIME

Published by WND Books, Washington, DC WND Books is a registered trademark of WorldNetDaily.com, Inc. ("WND").

Cover by Vi Yen Nguyen

WND Books are available at special discounts for bulk purchases. WND Books also publishes books in electronic formats. For more information call (541) 474-1776, e-mail orders@wndbooks.com or visit www.wndbooks.com.

Hardcover ISBN: 978-1-944229-33-7
eBook ISBN: 978-1-944229-34-4

Library of Congress Cataloging-in-Publication Data
Names: Corsi, Jerome R., author.
Title: Partners in crime : the Clintons' scheme to monetize the White House for personal profit / Jerome R. Corsi, Ph.D.
Description: Washington, DC : WND Books, 2016. | Includes bibliographical references and index. | Description based on print version record and CIP data provided by publisher; resource not viewed.
Identifiers: LCCN 2016020894 (print) | LCCN 2016010875 (ebook) | ISBN 9781944229344 (ebook) | ISBN 9781944229337 (hardcover : alk. paper)
Subjects: LCSH: Clinton, Bill, 1946---Finance, Personal. | Clinton, Hillary Rodham--Finance, Personal. | William J. Clinton Presidential Foundation. | Political corruption--United States.
Classification: LCC E886.2 (print) | LCC E886.2 .C67 2016 (ebook) | DDC 364.1/323--dc23
LC record available at https://lccn.loc.gov/2016020894

Printed in the United States of America
16 17 18 19 20 21 LBM 9 8 7 6 5 4 3 2 1

33614057642539

FOR DINESH D'SOUZA

WITH GREAT RESPECT FOR THE COURAGE HE CONTINUES TO DEMONSTRATE
CHAMPIONING AMERICA

TABLE OF CONTENTS

ACKNOWLEDGMENTS

My interest in the Clinton Foundation as a criminal enterprise began when my longtime New York associate Charles Ortel brought to my attention his research on the Clinton Foundation financial statements. Ortel, a well-known Wall Street analyst and private investor, has a long history of financial analytic work that, while often controversial, has generally been devastating in its conclusions and consequences.

Ortel, a frequent guest on Bloomberg television and a contributor to several print and Internet publications, including the *Washington Times*, began his Wall Street career working from June 1980 through July 2002 with Dillon, Read & Co., followed by the Bridgeford Group and the Chart Group. His international investment expertise frequently involves complex legal and financial structures in many different countries. He is currently managing director of Newport Value Partners, which provides independent investment research to professional investors.[1] He is a graduate of the Horace Mann School, Yale College, and the Harvard Business School. In an article published on August 4, 2009, citing financial analysis for which Ortel is perhaps best known on Wall Street, *Forbes* magazine noted that Ortel first broadcast his concerns about General Electric's earnings in 2008, when the stock was trading above $30 a share, compared to the date of publication, when GE's market value had plunged by about $200 billion, to $13 a share.[2]

On April 22, 2015, I published in WND my first article featuring Ortel's analysis of the Clinton Foundation, titled "Wall Street Analyst Uncovers Clinton Foundation Fraud."[3] Over the next few months, I published more than twenty articles in WND detailing Ortel's ongoing research, reporting his conclusion that the Clinton Foundation is "a vast criminal conspiracy" the Clinton family and their close associates have perpetrated "to defraud the general public, enrich themselves and entrench their political influence."[4] Ortel was the first to elucidate to me the criminal enterprise described by state and federal charity laws as "inurement." It's a scheme designed by the operators of a philanthropy to defraud donors by diverting their funds from the stated charitable purpose to personally enrich themselves and their associates. Ortel's brilliant analysis is featured prominently in this book, with the work duly attributed to him. Readers with a background in financial analysis are invited to read Ortel's work directly, published on his website at CharlesOrtel.com.

I have been reporting on Dinesh D'Souza's documentary films and best-selling books for years. This book is dedicated to Dinesh. I attended his various criminal proceedings, including his sentencing hearing, in federal court in Lower Manhattan, reporting for WND. As a result, I have experienced firsthand what I conclude is selective criminal prosecution because he dared speak out and oppose Barack Obama, starting in 2008. With great courage and equanimity, Dinesh has suffered the intolerance of the far left currently leading the Democratic Party. The far left represented by Barack Obama and the Clintons has no compunctions about politicizing the IRS and the Department of Justice, violating the spirit and meaning of "equal justice under law." The Obama administration has allowed the Clintons to perpetrate a philanthropic criminal fraud of massive proportions, with the mainstream media complicit in lavishing praise on the "good works" accomplished, as if the Clinton Foundation were a legitimate charity. The IRS and DOJ have failed to be vigilant regarding regulatory filing deadlines, organizational structure, the legitimacy of audited financial statements, and a host of other irregularities that should have closed down the Clinton Foundation decades ago. At the same time, the Obama DOJ sought to incarcerate D'Souza for a technical offense that would have received an IRS fine and a DOJ reprimand, had only Dinesh made his inconsequential straw contribution to a Democrat running for office.

Peter Schweizer is another true hero of this book. For years, I have interviewed and reported on Peter as he has sought to expose political corruption of both Democrats and Republicans. My determination to write this book intensified after Peter published his 2015 best-selling book, *Clinton Cash*.[5] The personal abuse the Clintons and their supporters heaped on Schweizer after the book's publication convinced me that the Clintons were up to their usual low-road modus operandi. Ad hominem insults were hurled against Peter precisely because the substance of what he was arguing was irrefutably true—so true that the Clintons could not afford politically the risk that the American public might read the book for themselves and see how accurately he had described the Clintons' criminal "get-rich-quick-and-often" scheme. This book adds new evidence to the many Clinton Foundation scams Peter first explored, providing added credibility to his accusation that the Clinton Foundation involves a massive "pay-to-play" bribery scheme in which seven-figure charitable donations and six-figure speaker's fees were sought in return for favorable policy decisions engineered by a secretary of state running the Clinton Foundation via a private e-mail server, in direct violation of national security laws.

Over the years, I have interviewed investigative reporter Ed Klein many times, and I always find his inside information to be accurate, even if often highly controversial. In writing his 2014 best-selling book *Blood Feud*,[6] Ed opened my eyes to the depth of the enmity between the Obamas and the Clintons that stems from the 2008 campaign. During that campaign, it was Hillary Clinton "hatchet man" Sidney Blumenthal who began circulating underground the research he had accumulated exposing Obama's largely undocumented past. Ed's 2015 best-selling book *Unlikeable*[7] provided an eye-opening account of the inner workings of the Clinton family and the Clinton Foundation that aided me greatly in understanding how the criminal husband-and-wife team operated.

Tom Fitton, president of Judicial Watch, has been a stalwart friend since 2004, when I coauthored with John O'Neill the Swift Boat book that confronted John Kerry's presidential campaign.[8] Tom has been a dogged researcher, and without Judicial Watch, many of the fundamental disclosures underpinning the central arguments of this book would not have been possible. Like Tom, Joe diGenova has played an important role in Washington as a former Justice Department insider. Joe's insights about the FBI criminal investigation of Hillary Clinton's private e-mail server at the Department of State was critical in understanding how the e-mails—largely unearthed through Judicial Watch FOIA lawsuits—morphed inevitably into an investigation of the Clinton family criminal exploitation of the Clinton Foundation through various "pay-to-play" schemes.

Roger Stone, another long-term associate whom I have interviewed repeatedly, added with his 2015 best seller *The Clintons' War on Women* a deeper understanding of how Hillary worked overtime, even as secretary of state, to cover up alleged sexual abuse by her husband.[9] Stone, who worked in the White House with presidents Nixon and Reagan, has added new dimensions to my understanding of how central the Clinton Foundation has been to the Clintons' ability to pay off those with firsthand knowledge of Bill's sexual behavior.

Finally, WND founder and CEO Joseph Farah was the first to urge me to write this book. Since 2004, I have worked at WND under his direction and guidance, grateful also for the insight and encouragement of WND cofounder Elizabeth Farah. Once again, I want to express in print my gratitude to Joseph and Elizabeth, not only for a dozen years of friendship, but also for their always-thoughtful advice and counsel.

Finally, this book would not have been possible without the hard work and dedication of WND Books's excellent staff, under the direction of Geoffrey Stone.

PREFACE

In *Partners in Crime*, my goal is to present the various Clinton Foundation criminal scams, with each narrative backed up by detailed research, extensive footnoting largely from mainstream media and government sources, and expert testimony, proving beyond a shadow of a doubt that the Clinton Foundation is "a vast, criminal conspiracy,"[1] and "a slush fund for grifters."[2] From taking over the governor's office in Little Rock to lying their way to the White House to skimming money from their lucrative foundation, the Clintons are known for criminal behavior.

The Clintons have advanced a criminal scheme since leaving the White House in 2000 that has enabled them to amass hundreds of millions of dollars in personal net worth, while building a $2 billion empire in the Clinton Foundation and raising an additional $1 billion to fund their political campaigns, including Hillary's second run for the presidency. The victims are countless thousands of honest people who contributed their hard-earned money to what they thought were philanthropic causes, while the Clintons used the Clinton Foundation to exploit for their personal profit impoverished millions in the United States and around the world, victims of earthquakes in India and Haiti, and sufferers of HIV/AIDS in the Third World.

Copying the World Economic Forum in Davos, Switzerland, the Clintons have held since 2005 the Clinton Global Initiative annual meeting in New York City as a personal public relations show funded by diverting philanthropic contributions. It's a stage for Bill, Hillary, and Chelsea to promote leftist ideologies, including climate change and "sustainability."

Partners in Crime recounts how the Clinton family has diverted money from the Clinton Foundation to subsidize their global, five-star, luxury travel lifestyle. In the process, the Clintons have partnered with some of the most questionable criminal exploiters of Third World misery and with international philanderers who subsidize Bill Clinton's sex exploits in offshore hideaways known both as "Orgy Island," or alternatively, as "Lolita Island."

Partners in Crime provides additional evidence to support the charges of "pay-to-play" offenses, commonly known as "bribery," that Peter Schweizer made in his book *Clinton Cash*. Advancing Schweizer's indictment, I argue here that the Clintons are also guilty of the crime known as "inurement," the diversion of charitable funds for the Clintons' personal profit, as well as for the financial gain of top aides and associates, including Doug Band, Ira Magaziner, Cheryl Mills, and Huma Abedin.

Along with a technical analysis of Clinton Foundation accounting fraud and a recounting of the organization's history of lying to federal and state regulators, *Partners in Crime* offers a gripping narrative of Clinton scams, spanning the globe from the Caribbean to Kazakhstan to Canada. The various scams discussed in the book demonstrated exactly how Bill and Hillary schemed to monetize the White House and utilize Hillary's position as secretary of state to win lucrative deals and six-figure speaking fees for Bill Clinton.

The sordid tale includes suspicion of Enron-like fraudulent accounting practices by none less than "Big Four" accounting firm PricewaterhouseCoopers. *Partners in Crime* reveals how Bill Clinton created "shell corporations" and "pass-through" bank accounts to hide millions of dollars he passed through secret corporations largely unknown to the American public, thinly disguised by a creative use of his William Jefferson Clinton initials to devise WJC LLC, WJC Investments, and WJC International Investments. The shell corporations also turned out to be convenient hiding places for the stock-option and percentage-participation side deals Bill Clinton cut in the process of providing favors to Clinton Foundation donors, including access to his wife via her private e-mail server for favorable public policy decisions at the State Department.

Not satisfied with the hundreds of millions the Clintons have made with Hillary as secretary of state, they are eyeing the billions to be made should Hillary win the White House in 2016. Already, Bill and Hillary have positioned Chelsea as the future Clinton Foundation chief operating officer, in training to advance the foundation criminal scheme to the next generation.

As the book concludes, I stress that many well-known donors, including Donald Trump, have the standing to file civil and criminal lawsuits against the Clinton Foundation. Trump and others who contributed generously to the Clinton Foundation could allege in lawsuits that they were defrauded by the Clintons into believing the foundation was a legitimate charity, not a criminal scheme in which some or all of their generous donations were diverted to the personal profit of the Clinton family and their close associates.

Partners in Crime concludes by providing readers the names and addresses of state attorneys general throughout the country, explaining that donors to the Clinton Foundation may file complaints with the attorney general in the state from which the contribution was made. Any one attorney general in any state in the Union can get a temporary restraining order from a state judge to call a stop to the Clinton Foundation nationwide, simply by placing the Clinton Foundation in receivership until the state attorney general seeking the temporary restraining order from a state judge has the time required to conduct a thorough law enforcement examination of Clinton family philanthropic fraud accomplished not just in the state bringing the action, but also on a global scale.

I wrote *Partners in Crime* to encourage all patriotic and law-abiding Americans to understand it is not enough for Hillary Clinton to withdraw from the 2016 presidential race in disgrace. A national campaign to "Shut Down the Clinton Foundation" must be launched, even if Hillary is indicted for criminal charges or drops out of the presidential election for other reasons. The goal of this book ultimately is to prevent Barack Obama and other heads of state worldwide from following the Clinton family crime formula to create their own "charitable foundations" to enrich themselves after they leave office.

PART ONE

CRIMINAL PHILANTHROPY— CLINTON-STYLE

Although estimates vary, it is acknowledged that each year charitable fraud is a multi-million dollar business.

—NEW YORK SCHOOL OF LAW REVIEW, 1988

Part 1 consists of three chapters, each of which presents vignettes that question whether the Clinton Foundation is a legitimate charity or a massive criminal fraud designed to operate as a private piggy bank for Clinton family members and their friends.

The evidence cited in each of the three snapshots makes clear that the Clintons are driven by insatiable greed, justified by a sense of being always near broke that is difficult for the average American today to understand. Displaying a willingness to engage in behavior involving questionable ethics, the Clintons have devised "get-rich schemes" that extend somehow even to justify leaving the White House at the end of the Clinton presidency by walking off with the White House silverware.

At the heart of the Clintons' drive for riches in the post-presidency is the Clinton Foundation, a philanthropic foundation the Clintons appear to use as a personal piggy bank.

Chapter 3 ends with a discussion that forms the first part of the "India scams," which are revisited in chapter 8. From a supposedly well-intentioned desire to help the victims of a devastating earthquake in India, Bill Clinton partnered with India-born Americans whose criminal behavior have two of them now in federal prison. Meanwhile, the American India Foundation, cofounded by Clinton, continues to raise millions in widely publicized gala events held in many states where the foundation is not registered as a charity.

1

CRYING POOR

We came out of the White House . . . dead broke.   —HILLARY CLINTON

In a television interview with ABC News on June 9, 2014,[1] Diane Sawyer posed to Hillary Clinton: "It has been reported you've made $5 million making speeches, the president's made more than $100 million."

"Well, if you—you have no reason to remember, but we came out of the White House not only dead broke, but in debt," Hillary responded.

"We had no money when we got there and we struggled to, you know, piece together the resources for mortgages for houses, for Chelsea's education, you know, it was not easy," she continued.

"Bill has worked really hard and it's been amazing to me," Hillary pleaded. "He's worked very hard, first of all, we had to pay off all our debts which was, you know, we had to make double the money because of obviously taxes, and pay you have at debts, and get us houses and take care of family members."

Not satisfied with the response, Sawyer pressed forward, asking, "But do you think Americans will understand five times the median income in this country for one speech?"

"Well, let me put it this way: I thought making speeches for money

3

was a much better thing than getting connected with any one group or company as so many people who leave public life do," Hillary claimed, insinuating remarkably that the Clintons had selected the lesser of available evils by accepting outrageously high speaking fees that bore the appearance of influence buying, rather than going to work for a legitimate business corporation after leaving the presidency.

"SCORCHED-EARTH LEGAL WARFARE"

Bill Clinton's departure from the White House was arguably one of the low points in his life and the history of the US presidency. On January 20, 2001, inauguration day, the *New York Times* characterized this last day of Bill Clinton's presidency as "a stunning end to the long melodrama and pitched legal battles" over his relationship with a White House intern.[2] The day before, Robert Ray, the head of the Office of Independent Counsel who had been investigating whether to charge Clinton with various crimes including perjury, reached a settlement with Clinton under which Clinton agreed he had lied under oath in the Paula Jones sexual misconduct case about his sexual affair with Monica Lewinsky, who was then a White House intern, with Clinton accepting a five-year suspension of his law license in exchange for avoiding criminal prosecution.[3]

On January 19, 2001, in Pulaski County, Arkansas, where Clinton faced a trial after he left office on charges brought by a bar committee that he was unfit to practice law, a circuit court judge accepted a $25,000 fine Bill Clinton paid to the Arkansas Bar Association in lieu of disbarment for having lied under oath that he "did not have sex with that woman," Monica Lewinsky.[4]

Three years earlier, Bill Clinton settled for $850,000 the Paula Jones lawsuit in which Jones agreed to drop the sexual harassment lawsuit she had pursued after "more than 4 ½ years of scorched-earth legal warfare."[5]

In response to Hillary's protestation of poverty upon leaving the White House, the Associated Press reported the Clintons faced legal bills, possibly as high as $10.6 million, incurred defending themselves in the Whitewater affair and the Monica Lewinsky scandal. This did not include the legal expenses the Clintons incurred to settle the Paula Jones lawsuit and to suppress what the media came to characterize as Bill Clinton's "bimbo-eruptions," including Kathleen Willey's claim that she was sexually assaulted by Bill Clinton in the Oval Office on November 29, 1993,[6] and the twelve-year sexual affair with Gennifer Flowers, dating back to his time as Arkansas attorney general.[7]

Predictably, the GOP pushed back against Hillary's protestation of poverty upon leaving the White House. "I think she's been out of touch with average people for a long time," Republican National Committee chairman Reince Priebus told the AP. "Whether she was flat broke or not is not the issue. It's tone deaf to average people."[8]

"CRYING POOR"

The AP also reported that Hillary had received an $8 million book advance in December 2000 from Simon & Schuster for the 2003 publication of her memoirs, *Living History*.[9]

PolitiFact pointed out that in 1999, the Clintons bought a five-bedroom home in Chappaqua, New York, for $1.7 million. Then, in December 2000, just as they were leaving the White House, they bought a seven-bedroom house near Embassy Row in Washington, DC, for a closing price of $2.85 million, on which they put $855,000 down.[10]

Hillary gave an exclusive interview in 2014 on ABC's *Good Morning America* with Robin Roberts, in which she walked back her earlier statement by noting that to repay the debt she and Bill Clinton faced after leaving the White House, the couple had to "keep working really hard" in the years that followed.[11]

"As I recall we were something like $12 million in debt," Hillary explained to Roberts, referring to the hefty legal bills the couple faced after Bill Clinton's second term.

"What we faced when he got out of the White House meant that we just had to keep working really hard," she added.

It is worth remembering that Bill Clinton complains he entered the presidency poor. "I think I had the lowest net worth of any American president in the 20th century, when I took office," he lamented to host David Gregory during an NBC *Meet the Press* show that aired June 29, 2014. PolitiFact rated the claim as "Half True," noting that Harry Truman entered the White House poorer, due, in part, to "money problems and bankruptcy-dodging" as a result of a failed haberdashery business.[12]

The reality is, the Clintons left the White House some $10 million in debt, a deficit that was largely avoidable if Bill Clinton had remained faithful to his wife. The other reality, obvious from Hillary's comments to ABC News, is that the Clintons feel money-deprived, analyzing their debt leaving the White House without balancing it against assets that allowed them to buy lavish private homes for their life outside 1600 Pennsylvania Avenue.

"HOW DID THEY GET SO RICH?"

Forbes reporter Agustino Fontevecchia puzzled over how Bill and Hillary Clinton, who "left the White House essentially broke in 2001," managed to make what he estimates to be $230 million "over the next 14 years through speaking engagements, book deals and consulting gigs. To our own astonishment," he wrote, speaking for himself and fellow staff writer Dan Alexander, "their latest public disclosure lists a maximum of $53 million in assets (we valued them at $45 million). The Clintons make it crystal clear that despite disclosure requirements by the Federal Election Commission and the Office of Government Ethics, and even adding voluntarily revealed tax filings, the relationship between money and power remains fraught with obscurity. To a certain extent, financial transparency is an illusion in Washington. Leaving the highest offices a public servant can aspire to, such as the Presidency or the State Department, can be exceptionally fruitful."[13]

Dan Alexander himself documented that since the Clintons left the White House in 2001, they have earned more than $250 million, with *Forbes* estimating their combined net worth is $45 million. "Where did all the money go?" he asked.

"From 2001 to 2014 the power couple spent $95 million on taxes," Alexander wrote. "Hillary's 2008 presidential run cost her $13 million. Their two homes cost a combined $5 million, and the Clintons have given away $22 million to charity. All of this is according to FEC filings, property records and years of tax returns. Add it up and you get $135 million. If the Clintons made $230 million, spent $135 million and have just $45 million left over, what happened to the other $50 million? . . .

"Where could that much money have disappeared?" Alexander continued. "The Clintons did not respond to repeated requests for comment. Others were just as perplexed as we were."

"I don't see how that would be possible," Jeff Mussatt, a certified financial planner who helped put together the financial disclosures for Republican presidential candidate Jim Gilmore, told Alexander. "That's quite a mystery you have on your hands."[14]

These discrepancies in how the Clintons report about their money—how they got the money, how much they have, and what happened to the amount they admit accumulating—are the central themes of this book, especially as regards the Clinton Foundation.

STEALING THE WHITE HOUSE CHINA

In February 2002, at the conclusion of a yearlong investigation, the House Government Reform Committee concluded that the Clintons took $360,000 worth of large gifts with them when they left the White House in January 2001.[15]

The *Washington Post* reported that among the gifts at issue were two sofas, an easy chair, an ottoman worth $19,900 from a New York furniture maker, a $2,843 sofa from Henredon, and a $3,650 breakfast set.[16]

According to the AP, the Clintons protested that seventeen gifts of china, cutlery, and furniture worth more than $75,000 arrived in December 2000 alone, at a time when the Clintons were looking to furnish their two newly purchased homes, one in Chappaqua, New York, and the other in Washington.[17]

Interestingly, the AP reported that Clinton confidant Bruce Lindsey refused to testify at the House Government Reform Committee investigation.[18] Lindsey joined the Clinton Foundation in 2001 as general counsel and served as CEO from 2003 to 2013, according to a biography on the Clinton Foundation website.[19] He currently serves as the foundation's chairman of the board.

Lindsey was an assistant and a deputy counsel to the president throughout Clinton's two terms in office. In 1993, he was also director of the Office of Presidential Personnel, where he supervised the selection and approval of political appointees in the Cabinet departments and to presidential boards and commissions. During the 1992 presidential campaign, he served as Bill Clinton's national campaign director. He previously was a partner at Wright Lindsey Jennings law firm in Little Rock, Arkansas, where he remains of counsel.[20]

Amid protests that continued into 2002 alleging the Clintons had stolen national treasures from the White House inner sanctum, including from the Lincoln Bedroom, the Clintons decided to resolve the controversy by making a settlement with the federal government. Bill and Hillary agreed to send $28,000 worth of household goods back to Washington and pay $86,000 for gifts.

CLINTON, INC.

It should not be surprising that Bill and Hillary sought to monetize the White House by stealing gifts and furniture on their departure. Clinton watcher Daniel Halper in his 2014 book, *Clinton, Inc.*, provides ample evidence that the Clinton "marriage" was never as much about love and sex as it was about power and money.

"It is commonly said that marriages are in many ways like business partnerships," Halper wrote. "And after thirty-eight years of marriage, that is what the Clintons are these days: dueling CEOs of a multimillion-dollar empire, Clinton, Inc."[21]

Still, the Clintons as individual citizens are subject to federal and state laws, as are all American citizens. But the Clintons as founders and principals, and Hillary as a sometimes director of the Clinton

Foundation, bear additional responsibilities. They are obliged by state and federal law to operate their foundation as a legitimate charity, taking pains not to enrich themselves and their associates, but instead, to make sure the organization serves only the charitable purposes the IRS determines in writing are acceptable.

Included among the operational responsibilities are the legal requirements to register as a charity with the federal government and with the states in which the foundation operates, along with the timely filing of audited financial reports, IRS tax Form 990s, and other regulatory documents as specified by federal and state law.

Claims to having been cash-poor, even if once true, and discrepancies between public statements of net worth and sums reported in tax filings, even if resulting from honest error, cannot under applicable laws and regulations be used to excuse errors and irregularities in preparing audited financial reports and filing required regulatory forms.

What we must never forget, regardless of how poor the Clintons may cry they once were, or how justified they may feel in becoming wealthy today, is that the Clinton Foundation has an importance beyond the Clintons themselves.

If we demonstrate in this book that the wealth the Clintons currently enjoy has derived even in part by fraudulently diverting charitable donations to personal enrichment, the legal consequences should be immediate and severe, including the filing of criminal charges on the state and federal level.

Ultimately, what is at stake in this inquiry regarding whether or not the Clinton Foundation is a legitimate charity is not precisely Hillary Clinton's future political career, but the paramount importance of preserving the integrity of charitable giving in the United States and abroad.

"I GOTTA PAY OUR BILLS . . ."

On May 4, 2014, NBC reporter Cynthia McFadden asked Bill Clinton, then in Africa for the foundation, to respond to critics, noting he had been paid $500,000 or more for eleven speeches he made while his wife was secretary of state. "I gotta pay our bills," Clinton explained. "I spend a couple of hours a day just doing the research. People like to hear me speak."[22]

Predictably, the comment set off a wave of criticism. Mike Halperin, cohost of Bloomberg's *With All Due Respect*, told cohost John Heilemann, "I can't understand the things he said."

Heilemann agreed. "Just all of these things—you think that it's Hillary Clinton who is tone deaf when she says we were dead broke when we came out of the White House. This is the same thing," he said. "It's like up in Chappaqua—the gas bills, the electric bills . . . this is why I have to give a half-million dollar speech. It's ridiculous."[23]

Jennifer Rubin, author of the *Washington Post's Right Turn* blog, was equally incredulous.

"On one level, who can be surprised?" Rubin asked in May 2015. "The idea of 'enough is enough' does not cross the Clintons' minds, nor do they understand the notion of foregoing personal enrichment. On the other hand, the degree to which average people may find their conduct piggish may be underestimated. You do wonder how long her Democratic opponents will resist attacking them both for their excess and their disdain for ethical boundaries."[24]

Yes, we do wonder …

2
PROFITING IN INDIA

I intend to come back to India for the rest of my life.   —BILL CLINTON

On January 26, 2001, six days after Bill Clinton left the White House and the day India celebrated its fifty-second Republic Day, the western part of the nation suffered one of the worst earthquakes in history.

The quake, which began at 8:46 a.m. local time, lasted more than two minutes and killed more than 19,727 people, with 166,000 injured, and property damage estimated at more than $4.5 billion. Registering a massive 7.9 on the Richter scale, it produced more than five hundred aftershocks, lasting until March and destroying twenty-one of the twenty-five districts in India's state of Gujarat, according to the Indian Metrology Department.[1]

It also was the third anniversary of the day Bill Clinton went on national television to explain, red-faced and right index finger wagging, a statement he came to regret, regarding what then was only alleged as a sexual affair with Monica Lewinsky.

"I want to say one thing to the American people. I want you to listen to me. I'm going to say this again: I did not have sexual relations with that woman, Miss Lewinsky," Clinton famously insisted.[2]

"SERIOUSLY CONCERNED"

One week after the earthquake, on February 1, 2001, Bill Clinton spoke over the phone with Indian prime minister Atal Bihari Vajpayee to see what he might do to assist the earthquake victims in India.

Indian news reports quoted Prime Minister Vajpayee concerning the telephone call: "'I told [Bill Clinton] that NRIs in the U.S. could be asked to adopt and rebuild affected villages,' he said, adding that despite his not remaining in office, Clinton was seriously concerned over the situation in Gujarat."[3]

NRIs are nonresident Indian citizens traveling on an Indian passport who temporarily live in a foreign country for six months or more, typically for education or employment. Indian-born immigrants to the United States are one of the fastest-growing immigrant populations, increasing from only 12,000 in 1960 to an estimated 1 million in 2000, making NRIs the third largest group of immigrants to the United States, behind only Mexicans and Chinese.[4]

In his 2007 book, *Giving: How Each of Us Can Change the World*, Bill Clinton recounted that Vajpayee told him the government could rebuild the larger areas but needed support for reconstruction of hundreds of smaller businesses.

Clinton said he knew many Indian Americans were already contributing individually to India to build hospitals, clinics, and schools, and to provide scholarships for worthy students. "After the earthquake many others were eager to join in," he observed. "Soon the American Indian Foundation was born, with a board of directors chaired by Rajat Gupta, senior partner of McKinsey and Company, and Victor Menezes, now retired senior vice chairman of Citigroup. The president is Lata Krishnan, an information technology entrepreneur from Northern California."[5]

AN ENORMOUS SUM OF MONEY

In the aftermath of leaving the White House, Clinton's reputation was racked not only by sexual scandals but by a last-hour pardon to the swashbuckling commodities trader, hedge fund manager, and notorious tax evader Marc Rich. Clinton pardoned Rich despite the fact Rich had fled to Switzerland to escape indictment in the United States for, among other criminal charges, tax evasion and illegally trading with Iran while American embassy personnel were still being held hostage in Tehran. Rich received the controversial pardon from Clinton on January 20, 2001, Clinton's last day as president. Despite the pardon, Rich never returned to the United States before his death on June 26, 2013, at seventy-eight years of age.

The Rich scandal involved Denise Joy Eisenberg, a songwriter for a long list of prominent singers, including Aretha Franklin, Natalie Cole, and Diana Ross. She married Marc Rich in 1966 and divorced him thirty years later, after they had three children together. In 1998, Denise Rich helped bundle a $450,000 contribution to what was then known as the William J. Clinton Presidential Foundation to help fund the building of the Clinton presidential library. According to the *Washington Post*, the contributions were made in three payments, from July 1998 to May 2000, at the urging of her friend Beth Dozoretz, then well known as a major Democratic Party fund-raiser.

The *Washington Post* further reported on February 10, 2001, that Denise Rich's attorney, Carol Bruce, told a House Government Reform Committee hearing on the Marc Rich pardon that her client gave "an enormous sum of money" to the Clinton library fund, but the amount and timing of the gifts were not disclosed. The newspaper added that Dozoretz spoke with Bill Clinton ten days before he pardoned Marc Rich, while she and Denise Rich were visiting Aspen, Colorado.

The article also noted that Grammy- and Oscar-nominated songwriter Denise Rich had "in recent years" donated $867,000 to Democratic Party Committees, $66,300 to individual Democratic candidates, and $70,000 to a fund established for the Senate campaign of Hillary Clinton, according to records obtained from the Center for Responsive Politics. Additionally, she had given $10,000 to the Clinton legal defense fund, while donating to Bill and Hillary furniture worth $7,375. "E-mail messages released by the House committee make repeated mentions of Denise

Rich's role in seeking a pardon for her ex-husband, including several that indicate Marc Rich's attorneys believe she could persuade the president," wrote *Washington Post* reporter James Grimaldi.[6]

It is worth noting that reporter Josh Gerstein, writing for Politico in August 2014, noted that key documents pertaining to the Marc Rich pardon remain under seal at the Clinton Library, hidden from public view yet today.[7]

DESIGN, CONSTRUCTION, AND ENDOWMENT

Key here is to understand that when the William J. Clinton Presidential Foundation was created in 1997, its sole purpose was to solicit charitable donations to build the Clinton presidential library.

On January 29, 1998, an IRS "determination letter" notified the William J. Clinton Presidential Foundation that, based on the foundation's application for recognition of tax exemption, the William J. Clinton Presidential Foundation was permitted to accept tax-exempt donations as a 501(c)(3) organization.[8]

The William J. Clinton Presidential Foundation submitted to the IRS the application for permission to allow charitable donors to make tax-deductible contributions on December 23, 1997, IRS Form 1023, which the IRS describes as "an application for recognition of tax-exemption." The submitted Form 1023 makes clear the only purpose for which the foundation was applying to the IRS for tax-exempt status was for the design, construction, and endowment of the Clinton Presidential archival depository, otherwise known as the Clinton Library.[9]

HONORARY CHAIR

The website of the American India Foundation, AIF, attributes the formation of the group not solely to Rajat Gupta, Victor Menezes, and Lata Krishnan, but to Bill Clinton as well. "Amid the tragic devastation caused by the Gujarat earthquake in 2001, President Bill Clinton and Prime Minister of India Atal Bihari Vajpayee recognized the need for a philanthropy platform that would connect the world's two largest democracies and provide a trusted bridge for meaningful participation in India's democratic and economic growth for both Americans and Indians," the AIF website notes.[10]

A *New York Times* article on April 5, 2001, reported that Rajat Gupta, then managing director of the international consulting firm McKinsey & Company, and Victor J. Menezes, the president and chief executive officer of Citibank, both identified as the AIF's two vice chairmen, "were among those who met with Mr. Clinton in early February to discuss what to do in response to the earthquake." *Times* reporter Celia W. Dugger further noted that by April 4, 2001, Clinton had joined Gupta in a trip to India.[11]

A *Times of India* report on August 24, 2003, titled "Clinton's India Connection" provided a similar story regarding the seminal role Bill Clinton played in creating the AIF in the aftermath of India's 2001 earthquake. "The senior vice-chairman of Citigroup, recalls receiving a phone call from Bill Clinton soon after the Gujarat earthquake."

The story noted that Clinton asked Menezes to help galvanize the Indian American community to aid victims of the disaster. "Menezes promptly made a couple of calls to his friends and the first meeting of the American India Foundation was held at the Citigroup Centre in New York," the *Times of India* story concluded. "Clinton is incredibly focused on building a bridge between the U.S. and India, and the non-resident Indian community in the U.S.," Menezes explained to his friends.[12]

Even today, the AIF still lists Bill Clinton as its "honorary chair."[13]

SCANDAL-TINGED EXIT

In her 2001 article, quoted earlier, *New York Times* reporter Celia Dugger noted that the scandals at the end of his presidency were the backdrop for Clinton's relief trip to India.

"Thousands of people, precariously balanced on mountains of rubble in this earthquake-ravaged town, chanted 'Clinton, Clinton!' as the former president toured the ruins today, solemnly laying roses in a lane where 150 schoolchildren were buried alive when the ground shook on Jan. 26," Dugger wrote. She continued:

> Bill Clinton, with his scandal-tinged exit from office, may elicit an exhausted sigh from many Americans, but here he still draws adoring throngs of ordinary Indians a year after he became the first American president to visit this country of one billion people in 22 years.
>
> And he basked in their affection today on the first full day of a week-long visit that will also take him to Bombay, Calcutta and New Delhi. At the devastated villages and towns he visited, Mr. Clinton ardently declared, "I intend to come back to India for the rest of my life."

Dugger noted that Clinton was then visiting India as "the chairman of the new American India Foundation," commenting that wealthy Indian-American entrepreneurs, executives, and doctors formed the AIF.

"They have set themselves a goal of raising $50 million to rebuild 100 of the 1,000 villages that were more than 50 percent destroyed by the earthquake here in the western state of Gujarat," the *New York Times* story stressed. "So far, they said they had collected more than $8 million."[14]

On April 4, 2001, *India Abroad* reporter K G Suresh described cheering crowds wherever Clinton visited following the disaster.

"Storming quake-hit Kutch and sharing the people's grief, former U.S. president Bill Clinton on Wednesday promised a focused action plan incorporating education and employment opportunities to rebuild the region," Suresh wrote.

"The U.S.-based America India Foundation [*sic*], which was formed to help out the victims of the Gujarat quake, is organising Clinton's visit."

Suresh quoted Clinton as telling Indian crowds, "We thought we should meet people on the ground and decide whether to have a macro approach or to build schools and houses," noting that Clinton was accompanied in India by a forty-member delegation of influential U.S.-based NRIs. Suresh continued:

The former president who has brought with him keys to a $50 million fund put together by the American India Foundation to help quake victims visited Anjaar and Ratnal, a village completely devastated by the quake.

Holding hands of two survivors, he laid flowers at the spot in Anjaar where about 150 children participating in a Republic Day parade were buried alive when the buildings along the narrow lane in which they were walking collapsed on them.

About 3,000 people watched Clinton as he bowed his head for a moment in memory of those who perished.

Clinton went around the rubble-strewn streets of Bhuj, Ratnal and Anjaar, holding out his hands to children and others during his whirlwind five-hour tour of Kutch.[15]

Suman Guha Mozumder, an *India Abroad* correspondent working out of New York, described an American India Foundation gala dinner in New York "attended by a galaxy of Indian American entrepreneurs, professionals and academics" that raised $800,000 for the Gujarat earthquake victims. According to Mozumder, the approximately three hundred guests paid $4,000 per plate or $25,000 for a table of ten for the dinner in the sixty-fourth-floor Rainbow Room of the Rockefeller Plaza in Manhattan. "Although former president Bill Clinton, who is a member of the board of the AIF, was not present, the speakers mentioned him many a time," Mozumder reported.[16]

The Clinton Foundation has generated publicity and news stories regarding charitable donations raised for India from 2001 through today. A 2014 article from *India Real Time*, a blog of the *Wall Street Journal*, highlighted Clinton's weeklong trip to India to raise awareness about the health and food programs the Clinton Foundation was funding there.[17]

Wall Street analyst Charles Ortel has insisted that the title "honorary" chairman is misleading if one assumes Bill Clinton as honorary chairman had no detailed duties and expected minimal compensation. Clinton played a prominent role in creating AIF in 2001. Ortel pointed out AFI trustees and donors boasted openly of their connection to

Clinton and likely used their association with Clinton to boost their prestige and influence worldwide.

There is no evidence in Clinton Foundation public filings that Bill Clinton or the Clinton Foundation had IRS approval and legal authority to conduct earthquake relief efforts targeting victims in India, Ortel stresses. And there is no evidence of IRS approval and authority in key U.S. states to solicit donations from the general public, yet the foundation certainly did so, as the public record amply demonstrates.

Bill Clinton is and was a person "in position to exercise significant influence"[18] over the American India Foundation from February 2001 to present. Yet his role as AIF honorary chairman was never declared on Clinton Foundation IRS Tax Forms 990s from 2001 forward, despite IRS regulations requiring the disclosure of affiliated charitable activities. Nevertheless, with Bill Clinton's blessing, the AIF is a member in good standing of the Clinton Global Initiative.

A SECRET PIPELINE

On October 24, 2012, Rajat Gupta, a Clinton Foundation donor, was convicted in federal court and sentenced to two years in prison plus an additional year on supervised release and a $5 million fine for his role in a massive insider-trading scheme on Wall Street.[19]

Gupta is one of four former board members of the AIF to have been accused or convicted of insider trading, campaign finance violations, or other schemes, Alana Goodman of the *Washington Free Beacon* reported. Among the others are AIF former trustee Raj Rajaratnam, who was listed as AIF cochairman as recently as in 2010. Rajaratnam was forced to pay a criminal and civil penalty of over $150 million, and is currently serving an eleven-year sentence for the insider-trading scheme that took down the Galleon Group hedge funds in 2011. Goodman noted Rajaratnam's sentence was the longest ever handed down in an insider trader case, "for allegedly using illegal stock tips to amass a $63 million fortune."

Goodman further reported that Gupta's attorneys in a sentencing memo noted: "Rajat worked with former U.S. President Bill Clinton and Victor Menezes, former Senior Vice Chair of Citigroup, to found the American India Foundation (AIF). Under their leadership, within its first year AIF raised millions of dollars to support earthquake relief efforts."[20]

Given this history, it will be hard for Bill Clinton to distance himself from the American India Fund in Hillary's 2016 run for the White House. Clinton himself, writing in his 2007 book, *Giving*, openly acknowledged the AIF has been successful raising money, noting that in the aftermath of the Gujarat earthquake, the AIF quickly raised $4 million for the relief, reconstruction, and rehabilitation of victims in India.[21]

Michael Rothfeld of the *Wall Street Journal* reported in 2012 that beginning around 2003, Gupta and Rajaratnam began investing millions of dollars together in financial investments related to Galleon and in an Asia-focused private-equity fund Gupta had helped to start. Prosecutors alleged that Gupta "became a 'secret pipeline' to Rajaratnam from 2007 until early 2009, supplying to Rajaratnam at Galleon inside information that Gupta gained as a result of his membership on the boards of Goldman and Proctor & Gamble." Prosecutors argued Gupta "provided advance tips about, among other things, a $5 billion investment in Goldman by Warren Buffett's Berkshire Hathaway Inc., at the height of the financial crisis and the investment bank's first quarterly loss as a public company." For their involvement in the Galleon inside-trading scandal, both Rajaratnam and Gupta are in federal prison today.[22]

This brings us to another Gupta, namely, Vinod, yet another AIF board member. Vinod Gupta, who is not related to Rajat Gupta, collaborated with Rajat in forming AIF and was an early AIF board member. Vinod, CEO of InfoUSA, was charged by the Securities and Exchange Commission with misappropriating company funds to pay almost $9.5 million in personal expenses to support his lavish lifestyle, causing the company to enter into $9.3 million of undisclosed business transactions between InfoUSA and other companies in which he had a personal stake—an amount he was ultimately forced to pay back to the company. The SEC's complaints, filed in federal district court in Nebraska, alleged that from 2003 to 2007, Gupta improperly used corporate funds for more than $3 million worth of personal jet travel for himself, family, and friends to such destinations as South Africa, Italy, and Cancun. He also used investor money to pay $2.8 million in expenses related to his yacht; $1.3 million in personal credit card expenses; and other costs associated with twenty-eight club memberships, twenty automobiles, homes around the country, and three personal life insurance policies.[23] In 2010, Vinod Gupta stepped down as chairman and CEO of InfoGroup, agreeing to pay more than $7.3 million to settle U.S. Securities and Exchange Commission allegations that he improperly used the company "as a piggy bank."[24]

Jonathan Allen, in a January 29, 2015, Bloomberg News article titled "Hillary Clinton Faces Scrutiny for Use of Private Jets," reported that Hillary flew from White Plains, New York, to Washington to pick up top aide Huma Abedin on the way to Charleston, South Carolina, on December 30, 2005, according to records kept by the Senate. "They rode aboard InfoUSA's jet, which company founder Vinod Gupta, a close family friend, often used to transport and entertain the Clintons and other recognizable figures, according to court filings," Allen wrote. "Hillary Clinton billed the Senate for $858 to fly on his company's plane."

He went on to note that "Bill Clinton made more than $3 million as an adviser to InfoUSA after leaving the White House in January 2001 and also was given options on 100,000 shares of stock, which were never exercised."[25]

Bill McMorris, writing in the *Washington Free Beacon*, reported that Rajat Gupta "presented Bill Clinton with an opportunity to cash in on their relationship" in 2001.[26] In a deal secretly engineered by Gupta and Anil Kumar, a McKinsey consultant who later testified against Gupta in the criminal trial in which Gupta was found guilty of insider trading with Rajaratnam's Galleon hedge fund, Gupta and Kumar set up their own consulting company. Called Mindspirit it was registered in the names of their wives, Anita Gupta and Malvika Kumar, without disclosing to McKinsey that Rajat Gupta had an ownership of the consultancy. For advice that Mindspirit gave Vinod Gupta in his role as InfoGroup CEO, InfoGroup compensated Mindspirit with 200,000 stock options that Rajat Gupta and Kumar exercised for an undisclosed amount. According to an SEC filing that exposed the scam, Bill Clinton, the honorary chairman of the American India Fund, as part of the deal, was granted 100,000 InfoGroup stock options that Clinton claimed he never exercised.[27]

Additionally, McMorris reported, Clinton received $3.3 million from 2002 through 2008 for advising Vinod Gupta, during which time Clinton got the free personal use of Gupta's InfoGroup corporate jets for the entire Clinton family.[28] The SEC complaint against Vinod Gupta noted, "Former President Clinton and his family, and other prominent individuals made improper, personal use of the Company's private jets, and Vinod Gupta did not reimburse the Company. The consulting agreements executed between the Company and former President Clinton in 2002 and 2005 were without any consideration to the Company, and the agreements were arranged without Board or Committee approval."[29] Despite Vinod Gupta having to pay back $9.3 million to InfoUSA and $7.3 million to settle the SEC suit against him, he still managed to contribute between $1 million and $5 million to the Clinton Foundation, with his most recent contribution being in 2014, as reported by McMorris.

"Before his arrest, [Rajat] Gupta was a top player in Democratic circles with close personal ties to the Clintons," McMorris wrote. "He served as global managing director of consulting giant McKinsey & Company from 1994 to 2003 before the company's board removed him from the position and reduced his role to senior partner. On his way out the door he presented a 23-year-old Oxford graduate with no experience a six-figure consulting job."[30] Of course, that Oxford grad was Chelsea Clinton.

While the Clintons may want to represent their fund-raising efforts in India following the Gujarat earthquake as an exercise in noble sentiments, the record suggests opportunism might be the better explanation.

In 2001, Bill Clinton sided with India after the earthquake served for him the political purpose of rehabilitating the tarnished reputation with which he left the presidency. By stepping forward to be a cofounder of the American India Foundation, he used India and the earthquake to cloak himself in a philanthropic mantle that helped him change the channel on his public image as he transitioned back to private life. As we shall see in chapter 8, when the Clintons quickly realized how much money they could make working with India, it did not take long before they figured out their 501(c)(3) foundation could be put to better use if its purpose could be expanded from just building a presidential library in Little Rock. Chapter 8 will conclude with a reflection on Raj Rajaratnam and Rajat Gupta as convicted felons doing time at the same federal prison facility in Massachusetts.

$1 BILLION RAISED

On November 1, 2011, after Gupta was indicted on federal criminal charges of insider trading, *India West* published a report attempting to resurrect his tarnished reputation. The article disclosed that the American India Fund, with the assistance of cofounder Bill Clinton, had raised more than $1 billion to assist the victims of the Gujarat earthquake.[31]

A WND story in October 2015, "Clinton Foundation 'Fraud Began with Exploiting Earthquake,'" featured the sharp criticism of Ortel, who was then in the midst of conducting a comprehensive study of Clinton Foundation financial reports. Ortel alleged that Bill Clinton had developed a methodology of exploiting epidemics and natural disasters to raise hundreds of millions in "charitable donations" that in a relaxed regulatory environment could be diverted to personal gain, funding Hillary's political campaigns and supporting Democratic Party causes.

"The Clinton Foundation financial fraud began with the illegal disaster relief efforts started in February 2001, when Clinton started chasing donations for Gujarat, India, without IRS authorization and subsequently substantial funds went missing, diverted from helping disaster victims by a bevy of scoundrels, including Rajat Gupta, now incarcerated," Ortel wrote in a report published on his website, CharlesOrtel.com.

"All years from 2001 onward when the Clinton Foundation operated are not audited as required, so it is difficult to be precise, but total Clinton Foundation fraud runs to hundreds of millions of dollars," Ortel alleged to WND, "with diversions for political purposes and personal enrichment likely to exceed $200 million."

Ortel further charged that the American India Foundation had been operating flagrantly in violation of state, federal, and foreign laws since its inception in 2001. "Instead of a charity, legally constituted and validly pursuing authorized tax-exempt purposes, it has been a false front that attracts donations, allows unknown sums to be diverted and then manufactures deductions for cronies," he said.[32]

BLACK-TIE GALAS

The AIF continues to run afoul of the laws and regulations governing charities operating in the United States. Regulators in Maryland, Virginia, and Illinois as recently as 2015 turned a blind eye to shutting down gala fund-raisers planned by the AIF despite the fact the AIF was not registered in the states as a nonprofit organization with authority to raise charitable donations.

A search of the Maryland Charities Database maintained by the Maryland secretary of state's website provided no listing for the American India Foundation at the time the gala was held.[33] This changed only after public attention had been drawn to the issue. As this book is being written, an application pending can be found for the American India Foundation in a search of the charitable organization database on the Virginia Department of Agriculture and Regulatory Programs, Office of Charitable and Regulatory Programs website.

As he explained in an e-mail to WND, Ortel's search of corporate filings with the Illinois secretary of state led him to conclude the American India Foundation had its charitable license in the state revoked twice, the first time on May 1, 2003, and the second time on August 14, 2015, with both revocations listed for a duration date specified as "perpetual."

Ortel also explained to WND that the AIF also appears to have held an inaugural gala March 27, 2015, in Atlanta, raising $100,000 in "charitable donations" without first being registered as a foundation in Georgia, as required by state laws regulating charitable solicitations. The Georgia inaugural gala featured progressive activist Carl Pope receiving the inaugural Lillian Gordy Carter Award for Exceptional Service to India, instituted in honor of the mother of President Jimmy Carter.

In March 2016, a search by Ortel of the charitable organization database for the state of Georgia failed to find an organization registered with the name "American India Foundation."[34] Under the Georgia Charitable Solicitations Act of 1988, it is a criminal felony for an organization to hold itself out as a nonprofit organization duly authorized to raise tax-deductible charitable donations without first registering in the state as a charity.

Ortel has repeatedly argued that at the crassest level, the Gujarat earthquake proved the Clintons are not above being "merchants in misery." Where Rahm Emmanuel, President Barack Obama's first White House chief of staff, achieved notoriety for admonishing that "no crisis should go to waste," the Gujarat earthquake demonstrates the Clinton Foundation acts as if Bill and Hillary believe that "no natural disaster should go to waste."

Unfortunately, a family willing to abscond with the White House silver clearly has the capacity to view earthquakes, hurricanes, and floods as just another opportunity to cash in on human misery. It should not surprise us, then, that the Clintons were drawn to AIF founders and trustees who today are in federal prison.

Meanwhile, the AIF holds well-publicized galas raking in additional millions of dollars in states where the fund is not registered as a charity. While examining the financial records of the AIF is beyond the scope of this book, the Clintons even today realize how profitable working with India can be. That profit potential was made clear by the stock options Vinod Gupta granted Clinton, which he managed to hide from public view until the Securities and Exchange Commission began its investigation of Gupta.

As of March 2016, Bill Clinton remained in his position as honorary chair of the American India Fund.

3

REINVENTING DAVOS

The [Clinton] foundation . . . accepted millions from seven foreign governments while Hillary Clinton served as secretary of state.

—WASHINGTON POST

Among the various similar versions of the story of how Bill Clinton got the idea to create the Clinton Global Initiative, the version with the most credibility was told by journalist Alec MacGillis in the *New Republic*. His article, "Scandal at Clinton Inc.: How Doug Band drove a wedge through a political dynasty," was highly critical of the Clinton Foundation and, in particular, of Doug Band. As Bill and Hillary soared to billions of dollars in Clinton Foundation riches, Band emerged from his lowly start serving first in White House as Bill Clinton's "body boy," to became a multimillionaire at the helm of his own Clinton-related international consulting firm.

MacGillis appears to have gotten the story from Paul Begala, the longtime Clinton loyalist who transitioned from being a key strategist in Clinton's 1992 run for the White House to serving as cohost of CNN's heavily partisan political program *Crossfire*, along with James Carville, another top Clinton strategist from the 1992 presidential campaign.

"As Begala tells it," MacGillis narrated, "the idea came to Band at that font of grand ideas, Davos." The reference to Davos is to the World Economic Forum, the high-level meeting of the global business elite.

MacGillis continued:

Given that Clinton's political stock was still languishing, Band was "astonished with the billionaires and CEOs standing in line to talk to him," Begala says. "He was rigorously assessing the president's strengths and attributes and maximizing them. I remember him saying, 'The president has a convening power, the power to bring people together.'" Why not create an annual event that harnessed the desire of wealthy celebrities to get close to Clinton to advance the aims of his foundation? Thus, in 2005, the Clinton Global Initiative (CGI) was born.[1]

A $2 BILLION GLOBAL EMPIRE

The *Washington Post* provided a slightly different version, repositioning Band's offhand observation that resulted in a historic reformation of the Clinton Foundation enterprise as having happened not while Clinton was shaking hands at Davos, but on the airplane carrying Clinton to Davos in 2005.

"Chevy Chase was on the plane with Bill Clinton," began *Post* reporters David A. Fahrenthold, Tom Hamburger, and Rosalind S. Helderman. "So was a former president of Brazil. The Founders of Google. A former president of Mexico. And [actor] John Cusack.

"They were all going to Davos, the Swiss resort that holds an annual conclave of the wealthy and powerful," the article continued. "The jet—arranged by a Saudi businessman—provided a luxurious living-room setting for a rolling discussion: Couldn't the big names at Davos be doing more to solve the world's big problems?

"In the background, a Clinton staff member named Doug Band had an idea that would change the ex-president's life," the *Post* reported. "'Only Bill Clinton could bring a group like this together,' Band thought.

"Bill Clinton didn't need Davos. He could do this himself.

"From that revelation came the Clinton Global Initiative—an annual gathering of the wealthy and powerful centered not on a place but on a man," the *Post* story concluded. "In the decade since, that program has become the public face of the Bill, Hillary and Chelsea Clinton Foundation, the sprawling organization that is now at the center of the Clintons' public and professional lives and a springboard for Hillary Rodham Clinton's presidential campaign."[2]

The writers of this story, obviously entranced by the Clintons' accomplishments, noted that the creation of CGI was an "evolution of the foundation, which began as a modest nonprofit focused largely on the ex-president's library in Arkansas," without disclosing the violations of charitable foundation law involved in its formation. When implementing Band's suggestion, the Clinton Foundation failed to apply to the IRS with a new application requesting a new determination letter for the Clinton Global Initiative, an entity the Clintons have tried to pass off as a mere subsidiary of the existing foundation.

Over time, the Clinton Foundation "evolved" from being the William J. Clinton Presidential Foundation, authorized by the IRS to accept tax-exempt contributions for the building of the Clinton presidential library, to being what the *Washington Post* article described as "a global philanthropic empire run by a former U.S. president and closely affiliated with a potential future president, with the audacious goal of solving some of the world's most vexing problems by bringing together the wealthiest, glitziest and most powerful people from every part of the planet."

With the "evolution," the name of the foundation subtly changed, as did its internal corporate structure, external receipt of funds, operational cash flow and expenditure structure, and the compensation packages arranged for those lucky enough to be included on the gravy train ride while it lasted. The William J. Clinton Foundation first became the Clinton Foundation, then from 2013 to 2015 the Bill, Hillary and Chelsea Clinton Foundation, used interchangeably with the Clinton Foundation once again, when Hillary launched her second presidential campaign.

Certainly Band, the former "body man," was not sufficiently expert in charitable foundation law to advise the Clintons or their board of trustees. Should CGI be a subsidiary consolidated into a single audited report prepared for the foundation as a whole? Or, should it be a stand-alone organization functioning to convene an annual conference, with all the attendant expenses of travel, honorarium payments, and hotel reservations required to operate a Davos look-alike?

Would holding an annual CGI conference designed to compete with Davos draw down on the resources needed to build the Clinton library? Or, had the Clinton library already become an afterthought, as the new focus shifted to helping earthquake victims in India, as it also continued shifting to fighting HIV/AIDS in the Third World and aiding flood victims in Haiti?

In the celebrity world to which Bill and Hillary had graduated in the post-presidency, did such distinctions, although required by federal and state law for all other foundations, really matter to the Clinton Foundation?

What was important, as far as the *Washington Post* was concerned, was that the Clintons not be deterred by the legal technicalities that applied to all other foundations, but that they be praised for the supposedly good work accomplished in the process of accumulating what the paper aptly described as the Clinton family "$2 billion global empire."

"The foundation now includes 11 major initiatives, focused on issues as divergent as crop yields in Africa, earthquake relief in Haiti and the cost of AIDS drugs worldwide," the *Post* gushed, lavishing praise on the Clintons for their assumed philanthropic accomplishments. "In all, the Clintons' constellation of related charities has raised $2 billion, employs more than 2,000 people and has a combined annual budget of more than $223 million.

"In the middle of it all is Bill Clinton," the writers went on, "a kind of post-presidency celebrity: a convener who wrangles rich people's problems. In the process, the foundation elevates the wealthy by giving them entrée to one of the nation's most prominent political families."

The themes, viewed in a less adoring fashion, raise troubling issues of how much Bill and Hillary felt they could charge those wanting political favors. Who would keep the books? Who would make sure the audited financials were honest, not merely rubber-stamped approvals of numbers generated by Clinton Foundation political operatives now elevated to hold positions as officers and trustees of the Clinton Foundation in its various gestations and manifestations? Who would ride herd on the Doug Band types surrounding Clinton, who believed the post-presidency was their chance to cash in on years of loyal service. So what if Doug Band's White House job demanded making sure Bill Clinton had a cold Diet Coke at hand whenever and wherever he might want one? This was the post-presidency. Now it was time for Doug Band to cash in.

WHO IS DOUG BAND?

MacGillis, in the *New Republic* article cited earlier, noted that Band "entered Clinton's orbit," at age twenty-seven, "as that lowliest of Washington archetypes," namely, the body man. "He was the all-purpose aide who carried the bags, provided the pen, watched the clock, kept the cigars close, and ensured the Diet Cokes were always chilled." He continued:

> And after the inglorious end of Clinton's presidency, Band had stayed on. It was he who had engineered Clinton's transformation into a philanthropist-king, and over the years, the pair had formed a bond that was more like father and son than boss and factotum. "The most important thing about Doug is that he sort of took control of President Clinton's career at a moment when he was dropping from about sixty percent [favorability] to thirty-nine percent," says Paul Begala, the former Clinton adviser. "You look up today and Bill is in a league inhabited only by himself and Nelson Mandela and the Pope. He's one of the most beloved people on the planet and an American political colossus as well. That's just astonishing—and Doug's been central to that."

But in 2011, noted MacGillis, Band struck out on his own, forming with Irish businessman Declan Kelly a corporate advisory firm that was known as Teneo. Band did not respond to an extensive list of questions posed for the *New Republic* article. But over the course of nine months, MacGillis managed to interview more than three dozen people who have worked with Band throughout his career. The results were less than flattering.

"There are those who worry about the overlap between his work for the Clinton Global Initiative—which he conceived and helped run for six years—and his energetic efforts to expand Teneo's client base," MacGillis wrote. "And there are those who worry about how some of the messier aspects of the charity's operations could create trouble for Hillary Clinton, who has made the family foundation her base as she contemplates a presidential run. But the real cause for these anxieties runs deeper. At its heart, the unease with Band reflects an unease with the phenomenon of post-presidential Clintonism itself."

According to MacGillis, Band traced his interest in politics to a campus visit Bill Clinton and Al Gore paid to the University of Florida, where Band was an undergraduate. After moving to the White House, Band can list as one of his accomplishments that he escorted Monica Lewinsky to the White House Congressional Ball in December 1995, shortly after Clinton began the sexual affair with her.

CGI, Band's brainchild, as described by MacGillis, was fraught with the type of conflicts of interest that can gray the hair of defense attorneys representing foundations being investigated by state attorneys general for the crime of "inurement," the technical term for diverting charitable funds into personal gain and profit. MacGillis noted Band's pivotal role in operating CGI "like an economy in which celebrity is the main currency," as CGI charged $20,000 to attend its annual conference held in a ritzy midtown Manhattan hotel. By 2013, MacGillis noted, after only eight years of operation, CGI had secured corporate pledges worth $74 billion for various charitable activities all over the globe. By comparison, the Gates Foundation had given away only $28 billion since its inception in 1994.

But always, the article makes clear, influence peddling was part of the celebrity dealing at CGI's core. "For corporations, attaching Clinton's brand to their social investments offered a major [public relations] boost," MacGillis noted. "As further incentive, they could hope for a kind word from Clinton the next time they landed in a sticky spot. 'Coca-Cola or Dow or whoever would come to the president,' explains a former White House colleague of Band's, 'and say, "We need your help on this."' Negotiating these relationships, and the trade-offs they required, could involve some gray areas. But for that, Clinton had Band.

Band's job at CGI was not without reward. "From outward appearances, Band had transcended his body-man beginnings at startling speed," MacGillis observed. "In 2003, he had purchased a $2.1 million condo in the sought-after Metropolitan Tower on West 57th Street. His salary from the Clinton Foundation remained relatively modest— $110,000 by the time he left in 2011, plus an additional payment from Clinton's personal office. Yet his official salary didn't account for the ways in which he benefited financially from his singular relationship with Clinton."[3]

MacGillis noted the same suspicious quid pro quo dealings that led investigative reporter Peter Schweizer to write his 2005 best-selling book *Clinton Cash: The Untold Story of How and Why Foreign Governments and Businesses Helped Make Bill and Hillary Rich:*

> And questions were surfacing about some of the people getting through the gate. There was London businessman Victor Dahdaleh, who touted Clinton as a close friend and gave the foundation around $5 million in 2010. The next year, British authorities charged him with bribing a Bahraini company, for as much as $9.5 million. (The trial has been delayed until November.) There was Canadian businessman Frank Giustra, who often made his luxury jet available to Clinton and Band. In 2005, Giustra and Clinton overlapped on a visit to Kazakhstan, and at a dinner, Clinton praised the country's autocratic ruler, Nursultan A. Nazarbayev. Days later, according to

The *New York Times*, Giustra secured a huge uranium-mining deal in the country. In early 2006, Giustra donated $31.3 million to the foundation, followed by another $100 million pledge. (He also "co-produced" Clinton's sixtieth birthday party in Toronto, which raised another $21 million.)[4]

The Clintons left their fingerprints on these and other scams, as will be documented in subsequent chapters, in the details of fraudulent audited financial reports and erroneous and otherwise misleading regulatory forms, including IRS Tax Form 990s that the Clinton Foundation has filed since inception. A key contention of this book is that should state attorneys general and federal Department of Justice investigators examine the Clinton Foundation, multiple-count criminal prosecutions would be filed against the Clintons and their various associates, including Band, for a trail of crimes committed under the less-than-watchful gaze of a loving mainstream media.

As Band transitioned from CGI to Teneo, his lifestyle took on even more grandiose proportions. MacGillis observed how Band coveted his American Express "invitation-only black card for high-rollers" and flashed his roll of one-hundred-dollar bills around town as he became a regular at expensive Fifth Avenue restaurants and A-list nightclubs requiring a nod from the bouncers to be admitted. In the process of moving up, Band sold his apartment in the Metropolitan Tower in New York City to purchase a $7.1 million condo plus an adjoining unit for another $1.7 million in the Essex House on Central Park South.

"From the beginning, Teneo resembled an outpost of Clintonland more than an independent entity," MacGillis wrote.

"A number of key Teneo clients were also closely involved with Clinton's charitable work." MacGillis noted that one month before the Rockefeller Foundation presented Clinton with an award for philanthropy, it gave Teneo a $3.4 million contract to propose "tangible solutions to global problems." Another early Teneo client was Coca-Cola, "which helped build the distribution system for medicine in Tanzania, Mozambique, and Ghana, for a CGI project." Band had served on

Coca-Cola's international advisory board with a former Coca-Cola CEO, Donald Keough, who chaired the boutique investment bank Allen & Company, a group that also holds a financial interest in Teneo. Among other Teneo clients, MacGillis listed the hospital chain Tenet, a lead partner in the new Clinton Health Matters Initiative, and UBS Americas, which launched a Small Business Advisory Program with the Clinton Foundation. Band's "pitch," MacGillis noted, left Clinton Foundation donors with "the distinct impression that Clinton had encouraged the donors to avail themselves of Band's services."[5]

THE DAVOS SCAM

Theodore Roosevelt Malloch, who teaches business ethics at the University of Oxford,[6] presents an insider's view of the Davos World Economic Forum in his 2016 memoirs *Davos, Aspen and Yale: My Life Behind the Elite Curtain as a Global Sherpa.*[7] Malloch is a Christian conservative whose expertise in both his academic endeavors and his business career has centered on the theme of "spiritual capital," arguing that business and government in a global economy must retain an ethical compass to be truly successful.[8]

In 1990, Klaus Schwab, founder and CEO of the World Economic Forum (WEF),[9] recruited Malloch to serve on the WEF's executive committee, taking responsibility for the organization and management of the annual Davos summit, a job Malloch did for four years. Malloch was sanguine in his evaluation of Schwab's World Economic Forum. "Today Davos is synonymous with a different kind of cult," he wrote. "It is the cult of business celebrity; elites from every avenue of life, every industry, every country, leaders and . . . wannabes, will do anything to be seen there, especially during the last week of January, when the World Economic Forum conducts its annual meeting." But, at bottom, for Schwab, the meeting was about money. "They pay over seventy thousand dollars just to be invited; over a million to be members according to The Guardian," Malloch noted. "It has become the hub of political, economic, cultural, and every other kind of power imagined by postmodern man. In fact, it is about the emergence of what the ringmaster at Davos calls 'Davos-Man' [a phrase he borrowed from the late Harvard professor Samuel Huntington], a kind of *übermensch* that can transform the world. Nietzsche would be proud."

Malloch was also clear that the meeting had an underlying agenda. "It [the World Economic Forum] has also placed itself as the epicenter of [New Age] globalism—a new ideology. Globalism is not the same as the gradual process of globalization, which sees countries involved in more and more trade and investment across borders. Globalism is a movement to and a belief in one world government," This objective, Malloch concluded, was the underlying ideological purpose that permeated the annual Davos summit. "The WEF logo itself puts the organization in the center of the globe's sphere; and Herr Professor Dr. Schwab is the 'Wizard' of this 'Oz,' behind the curtain, who makes the whole thing run—just as in the movie," he wrote. Here is where the global elite in business, academics, and consulting met to be seen, trade business cards, and make deals. "At Davos two bankers met from UBS and Swiss Bank Corp, and later you read of a merger," Malloch observed. "The steel company of Holland sold out to their counterparts in India. Investment dollars flew like sand in the desert wind."

Malloch learned that central to the Davos globalism is the presumption that big government was good and capitalism was bad. "Is Big Government good government? Do markets always fail when left to their own devices? These questions are verboten in Davos—for the hallmark of all believers here gathered is that government is the solution—perhaps assisted by some special council, formed of course by 'FOK'—friends of Klaus (Schwab)," Malloch noted.[10]

BILL CLINTON AS HIS OWN WIZARD OF OZ
Doug Band obviously saw the Davos World Economic Forum for what it was – an opportunity to make for Clinton and for himself an enormous amount of money. Band understood that Clinton, accepted as a Rhodes Scholar even though he never graduated Oxford, was a near

genius when it came to the academic analysis of social and economic problems from a leftist perspective. Why couldn't Clinton be his own Wizard of Oz? Band quickly realized that Clinton could charge attendees of his own annual summit tens of thousands of dollars to attend. This would place Clinton, not Schwab, at the center of the wealth, business deals, and global agenda setting. Even better, Clinton could conduct the meeting under the guise of his philanthropic foundation, topping Strauss by giving the impression his annual summit was aimed squarely at doing good. When Band realized Clinton could top Strauss in his "Wizard of Oz" act, the Clinton Global Initiative was born.

In 2005, Clinton held the first CGI annual meeting at a swanky New York City hotel, with the world press dutifully attending to report chapter and verse on the billions of dollars in philanthropic pledges the attendees would make to causes such as eliminating world poverty, and fighting HIV/AIDS in the Third World—all overlaid with the current leftist ideological cause in vogue, combating global warming. And when the data did not support the assertion that the earth was warming up from human consumption of carbon-based fuels, the ideological agenda could morph into "ending climate change," all with the blessing of the CGI global elite, who pay tens of thousands to be seen on stage with their Clinton family emcees. The CGI version of Davos-like globalism shows up in the constant references to "suitability"—a term drawn directly from the United Nations Agenda 21 globalism—as a measure of determining when a CGI-backed social engineering project is successful.

CGI quickly developed into a four-day public relations forum that positioned the Clinton Foundation at the center of all philanthropic good worth doing worldwide. The event became the stage-show version of the glossy Clinton Foundation annual report, where instead of showing a photograph of Bill Clinton with Nelson Mandela fighting HIV/AIDS in Africa, Clinton could host a panel with Mandela onstage, with a web broadcast allowing a global audience to watch the revered former South African leader congratulate the former president of the United States for tackling monumental social problems he had not been able to solve in government. If just given enough time—and unlimited money—Clinton through the CGI could end poverty, cure disease, and save the planet, while establishing his leftist ideology as the only acceptable way for a person who cared about others to think.

Maybe Band did not come up with the CGI idea without copying Strauss and his Davos World Economic Forum. But Band had to feel he had truly cracked the formula for wealth beyond his and the Clintons' wildest imagination in 2006, when Schwab attended the CGI forum to congratulate Bill Clinton, who stood proud at center stage as host. Even better, U.S. journalists did not have to travel to Switzerland to write their praise of the Clinton Foundation as the new solution to the world's problems.

CLINTON GLOBAL INITIATIVE "FOR SALE"

From the start, the pinnacle of attending CGI's annual meeting quickly became time on stage with Bill, either as a panel participant, a featured guest, or an honoree. The participation in the program, often consisting of nothing more than an introduction to the audience, meant recognition from the high-dollar contributors attending the meeting. Everyone paid $20,000 just to attend the meeting. The true high-dollar attendees sponsored the meeting as global businesses, academics, consultants, and even governments. "Friends of Bill," known to insiders simply as "FOBs," soon figured out six- and seven-figure donations or pledges announced publicly at the Clinton Global Initiative annual meetings could translate into camera time with Bill Clinton onstage. Rogues and international criminals attending CGI knew stage time brought the instant credibility they needed to advance their shady deals, sometimes requiring the Clintons to work behind the scenes to get the U.S. government bureaucracy to change rules.

The saga of Ron Burkle's association with Bill Clinton and the Clinton Foundation shows how the Clintons used the Clinton Global Initiative to profit. CGI solicited "sponsorships" from corporations and wealthy individuals, expecting to receive millions of dollars in fees paid to them directly in exchange for plugging CGI sponsors into a network of political influence, investment bank financing, and lucrative international opportunities. The Ron Burkle saga also demonstrates that the least savory CGI sponsors were often the most successful with the Clintons.

California-born Burkle, the son of a grocery store manager, dropped out of college and spent fifteen years working at his dad's store, according to a 2006 profile published in *Forbes*.[11] "In 1981 he mounted a botched buyout attempt of the chain and was fired," the *Forbes* profile noted. "And then he got very serious about investing, parlaying a few lucky bets on regional grocery chains into a controlling stake in giant Pathmark, management of four private equity funds with $4 billion from investors, stakes in some 35 companies and a personal fortune that FORBES pegs at $2.5 billion." Burkle established a presence making friends with young Hollywood stars, investing $50 million into the apparel company of rap producer Sean "Diddy" Combs and rehabbing a New York apartment as a "crash pad" with actor Leonardo DiCaprio, twenty-two years his junior. He established himself in politics and met Bill Clinton by raising $50 million for the Democratic Party, holding up to forty political fund-raisers in a year at his 50,000-square-foot mansion on eight acres in Beverly Hills.

Burkle's attendance at the Clinton Global Initiative's second annual meeting in 2006 was documented in a CGI press release September 22, 2006, which said he had joined a team formed "to pursue opportunities in the areas of clean alternative and renewable energy sources." The move was described as a CGI "tangible step" that "will enhance the work of the President's Climate Change initiative."[12] The *Los Angeles Times* published a photo of Burkle and Clinton onstage at the CGI 2006 annual meeting, posing with film producer Stephen Bing, another member of the clean energy team. The photograph, attributed to Stephen Hilger of Bloomberg News, ran with a caption explaining that Bing had contributed to the Clinton Foundation, and Burkle "is a longtime Clinton supporter."[13]

The *New York Times* noted that at the CGI 2006 annual meeting, "three of the world's richest men—Richard Branson, Ronald W. Burkle and Vinod Khosla—trooped onto a New York ballroom stage with former President Bill Clinton to pledge support for renewable energy projects to combat global warming and create jobs." Several months earlier, Senator Clinton had sponsored legislation to provide billions in new federal incentives for ethanol, the *Times* noted.

> One potential beneficiary is the Yucaipa Companies, a private equity firm where Mr. Clinton has been a senior advisor and whose founder, Mr. Burkle, has raised hundreds of thousands of dollars for Mrs. Clinton's campaigns. Yucaipa has invested millions in Cilion Inc.—a start-up venture also backed by Mr. Branson, the British entrepreneur, and Mr. Khosla, a Silicon Valley venture capitalist—that is building seven ethanol plants around the country. Two are in upstate New York.

The article noted that Senator Clinton had worked especially hard "to foster a business climate [in New York state] that favors the sort of ethanol investments pursued by her husband's friends and her political supporters."[14]

Because Burkle's Yucaipa funds are private, the Clintons had refused to release tax returns that would detail their Yucaipa investments. In 2007, however, Hillary's 2008 presidential campaign forced the release of her 2000–2007 tax returns. Thomas Edsall, reporting in the *Huffington Post*, revealed that Burkle's Yucaipa Global Opportunities Fund had paid Bill Clinton $15 million in consulting fees between 2003 and 2007. Edsall concluded that the $15 million was for Clinton's role as "rainmaker" and "door opener" to Burkle's Yucaipa Global Opportunities Fund.[15]

In January 2008, when Clinton sought to terminate his relationship with Burkle to avoid creating yet another headache for Hillary's 2008 presidential campaign, John Emshwiller reported in the *Wall Street Journal* that Clinton stood to earn $20 million by cashing in on an agreement with two of Burkle's Yucaipa domestic funds dating back to 2002 that paid Clinton a percentage of earnings should fund returns grow above certain thresholds. The *Wall Street Journal* also reported Clinton had invested an undisclosed sum of his own money in Burkle's global fund, in return for a limited partnership interest. Clinton was also one of three owners of the global fund's general partner, along with Burkle, who was the managing partner, and an entity connected to the ruler of Dubai, Sheikh Mohammed bin Rashid al-Maktoum.[16]

Todd Purdum's June 30, 2008, *Vanity Fair* article, "The Comeback Id," featured a photograph of Bill Clinton in Richmond, Virginia, speaking on behalf of his wife during the run-up to the 2008 Virginia primary, which Hillary lost to Barack Obama. The article provided salacious details that added typical Bill Clinton color to the relationship with Burkle. It discussed Band's wedding in Paris, attended by Clinton and Burkle, the "supermarket billionaire and investor who is Clinton's bachelor buddy, fund-raiser, and business partner." Burkle arrived with an attractive blonde, Purdum wrote, described by a fellow guest as "not much more than 19, if she was that." This was followed by a paragraph that has become legend in the lore of Bill Clinton sexual escapades:

> Burkle's usual means of transport is the custom-converted Boeing 757 that Clinton calls "Ron Air" and that Burkle's own circle of young aides privately refer to as "Air F**k One." Clinton himself had arrived on the private plane of another California friend, the real-estate heir, Democratic donor, liberal activist, and sometime movie and music producer Steve Bing, whose colorful private life includes fathering a child out of wedlock with the actress Elizabeth Hurley and suing the billionaire investor Kirk Kerkorian for invasion of privacy, alleging that private investigators for Kerkorian swiped Bing's dental floss out of his trash in a successful effort to prove that Bing's DNA matched that of a child delivered by Kerkorian's ex-wife, the former tennis pro Lisa Bonder. (The suit was later settled out of court.)[17]

But by 2016, the relationship between Clinton and Burkle had soured, apparently beyond repair. Evan Halper reported in the *Los Angeles Times* that Burkle had startled the Hollywood left by declaring that in 2016 he was going to fund not Hillary Clinton, but GOP candidate John Kasich, the Republican governor of Ohio. "As much as I like Gore, Kerry and [Hillary] Clinton, nobody can ever remember what they stand for," Burkle said. "They overcomplicate it . . . They don't win on vision—they make it too complicated. They don't win on likability." Halper further reported that Burkle also told him that President Obama has been a bitter disappointment, failing to deliver on his promise to work with Republicans.[18]

The fallout between Clinton and Burkle appears to trace back to a business deal gone bad. In 2010, the *Daily Beast* reported that Clinton was angry because Burkle did not make a $20 million "final payment" Clinton expected from the profits of their decade-long partnership.[19] According to *Wall Street Journal* reporter John R. Emshwiller, the disagreement centered on the deal Burkle had made to share with Bill Clinton a percentage of the profits from two of Burkle's domestic Yucaipa investment funds, provided the returns reached a certain threshold. The disagreement apparently also involved the Yucaipa Global Partnership, LP, focusing on investing in foreign companies. Emshwiller reported that Clinton had invested some of his own money in the foreign fund and had a limited partnership interest in the fund as a result.

"Mr. Burkle made his fortune by investing in a range of industries, particularly the supermarket business, and is believed to have become a billionaire," Emshwiller wrote. "He also has become a major fund-raiser for and backer of Democratic Party candidates, including the Clintons. He often opens his Beverly Hills estate, Green Acres, for fund-raising events, and Mr. Clinton has been a frequent houseguest there." The exact nature of the business arrangements between Clinton and Burkle had never been made fully clear, wrote Emshwiller. "He has met at times with people involved in various Yucaipa business deals. And the former president's vast global network of contacts probably has been an asset for Mr. Burkle in dealings with business, labor and political leaders. Over the years, Mr. Burkle has said publicly that Mr. Clinton's prestige and connections have helped Yucaipa get its business proposals in front of top corporate decision makers."[20]

What should be clear from this narrative is that Bill Clinton has engaged with his campaign contributors and foundation donors in business dealings that were never fully disclosed publicly. The disagreement with Burkle first surfaced in 2008, as Hillary Clinton was making a bid for the White House, much as the disagreement resurfaced in 2016, as Hillary Clinton was deeply involved in her second presidential campaign. For the Clintons, it seems that the easy mixture of campaign funding, philanthropy, and undisclosed business dealings make them oblivious to the moral rules of conduct, especially when times are good and the deals come easy.

THE FOLLIERI CHARADE

The discussion of Burkle is not complete without a brief narrative recounting the scam perpetrated on Bill Clinton and Burkle by a then twenty-five-year-old Italian businessman, Raffaello Follieri, whom the *Wall Street Journal* described as "handsome and charming."[21] Follieri came to New York in 2003, to launch a business buying and redeveloping Roman Catholic Church properties, claiming he had close ties with Vatican officials who would smooth the way for deals, according to business associates and material issued by his company, Follieri Group. In 2005, Follieri met Band, representing that he could help Hillary Clinton with Catholic voters during her presidential campaign.

Reporter Alec MacGillis, in his scathing September 2013 *New Republic* article on the Clinton Foundation, explained that when Follieri arrived in New York, Band was already dating his future wife, Lily Rafii, who was then working in mergers and acquisitions at Morgan Stanley. Follieri, who was then dating actress Anne Hathaway, invited Band and his future wife to dine with him at trendy New York restaurants where he could introduce Band to his "Euro jet set." Swept up by Follieri, Band introduced him to Clinton, Burkle, and Mexican billionaire Carlos Slim, then the richest man in the world, aboard Slim's yacht in the Sea of Cortez. Slim declined to invest. But that did not deter Band, who then introduced Follieri to Michael Cooper, the head of Toronto-based Dundee Realty Corporation, who had just returned from a summer trip with Bill Clinton to Africa, where Cooper invested $6 million.[22] The *Wall Street Journal* reported that Follieri paid Band a $400,000 finder's fee for introducing Follieri to Cooper. The same article reported that in 2005, Burkle's Yucaipa fund agreed to invest up to $100 million in Follieri's church property venture. In the mix, Follieri's foundation pledged to the Clinton Global Initiative $1 million to vaccinate Honduran children against hepatitis.[23]

On September 20, 2006, Follieri and Hathaway were photographed at the opening reception of the Clinton Global Initiative annual meeting at the Museum of Modern Art.[24] A Clinton Global Initiative press release the next day documented the Follieri Foundation had committed $1 million to vaccinate 10,000 children in Honduras from Hepatitis A in 2006, "with the ultimate goal of eradicating poverty and significantly improving the condition of children's health, housing, and education throughout the world." The press release further noted Follieri "was inspired to make this commitment as a result [of] his participation in the inaugural meeting [of the] Clinton Global Initiative, during which he committed to bringing 1000 Hepatitis A vaccines to children in San Marcos, Nicaragua."[25]

Michael Shnayerson reported in *Vanity Fair* the importance of the Band introduction that led to the relationship with Clinton and Burkle. "If Follieri had charmed only Ron Burkle at that fateful New York Palace Hotel meeting, that would have been, as Hathaway might say, brilliant," Shnayerson wrote. "But he had impressed Doug Band too. And Follieri, in turn, was salivating at the thought of all the other prospective investors to whom the keeper of Bill Clinton's Rolodex might introduce him. Almost every day, it seemed, Band would get excited e-mail suggestions from his new friend. 'They were BlackBerrying each other,' says one former employee, 'all the time.'"[26]

Follieri's investment scam began to come apart in April 2007, when Burkle's Yucaipa companies filed suit in Delaware court, accusing Follieri and his firm, the Follieri Group, with "willfully and systematically misappropriating" at least $1.3 million of the over $55 million Yucaipa had invested into their joint venture company, Follieri/Yucaipa Investments.

The suit alleged that the misappropriations went to finance Follieri's "personal extravagances and budget mismanagement," including among the alleged improprieties private jet travel for Follieri and Hathaway; a penthouse apartment in the Trump Tower in the heart of midtown Manhattan used by Follieri; and "massive charges for 'five-star' lodging, meals and entertainment" as well as medical care for Follieri relatives and a dog. Additionally, the suit alleged hundreds of thousands of dollars were improperly loaned to the Follieri Foundation, a nonprofit charity run by Follieri and his family.[27]

On June 24, 2008, Follieri was arrested and charged with defrauding investors of up to $6 million by posing as an agent of the Vatican. "He is a con man," Reed Brodsky told Federal Magistrate Judge Henry Pitman, as reported by the *New York Daily News*. "He was able to con a lot of people out of a lot of money over a long period of time."[28] He pled guilty to fourteen counts of conspiracy, money laundering, and fraud, and served almost five years in a Pennsylvania prison before he was deported back to Italy. ABC News noted that at the height of his scam, Follieri spent $97,000 on a private airplane to take him and Hathaway to the Dominican Republic, where they spent New Year's Eve partying with Bill Clinton at designer Oscar de la Renta's house.[29]

The tangled inter-dealings between the Clinton Foundation "charity" and fund-raising for Hillary Clinton's Senate and presidential campaigns; the fees and outside business deals on which Bill Clinton personally profits, including at times undisclosed stock options; and the client referrals to consulting firms owned by Clinton associates, as exemplified by Band and Teneo, raise conflict-of-interest questions that should keep scrupulous law enforcement officials busy for years.

A thorough search of the audited financial reports and the IRS Tax Form 990s filed by the Clinton Foundation and the Clinton Global Initiative uncovers no reference to Burkle and his various Yucaipa funds, or to Follieri and the $1 million pledge he made at the CGI 2006 annual meetings, despite strict federal and state requirements that principals of a charitable foundation must report all relevant financial transactions with donors. Unfortunately, there are dozens of Clinton Foundation stories that echo the Burkle and Follieri escapades. However, line items in audited financial statements and regulatory reports requiring the charity to report all grants received simply lump together all donations without detail or accompanying documentation into a summary number that federal and state regulators regularly fail to scrutinize.

Pledges of contributions made at each CGI annual meeting since 2005 often seem to dematerialize after those making the pledge get time on the Clinton CGI stage to brag about their philanthropic intentions. The point of CGI, it would appear, is to produce a public relations event in which Bill, Hillary, and Chelsea can be held up for praise for their good deeds, while the Clintons arrange to cash in on side deals. Unfortunately, federal or state regulators have failed to demand legitimately audited financial statements with detailed accounting reports that prove the CGI show is something other than an elaborate Clinton family con game.

THE HUMA PROBLEM

On May 15, 2013, *Politico* broke the story that longtime Hillary Clinton aide Huma Abedin spent her final months at the State Department working as a "special government employee" in a part-time consultancy, beginning during her pregnancy in the summer of 2012, while she worked a second job as a part-time consultant to Teneo.[30] The *New York Post*, in September 2013, reported Abedin was being paid $355,000 as a consultant to Teneo, while receiving $135,000 in government pay as a part-time consultant for Hillary.[31]

The *Washington Post* revealed in August 2015, that Abedin actually held four different jobs simultaneously, being paid also by the Clinton Foundation, where she was a contractor preparing for Hillary's eventual transition from the State Department to the charity. The *Washington Post* story used a dinner at a private club in Dublin, Ireland, that Huma had arranged in December 2012 as Hillary was preparing for her farewell international trip as secretary of state to illustrate how Abedin was working for four different employers at the same time. The newspaper recounted the Dublin dinner as follows:

> The invitation was sent from Abedin's State Department account as Clinton planned for an official trip in her role as secretary. The dinner was attended by the chief executive of the private consulting firm Teneo, which has close ties to the Clintons and employed Abedin as an adviser. Seated around the table were donors to Hillary Clinton's campaigns as well as to the Clinton Foundation, where Abedin was a contractor preparing for Clinton's eventual return to the Charity. And Clinton, who was also paying Abedin out of her personal funds to prepare for her transition from secretary of state to private life, showed up for about an hour.[32]

Abedin, who has worked since the 1990s as one of Hillary Clinton's top aides, is the wife of disgraced former congressman Anthony Weiner, who was forced to leave the House of Representatives over his extramarital sex texting. Abedin also has connections to the Muslim Brotherhood, having served for a dozen years as an assistant editor for the *Journal of Muslim Monthly Affairs* for the Institute for Muslim Minority Affairs, founded by her late father and currently directed by her mother. The Institute for Muslim Minority Affairs is backed by the Muslim World League, an Islamic organization in the Saudi holy city of Mecca that was founded by Muslim Brotherhood leaders in the Middle East.[33]

In Hillary Clinton's 2008 presidential campaign, Abedin served as her traveling chief of staff. From there, Abedin transitioned to being Clinton's deputy chief of staff at the State Department. Currently, Abedin serves as vice chair for Hillary Clinton's 2016 presidential campaign. In an interview given in April 2016, Abedin recalled the first time she saw Hillary was when she was working as a White House intern, starting in 1996, assigned to the then First Lady Hillary Clinton's staff. "You know these things that happen in your life that just stick?"

Abedin recalled. "She walked by and she shook my hand and our eyes connected and I just remember having this moment where I thought, 'Wow, this is amazing.'" The impact evidently was permanent. "And it just inspired me," Abedin continued. "You know, I still remember the look on her face. And it's funny, and she would probably be so annoyed that I say this, but I remember thinking: 'Oh my God, she's so beautiful and she's so little!'"[34]

Politico reported in August 2015 that the scandal over Hillary's private e-mail server at the State Department had turned to Abedin, described in the article as "Hillary Clinton's most trusted confidante." Abedin had her own e-mail account for State Department business on Clinton's private e-mail server, an arrangement Politico considered "unusual," even for top brass at the State Department.[35] As FOIA requests from watchdog groups, including Washington-based Judicial Watch, forced the public release of thousands of Hillary Clinton e-mails from the State Department, various e-mails revealed that Abedin, while working as Hillary's State Department aide, continued to interact with individuals connected with Teneo, including Band, as well as with the Clinton Foundation.[36]

Politico reported that Senate Judiciary Committee chairman Chuck Grassley, R-IA, had sent a letter to FBI director James Comey, asking for confirmation of a report that the Office of the Inspector General for the State Department had opened an investigation involving potential criminal conduct by Abedin while she worked for the State Department under Clinton.[37] Grassley's concerns centered around possible conflict-of-interest suspicions that Abedin's maternity leave pay had been inflated, especially in consideration of her side work for the Clinton-linked consulting firm Teneo.[38]

SHAKE-UP IN THE CLINTON FOUNDATION

Just weeks before Hillary Clinton kicked off her 2016 campaign for president at an event for Roosevelt Island adjoining New York City, the Clinton Foundation cut all ties with Band, a man the *New York Post* described as "once so close to Bill Clinton that he was considered a surrogate son." *Post* writers Isabel Vincent and Melissa Klein quoted Daniel Halper, author of the 2014 book *Clinton, Inc.*, who explained Band's departure as an attempt to reposition the Clinton Foundation before conflicts of interest surface to tank Hillary's second run for the presidency.

"I think Teneo is not just emblematic of how Clinton Inc. works, it shows the political and financial mess that this whole thing has created," Halper told the newspaper.

"There's an undertow of transactionalism in the glittering annual dinners, the fixation on celebrity and a certain contingent of donors whose charitable contributions and business interests occupy an uncomfortable proximity," Halper said. "More than anyone else except [Bill] Clinton himself, Band is responsible for creating this culture. And not only did he create it, he has thrived in it."[39]

The London *Daily Mail* reported in September 2015 that Chelsea Clinton was responsible for pushing Band out of the Clinton Foundation. Chelsea is "becoming a powerful player in the palace intrigue among the three Clintons" the paper said, and "has moved into being a major player in the Clinton Foundation" since the foundation was renamed to include her in 2013. According to the *Daily Mail*, Chelsea resented Band's closeness to her father and insisted that old Clinton cronies had to go.[40]

The *Daily Mail* report was based on information developed by veteran investigative reporter Edward Klein in his 2015 best-selling book *Unlikeable: The Problem with Hillary*.[41] Klein wrote that in a confrontation with her father in 2013, Chelsea told Bill Clinton: "You treat these [people] like family [referring to Band], and you blindly trust them. They pay you back by screwing up the foundation's finances so badly it may be impossible to fix it. You assume that people are loyal because you are. But they are not. And this proves it."[42]

Klein noted Chelsea's concern about the way the Clinton Foundation was being run had first been reported by the *New York Times* in August 2013. Reporters Nicholas Confessore and Amy Chozick exposed Chelsea's alarm at learning that the Clinton Foundation had run multimillion-dollar deficits for several years, despite vast amounts of money flowing in. The article pointed out that "after years of relying on Bruce R. Lindsey, the former White House counsel whose friendship with Mr. Clinton stretches back decades, to run the organization while living part-time in Arkansas, the family has hired a New York–based chief executive with a background in management consulting." Lindsay's association with Clinton stretched back to the early days, when he was Clinton's attorney in Arkansas.

To replace Lindsey as Clinton Foundation CEO, Chelsea chose thirty-eight-year-old Eric Braverman. The *New York Times* described Braverman as an associate of Chelsea Clinton when both worked for consulting firm McKinsey who "had helped the Clintons with philanthropic projects in Haiti after the earthquake there."[43] As noted earlier, although Lindsey resigned as CEO of the Clinton Foundation in 2013, he has continued to serve as chairman of the foundation's board of directors, a position he has held since 2005.

In a press release July 2, 2013, the Clinton Foundation announced the decision to hire Braverman to replace Lindsey as CEO. "Prior to joining the Clinton Foundation, Braverman garnered experience advising governments, non-profits, and businesses with McKinsey & Company, where he has worked since 1997," the press release read. "He served as a partner in their public sector practice, directing McKinsey's work on government innovation and counseling clients on strategy, organization, and partnership between the public, private, and social sectors. He also has experience with disaster relief and reconstruction, including work with the Clinton Foundation on its recovery efforts in Haiti following the January 2010 earthquake."[44]

The careful reader should keep in mind the McKinsey connection that continues to weave through the Clinton Foundation saga. Recall that Rajat Gupta was CEO of McKinsey in 2001, when he formed the American India Foundation after the Gujarat earthquake, the event that triggered Bill Clinton's pivoting of the Clinton Foundation from building the presidential library to a widening range of purposes. In chapter 7, we will examine in much closer detail the involvement of

Braverman and McKinsey with the Clinton Foundation's involvement in Haiti's post-earthquake recovery. Also figuring in the drama involving McKinsey is another longtime Clinton friend and adviser, Ira Magaziner. In chapter 5, we will examine how the Clinton Foundation's scope spread to Ira Magaziner directing an effort to raise funds for HIV/AIDS victims in the Third World, at the suggestion of Nelson Mandela, a year after Clinton began raising money for the earthquake victims in India. In 2003, Chelsea was offered a job at McKinsey management consultants in New York for a sizable starting salary.

"When Chelsea Clinton was headhunted for a £40,000 first job [equivalent to approximately $120,000 a year in 2015 dollars] at management consultants McKinsey & Company earlier this week, there were a few raised eyebrows and rather more snarlingly envious comments," wrote columnist Stuart Jeffries in the *Guardian* of London.

> What does that gawky brat have that others don't? How could a 22-year-old woman with no business experience justify such a lavish per annum wedge? Would her master's degree in international relations from Oxford and a history BA from Stanford really help one of McKinsey's current clients, say, the steel group Corus, which is poised to undertake a strategic review after a 20% share plummet that followed a planned merger with a Brazilian outfit? Are you sure? Did she only get the job on the back of daddy's old job and mommy's highly regarded intellectual capabilities?[45]

The McKinsey connection was not lost on Evgenia Peretz, who reported in an August 2015 *Vanity Fair* article titled "How Chelsea Took Charge of Clintonworld" that Chelsea had worked with Braverman at McKinsey. Peretz noted that as part of the transition in 2013, Chelsea did her best not only to distance the Clinton Foundation from Band, but also to greatly reduce Magaziner's influence. As we will see in chapter 5, Magaziner built the Clinton Foundation HIV/AIDS initiative into its largest single activity, beginning in 2003. "It was felt in some quarters that Chelsea, who hadn't paid her dues—by, say, spending real time in Africa, or cutting her teeth at one of the programs—was coming in and throwing her weight around. Lindsey and others complained to President Clinton but to no avail," Peretz wrote. "'He has no ability to say no to her,' says a source familiar with the shake-ups."[46]

In their 2013 article, *New York Times* writers Confessore and Chozick also pointed out that replacing Lindsey was not Chelsea's only concern. She was clearly focused on Band, who had left his paid position with the Clinton Foundation in late 2010, despite continuing his relationship with the Clinton Global Initiative. Confessore and Chozick stressed that in 2013, the Teneo had several important clients that also remained very important to CGI, including Coca-Cola, Dow Chemical, UBS Americas, and Standard Chartered, a British financial services company. Standard Charter, a 2012 sponsor of CGI, had paid a $340 million fine to New York regulators in 2012 to settle charges that it had laundered money from Iran.

The article made clear just how handsome was the financial reward to Teneo involved in contracting clients that were Clinton Global Initiative sponsors. The typical Teneo contract, according to the *Times* report, included a retainer, plus monthly fees as high as $250,000. Teneo also frequently recruited clients who were Clinton Foundation donors, even if they were not sponsors of the Clinton Global Initiative. In return, Teneo encouraged its clients to become new Clinton Foundation donors and to sponsor the Clinton Global Initiatives. "Some Clinton aides and foundation employees began to wonder where the foundation ended and Teneo began," Confessore and Chozick concluded.

The two reporters had no doubt that coincident with Braverman's hiring, Chelsea Clinton had taken a major step toward gaining control over the Clinton Foundation. When Braverman was hired in July 2013, Chelsea was appointed vice chair of the Clinton Foundation board, where she would "bear significant responsibility for steering her family's philanthropy, both in the causes it tackles and in the potential political and financial conflicts it must avoid." The *New York Times*, however, signaled that the problems with Band remained, noting that

Chelsea had become "increasingly concerned with the negative impact Mr. Band's outside business might have on her father's work and that she cited concerns raised during the internal review about potential conflicts of interest involving Teneo."[47]

The highly profitable nature of the incestuous arrangement between Clinton and Band, obvious from the way Teneo and the Clinton Foundation double-teamed clients, was a major reason it took Chelsea until 2015, when her mother was preparing to run for president, to get rid of Band. To appreciate the client double-teaming, consider that a major corporation wanting political favors understood that contributing to the Clinton Foundation and/or sponsoring the Clinton Global Initiative would be a good idea. Paying the Clinton Foundation and/or the CGI tens or hundreds of thousands of dollars allowed participating corporations for many years to benefit from the political connections of both Bill Clinton as former president and Hillary as a U.S. senator from New York. To complete the circle, however, the corporation donating to the Clinton Foundation and/or sponsoring the Clinton Global Initiative would next be solicited by Band to hire Teneo. The management consulting advice Teneo provided would ensure that the corporation would be positioned to receive the maximum benefit possible from the political influence Bill and Hillary could wield. All this, of course, had to recede from public view before Hillary launched her 2016 presidential bid. Hence, the importance of elevating Chelsea to vice chairman of the Clinton Foundation and giving her license to clean house.

The problem was that as the Clinton Foundation was growing in size, the incestuous ties between Bill Clinton and Teneo were becoming too obvious to be long sustained, if the ties remained in public view. In 2012, Bill finally "changed his relationship" with Teneo. The scandal that caused the change involved Jon Corzine, the former Democratic New Jersey governor and a client paying Teneo $125,000 a month. The scandal broke nationwide when Corzine bankrupted his MF Global hedge fund. In the wake of the Corzine debacle, Teneo announced that Bill Clinton would no longer be a paid adviser to the firm. Yet in typical Clinton fashion, the public attention drawn to the incestuous nature of the relationship between the Clinton Foundation and Teneo was sufficiently diverted by a change in Bill's relationship with Teneo that was more cosmetic than fundamental.

"His advisory board role at Teneo transitioned at the end of 2011," Teneo spokesman Matt McKenna told Politico blogger Maggie Haberman in February 2012, carefully noting that Teneo would continue to represent Bill Clinton "in a personal capacity." This had to be admitted because Haberman/Politico knew that despite the decision to stop paying Bill Clinton, Teneo was still delivering favors for him, especially in Ireland. "Declan Kelly, one of Teneo's founders, was instrumental in setting up the recent Irish investment forum and working with President Clinton to bring American companies to the table," Haberman continued in her blog post. "In addition to representing President Clinton personally, Teneo will continue to work on a pro bono basis to expand participation in the Clinton Global Initiative and support for the Clinton Foundation's activities around the world."[48]

While the Corzine scandal may have been the final straw requiring that Teneo stop sending Bill Clinton checks directly, the double-teaming game obviously had only gone underground, substituting a more indirect way of compensating Bill than by having Teneo writing him the regular checks Bill enjoyed while his formal relationship with Teneo was allowed to remain in place.

BRAVERMAN QUITS

In a surprise move Clinton Foundation CEO Eric Braverman stepped down in January 2015, only some eighteen months after he had agreed to take the job.[49]

Two months later, Kenneth P. Vogel, Politico's chief investigative reporter, published an important background story titled "Eric Braverman Tried to Change the Clinton Foundation. Then He Left." According to Vogel, Braverman's abrupt decision to resign as Clinton Foundation CEO "stemmed partly from a power struggle inside the foundation between and among the coterie of Clinton loyalists who have surrounded the former president for decades and who helped start and run the foundation." His departure was a blow to those Clinton insiders who felt that his appointment as CEO validated Chelsea Clinton's view that the foundation needed to tighten its governing and budget, and implement more comprehensive policies to vet donors and avoid conflicts of interest.

"When Braverman arrived to replace Lindsey as CEO, he moved quickly to adopt the auditor's recommendations, and then some," Vogel noted. "He diversified the foundation's board beyond the Clintons and their longtime political allies and restructured its finance department. . . .

"No public explanation was offered for Braverman's resignation," Vogel reported. "But sources say Braverman's modernization efforts were hampered by the occasionally conflicting visions of the three Clintons, and their rival staff factions."[50]

Braverman's abrupt departure was widely viewed as a signal from the inside that the history of irresponsible management and reckless accounting endemic to the Clinton Foundation since inception might have become so entrenched as to be impossible to correct, even though the criminal corruption at the heart of the Clinton Foundation was obvious to anyone who bothered to look. The suspicion remains that Braverman quit before he was forced to put his signature on audited financial statements and regulatory filings that would have implicated him in criminal proceedings.

On March 11, 2015, the Clinton Foundation announced that Donna Shalala, who had served as secretary of health and human services under Bill Clinton, had agreed to replace Braverman as Clinton Foundation CEO. What was becoming obvious was that while Chelsea may have asserted her control over the Clinton Foundation starting in 2013, she was not sufficiently strong to clean house. By 2015, Hillary stepped in, determined to put the lid on Clinton Foundation corruption, so as not to upset her continuing aspirations to be president. Within the Clinton Foundation, the power shifted to Hillary, who found with

Shalala a Hillary loyalist with proven administrative skills to replace Chelsea's departing McKinsey friend.

"As Hillary Rodham Clinton prepares to run for president, the foundation has also faced increased scrutiny, particularly for its vigorous fundraising from major corporate interests and its receipt of donations from foreign governments and organizations," the *Washington Post* wrote, reporting Shalala's appointment as Clinton Foundation CEO.

"A *Washington Post* analysis found that more than a third of the foundation's largest donors were based outside the United States," the newspaper continued. "The foundation also accepted millions from seven foreign governments while Hillary Clinton served as secretary of state."[51]

With Hillary firmly in charge of the Clinton Foundation, the gears of the moneymaking machine Bill and Hillary had orchestrated to benefit personally, most recently from Hillary's position as secretary of state, were well oiled as Hillary faced the need to raise a war chest for her 2016 presidential campaign.

Chelsea had been given her chance to clean house and she failed.

Now, Shalala's job was to keep the lid on Clinton Foundation scams until Hillary was firmly ensconced in the White House. With Hillary as president and Bill as "First Spouse" the Clintons would be protected from criminal investigations of the Clinton Foundation, with their moneymaking game positioned to advance to a new and much higher level.

CRIMINAL PHILANTHROPY— CLINTON SCAMS

How did the Clintons amass so much wealth in such a short period of time?

—PETER SCHWEIZER, *CLINTON CASH*

Part 2 consists of five chapters, each of which presents a Clinton Foundation scam in a different area of activity, starting in chapter 4 with the scams perpetrated in concert with Canadian mining executive Frank Giustra, and continuing in chapter 5 to describe how the Clintons have sought to game the HIV/AIDS epidemic for personal profit.

Chapter 6 highlights how Hillary Clinton violated, virtually even as it was being agreed upon, the Memorandum of Understanding, or MOU, required by the Obama transition team as a precondition of her being nominated secretary of state.

Chapter 7 is devoted to detailing how the Clintons swindled survivors of the 2010 earthquake in Haiti who had mistakenly relied upon the Clintons to alleviate their misery. In reality what they suffered was exploitation that added to the almost unbearable hardship imposed upon them by the earthquake itself.

Chapter 8 provides more detail, adding to the narration in chapter 2 of the earthquake that hit India in 2001, showing in more detail the extent to which the Clintons buddied with criminals from India.

4

THE CANADA SCAM

All of my chips, almost, are on Bill Clinton. He's a brand, a worldwide brand, and he can do things and ask for things that no one else can.

—FRANK GIUSTRA, QUOTED IN THE *NEW YORKER*

Intense scrutiny of the relationship between Bill Clinton and Canadian mining financier Frank Giustra arguably began with an article reporters Jo Becker and Don Van Natta Jr. wrote in the *New York Times* on January 31, 2008, titled "After Mining Deal, Financier Donated to Clinton."

The essence of the article was that Giustra brought Clinton with him to Kazakhstan on Giustra's luxurious private jet for Clinton to use his political influence to get Kazakhstan's president, Nursultan A. Nazarbayev, to agree to grant Giustra a "monstrous deal." When the deal was done, Giustra's "unknown shell company" would get exclusive rights to buy at a bargain price into three uranium projects controlled by Kazakhstan's state-owned uranium agency. As a result of the transaction, Giustra would reap tens of millions of dollars in windfall profits. In return for Bill pulling the right strings with various principals in Kazakhstan and for Hillary using her power and influence at the State

Department to make sure all roadblocks were removed, the Clintons would get paid handsomely.

The payments to the Clintons would come in the usual manner— publicly disclosed as six-figure speaker's fees for Bill and as seven-figure "donations" to the Clinton Foundation, with the possibility of additional under-the-table secret payments and percentages paid through Bill Clinton's "shell company" pass-through bank account. Clinton secretly established the account at WJC, a limited liability company registered in Delaware using his initials as a code easily recognizable by Clinton family insiders.

The *New York Times* article suggested that once the 2005 uranium agreement with Kazakhstan was final, Giustra returned the windfall to Clinton by donating $31.3 million to the Clinton Foundation. "The gift, combined with Mr. Giustra's more recent and public pledge to give the William J. Clinton Foundation an additional $100 million, secured Mr. Giustra a place in Mr. Clinton's inner circle, an exclusive club of wealthy entrepreneurs in which friendship with the former president has its privileges," the *Times* reported.

The paper went on to suggest that with Hillary Clinton's 2008 bid for the presidency heating up, Bill's ties with Giustra might be problematic. "As Mrs. Clinton's presidential campaign has intensified, Mr. Clinton has begun severing financial ties with Ronald W. Burkle, the supermarket magnate, and Vinod Gupta, the chairman of InfoUSA, to avoid any conflicts of interest," the *New York Times* reported. "Those two men have harnessed the former president's clout to expand their businesses while making the Clintons rich through partnership and consulting arrangements." Still, the newspaper noted, Bill Clinton had no intention of discontinuing his activities to raise money for the Clinton Foundation, even if Hillary were elected president. While Giustra discounted that his relationship with Bill had done anything to directly affect his business transactions, other than to raise his media profile, the *New York Times* noted that mining colleagues and analysts agree that "it has not hurt." The newspaper quoted Neil MacDonald, the CEO of a Canadian merchant bank that specializes in mining deals, as commenting that Giustra's financial success was due to a "fantastic network" that was "crowned by Mr. Clinton." The article further suggested a quid pro quo by quoting MacDonald as saying: "That's a very solid relationship for him [Giustra]. I'm sure it's very much a two-way relationship because that's the way Frank operates."[1]

MUCH-TALKED-ABOUT FRIENDSHIP

Douglas Todd in the *Vancouver Sun*'s blog *The Search*, reported that Giustra had donated the $31.3 million to the Clinton Foundation specifically to help fund the foundation's HIV/AIDS project in Africa. Todd's reporting was based on an interview he had conducted with Giustra in the boardroom of Giustra's "global empire" on the top floor of a tower in downtown Vancouver that "has the luxurious-yet-antiseptic quality of most corporate offices, despite its panoramic view of the North Shore Mountains."

In the interview, the then fifty-one-year-old "mining and financial whiz" said he was worried economic globalization had not been friendly to poor people, "especially those in developing countries where resource-extraction industries like his own has made a lot of money." So, in his friendship with Bill Clinton, Todd reported, Giustra "is trying to do something about it, something he hopes may head off, at its most extreme, revolution." Todd further stated that that is why Giustra, in his "much-talked-about friendship" with Bill Clinton, decided to begin by making "a $31-million donation to Clinton's anti AIDS/HIV project in Africa." After that contribution, Giustra told Todd, he "no longer has the luxury of staying out of the media spotlight."[2]

STAR-STUDDED BASHES

In the process of consummating the big deal, Giustra set up the Clintons to understand how profitable a "friendship" with him might be. In 2006, he threw a "star-studded 60th birthday bash" for Bill Clinton at the Fairmont Royal York Hotel in Toronto. According to the Toronto

Star, actor Kevin Spacey emceed the event, which included appearances by Billy Crystal and Bon Jovi.[3] The Clintons' take from the birthday ball? The *Vancouver Sun* reported the birthday party netted a $21 million "donation" for the Clinton Foundation.[4]

Then, in May 2008, Giustra threw another fund-raiser bash in Toronto that raked in $16 million for the Clinton Foundation. By 2008, Clinton and Giustra had spent enough time together to appreciate the mutual profitability of concocting what they called the "Clinton Giustra Sustainable Growth Initiative," a new program to be managed under the auspices of the Clinton Foundation in the United States. While Clinton and Giustra were somewhat vague when it came to defining the specifics of their "Sustainable Growth Initiative," the title included the right United Nations Agenda 21–type catchphrases to guarantee support from politically correct left-leaning globalists. When featured on the Clinton Foundation website, the Clinton Giustra Sustainable Growth Initiative was typically described as managing projects "that organize market-driven activities to meet the private sector's requirements of local supply chains." Even though Giustra began his career as a penny-stock jockey who graduated to producing feature films and buying mining companies, the idea seemed to be that he was an entrepreneur businessman who would understand the global dynamics generating economic growth without abusing the environment or exploiting natural resources. In other words the concept "Sustainable Growth Initiative" was sufficiently broad and inoffensive sounding to draw millions of dollars in funding for whatever Clinton and Giustra decided to do.

The party Giustra held for Clinton in Toronto in 2008 was another huge success. Margaret Wente reported on March 4, 2008, in the Toronto *Globe and Mail* that some of Canada's well-healed mining firms "forked over" as much as $300,000 for a table at what she described as "Toronto's most spectacular fundraiser of the year."[5] Wente wrote that the evening was "a classic mix" of business, philanthropy, power, and influence. "Bill was in great form," she added. "The event was so important that he abandoned his wife's campaign trail to be there. As the crowd chowed down on organic beef, they were entertained by the likes of Elton John, Norah Jones, Robin Williams and John Travolta. The stretch limos and private jets were stacked three deep."

Wente also noted there was something for everyone attending the 2008 Toronto bash. "When you're chasing big contracts, friends like Bill can come in handy," she commented, noting the obvious benefit Giustra could seek to derive. "Of course, Bill's rich friends get something too," she continued. "They get to name-drop, network and laugh at Robin Williams, and they get to feel good. In keeping with the Sustainable Growth Initiative, the Westin gala was even super-eco-friendly. It had organic local food and used electricity that was partly generated by wind. Guests were urged to take home and plant their table's floral centerpiece. It's unknown how many of them went home by corporate jet."

As was standard operating procedure for the Clinton Foundation, neither the $21 million reportedly raised in the 2006 Toronto fund-raiser nor the $16 million raised at the 2008 Toronto fund-raiser were separately listed, accounted for, or otherwise described in the Clinton Foundation annual reports, audited financial statements, or IRS Form 990s filed with federal regulators in 2006 or 2008. Because of the lack of detail in the Clinton Foundation audited financial statements and regulatory filings, it is impossible to tell whether or not the dollars raised in either Giustra-sponsored fund-raiser in Canada were even deposited in the Clinton Foundation accounts. The only relevant number reported in Clinton Foundation annual audited financial reports and IRS Form 990s is a number that lumps together all "contributions" to the Clinton Foundation, without specifying what the fund-raisers were or how much money each contributed.

Even more confusing, the totals in the Clinton Foundation audited annual reports and IRS Form 990s for the same year do not agree. The Clinton Foundation annual audited financial report prepared by accounting firm BKD in Little Rock listed total contributions for the year at $134,217,961 and grants at $1,599,407. The Clinton Foundation IRS Form 990 filed for 2006 listed total contributions and grants at

$135,817,368. There is no mention of the 2006 Giustra Toronto birthday bash in either document. The same pattern holds for 2008.

LIKE THE ROOSTER CROWS . . .

Clinton defenders predictably entered the fray to rejoinder the allegations, denying there was any "pay-to-play" involved in the Kazakhstan uranium deal.

One of the more prominent to come to the Clintons' defense was *Forbes* contributing editor Robert Lenzner. "An article in *The New York Times* on January 31, 2008, though carefully worded, seemingly implied that former president Bill Clinton used political influence in Kazakhstan to allow Canadian mining magnate Frank Giustra, 51, to invest in what turned out to be a very profitable uranium venture in return for Giustra's major donations to Clinton's foundation," Lenzner wrote. "Other media outlets parroting the story in the wake of Hillary Clinton's nomination as secretary of state have been less subtle, suggesting there was an outright quid pro quo."

Lenzner continued, "The *Times* story is premised on the coincidence that Giustra and Clinton were both in Almaty, Kazakhstan, on September 6, 2005, exactly the time when Giustra was pressing his case to invest in several uranium properties there. Clinton was in Kazakhstan to announce a Clinton Foundation agreement enabling the government to buy low-cost HIV drugs. The *Times* seems to suggest that Clinton's appearance with Giustra, together with his public praise of the president of Kazakhstan, somehow helped Giustra with his uranium deals."[6]

In 2015, with Hillary Clinton preparing for a second run for the White House, investigative reporter Peter Schweizer took up again the Kazakhstan story in his book *Clinton Cash*, devoting two chapters to investigating further insinuations of a "pay-to-play" relationship between Bill Clinton and Frank Giustra, first given national play by the *New York Times* in the 2008 article by Becker and Van Natta.[7] "Bill maintained that the entire visit was about dealing with HIV/AIDS in Kazakhstan," Schweizer wrote. "Giustra insisted that the mining deal he wanted to secure did not involve Nazarbayev or the Kazakh government." But Schweizer dismissed both explanations as subterfuge, writing that they were "at best elaborate evasions."[8]

For this conclusion, Schweizer advances several supporting arguments, pointing out, for instance, that at the time of Clinton's visit, the World Health Organization and the United Nations Program on HIV/AIDS estimated only fifteen hundred Kazakhs needed treatment for the disease.[9] Schweizer also noted that in a 2009 video, Mukhtar Dzhakishev, then president of Kazatomprom, the government agency that runs Kazakhstan's uranium mines and nuclear energy industry, revealed that then senator Hillary Clinton had pressured Kazakh officials to secure the deal for Giustra.[10]

In his *Forbes* article, Lenzner said that Becker and Van Natta had mistakenly reported in the *New York Times* that Bill Clinton and Giustra first met at a fund-raiser for tsunami victims at Giustra's Vancouver home in June 2005. "Actually that fundraiser was in January 2005, and Clinton was not present. He sent a video message instead," Lenzner corrected. "The two men did meet in June 2005, but on a philanthropic trip to Mexico and Colombia organized by the Clinton Foundation." Getting this type of a detail wrong is typically what Soros-funded left-leaning advocacy groups like Media Matters use to "discredit" reports threatening their ideological point of view.

The same tactics were used to attack Schweizer's 2015 book alleging the Clintons had traded political intervention for contributions. The problem is that bribery, the specific charge Schweizer alleged, requires proof of a quid pro quo. Law enforcement investigators would need access to e-mails that criminals typically hide or destroy in their effort to avoid establishing proof of wrongdoing. At any rate, minor mistakes, such as incorrectly identifying the circumstances of Bill Clinton's first meeting with Giustra, are used by Clinton defenders on the political left to undermine confidence in the accuracy of the accuser's information overall.

On *Fox News Sunday* April 26, 2015, anchor Chris Wallace interviewed attorney Lanny Davis, a longtime Clinton family defender, about the Schweizer book.[11] Giving left-leaning voters reasons to dismiss critics of the Clintons is a Davis specialty, honed through Clinton White House crises that go back to the death of Vince Foster, the conviction of Webb Hubbell in the Whitewater scandal, and the demonization of Monica Lewinsky in the Clinton Oval Office sex scandal in which Bill was impeached by the House of Representatives for lying under oath.

The background of Wallace's questioning is complicated, but important. In 2004, Giustra had attracted investors to put together a company that was eventually called UrAsia Energy Ltd. In 2005, when UrAsia acquired the uranium contracts from Kazakhstan, uranium was trading at $22 per pound. In February 2007, when a South African mining company agreed to pay $3.1 billion to acquire UrAsia in a reverse merger, uranium was trading at $113 a pound. When the reverse-merger acquisition was completed, the surviving company assumed the name Uranium One. To appreciate Giustra's windfall profits, consider that Uranium One paid $7.05 a share to acquire UrAsia, a company whose shares two years earlier, in 2005, were trading at merely 10 cents a share.[12] As noted, the Uranium One acquisition was a reverse merger. When the complex transaction was final, Giustra and his shareholders ended up owning 61 percent of Uranium One.

Then, in June 2008, the Russian State Atomic Nuclear Agency, Rosatom, began negotiations to make an investment in Uranium One. In June 2009, Rosatom subsidiary ARMZ bought a 17 percent stake in Uranium One. According to a *New York Times* timeline, between 2008 and 2010, Uranium One and UrAsia investors made $8.66 million in donations to the Clinton Foundation.[13]

By 2010, Uranium One had purchased such extensive uranium assets in the United States that it was projected to control half of all U.S. uranium output by 2015. In June 2010, ARMZ, the wholly-owned subsidiary of Rosatom that originally bought a 17 percent share in Uranium One, sought to buy a majority 51 percent control of the company. The transaction, subject to approval by the Committee on Foreign Investment in the United States, CFIUS, would give Russia access not only to the Kazakhstan uranium assets owned by Uranium One, but also the U.S. uranium assets owned by Uranium One. That same month, June 2010, Bill Clinton was in Moscow, being paid $500,000 to give one speech for Renaissance Capital, RenCap, a Cyprus-registered corporation controlled by former Russian intelligence officers with close ties to Russian president Vladimir Putin.

On *Fox News Sunday*, Wallace asked Davis:

Do you think it was a coincidence all these Canadian mining executives are giving millions to the foundation, that a company with close ties to Vladimir Putin's government in Russia is giving half a million dollar speech? Do you think that's a coincidence that's happening while the Russian company that wants to buy Uranium One has business before the State Department? Do you think that's a coincidence?[14]

Once again, note CFIUS is the acronym for the Committee on Foreign Investment in the United States, the interagency committee of the U.S. government, operating out of the U.S. Treasury, that is responsible to review and authorize transactions of a U.S. business that could result in a foreign person or entity undermining U.S. national security interests.[15] As secretary of state, Hillary Clinton was a member of CFIUS. Running for the White House in 2008, she was the only presidential candidate to make an issue of the importance of strengthening CFIUS to protect U.S. national interests, U.S. economic sovereignty, and U.S. national security.[16] In October 2010, CFIUS reviewed and approved the Rosatom acquisition of majority control in Uranium One before the deal was finalized.[17] In 2013, after receiving the approval of CFIUS with Mrs. Clinton a member of CFIUS, Rosatom acquired all remaining shares of Uranium One.[18]

This is how Lanny Davis answered Wallace's question on *Fox News Sunday*:

I don't use the word "coincidence." Of course, it's a coincidence, but it's a false inference. It sounds like if two incidents occur side by side, like the rooster crows and then the sun rises, it's a coincidence that the sun rises after the rooster crows. The rooster doesn't cause the sun to rise. In this case, the man on CFIUS from State has been publicly quoted, not by Mr. Schweizer, not by The *New York Times*, that nobody from the State Department, Hillary Clinton never once intervened on that decision or any other decision. That's a fact omitted by Mr. Schweizer.[19]

The point Davis was making is that even though the sequence of events looks suspicious, the e-mail or other written evidence of a quid pro quo deal proving the Clintons were paid to allow Giustra's uranium bonanza to proceed to fruition was lacking. Yes, Mrs. Clinton as secretary of state voted with CFIUS to approve the Giustra uranium deal. But can anyone prove she was paid under the table for her CFIUS vote? That was Lanny Davis's point. In a criminal court, coincidence is not enough to convict.

The question before CFIUS was whether Russia's gaining control over perhaps as much as half all U.S. uranium production threatened U.S. national security interests because uranium is a strategically important natural resource and Rosatom is a state nuclear agency owned by the Russian government. With Rosatom acquiring a majority stake in Uranium One, Russia got access to a substantial proportion not only of U.S. uranium reserves, but also of uranium reserves in the former Soviet republic of Kazakhstan.

But the question was not altogether simple. Increasing demand for energy in developing countries, including both India and China, meant worldwide demand for uranium was growing dramatically, as nuclear energy became a cost-effective alternative to oil and gas. Perhaps CFIUS had made a justifiable economic decision approving the acquisition. In a global economy, it may not be reasonable for the United States in future decades to demand control of all U.S.-based natural resources, especially given the large and growing U.S. national debt resulting from continuing large U.S. federal government budget deficits. CFIUS is not a law enforcement agency or a court of law authorized to investigate or adjudicate crimes such as bribery. Nor is CFIUS an agency of national defense on a par with the Department of Defense and the Pentagon. As long as the United States still had enough uranium to meet projected needs for the foreseeable future, what was wrong with approving the sale to foreign nations of access to U.S. uranium mine?

Still, the transaction bristled in that the profit of selling the U.S. uranium resources rebounded primarily to a Canadian firm. With the Clinton Foundation benefiting financially from Bill's growing friendship with Giustra, the question of wrongdoing was in the air, even if the specific proof required to obtain a criminal conviction on a bribery indictment was lacking.

WAS THE $500,000 SPEAKER'S FEE A CHARITABLE DONATION?

As noted earlier, the main inquiry of this book differs from the central question of Schweizer's book, in that the issue here is inurement, not bribery: Did the Clintons use the Clinton Foundation to benefit personally from the transactions with Giustra involving Kazakhstan, UrAsia, and Uranium One? Here the offense involves inurement, using a charitable foundation for personal gain, and the burden of proof is on the Clintons, with the law demanding that they prove they ran their 501(c)(3) foundation as a legitimate charity, deserving IRS tax-exempt status.

In the prosecution of allegations of inurement, the relevant legal questions turn not on whether or not the defendants had intent to commit bribery, but on whether or not they ran a charity to financially benefit themselves and their associates. Even if the FBI were able to recover the thousands of e-mails Hillary Clinton destroyed on the personal server she used to transact e-mail business as secretary of state, do we really expect we would catch the Clintons openly transacting a quid pro quo with Frank Giustra? Probably no, as the e-mails may have been carefully worded so as not to describe in detail the contribution the Clintons expected to be made to the Clinton Foundation in return for favorable policy decisions

Hillary made at the State Department. But if it is established that Bill and Hillary Clinton benefited financially through donations to the Clinton Foundation resulting from Bill's friendship with Giustra and the generosity of Giustra's associates in Canada who stood to benefit from the Uranium One deal, we have advanced down the path of establishing the first element of an inurement allegation. Now the only question is whether or not the Clintons, in accepting donations to the Clinton Foundation from Giustra and his Canadian associates, diverted those funds to the financial benefit of themselves and/or their close associates, or whether the Clintons followed all the rules and regulations required to run their foundation legitimately.

What we are much more likely to find by comparing the public record with information uncovered through a detailed examination of the Clinton Foundation audited financials and regulatory reports is evidence that the Clintons took steps to hide the full extent of their financial interactions with Giustra and with those they met through him. Instead of trying to prove Clinton's $500,000 speaking fee in Moscow was a payoff for the uranium deal, we are more concerned here with investigating whether the $500,000 fee was booked to the Clinton Foundation financials, treated as a charitable contribution, and fully reported to the IRS as such. Then we are interested in finding out how much of the $500,000 was spent by the Clinton Foundation to support the Clintons' lavish lifestyles, including paying for private jet travel, paying for expensive hotels in resort or other high-dollar destinations in the United States and abroad, as well as paying unusually high salaries and benefits to themselves and their top Clinton Foundation employee associates.

An examination of the relevant audited financials and IRS Tax Form 990s filed by the Clintons for the years 2008 through 2010 reveals no listing of Bill Clinton's $500,000 speaking fee in Russia as a payment made to the Clinton Foundation, instead of to Bill Clinton personally, or to a separate corporate entity designated by Clinton for payment.

WHO IS FRANK GIUSTRA?

Born in 1957 in Sudbury, Ontario, Canada, to a nickel miner, Frank Giustra spent part of his childhood in Italy and Argentina.[20] He began his career as an assistant trader and graduated to stockbroker with Merrill Lynch in 1978 and was known as a dealer in penny stocks in the Howe Street financial district of Vancouver, British Columbia. In the early 1980s he joined Yorkton Securities and moved to Europe, where he concentrated on international mining finance.[21] After becoming an investment banker, Giustra financed several feature films, and as he reached age forty, he decided he wanted to enter the entertainment business.[22] In 1997, Giustra put up $16 million of his own money to found what was to become Lionsgate Entertainment Corporation with a $40 million total investment that included former executives from Yorkton Securities.[23] In November 1997, shortly after forming the company, Giustra arranged to merge Lionsgate with Toronto Stock Exchange–listed Beringer Gold Corporation, taking his new company public in a transaction that netted him an estimated $64 million. Giustra next sold off Beringer's gold assets, and began purchasing Canadian film businesses with the proceeds.

Displaying skills for wheeling and dealing in finance that prefigured Giustra's return to mining with the UrAsia/Uranium deals, Giustra in 1998 gambled Lionsgate's future in a complicated deal with Mandalay Pictures. The deal called for Giustra's company to put up $80 million, with more than $700 million coming from Paramount Pictures and other companies that would share distribution rights. In the deal, Giustra pledged that Lionsgate would produce twenty films over a five-year period, the first due in 2000, with Lionsgate not scheduled to receive any earnings until distributors had recouped their costs. In the same year, Lionsgate picked up a bankrupt film distributor named International Movie Group, which, ten years earlier, Giustra and Yorkton Securities had financed at a cost of $14 million. The deal resembled the type of "reverse merger" Giustra orchestrated between UrAsia and Uranium One in that in both instances he managed to leverage the assets of a relatively large company to allow his relatively small company to leapfrog into a major industry position.

In 2000, Giustra stepped down as CEO of Lionsgate, retaining his position as chairman. From 2001 to 2007, he was chair of British Columbia–based Endeavor Financial, a merchant bank specializing in launching natural resource companies. At Endeavor Financial, Giustra and his business partner and friend Ian Telfer took a relatively small company, Wheaton Rivers Mineral, and merged it into Goldcorp, then the world's third-largest gold mining company with a market capitalization at the time of nearly $30 billion.[24] Currently, Giustra serves as president and CEO at Fiore Capital Corporation, a company that since July 2007 has been an exclusive adviser to Endeavor Mining Corporation.[25] In 2015, Giustra was reportedly largely divested of his interests in Lionsgate, no longer serving on its board of directors.[26]

In 2004, Lionsgate distributed progressive Michael Moore's documentary attacking then president George W. Bush, *Fahrenheit 9/11*. In 2014, Lionsgate agreed to distribute conservative Dinesh D'Souza's political documentary feature film *America: Imagine a World Without Her*.[27] While Lionsgate is well-known in the movie industry for both projects, Giustra had no involvement in the films. Today, Lionsgate is a major New York Stock Exchange–listed distributor based in Santa Monica, California, with annual gross revenues in 2013 exceeding $2 billion.[28]

ALL THE CHIPS ON BILL

Bill Clinton began flying on Giustra's private airplane in June 2005, when Clinton's staff asked to borrow Giustra's aircraft to fly the former president to a series of Clinton Foundation events.[29] The *Washington Post* noted that Giustra agreed on the condition that he could join the trip. Giustra's airplane touched down at White Plains, New York, the closest airfield to Clinton's home in Chappaqua. Giustra ferried Clinton to Arkansas, then on to Mexico, Colombia, and Brazil. The luxury plane was a full-sized passenger jet with comfortable seating areas and a private bathroom that included a shower. The interior doors had gold-colored fixtures, and an art collection was on the walls.[30]

"On their first meeting, the two men bond immediately," *Washington Post* reporter Anu Narayanswamy wrote, adding that between 2014 and 2015 Clinton used Giustra's jet in at least twenty-six foundation trips, with Giustra accompanying Clinton for thirteen of them. There is nothing to indicate in Clinton Foundation financial reports that the cost of these trips was recorded as revenue to the foundation, or separately reported by Bill Clinton so personal income tax rules could be applied appropriately. The *Washington Post* article noted that in the period September 3–6, 2005, Clinton and Giustra flew separately to Kazakhstan, where the two joined fifty others at a state dinner. "Two days later, Giustra's company finalizes a $500 million deal to acquire three rich deposits of uranium in the former Soviet republic," Narayanswamy wrote. "The following year, Giustra makes a donation of $32.7 million to the Clinton Foundation."[31] The *Post* article carefully avoids drawing any conclusion that the Giustra contribution was a quid pro quo that "paid off" Clinton for any influence he may have exerted on the Kazakhstan leaders to get the uranium deal done.

In a September 16, 2006, *New Yorker* magazine piece, left-leaning author and reporter David Remnick described seeing Bill Clinton and Giustra at a Government Leaders Forum sponsored by Microsoft. "Giustra told me that he was still heavily involved in business—he travels frequently to Kazakhstan, to check on mining interests he has there—but that his wife had been pushing him to give away more of his money." Remnick evidently asked Giustra what he thought of Clinton. "All of my chips, almost, are on Bill Clinton," he said. "He's a brand, a worldwide brand, and he can do things and ask for things that no one else can."[32]

Financial Times reporter Andrew Jack described a Clinton trip to Africa on Giustra's private airplane, with Giustra introduced into the narrative as one of the major funders of what was to become the Clinton HIV/AIDS Initiative. Jack described Giustra's donation as if Giustra were donating directly through the Clinton Foundation, with no mention of Giustra donating through a separate foundation structure incorporated in Canada. "On the plane the following day, Frank Giustra effuses about Mandela: 'For me, he's up there with Mahatma Gandhi,'" Jack wrote. "An Italian-Canadian with close-cropped white hair, Giustra is part of the most exclusive group in the Clinton entourage: the corporate sponsors. In fact, he is not travelling with us. We are travelling with him. Clinton is flying on Giustra's luxurious personal MD-87 jet, and his donations are substantially underwriting the foundation's pediatric HIV medicines programs." From what Jack observed and reported, Giustra fit right in with the gang of Clinton regulars on the trip. "That gives him a regular place at the president's side, including the card table, where the two men and others gather on the flights and late at night in palatial hotel suites across Africa," he continued. "They play 'oh hell,' a card game the film director Steven Spielberg taught Clinton when he was president."[33]

SECRET GIUSTRA-RELATED MILLIONS DONATED TO CLINTON FOUNDATION

Schweizer devotes considerable attention to the Russian uranium deal in *Clinton Cash*. A key figure in the narrative is Ian Telfer, a Canadian longtime associate of Giustra who made a fortune as a gold investor and has served as the chairman of the World Gold Council. Telfer, it turns out, was also chairman of Uranium One. "The Clinton Foundation also failed to disclose major contributions from entities controlled by those involved in the Uranium One deal," Schweizer wrote. "Thus, beginning in 2009, the company's chairman, Telfer, quietly started funneling what would become $2.35 million to the Clinton Foundation through a Canadian entity he controlled called the Fernwood Foundation."

Schweizer searched the records of the Canadian government revenue agency's charity reports and found that the Fernwood Foundation donated more than $2 million to the Clinton Foundation while Hillary was secretary of state. Schweizer reported that in 2009, Fernwood contributed $1 million to the Clinton Giustra Sustainable Growth Initiative; in 2010, the Fernwood Foundation contributed $250,000; in 2011, a total of $600,000; and in 2012, another $500,000. This would put total Fernwood Foundation donations to the Clinton Foundation in excess of $4 million from 2009 to 2010.[34]

"THE CLINTON FOUNDATION DOES ALL THE WORK"

This section may be a challenging read, but the point is to document the confusing array of names the Clinton Foundation has given to various entities and programs related to Giustra in Canada and the United States. The reason the section is important is that experienced law enforcement investigators consider a telltale sign of fraud the creation by criminals of multiple organizational structures with nearly identical names and uncertain legal registration status. Especially when the organizational structure appears overcomplicated and confusing by design, law enforcement investigators suspect entities created with no clear specification of what the various entities really do may have been created to construct a shell game in which assets can be hidden from state and federal regulators, including tax collectors.

Schweizer further noted that, according to Canadian tax records, nearly all the funds the Clinton Giustra Sustainable Growth Initiative (CGSGI) collected were transferred directly to the Clinton Foundation in New York. This results in the conclusion the Clinton Foundation accounted for CGSGI not as a separate foundation, with its own IRS 1023 application and separate legal subsidiary documentation, but as a part of the Clinton Foundation. CGSGI financials appear to have been consolidated into Clinton Foundation financials in all financial audits and IRS Form 990s for the relevant years.[35] Schweizer correctly noted the Clinton Foundation's failure to report these transactions was a clear violation of the Memorandum of Understanding negotiated with the Obama transition team as a condition for Hillary Clinton to be nominated as secretary of state, which required public disclosure of all foreign contributions, as we shall see in chapter 6.

It took the Clinton Foundation until the publication of Schweizer's book in 2015 to respond to allegations that it had failed to report $2.35 million in donations from the Fernwood Foundation. On April 26, 2015, the *Wall Street Journal* reported that Clinton Foundation CEO Maura Pally said the donations from Fernwood went into "a separate Clinton charity," the Clinton Giustra Enterprise Partnership-Canada. Yet, reading deeper into the article, it was clear Pally and the Clinton Foundation were admitting the Canadian contributions reached the Clinton Foundation in the United States. "The Fernwood donation went to the Clinton Giustra Enterprise Partnership-Canada, which is named for former president Bill Clinton and longtime supporter Frank Giustra, a Canadian mining executive who also has been a business partner and is a friend of Mr. Telfer's," reporters Siobhan Hughes and James V. Grimaldi wrote. "The Clinton Giustra Enterprise Partnership-Canada, a charity, in turn, provided funding to the Clinton Giustra Enterprise Partnership, a program." The article further disclosed that the Clinton Foundation "does all the work" of the Clinton Giustra Enterprise Partnership, according to Pally. "CGEP (Canada) provides funding on a project-by-project basis and this money goes exclusively to CGEP projects, not to the Foundation's general operating fund," Pally said in a statement the previous Sunday, according to the *Wall Street Journal*.[36]

In 2007, Clinton and Giustra launched the Clinton Giustra Enterprise Partnership "with the focus of creating social and economic development programs in parts of the world where poverty is widespread, including Colombia, Peru, Mexico and Haiti."[37] A note in the William J. Clinton Foundation IRS Form 990 filed for 2007 documents that the Clinton Giustra Sustainable Growth Initiative, also launched in 2007, is a Clinton Foundation program designed to work with local communities, the private sector, governments, and other nongovernmental organizations "to develop new, practical models for businesses to spur sustainable social and economic development as an integral part of their operations in the developing world." The note in the 2007 IRS Form 990 further specified that CGSGI was beginning in Latin America "to strengthen child nutrition, expand access to health care in remote areas, and strengthen entrepreneurship in Colombia and Peru."[38]

This rather general language, typical for Clinton Foundation annual reports, audited financial statements, and IRS Form 990s, when compared against Pally's statement, noted earlier on the Clinton Foundation website, suggests there are three entities: the Clinton Giustra Enterprise Partnership (Canada), the Clinton Giustra Enterprise Partnership (USA), and the Clinton Giustra Enterprise Partnership. The Clinton Giustra Enterprise Partnership (Canada) was registered as a charity in Canada in 2007, but the other two entities appear never to have been registered in the United States, as of March 2016. The two U.S. programs appear to have been used interchangeably, more as "brand names" for various Clinton Foundation programs than as separately incorporated entities. The confusion is compounded by the Clinton Foundation's general failure to identify any specific program details about what exactly CGSGI funded in 2007, if anything.

Jo Becker and Mike McIntire reported in the *New York Times* that Schweizer was correct in reporting that Telfer, as chairman of Uranium One according to Canadian government records, had used his family foundation to make four previously undisclosed donations to the Clinton Foundation totaling $2.35 million. Again, the two reporters assumed the relevant allegation against the Clintons was bribery. "Whether the donations played any role in the approval of the uranium deal is unknown," Becker and McIntire wrote. "But the episode underscores the special ethical challenges presented by the Clinton Foundation, headed by a former president who relied heavily on foreign cash to accumulate $250 million in assets even as his wife helped steer American foreign policy as secretary of state, presiding over decisions with the potential to benefit the foundation's donors."

Again, these were charges Clinton supporters could easily dismiss. "In a statement, Brian Fallon, a spokesman for Mrs. Clinton's presidential campaign, said no one 'has ever produced a shred of evidence supporting the theory that Hillary Clinton ever took action as secretary of state to support the interests of donors to the Clinton Foundation,'" Becker and McIntyre continued. "He [Fallon] emphasized that multiple United States agencies, as well as the Canadian government, had signed off on the deal and that, in general, such matters were handled at a level below the secretary. 'To suggest the State Department, under then-Secretary Clinton, exerted undue influence in the U.S. government's review of the sale of Uranium One is utterly baseless,' he [Fallon] added."[39]

PROTECTING THE PRIVACY OF DONORS, OR THE SECRECY OF DONATIONS?

In a follow-up *New York Times* article, titled "Canadian Partnership Shielded Identities of Donors to Clinton Foundation," Becker and McIntire reported that the Clintons had engineered with Giustra a complex international structure of interlocking foundations designed to permit the Clintons to hide identities of the Fernwood Foundation donors:

> The nonprofit, the Clinton Giustra Enterprise Partnership (Canada), operates in parallel to a Clinton Foundation project called the Clinton Giustra Enterprise Partnership, which is expressly covered by an agreement Mrs. Clinton signed to make all donors public while she led the State Department. However, the foundation maintains that the Canadian partnership is not bound by that agreement and that under Canadian law contributors' names cannot be made public.

Subtly, the Clinton defenders were trying to shift the ground to insist that the goal had not been to keep secret sizable Canadian donations with ties to the Uranium One deal but to hide the identity of the Canadian donors.

Again, the Clinton Foundation attempted to deny that the failure of the Clinton Foundation to disclose Giustra-related contributions publicly violated the Clinton MOU, with Clinton defenders now trying to insist the Clintons had no choice. The argument seemed to be this: If Canadian law demanded the Clintons keep secret the identity of the Canadian donors, then how could the Clintons be blamed for doing just that? "'This is hardly an effort on our part to avoid transparency,'" insisted Maura Pally, acting chief executive of the Clinton Foundation. "Instead, the foundation said that the partnership was created by the

Canadian mining financier Frank Giustra to allow Canadian donors to get a tax benefit for supporting his work with Mr. Clinton—a benefit that came with the price of respecting Canada's privacy laws," McIntire and Becker reported.

Nor did the *Times* reporters appear to buy additional assertion by the Clinton defenders that the complex international structure was necessary to provide the Canadian donors a tax deduction. "However, interviews with tax lawyers and officials in Canada cast doubt on assertions that the partnership was necessary to confer a tax benefit; an examination shows that for many donors it was not needed, and in any event, since 2010, Canadians could have donated to the foundation directly and received the same tax break," McIntire and Becker reported in this second article, dated April 29, 2015. "Also, it is not at all clear that privacy laws prohibit the partnership from disclosing its donors, the tax lawyers and officials in Canada said."

What the *Times* appeared to be suggesting is that the complex international structure, as well as the Clinton Foundation explanation for refusing to disclose the names of the Canadian donors, constituted an elaborate scheme to hide both the identities of the Guistra-related donors and the facts of their contributions to the Clinton Foundation information from the public. "The partnership [between Clinton and Giustra], established in 2007, effectively shielded the identities of its donors—and the amount they gave—by allowing them to bundle their money together in the offshoot Canadian partnership before it was passed along to Clinton Foundation programs. The foundation, in turn, names only the partnership as the source of those funds." The article stressed that in 2010, the Canadian government had authorized the Clinton Foundation to receive tax-deductible donations directly from Canadians, without requiring the donations to first pass into a charity registered in Canada.

McIntire and Becker also challenged the contention that the Canadian Giustra partnership was needed to protect the privacy of the donors. "A spokeswoman for the Canadian Revenue Agency, Magali Deussing, said that the tax law 'does not regulate whether a registered charity or other qualified donee can disclose donor information.' However, other federal or provincial privacy laws may apply, she said." The *Times* then reported that Malcolm Burrows, the head of philanthropic advisory services at Scotiabank in Toronto, said that "general Canadian privacy rules" could apply to charities, but that "in most cases it is not a concern because charities and their donors want the publicity." Burrows said the "irony here is that the foundation is saying they're not allowed to do it. But many foundations want to put that information out there."

The *Times* went on to quote Mark Blumberg, a tax lawyer in Toronto, who said that while privacy laws would prohibit charities from misusing donor information for commercial purposes, they generally did not otherwise prevent disclosure of donors. "If an organization operating in British Columbia wants to be transparent about who their donors are, then they could easily provide an opportunity for donors to consent to the disclosure of their name and/or donation amount," Blumberg said.[40]

With the controversy over the Fernwood Foundation donations surfacing, Clinton defenders were caught in a lie. Canadian law did not require that Canadians could get a tax deduction only if they invested in a Canadian charity, and it did not require Canadian foundations to keep the names of donors private. What the *Wall Street Journal*'s and *New York Times*'s reporting established after the publication of Schweizer's book was that the real purpose of the secrecy was to shield sizable foreign donations to the Clinton Foundation from Canada that were from donors related to Giustra. The *Journal*'s and *Times*'s reporting in 2015 buttressed Schweizer's conclusion that the Giustra–Clinton partnership in Canada had been set simply to "operate as a pass-through" to hide the identities and amounts contributed by Giustra and others who had benefited financially from the Uranium One deal.[41]

$33.3 MILLION IN DONATIONS FROM CANADA

A list of lifetime cumulative donations to the Clinton Foundation, referenced by the second *New York Times* article, made clear that Clinton Giustra Enterprise Partnership (Canada) was one of the Clinton

Foundation's top seven donors through December 2015, along with the UNITAID donation to the Clinton Health Access Initiative, and the money the Bill & Melinda Gates Foundation had donated to Clinton Global Initiative membership, sponsorship, and fees. The Clinton-Giustra partnership in Canada is listed on the Clinton Foundation website as having contributed "more than $25 million" through December 2015.[42] Canadian tax records show the partnership in Canada took in $33.3 million in donations between 2008 and 2013. This total appears to suggest that if Ian Telfer and the Fernwood Foundation contributed in excess of $4 million, Giustra could not have contributed the $31.3 million he claimed to have donated immediately after the initial Kazakhstan uranium deal was completed, plus the $100 million he pledged to contribute from the earnings of that deal. Or, perhaps Giustra donated his $31.3 million in 2008 directly to the Clinton Foundation to fund the foundation's HIV/AIDS work in Africa.

The public record remains unclear regarding who precisely in Canada contributed what amount exactly to the Clinton Foundation. It is also unclear on how the donations from Giustra and his Canadian associates was received by the Clinton Foundation, as direct contributions, or as contributions to Clinton Giustra Enterprise Partnership (Canada) that were bundled in Canada before the partnership sent the contributions to the Clinton Foundation in the United States. Adding to the confusion, the New York Times reported that about half of the $33.3 million donated through the Clinton Giustra Enterprise Partnership (Canada) came from various charities, including $10.5 million from the Radcliffe Foundation. The New York Times concluded that of the $33.3 million donated from Canada via the Clinton Giustra Enterprise Partnership (Canada), the origin of about $20 million comes from "donors whose identities remain a mystery, at least for now."[43]

In addition to Telfer, Schweizer named other Canadian contributors to the Clinton Foundation that had benefited from Giustra's uranium transactions. The Times, agreeing with Schweizer, identified the following four Clinton Foundation donors along with their specific connection to Giustra's Uranium One deal:

- Frank Holmes, another major shareholder in the deal, who wrote a check to the Clinton Foundation for between $250,000 and $500,000. Holmes was CEO of U.S. Global Investors, which held $4.7 million in Uranium One shares in the first quarter of 2011.

- Paul Reynolds, who donated between $250,000 and $500,000 to the Clinton Foundation, was an adviser on the 2007 UrAsia/Uranium One merger. Reynolds later helped raise $260 million for Uranium One.

- Neil Woodyer, who donated $50,000 to $100,000 to the Clinton Foundation, was, with Giustra, a cofounder of Endeavor Mining, and also advised Uranium One.

- GMP Securities Ltd. worked on a debt issue that raised $250 million for Uranium One, donating a portion of the profits to the Clinton Foundation.[44]

Among the others Schweizer mentioned were Robert Disbrow, a broker at Haywood Securities, a company that provided $58 million in capital to float shares of UrAsia's private placement. Disbrow donated between $1 million and $5 million to the Clinton Foundation. Another was Sergei Kurzin, a Russian deal maker involved in the Kazakhstan uranium deal and a shareholder in UrAsia Energy, who made a $1 million pledge to the Clinton Giustra Sustainable Growth Initiative.[45]

A review of the IRS Form 990s filed by Clinton Global Initiative for the years 2009 through 2013, as well as a review of the audited financials and the IRS Form 990s for the Clinton Foundation for the years 2008 through 2013, show no separate reporting of donations made by the Clinton Giustra Enterprise Partnership (Canada) or any of the individual donors related to the Giustra uranium deal, including Giustra himself, that Schweizer identifies in *Clinton Cash*.

Again, remember that in the audited financial statements and IRS

Form 990s of the Clinton Foundation filed since inception, and in the Clinton Global Initiative IRS Form 990s filed between 2009 and 2013, all donations are lumped together in a "contributions" and/or "grants" category in a single sum. There is no financial breakdown or textual notes that would allow a regulator or a law enforcement authority to determine the donor or amount given.

John Sexton, reporting at Breitbart News, noted the contributions from the Canadian charity dropped dramatically in 2013, the year Hillary Clinton resigned as secretary of state. The total amount the Clinton Giustra Enterprise Partnership (Canada) passed on to the Clinton Foundation in the United States in 2013 was $314,437, a small fraction of the $4.7 million the Canadian charity delivered to the Clinton Foundation in 2013, or the $4.6 million it gave in 2011.[46] This supports Schweizer's conclusion that Clinton's best years for high-paying speaker's fees, with much-higher-than-average fees being paid by foreign entities, occurred "while his wife was at the pinnacle of her power as secretary of state, a perch with enormous influence over issues that directly affect foreign governments."[47]

CLINTON'S SECRET BANK ACCOUNT

On May 25, 2015, the Associated Press broke the story that Bill Clinton had created and used a shell corporation, WJC, and a shell bank account for an undisclosed amount of time to hide an undisclosed amount of money from public reporting and accountability.[48] The disclosure came in response to questions the AP had posed regarding financial files the Clintons had released as a legal requirement for Hillary's 2016 presidential campaign, with the answers provided by Clinton officials who spoke on the condition of anonymity. The officials leaking the information confirmed that WJC was a pass-through account, designed to collect fees for consulting, possibly for speeches, and conceivably to receive payment on commercial "deals" in which the Clintons had delivered services, possibly including political favors, in return for payment.

WJC is the type of company that gun-running and drug-dealing criminal cartels involved in international money laundering create and operate to avoid law enforcement detection. By emptying the account to zero following each transaction, the Clintons could use a pass-through account at WJC in an attempt to avoid having to make public disclosure of the account. The existence of WJC as a corporation or as a shell bank account has never been mentioned in any Clinton Foundation audited financial statements or IRS Tax Form 990 since the foundation's inception in 1997. Because the WJC bank account might never show up with a positive balance in banking records reported to bank regulators, the Clintons could also seek to avoid disclosing the existence of the account in their income tax filings. What would be required to avoid detection is to make sure the amounts deposited into the account were quickly debited out of the account, such that the account never showed a positive balance for more than a few hours or a few days, at most. The account is called a pass-through account precisely because the Clintons never intended any money to remain deposited for long in WJC bank accounts.

"While Bill Clinton's lucrative speeches have provided the bulk of the couple's income, earning as much as $50 million during his wife's four-year term as secretary of state in the Obama administration, the former president has also sought to branch out into other business activities in recent years," the AP reported, adding that little is known about the exact nature and financial worth of Bill Clinton's non-speech business interests.

The AP story revealed that WJC was set up in Delaware in 2008 and again in 2013, and in New York in 2009. There was no mention of WJC in any financial disclosures made by Hillary Clinton between 2008, when she was first running for president, and 2013, when she held the position of U.S. secretary of state.[49]

For those versed in the requirements of the Bank Secrecy Act of 1970, BSA, widely known as the Currency and Foreign Transaction Reporting Act, and the various U.S. Department of Treasury publications on money laundering, the creation of shell companies operating pass-through bank accounts is an automatic red flag, signaling the possibility of illegal activity, including money laundering and U.S. income tax evasion. The U.S. Money Laundering Threat Assessment Working Group, composed of the U.S. Department of Treasury, the Department of Justice, the Department of Homeland Security, the board of governors of the Federal Reserve System, and the U.S. Postal Inspection Service, have consistently warned that legal entities, such as shell corporations formed in the state of Delaware, "because of their ability to hide ownership and mask financial details" have become "popular tools" for money launderers.[50] The Federal Financial Institutions Examination Council's *Bank Secrecy Act Anti-Money Laundering Examination Manual* currently warns that while there are certain legitimate reasons for the creation of shell companies, it remains common knowledge that shell companies "can be used for money laundering and other crimes because they are easy and inexpensive to form and operate." The manual further notes shell companies are frequently used for criminal purposes because "ownership and transactional information can be concealed from regulatory agencies and law enforcement, in large part because most state laws require minimal disclosures of such information during the formation process."[51]

Clearly, Bill Clinton's use of a shell company pass-through account for the receipt of personal income throws into complete doubt any ability to estimate accurately the income the Clintons might receive from undisclosed payments received in the United States or internationally for unspecified services rendered. What this means is that Clinton Foundation audited financials and IRS Form 990s are completely blind to any and all funds transferring to the Clintons through WJC even if the funds relate to a Clinton Foundation donor or associate, such as Frank Giustra. Finally, if the funds passing through WJC are not deposited into Clinton family bank accounts audited for tax purposes, the Clintons could conceivably offshore banking accounts to evade state and federal reporting requirements and the paying of income taxes. Without full reporting and disclosure by the Clinton Foundation and the Clintons personally, the funds passed through the WJC shell company account that ended up in offshore accounts, money market accounts, or other investments might never be found. Obviously, funds hidden through money-laundering activities would never be reported in the public disclosure requirements candidates Hillary Clinton faced as a U.S. senator from New York, as well as when she was secretary of state, or while she was running for the presidency in 2008 and again in 2016.

THE CLINTON GIUSTRA SHELL GAME

Writing in the Canadian mining publication the *Northern Miner*, Gwen Preston reported in 2007 that Giustra, then approaching his fiftieth birthday, had announced on June 21 that year that he was planning to donate $100 million plus half of his future mining earnings to the "new entity" known as the Clinton Giustra Sustainable Growth Initiative "to fight Third World Poverty with help from the mining industry." Giustra's intentions were stated as if they were completely philanthropic. "I really like what I do, which is creating wealth by investing in the mining industry, and I want to continue to do it—but the only twist is that now I get to do it to give it away," Giustra told the *Northern Miner*. "It's fun—it's actually a great position to be in."

The publication further announced that Giustra had spent the previous five months asking mining industry members and other industrialists to join the project. "The world's second-richest man, Mexican telecommunications tycoon Carlos Slim, is already matching Giustra's US$100-million donation, and more than 20 large mining companies and mining-focused brokerage firms have already signed on as partners, many of them committing a percentage of revenue to the fund," Preston noted. The article went on to point out that Colombia would be the first focus of the Clinton Giustra Sustainable Growth Initiative, but the goal was to get a coalition of "companies and organizations" to work with governments and nongovernment organizations "to improve health and education and promote sustainable development," with a goal ultimately of moving beyond Latin America to expand the initiative worldwide.[52]

An updated listing by the Clinton Foundation showed Slim had contributed dramatically less to the foundation than the $100 million promised,[53] the *Washington Free Beacon* reported, with cumulative contributions through 2015 between $250,000 and $500,000.[54]

Yet a page on the Clinton Foundation website detailing the Clinton Giustra Enterprise Partnership continues to credit Slim as a cofounder:

> The Clinton Giustra Enterprise Partnership (CGEP) was co-founded by President Clinton and Frank Giustra in 2007 and is currently funded by Frank Giustra and Fundación Carlos Slim in Latin America. CGEP creates, replicates, and oversees social enterprises that generate both social impact and financial returns by addressing existing market gaps in developing countries' supply or distribution chains. In order to increase their impact and quickly replicate their models, CGEP establishes strategic partnerships with large corporations.[55]

Typically, many pledges announced by the Clinton Foundation, especially those proclaimed during the Clinton Global Initiative annual meetings, never appear to materialize. But while the Clinton Foundation widely publicizes the pledges when made, the Clinton Foundation is typically silent on whether or not the pledged contributions ever materialized. The Clinton Global Initiative annual meeting press releases typically give the total of all pledges made during the meeting, without providing details on the individual pledge subtotals that contribute to the final summed-up total amount in pledges claimed. This failure of CGI to provide detailed reporting on individual pledges makes it virtually impossible to determine which specific pledges were fulfilled in total, partially fulfilled, or never fulfilled. In recent years, the Clinton Global Initiative has gotten much less dollar-specific about pledges made during the CGI annual meeting. "Attendees made 79 new Commitments to Action that, when fully funded and implemented, will positively impact the lives of more than 1.6 million people in the United States," a press release issued for the 2015 Clinton Global Initiative annual meeting announced.[56] But no cumulative dollars pledged were announced, nor was any explanation provided that detailed what the seventy-nine new "Commitments to Action" were or when they might be funded. This is very different from the 2006 Clinton Global Initiative's second annual meeting, attended by Slim, when a press release announced "hundreds of participants had made 215 commitments, totaling over $7.3 billion" that combined with the previous year's totals meant "CGI has resulted in nearly $10 billion worth of commitments in just its first two years."[57]

FONDO ACCESO

In early June 2010, the Clinton Foundation, Giustra, and the Carlos Slim Foundation announced the launch of Fondo Acceso, supposedly a $20 million private equity fund "set up to invest in small and medium-sized enterprises in Colombia."[58] The Clinton Foundation, reported Alana Goodman in the *Washington Free Beacon* in November 2015, was actually running Fondo Acceso in Colombia, "raising concerns from government and consumer watchdog groups who say the practice is unusual and could pose a significant conflict of interest."[59]

Goodman noted that Fondo Acceso was owned by the Clinton Foundation and being run out of the Clinton Foundation's Bogotá office and staffed by Clinton Foundation employees. "The firm is managed by Carolina Botero, who is also chief financial officer at the Clinton-Giustra Enterprise Partnership. It lists various Clinton Foundation and CGEP officials as directors in its corporate filings," Goodman wrote. "The Clinton Foundation's tax returns list Fondo Acceso as a related corporation in which the foundation holds a 50 percent stake." Goodman further reported that Colombian companies that want to apply for venture funding from the Fondo Acceso must also sign a contract turning over financial and internal information to both the private equity firm and the Clinton Foundation. "Vanessa Jimenez, chief administrator at the Clinton Foundation's Bogota office, answered the phone number listed for the private equity fund on Tuesday. She said she was not allowed to talk about Fondo Acceso's investments," Goodman wrote. "Jimenez said Fondo Acceso was based out of the office, but employees there technically worked for the Clinton Foundation." Goodman's reporting stressed the unusual nature of a charitable foundation running a private equity fund, noting that only $2 million in Fondo Acceso investments in Colombia could be documented, out of the $20 million investment initially promised by the Clinton Foundation and Slim.

Then, a few days later, Goodman reported that Fondo Acceso had never been registered as a private equity fund in Colombia. Instead, it was registered in Colombia as a "simple stock corporation," which legal experts told Goodman should have precluded the company from doing business as a private equity firm. She also reported that after her first article was published, the Fondo Acceso website was removed from the Internet. Those in Colombia interviewed by Goodman explained that by not registering as a private equity fund, Fondo Acceso could avoid the scrutiny and regulation of the Superintendency of Finance.[60]

Again, we see the confusion of corporate legal structures. While sounding similar, the Clinton Giustra Sustainable Growth Initiative and the Clinton Giustra Enterprise Partnership were always two different entities. Amy Davidson made this clear in an April 24, 2015, *New Yorker* article, writing that Craig Minassian, a Clinton Foundation spokesman, pointed out to her that these were legally separate entities. The Clinton Giustra Enterprise Partnership (Canada), Davidson wrote, is a Canadian registered corporation organized as a charity under Canadian law. The Clinton Giustra Sustainable Growth Initiative operates as a brand name to identify a program run by the Clinton Foundation.

Minassian predictably attempted to convince Davidson that the Clinton Giustra Enterprise Partnership was incorporated as a Canadian charity to get Canadian donors tax benefits and keep their names private. But when Davidson realized all money given to the Canadian entity was funneled to the Clinton Foundation in the United States and that, per an agency agreement, all the work of the Clinton Giustra Enterprise Partnership (Canada) was done by the Clinton Foundation in the United States, she saw through Minassian's explanation as a cover-up. "The Web site that has the C.G.E.P. [Clinton Giustra Enterprise Partnership] name on it also has the Clinton Foundation logo and Bill Clinton's picture; it also has a copyright notice naming the Canadian entity as the site's owner," Davidson wrote. "Anyone visiting the site would be justifiably confused. They are, in other words, effectively intermingled." Davidson appeared to understand the subterfuge, joining the *New York Times* reporters in getting to the heart of the Canadian ruse. "And what would it mean if the Canadian explanation flew—that the Clintons could allow a foreign businessman to set up a foreign charity, bearing their name, through which people in other countries could make secret multi-million-dollar donations to their charity's work?" she asked.[61]

So was Fondo Acceso a part of the Clinton-Giustra Sustainable Global Initiative or the Clinton Giustra Enterprise (Canada), or a program owned and operated by the Clinton Foundation as part of the U.S. Clinton Giustra Enterprise Partnership? What was Carlos Slim's corporate ownership in Fondo Acceso? Why were Fondo Acceso employees in Columbia employees of the Clinton Foundation in the United States? Law enforcement investigators examining Clinton Foundation financials should see if offshore accounts were established by Clinton–Giustra operatives in Colombia to evade U.S. taxes as one of the many strategies possibly being employed to enrich Clinton family members. Certainly it should be suspicious that Fundo Acceso would shut down its website the moment a U.S. investigative reporter begins asking questions. If Fundo Acceso were really established to put to work the $100 million pledged each by Giustra and Slim, why wasn't the fund registered as a charity in Columbia? If Fundo Acceso were a private investment fund, why wasn't the fund registered as a private equity fund in Colombia? And finally, why are the funds actually invested so small, when the initial pledge was represented to be $100 million?

SUSPICIOUS TRANSACTIONS

Experienced law enforcement investigators recognize transactions involving one foundation writing a check to another foundation as a signal a money-laundering operation may be taking place. At the level of the foundation transferring the money in Canada, a portion of a donor's contribution may be skimmed off and applied to another use, perhaps sent by wire transfer to an undisclosed account in the United States to pay personal expenses, or maybe even campaign expenses. Conceivably, the net remaining in Canada, after the funds are applied to campaign financing for Hillary Clinton in the United States, could then be wired from Giustra's Canadian foundation to the Clinton Foundation in the United States. The transaction is especially hard to track if there are multiple donors in Canada or in Mexico pledging publicly to contribute larger amounts than are actually donated. When the sums donated in Canada and/or Mexico do not tally with the records of donations received by the Clinton Foundation in the United States, the money-laundering opportunities are almost limitless.

Under the Bank Secrecy Act, banks operating in the United States are required to establish, implement, and maintain programs designed to detect and report suspicious activity indicative of money laundering and other financial crimes. The purpose of the Bank Secrecy Act is to protect the public from harm by identifying and detecting money laundering from criminal enterprises, terrorism, tax evasion, or other unlawful activities, including charity fraud.[62]

To ensure that the Clinton Foundation transactions with Giustra in Canada and with Carlos Slim in Mexico were legitimate, law enforcement authorities need to obtain all copies of checks, wire transfers, account statements, invoices, bills, delivery tickets, e-mail communications, other correspondence, incorporating documents, government registration applications, contracts, loan agreements, and other account books or official records for at least the following entities: the Clinton Giustra Enterprise Partnership (Canada), the Clinton Giustra Enterprise Partnership (USA), and the Clinton Giustra Sustainable Growth Initiative, Fundo Acceso (Columbia), and the Clinton Foundation in the United States. If audited financial statements are fraudulent, the auditors may bear their own criminal liability. The criminal liability of the auditors may be compounded if fraudulent audited financial statements were used as the basis for regulatory filings in the United States, including IRS tax Form 990 filings.

Instead of examining audited financial statements and IRS Form 990s that report only total contributions and grants, all transactions between Clinton–Giustra entities in Canada, Clinton–Giustra entities in the United States, and the Clinton Foundation need to be examined one by one. The tracking should start with documentation of each amount donated by each donor, following where the money was deposited, what intermediary entities booked the donation, and how the donation was transferred to the final Clinton Foundation donor entity in the United States. The same should hold true for any contributions and/or investments made by Carlos Slim in Mexico that may or may not be related to one or more of the various Clinton-Giustra entities. The concern is that financial schemes might be advanced by issuing phony statements or fraudulent payments from financial sources that were designed to cover up the transfer of the funds for personal use and/ or redistribution schemes.

Law enforcement needs to be on the watch for proxy accounts set up as pass-through accounts in shell corporations into which funds are initially deposited or transferred to monitor the potential for diversion. The FBI should interrogate individuals in the Clinton Giustra Enterprise Partnership in Canada and the United States, as well as the Clinton Foundation in the United States, for evidence of multiple schemes to falsify official audit statements and regulatory filing documents. The FBI also should investigate any and all official documents submitted by the Clinton Giustra Enterprise Partnership in Canada as well as in the United States and the Clinton Foundation in the United States for falsified entries, including the identification as donors under fictional names appearing on lists as individual, group, or corporate donors.

What should be clear from the investigations undertaken by news reporters after the publication of Schweizer's *Clinton Cash* is that the organizational complexity of creating a foundation in Canada to fund a foundation in the United States to fund programs in Latin and South America, with the involvement of Mexican billionaire Carlos Slim, demands Bank Security Act investigations. This is especially true when the identities of Canadian donors to the Clinton Giustra Enterprise Partnership (Canada) remain secret or uncertain and the amounts reportedly donated in Canada and received by the Clinton Foundation in the United States remain divergent. If the amount of donations recorded as donated in Canada differs from the amounts received by the Clinton Foundation in the United States, a money-laundering scheme to divert proceeds to Clinton family personal and/or personal purposes is almost certain.

CLINTON FOUNDATION SCRABBLES TO EXPLAIN

As noted earlier in this chapter, on April 26, 2015, Maura Pally, writing as acting CEO of the Clinton Foundation and a senior vice president of Women and Youth Programs, attempted to explain why Bill Clinton and Frank Giustra created the Clinton Giustra Enterprise Partnership in 2007. Taking a closer look at Pally's reasoning in this section, it should be clear that the explanation for why the Clinton Giustra Enterprise Partnership exists is shifting.

"The [Clinton] Foundation has 11 different initiatives, some of which function in organizationally different ways," Pally began in a posting on the Clinton Foundation website. "One of these 11 initiatives is the Clinton Giustra Enterprise Partnership (CGEP), which is focused on advancing innovative solutions to poverty alleviation on a global scale. CGEP has come under heightened scrutiny this past week and I want to explain how it operates." After the flurry of press investigations, Pally had no choice but to acknowledge the Clinton Foundation in Canada was a shell pass-through entity, not an operating foundation. "The Clinton Foundation executes all of the work that CGEP does," she openly admitted.

"CGEP does receive financial backing for projects from an independent Canadian charity called the Clinton Giustra Enterprise Partnership

(Canada), which Frank Giustra established so that Canadians could support the initiative's valuable work and receive a charitable tax credit," Pally continued, still holding on to the now-debunked tax-exemption reason for creating the Canadian foundation. But the real point of Pally's new explanation seemed to be the next sentence, in which she somehow suggested it was important the Canadian donors be able to support the Clinton Foundation on a project-by-project basis. Advancing this point, Pally wrote, "CGEP (Canada) provides funding on a project-by-project basis and this money goes exclusively to CGEP projects, not to the Foundation's general operating fund."

But even advancing the new explanation that a separate Canadian structure was needed so Canadian investors could pick which Clinton Foundation projects they wanted to support, Pally also refused to let go of the donor privacy reason. "Like every contributor to the Foundation, the Clinton Giustra Enterprise Partnership (Canada) is publicly listed as a donor on our website," Pally said. "But as it is a distinct Canadian organization, separate from the Clinton Foundation, its individual donors are not listed on the site. This is hardly an effort on our part to avoid transparency—unlike in the U.S., under Canadian law; all charities are prohibited from disclosing individual donors without prior permission from each donor."[63]

Dropped from Pally's description was any discussion of the Clinton Giustra Sustainable Growth Initiative, reinforcing the impression that CGSGI was nothing more than a brand name, used interchangeably with the Clinton Giustra Enterprise Partnership (USA) to designate Canadian money coming to the Clinton Foundation as a contribution from Giustra personally and/or from Canadian donors who profited with Giustra in their various mining finance ventures.

Perhaps bribery cannot be proved in Bill Clinton's relationship with Frank Giustra. But surely no one but a Clinton partisan could doubt the inurement allegations are worth investigation in an international corporate structure this complex that has suffered from shifting Clinton Foundation and discredited reasons for existing in the first place. What seems obvious is that the Clintons used Bill's friendship with Giustra to position the Clinton Foundation for the financial gain.

That the mix of structures involved in the transfer of money from Giustra to the Clintons involved pass-through bank accounts created within shell corporations identified only by Bill Clinton's initials suggests the possible diversion of Giustra funds for the personal use of the Clinton Family. Any serious law enforcement investigation of the Clinton-Giustra spaghetti structure to pass money internationally will inevitably raise questions about the honesty of auditors preparing audited financial statements as the basis for regulatory reporting.

5

THE HIV/AIDS SCAM

Ira Magaziner is busy saving the lives of people with AIDS.

—BILL CLINTON, *GIVING*

This chapter focuses on answering the question, how did a foundation granted IRS federal tax-exempt status for creating a presidential library in Little Rock, Arkansas, suddenly gain federal tax-exempt authorization to combat HIV/AIDS in the Third World?

The story begins at the World AIDS conference held in Barcelona, Spain, in July 2002. It continues through the Clinton Foundation's theft of UNITAID air levies imposed on French airline travelers by the French government. From there, we go to Geneva, Switzerland, where the United Nations World Health Organization bears the responsibility for managing the UNITAID funds.

The chapter next winds to India, where the Clintons, through their top political operatives, arrange to buy defective generic drugs to deliver to Third World HIV/AIDS victims. It concludes in Africa, where we ask if the Clinton Foundation followed through to make sure those drugs reached diseased patients.

Throughout, we ask the hard questions: Despite all the media hype, did the Clinton Foundation actually make any difference in controlling the HIV/AIDS epidemic in the Third World? If not, what happened to all the money?

Or, is the Clinton HIV/AIDS Initiative, also called the Clinton Health Access Initiative, or CHAI, just another Clinton family get-rich-quick inurement scheme, designed callously to rip off legitimate charity donors worldwide as well as HIV/AIDS-infected people in the Third World who desperately need effective medical assistance?

A NELSON MANDELA SUGGESTION

In his 2007 book *Giving*, Bill Clinton credits the idea to use the Clinton Foundation to fight HIV/AIDS in the Third World to a conversation he had with Nelson Mandela in 2002.

"After Nelson Mandela and I closed the World AIDS conference in Barcelona in [July] 2002, Prime Minister Denzil Douglas of St. Kitts and Nevis asked me to help the Caribbean nations establish and fund systems for the prevention, care, and treatment of HIV/AIDS," Clinton wrote. "I agreed to do what I could, but with limited staffing in Harlem and Little Rock and an already crowded list of commitments, I needed some help. I called Ira Magaziner, who had spearheaded our efforts in healthcare and e-commerce in the White House, and asked him to organize and lead the project."[1]

News reports at the time noted that Clinton and Mandela, the former president of South Africa, who cochaired the conference, gave upbeat closing speeches to the fourteenth International AIDS Conference in Barcelona in 2002. CNN reported that Clinton said "wealthy nations" should decide what should be each one's share of the $10 billion a year that "the secretary-general of the United Nations and the experts have said is required to spend" to battle AIDS. CNN also reported that Mandela said world leaders "must do everything" to fight the stigma associated with the HIV virus.[2]

While news reports at the time indicated Clinton and Mandela received enthusiastic applause, embracing on the platform after giving the conference's closing speeches, there was opposition to Bill Clinton's appearance. Act Up, the radical AIDS political activist group, attacked what it called Clinton's "dismal record" on HIV/AIDS, charging that Clinton had not "earned the right to address an International AIDS conference."

The group panned Clinton for betraying the promise he had made as a candidate for president in 1992 that he would create a "Manhattan Project" to launch an all-out, coordinated research effort to find a cure for AIDS. "Once elected to the White House, Clinton abandoned that promise, and the hopes of millions around the world who are still waiting and dying for a cure for AIDS," the group said on its website. Act Up further charged that as president, Clinton "neglected the global fight against AIDS," allocating only $100 million for Africa's AIDS orphans, but that since leaving the White House, Clinton suggested that the United States should spend $2.5 billion to fight AIDS internationally, something "the Clinton administration never did in eight budgets submitted to Congress, despite huge surpluses."[3]

In *Giving*, Clinton lavished praise on Ira Magaziner. "I had known Ira since the late 1960s, when we were students at Oxford," Clinton wrote. "From 1979 until he came to work in the White House, he founded and ran two successful corporate strategy firms from all across the world and wrote three books about the challenges of the emerging global economy. His long years of experience in the business world, his work on health care and electronic commerce in the White House, and his amazing ability to analyze complex problems and come up with creative solutions made him the perfect person for the job."

Clinton further praised Magaziner for assisting Hillary Clinton in heading the task force Clinton had appointed at the beginning of his first term as president to promote nationalized health care, a doomed effort that became known as "HillaryCare."

In positioning Magaziner to head the Clinton Foundation HIV/AIDS Initiative, Bill Clinton took pains to excuse him for the political fiasco HillaryCare became. "I was especially glad Ira was able to take on this challenge because I always thought he took an unfair share of the blame for the defeat of my health-care plan in 1994," Clinton continued. "As I explained in my memoir, our effort to reduce costs and cover everyone was killed by politics, not by the plan's particulars. Since 2000, all the cost and coverage problems have worsened, and there is a growing consensus among business, labor, consumers, and health-care providers that we finally have to change our system to rein in costs, cover everyone, and promote wellness, in addition to treating sickness." Setting the stage for the Clinton Foundation involvement in the HIV/AIDS fight, he added, "I am optimistic that we will finally address the challenge in the next couple of years."

Clinton concluded his praise seeming to suggest Magaziner would now try to achieve through the Clinton Foundation what the Hillary–Magaziner teamwork had failed to accomplish in the White House: "Meanwhile, Ira Magaziner is busy saving the lives of people with AIDS."[4]

Cynically, we could note that Clinton got religion over combating HIV/AIDS after he left the White House, when he realized he had discovered another human catastrophe, like the India earthquake, that could be leveraged to induce thousands of people worldwide to donate millions of dollars to the Clinton Foundation. To make the appeal to donor compassion even more compelling, the foundation, under Magaziner's direction, would find its particular philanthropic calling to combat AIDS in the Third World, where clearly the economics of poverty compounded the health problem.

WHO IS IRA MAGAZINER?

Magaziner was born in New York City in 1947. At Brown University in Providence, Rhode Island, in the late 1960s, he was a radical student activist opposed to the Vietnam War. He is remembered for having been one of the two architects of the "New Curriculum," which is typically defined as a liberal academic approach that includes no core course requirements.

During the 1968 black student walkout at Brown, Magaziner, as president of the Undergraduate Council of Students, held rallies to support the walkout and led the negotiation pushing the university administration to make concessions to get the students to return. Delivering the valedictorian address at graduation in 1969, Magaziner made national news by leading the students to express their protest to the war by turning their backs on Henry Kissinger, who was receiving an honorary degree.[5]

Upon graduation from Brown, Magaziner was named a Rhodes Scholar at Oxford University in England, where he met Bill Clinton, another student Vietnam War protestor. Clinton had been named a Rhodes Scholar in 1968, after getting his undergraduate degree from Georgetown University. Clinton and Magaziner were two of the rare U.S. students to drop out of the Rhodes Scholarship program without receiving a degree. Rhodes Scholars have all Oxford University tuition and fees paid by the Rhodes Trust and receive a monthly living stipend.

Clinton has never fully explained why he quit, though Nixon aide Roger Stone in a 2015 book alleges that Clinton was expelled for having sexually assaulted a nineteen-year-old undergraduate coed he met in a pub.[6] Magaziner has been equally vague about why he left Oxford without a degree, though he was known at the time for visiting U.S. military bases in England to organize servicemen to protest the war.

Upon returning to the United States, he pulled together a group of leftist organizers who descended upon working-class Brockton, Massachusetts, in what turned out to be a failed attempt to transform the town "into the young activists' idea of a model city."[7] Following that, Magaziner turned up at the Boston Consulting Group, where founder Bruce Henderson recalled him showing up for his job interview wearing dungarees and claiming he did not care about money, but that he needed to learn how business worked.[8]

In the August 13, 2013, *New York Times* article by Nicholas Confessore and Amy Chozick, "Unease at Clinton Foundation Finances and Ambitions," that threw Chelsea Clinton into an uproar, as noted in the previous chapter, Magaziner was singled out, along with Doug Band, for criticism. After acknowledging that Magaziner is widely credited as the driving force behind what had become the Clinton Foundation's largest project, the Clinton Health Access Initiative, or CHAI, the *Times* reporters noted the Clinton Foundation had still built up a $40 million deficit during 2007–2008, the years in which Hillary was running for president. Confessore and Chozick commented that Clinton Foundation officials had confided in them their view that Magaziner was "impulsive and lacking organizational skills."

"On one occasion, Mr. Magaziner dispatched a team of employees to fly around the world for months gathering ideas for a climate change proposal that never got off the ground," they wrote. "Another time, he ignored a report—which was commissioned at significant expense from the consulting firm McKinsey and Company—on how the foundation could get involved in forestry initiatives." The reporters recounted yet another incident in which Magaziner was lying on a conference table in the middle of an important meeting "because of terrible back spasms, snapping at a staff member." The newspaper reported that Band had repeatedly urged Bill Clinton to fire Magaziner, but Clinton refused, claiming that despite Magaziner's managerial weaknesses, he "was a visionary with good intentions."[9]

The article drew a surprise reaction from *New York Times* columnist Maureen Dowd, who pounded the Clintons and their foundation in an August 17, 2013, column titled "Money, Money, Money, Money, MONEY!" Dowd, who typically supports Democratic Party political candidates, bemoaned the "Clintons' neediness, their sense of what they are owed in material terms for their public service, their assumption that they're entitled to everyone's money."

Keying off the reporting of Confessore and Chozick, Dowd leveled an accusation at the Clintons that clearly sounds like an inurement indictment. The Clinton Foundation was not a legitimate charity, she wrote, but a source of Clinton family cash. Picking up on the theme that the Clintons under Magaziner's encouragement flew a team of employees around the world for months gathering data for a climate change proposal that was never issued, Dowd concluded, "We are supposed to believe that every dollar given to a Clinton is a dollar that improves the world. But is it?"

"Clintonworld is a galaxy where personal enrichment and political advancement blend seamlessly, and where a cast of jarringly familiar characters pad their pockets every which way to Sunday," Dowd continued. "The Clintons want to do big worthy things, but they also want to squeeze money from rich people wherever they live on planet Earth, insatiably gobbling up cash for politics and charity and themselves from the same incestuous swirl."[10]

After Chelsea Clinton began asserting her leadership over the Clinton Foundation in 2013, the tables turned on Magaziner. Writing in the *New York Times* November 18, 2015, reporter Maggie Haberman noted that an internal review from the CHAI board concluded "Mr. Magaziner had shown 'disdain' for the health initiative's board, exhibited 'duplicitousness with management' and displayed 'a lack of transparency' and 'dismissive behavior' toward Clinton family members."

Haberman noted Maganizer's performance review "also said that his underlings could find him 'prickly,' 'intimidating,' 'abrasive' and 'arrogant.' And it cited interviews with unnamed board members who savaged Mr. Magaziner, saying he treated them with disrespect and suspicion, had created needless divisions and was overly concerned with gaining independence from the Clinton family." In conclusion, the internal performance review accused Magaziner of "paranoia."[11]

START-UP IN THE CARIBBEAN

As noted above, the origin of the idea to transform the Clinton Foundation by combating HIV/AIDS in the Third World traces to the Barcelona AIDS conference in 2002, where Denzil Douglas, prime minister of the Caribbean country Saint Kitts and Nevis, told Clinton of the problem of middlemen marking up the price of generic drugs from a list price of $500 to $3,600 for each AIDS patient treated.[12] Here, Bill Clinton's narrative in *Giving*, quoted earlier, brings his old friend

Magaziner into the mix as the person to head the HIV/AIDS initiative for the Clinton Foundation.

On August 22, 2002, one month after the Barcelona conference, Magaziner signed a Memorandum of Understanding (MOU) with the Caribbean Community, CARICOM, that pledged the William J. Clinton Presidential Foundation's support of the region in efforts to combat HIV/AIDS. The press release announcing the agreement noted that a follow-up to the Barcelona conference took place in Saint Kitts and Nevis between Prime Minister Douglas and representatives of the Clinton Foundation that led to the signing of the MOU. "The CARICOM Secretariat is pleased to receive representatives from the William Jefferson Clinton Foundation," the press release noted. "Through our discussions today we are seeking to establish a firm footing for our relationship with the signing, by the Secretariat, of a Memorandum of Understanding. The MOU will then be taken back to the Clinton Foundation, by its representative here today, for signature by its President. This MOU will lay the basis for collaboration and support as the Region seeks to address the HIV/AIDS pandemic that is threatening the social and economic fabric of our society." The press release concluded by quoting Bill Clinton: "The Caribbean has cut a deal . . . it has a plan . . . but insufficient resources. . . . Let's find out what is the deficit and go and get the money."[13]

In *Giving*, Clinton made clear that raising money to fight HIV/AIDS was the first requirement. "Initially, the plan we developed called for assembling volunteers to work with governments that asked for our help to increase care in the Caribbean," he wrote. "As we were getting organized, I asked wealthier nations to commit the funds necessary to upgrade and expand developing nations' health services and to fund the purchase of generic drugs." Here Clinton sounds comfortable continuing in his post-presidency the same type of international leadership he would have been expected to exercise as president. "Ireland and Canada were our first donors, followed by Norway, Sweden, and France, with other nations contributing lesser amounts," he noted. "The foundation's expenses were covered by private citizens' donations from the United States, Canada, the United Kingdom, Ireland, and other nations."[14]

IRELAND PLEDGES €110

Then, on July 8, 2003, the Irish Examiner reported that Irish prime minister Bertie Ahern had signed an agreement with Bill Clinton to donate up to $158.2 million to fight HIV/AIDS in Mozambique, making Ireland the first government in the world to back the Clinton initiative.[15]

One major difficulty was that the Clinton Foundation at that time had neither applied for nor received an IRS determination letter authorizing the foundation to raise tax-exempt funds for the purpose of fighting HIV/AIDS. The only IRS determination letter that the William J. Clinton Presidential Foundation had received at that time was to build the Clinton presidential library in Little Rock.

Yet, there is no doubt the government of Ireland went into business with the Clinton Foundation to fight HIV/AIDS. The Development Cooperation Ireland, a part of the Irish government's Department of Foreign Affairs and Trade, commonly known as "Irish Aid,"[16] said in its 2004 annual report that "Ireland has prioritized HIV/AIDS in its overseas development program."[17]

Then, on September 29, 2006, Ahern signed a new agreement "under a renewed partnership with the Clinton Foundation," that would focus on addressing HIV/AIDS "in two of the worst affected countries in the world"—Mozambique and Lesotho—with the government of Ireland pledging under the new agreement to provide $76.1 million to Mozambique and $12.6 million to Lesotho over the next five years, making Ireland "the largest country donor to the Clinton Foundation HIV/AIDS Initiative."[18]

In the press release, Ahern made glowing comments about Ireland's partnership with Bill Clinton in the fight against HIV/AIDS. "Since the end of his U.S. Presidency, Bill Clinton has worked to transform AIDS from a death sentence into a manageable disease," Ahern said. "He has brokered deals to make HIV drugs affordable and readily available. He has used his influence with world leaders to make the plight of their HIV positive population a problem they could not ignore. Ireland is proud to support the President and the work of his foundation." Ahern said the relationship also "yielded real results for the people of Mozambique."[19]

A note at the end of the press release bragged about the progress Irish Aid had made with the Clinton Foundation in Mozambique in the years 2003–2006, claiming that more than 20,000 people were on anti-retroviral treatment.

CLINTON FOUNDATION STILL SOLICITING IN IRELAND

While the Clinton Foundation "swore off" donations from foreign governments when Hillary Clinton was secretary of state, that did not stop the Clinton Foundation from continuing to raise millions of dollars from foreigners with connections to their home governments, wrote James V. Grimaldi and Rebecca Ballhaus in the *Wall Street Journal*. The article documented that between 2009 and 2014, the Clinton Foundation accepted $6.5 million dollars from individuals in Ireland who contributed more than $50,000 each.[20]

Grimaldi later reported the Clinton Foundation planned to keep accepting foreign donations, even though the issue might become politically charged during Hillary's planned 2016 presidential campaign. The board of the Clinton Foundation had decided also to continue the policy that had been resumed in 2013, when Clinton had resigned as secretary of state, of allowing foreign governments as well as foreign individuals to contribute to the Clinton Foundation and participate in the Clinton Global Initiative.

Grimaldi further reported that Republican National Committee chairman Reince Priebus objected that the new policy came weeks after the Clinton Health Access Initiative failed to disclose millions of dollars in donations from countries including Australia, Canada, Ireland, Norway, and the UK. "The Clinton Foundation receiving foreign government funding as Hillary Clinton campaigns to be president should set off alarm bells," Priebus said. "The fact that the Clinton Foundation previously failed to disclose foreign government donations should cast even greater doubt on any new policy."[21]

The Irish Aid annual report for 2014 continued to reference Ireland's working relationship with the Clinton Foundation: "As a result of Ireland's continuing partnership with the Clinton Health Access Initiative and the ongoing commitment of the Government of Mozambique to expand HIV and AIDS services there are now over half a million people receiving antiretroviral treatment for the disease."[22]

CLINTON FOUNDATION NOT REGISTERED AS A CHARITY IN IRELAND

The question whether or not the Clinton Foundation was ever registered in Ireland as a charity under Irish law caught the attention of Wall Street analyst Charles Ortel. Irish tax and customs law is clear that a foreign charity must apply for a tax determination in Ireland under Sections 208A and 208B of the Taxes Consolidation Act of 1997.[23] Irish revenue law specifies criminal sanctions against any person soliciting funds in association with a false claim that the organization is a "registered charity" within the jurisdiction of Ireland.[24]

WND reported that Ortel had received e-mail confirmation from the Charities Regulatory Authority in Ireland that the Clinton Foundation under its various names, including the Clinton Health Access Initiative and the Clinton Global Initiative, is not registered as a charity in Ireland.[25]

On September 22, 2015, Brenda Ryan of the Charities Regulatory Authority in Ireland e-mailed Ortel, saying, "According to our records there are no charities or subsidiaries on the Public Register." To avoid confusion, Ryan's response listed Ortel's "Initial Query" word for word as part of her e-mail, including Ortel's specification of various Clinton Foundation subsidiaries, such as the Clinton Health Access Initiative and the Clinton Global Initiative.

"The record shows the Clinton Foundation virtually since its inception has raised hundreds of millions of dollars in Ireland, often in conjunction with the Irish government," Ortel explained to WND. "This raises the question whether the Clinton Foundation has violated both U.S. federal law regarding the operation of U.S. charities in foreign countries and Irish law with regard to the operation of a foreign charity raising donations in Ireland, that merit the serious consideration of federal and state regulators in the United States as well as regulators in Ireland."

On August 4, Brenda Wilson at the Irish Government's Department of Foreign Affairs and Trade e-mailed Ortel, confirming that the Clinton Health Access Initiative (CHAI) is a partner of Irish Aid in two of its partner countries, Mozambique and Lesotho.

"Within the current framework of Irish Aid cooperation with the Clinton Health Access Initiative (2011–2015), Irish Aid funding has been provided directly to the Ministries of Health in Mozambique (€60m) and Lesotho (€8.246m)," Wilson's e-mail continued. "During that period, funding to CHAI itself amounted to a total of €2.088m."

Wilson provided the following table to summarize total direct funding to CHAI:

	CHAI MOZAMBIQUE	CHAI LESOTHO
2008	€ 238,209	€
2011	295,000	
2012	200,000	
2013	250,000	343,007
2014	250,000	500,000
2015	250,000	
TOTAL	€ 1,438,209	€ 843,007

These numbers fall short of the sums the Irish government pledged to spend funding HIV/AIDS work in Mozambique and Lesotho, according to the Irish government's 2006 press release quoted earlier. Nor is it clear whether the money went to Mozambique directly, to the Clinton Foundation to spend on Mozambique, or into some offshore bank account controlled by the Irish government, the Clinton Foundation, or both. Ortel told WND that the Clinton Foundation audited financial statements provided to regulators and the annual reports dating back to the initiation of the Irish Aid program, which was set up to fight HIV/AIDS in Africa, fail to document where the missing millions initially pledged by the Irish government went, and whether or not the Irish Aid donations flowed through the Clinton Foundation, through CHAI, or were sent directly to the governments of Mozambique and Lesotho.

"The presumption seems to be that because the Clinton Foundation is fighting HIV/AIDS, the Clinton Foundation and its various subsidiaries have to worry about formalities, including whether or not the Clinton Foundation is acting as an agent of a foreign government, or violating charitable giving laws in the United States or in foreign nations," Ortel said. It also was clear that the Clinton Foundation and its various subsidiary organizations did not provide the accurate and meticulous accounting and regulatory financial reporting that would track precisely the Clinton Foundation's role in handling Irish Aid money targeted for Africa.

MASSIVE CORRUPTION IN MOZAMBIQUE

On January 25, 2011, Jason O'Brien of the *Irish Independent* provided reason for concern, reporting that Global Fund, a charity established by U2 singer Bono to fight AIDS, tuberculosis, and malaria in the Third World, confirmed that 25 million euros had gone unaccounted for in a 15-billion-euro development fund to which Irish Aid had contributed 115 million euros.

"The corruption includes millions spent on cars and motorbikes without receipts, millions more disappearing through faked invoices, and free drugs from donors being sold on the black market," the *Irish Independent* reported. O'Brien further commented that Global Fund admitted only a tiny fraction of the 8 billion euros claimed to have been allocated since 2002 to fight AIDS, tuberculosis, and malaria, had ever been audited.[26]

Under U.S. law, a U.S. charity must control its foreign operations. "If the U.S. charity acts as an agent of a foreign government furthering the work of that foreign government, donations to the charity likely will not be deemed eligible for tax deductions," Ortel explained to WND. "All U.S. persons operating U.S. charities in foreign countries must also be mindful of Foreign Corruption Practices rules, which would have been almost impossible to have avoided violating, given the massive corruption rampant in Mozambique, especially when the program started.

"Perhaps it is too much to expect primary U.S. regulators based in Arkansas, and even the IRS to monitor activities of a public charity like the Clinton Foundation that receives monies in a wide array of currencies and then, supposedly, allocates these donations to causes in numerous foreign locations," Ortel added. "On the other hand, the long pattern of late, confusing, and inaccurate public filings of Clinton Foundation entities is certainly one of many red flags for fraud of which experienced auditors and analysts are well aware."

NO IRS AUTHORIZATION

While the receipt of a sum as large as $158.2 million in 2003 would have been a blessing for any foundation in the world, the William J. Clinton Presidential Foundation failed to report the donation in its audited financial statements and the Tax Form 990s filed with the IRS in the years when the HIV/AIDS initiative was being launched. "Though there are numerous press releases and other accounts of extensive global activity by the Clinton Foundation fighting HIV/AIDS from July 2002 onward, companion financial disclosures filed for 2002 and 2003 do not explicitly document related inflows and outflows of the HIV/AIDS initiatives," Ortel told WND.[27]

In his second interim report published on his website, Ortel puzzled over whether the Clinton Global Initiative, the Clinton Health Access Initiative, and the Clinton HIV/AIDS Initiative were an elaborate smoke screen designed to cover the fact that the Clinton Foundation was operating outside the law for eight years. The foundation was raising "charitable donations" to combat HIV/AIDS when it had no IRS determination letter authorizing tax-exempt status for that purpose.[28]

Ortel noted the following in his report:

- "Between 12 July 2002 and 23 March 2004, the Clinton Foundation illegally held itself out as a tax-exempt organization authorized by the IRS to fight the HIV/AIDS pandemic internationally. Substantial efforts during this time period were not explicitly approved in advance by the IRS and therefore were not validly constituted under domestic and international laws."

- "On 24 March 2004, Clinton Foundation Trustees and others created an entity, the original Clinton Health Access Initiative, CHAI, that they later claimed falsely was an IRS-authorized tax-exempt organization, as and after they filed a false and materially misleading application in 2010 with the IRS and with numerous domestic and international counterparties, including regulators and donors."

- "By 31 December 2005, and afterwards, the Clinton Foundation falsely claimed that it had perfected a merger with the original Clinton Health Access Initiative inside the United States and in relevant foreign jurisdictions, a claim that was and remains materially misleading."

Ortel repeatedly has warned that the tax implications are dire for the Clintons personally, for the directors of the Clinton Foundation, and for donors around the world who believed they could take tax exemptions for donations, should the IRS and/or the courts determine that the Clintons solicited "charitable tax-exempt donations" for HIV/AIDS for eight years during which the IRS had not authorized tax-exemption for that purpose. This pattern of failing to provide detailed audited financials and line item–specified HIV/AIDS activity on Clinton Foundation audited financial statements and IRS Tax Form 990s continued through 2009.

The approach, Ortel stressed, was fraught with legal problems. Remember, in 2002 and 2003, the Clinton Foundation was still officially named the William J. Clinton Presidential Foundation and had authorization only to accept tax-deductible contributions to build the Clinton presidential library. When Bill Clinton got inspired by Nelson Mandela at the Barcelona AIDS conference in 2002 to start raising charitable donations to combat HIV/AIDS in the Third World, no new Form 1023 application was sent to inform the IRS of a change in organizational purpose. Not being notified, the IRS did not revise the original determination letter or write a new one to add HIV/AIDS as an additional purpose for which the foundation is allowed to solicit tax-deductible charitable contributions.

Through this critical period of time, when the foundation was transitioning to being an HIV/AIDS health powerhouse internationally, its auditor remained the relatively small, regional accounting firm BKD, headquartered in Little Rock, Arkansas. Remarkably, the Clinton Foundation through the end of 2015 still fails to list on its website a complete set of audited financial statements and IRS Tax Form 990s from inception in 1997 through 2004. From 2002 through 2004, the Clinton HIV/AIDS program operated under the title Clinton HIV/AIDS Initiative, or CHAI. A copy of the BKD 2004 audit for the William J. Clinton Presidential Foundation, Inc., was found on the Massachusetts attorney general's website for searching documentation submitted by nonprofit organizations and charities registered in the state.[29] At the end of 2015, this document was not archived for public view on the Clinton Foundation website.

The BKD 2004 audit did not restrict the Clinton Foundation to the purpose of building the Clinton library. "The mission of the William J. Clinton Presidential Foundation currently focuses its work in five critical areas," the BKD audit states in a paragraph titled "Nature of Operations." The five areas specified were: (1) economic empowerment of poor people; (2) racial, ethnic, and religious reconciliation; (3) health security, specifically combating AIDS; (4)

leadership development; and (5) citizen service. BKD specified the foundation had $44,529,126 in revenue from contributions in 2003 and $61,774,446 in 2004 but failed to provide any detail on where the contributions originated. The largest expenditure listed for the year ending December 31, 2004, was $43,522,300 as a grant or transfer to the National Archives, an expenditure not related to fighting HIV/AIDS, but to building the Clinton presidential library.

A separate 2004 Annual Report for the William J. Clinton Foundation (published dropping the word "Presidential" from the foundation's title), explained the foundation's HIV/AIDS accomplishments:

> Expanded the Clinton HIV/AIDS Initiative (CHAI) into a number of new partner countries in the Caribbean, Africa, Asia and Eastern Europe. Together CHAI's partner countries represent more than 33% of all HIV/AIDS cases in Africa, 95% of all cases in the Caribbean, and 85% of cases in Asia. CHAI helps its partner countries plan and implement large-scale integrated prevention, care and treatment programs by providing technical assistance, mobilizing financial and human resources, negotiating antiretroviral drug agreements and facilitating the sharing of best practices.[30]

The financial summary in this document broke out the contributions for the foundation for 2004 at $5,747,324, and the contributions for the HIV/AIDS initiative at $4,027,122, for a total 2004 contributions of $61,744,446. Again, no information as to whether the contributions came from foreign governments or individuals was included in the report.

An IRS Tax Form 990 for the Clinton HIV/AIDS Initiative, Inc., was also found on the Massachusetts charities website,[31] though not on the Clinton Foundation website. The form was separate from a IRS Tax Form 990 filed for the William J. Clinton Presidential Foundation for 2004. The 2004 Form 990 filed for CHAI listed total contributions for the year at $5,863,349, a number that differed from the financials presented in the 2014 annual report. The major expenditures listed were for travel, $2,369,202; consulting fees, $1,475,875; and compensation of officers and director, plus salaries and wages, listed at $1,173,182. What this 2004 CHAI Form 990 makes clear is that combating HIV/AIDS was not a major 2004 expense. Ira Magaziner is not listed in this Form 990 as being among the CHAI directors or officers receiving compensation.

The available records of Clinton Foundation audited financials and IRS Tax Form 990 reporting for the years through 2009 strongly suggest Bill Clinton impulsively seized the Mandela suggestion to morph the Clinton Foundation into a new, special purpose, somehow deciding that the millions raised and spent did not need to be documented in audited financial statements or reported to regulators. For law enforcement investigators experienced with charitable organization audit and regulatory reporting legal requirements, these types of failures to record and report are clear signs of financial fraud.

THE CLINTON FOUNDATION'S SHIFTING PURPOSE

After Ortel began publishing on his website his various analyses of the Clinton Foundation, a second IRS Form 1023 dated August 9, 2010,[32] and a second IRS determination letter dated October 6, 2010,[33] suddenly appeared on the Clinton website. Both were filed not by the William J. Clinton Presidential Foundation under any of the various names the organization has operated since inception, but under the auspices of the Clinton Global Initiative, Inc., or CGI, Inc. Interestingly, the IRS determination letter makes it clear the IRS was granting tax-exempt authority to CGI, Inc., but the letter was open-ended, failing to specify any particular charitable purpose for which the corporation was allowed to solicit tax-deductible contributions.

On December 11, 2009, CHAI in Massachusetts filed an IRS application for tax-exempt status. On March 15, 2010, the IRS issued CHAI in Massachusetts a determination letter. The Form 1023 application and the IRS determination letter are found only through the New York State Charity Bureau. Neither was archived on the Clinton Foundation website as of March 2016. The application by CHAI for an IRS determination letter came in 2009, as the Clinton Foundation prepared to break CHAI into a separate corporation, much as this section demonstrates was done with CGI. It will also be noted in the next chapter that the Memorandum of Understanding negotiated on behalf of Hillary Clinton with the Obama transition team as a condition of her nomination for secretary of state required that only CGI be made into a separate corporation, not CHAI as well. The 2010 IRS determination letter to CHAI was also open-ended, failing to specify any particular charitable purpose for which the corporation was allowed to solicit tax-deductible contributions.

The Clinton Foundation website admits the shifting organizational structure of CGI, noting that from 2005 to 2009, it "was an initiative of the Foundation," but that from 2010 to 2013, CGI "operated as a separate but affiliated non-profit organization as part of an agreement between the Foundation and the Obama Administration." While arguing CGI was a separate nonprofit organization, the Clinton Foundation website admits that from 2010 to 2013, the foundation "continued to consolidate CGI's finances into its annual financial reporting." Ortel argued this seems to suggest that the Clinton Foundation wanted to have it both ways. If CGI were a nonprofit organization separate from the Clinton Foundation, why would its financials be consolidated into the Clinton Foundation financials? Ortel's analysis stressed this would suggest there was an undisclosed joint services agreement between the two entities, such that CGI relied upon services and personnel hired under the Clinton Foundation organization.[34] Typically, this type of activity is associated with a charitable organization, such as a 501(c)(3) that wants to carry on an unrelated business activity that might threaten its tax exemption. Recall also that complicated structures created within a charitable organization should be a red flag to the possibility of fraud.

That CGI financials would be consolidated into the Clinton Foundation financials also seems to fly in the face of the 2010 CGI Form 1023 application submitted to the IRS in 2010 and the IRS determination letter in 2010 that both treat CGI as if they were a truly separate and autonomous organization. Ortel asks: Why else would CGI apply for its own IRS tax-exempt determination, unless it was intended to operate as a separate organization? The CGI Form 1023 filed in 2010 specifically states CGI was incorporated on September 4, 2009, meaning it must have been a corporation separate from the Clinton Foundation. But again, Ortel asks why, if CGI was truly a separate organization in 2009, were CGI financials being consolidated with the Clinton Foundation financials in the period 2010 through 2013? The formation of separately incorporated structures within 501(c)(3) organizations that remain financially consolidated within the parent foundation is a tricky transaction fraught with pitfalls when it comes to determining whether tax-exempt status is preserved, as well as other critical legal issues, including whether or not the restructuring limits liabilities.

As we shall see in the next chapter, the reorganization of CGI was necessitated by the agreement Hillary Clinton made with the Obama transition team as a precondition for her to be nominated as secretary of state. What is clear is that on September 4, 2009, the secretary of state in Arkansas issued CGI a certificate of incorporation, making it clear that after Hillary was nominated and confirmed as secretary of state, the Clinton Foundation broke out CGI as a separate corporation, that appears to have continued functioning as a subsidiary of the Clinton Foundation, with the financials of CGI consolidated into the Clinton Foundation.

What is also clear is that the Clinton Foundation operated without IRS authorization to solicit tax-deductible contributions for HIV/AIDS for as many as eight years. These years encompass the period between 2002, when Clinton first got the idea from Mandela that his foundation could rake in money by championing the international battle against HIV/AIDS, and 2010, when CGI finally got its own IRS determination letter. The problem is that the HIV/AIDS work in 2009 was operating under the auspices of the Clinton HIV/AIDS Initiative, also known as the Clinton Health Access Initiative, or CHAI. It is not clear that an IRS determination letter issued to CGI in 2010 would apply to the Clinton Foundation itself, or to CHAI. But it seems clear that, in any event, the

2010 IRS determination letter could not apply retroactively to the Clinton Foundation or CHAI. Another problem is that the IRS letter says nothing that would extend specific authority to the Clinton Foundation, CGI, or CHAI to solicit tax-deductible contributions to fight HIV/AIDS. The only specific authority the IRS granted was in the original determination letter that gave the William J. Clinton Presidential Foundation the authority to raise tax-deductible funds to build the library.

When filing the IRS Form 1023 in 2010, someone at the Clinton Foundation may have realized the foundation had not been authorized to solicit tax-exempt charitable donations to fight HIV/AIDS under the original IRS determination letter. But even after the issuance of the second IRS determination letter in 2010, it remains a stretch to argue IRS blanket authorization of CGI, Inc., authorized CHAI to solicit tax-exempt authority to raise charitable donations to fight HIV/AIDS. If CGI were a separate organization, operating under separately incorporated articles of incorporation in Arkansas, how could any IRS authorization issued to CGI, Inc., apply to a separately incorporated Clinton Foundation or to CHAI?

Ortel continues to insist the Clinton Foundation never validly changed its original tax-exempt purpose in July 2002, when the foundation expanded its purpose to address the HIV/AIDS pandemic. "Furthermore, acute, continuing concerns have only increased about 'inurement'—how individuals and other entities may have derived 'private benefit' that is more than 'insubstantial' through activities in concert and related to those of the Clinton Foundation," he wrote in his second interim report. Ortel is also correct in that the CGI Form 1023 dated August 9, 2010, and the IRS determination letter CGI, Inc., received, dated October 6, 2010, are the only documents the Clinton Foundation has ever produced as evidence the IRS granted tax-exempt status to the Clinton Foundation and its various incarnations for any purpose broader than building the Clinton library.

Ortel remains highly critical of the Clinton Foundation reorganization in 2009 and 2010, which resulted not only in a new incorporation status for CGI but in creating a "New CHAI" structure out of the "Old CHAI" structure, as we shall see in detail in the next chapter. "The purported reorganization of the Clinton Foundation during 2009 and 2010 and the subsequent merger of new CGI into the Clinton Foundation in 2013 were deceptive, intentionally misleading, sham transactions," he wrote in the executive summary to his second interim report, September 8, 2015. He continued:

> Between August 2010 and October 2010, Clinton Foundation trustees and others obtained a valuable tax-exempt authorization for new CGI from the IRS on the basis of a false and materially misleading application. Trustees of the Clinton Foundation and others submitted a false, incomplete, and materially misleading application to the IRS, yet managed to obtain tax-exempt authorization for New CGI. Among other defects, the application submitted to the IRS failed to explain material conflicts of interest, failed to highlight material uncorrected irregularities in informational returns, and failed to make full disclosure concerning the repeated practice that the Clinton Foundation, Trustees, Executives, and those in position to exercise influence demonstrated making false and materially misleading representations.[35]

ONLY "REASONABLE ASSURANCE"

To someone reading the BKD audited financial report for 2004, it would appear the HIV/AIDS initiative was an afterthought, given that the line items reported make it hard to imagine the William J. Clinton Presidential Foundation was doing anything but finishing off the presidential library, since the audited financial fails to make any mention whatsoever of the HIV/AIDS millions Bill Clinton claimed to have been collecting since July 2002.

Ortel has insisted questions remain to be answered: Where did all the money go that Ireland, Canada, Norway, and Sweden pledged to fight HIV/AIDS? Into what bank accounts was all that money deposited? How was that money transferred from these foreign nations to the

William J. Clinton Presidential Foundation bank accounts in Little Rock or to the CHAI bank accounts in Massachusetts? What were the HIV/AIDS expenditures in these formative years? What drugs precisely were purchased and where were they delivered? What was the cost not only of purchasing but also distributing the HIV/AIDS drugs?

It is hard to imagine a charitable foundation being less responsible than this in reporting and accounting for details of contributions and expenditures, and it is even more astounding to realize these were the supposedly audited financials filed by a foundation established by and named for a person who once was president of the United States.

One more point merits comment here. Ortel has pointed out a BKD audit found on the Massachusetts attorney general's charities website has a reliance letter by the accounting firm specifying that the standard BKD used in conducting the audit included "reasonable assurance about whether the financial statements are free of material misstatement." The BKD reliance letter went on to specify:

> An audit includes examining, on a test basis, evidence supporting the amounts and disclosures in the financial statements. An audit also includes assessing the accounting principles used and significant estimates made by management, as well as evaluating the overall financial statement presentation. We believe that our audits provide a reasonable basis for our opinion.

This remarkable statement is an admission that BKD did not conduct the type of full and independent audit required by federal and state regulators for registered charities for financial reporting. Instead, BKD admits it relied on numbers provided by Clinton Foundation management to form the substance of its audit, with BKD taking responsibility to check the numbers provided by management on a "test basis." Contrast this to a full audit that would trace each number provided by Clinton Foundation management back to original records that would include examining checks received as contributions and invoices paid on expenditures. Ortel's conclusion is blunt: What BKD provides could never be utilized by Clinton Foundation management or by federal and state regulators to give a complete and unbiased audit of all transactions traced back to their source during the audit period.

CLINTON HOOKS UP WITH RANBAXY IN INDIA

Mandela's argument that Bill Clinton should get into the business of combating HIV/AIDS seemed premised on the idea that Clinton could use his reputation as a former U.S. president to jawbone manufacturers to produce and sell generic antiretroviral (ARV) drugs at dramatically reduced prices. Mandela also thought Clinton might get sympathy from the pharmaceutical companies because the ARV drugs were aimed for distribution to impoverished HIV/AIDS sufferers in Third World countries. In 2002, Ira Magaziner approached Ranbaxy, a pharmaceutical company headquartered in India, to discuss this proposition.

Professors Ethan B. Kapstein at Arizona State University and Joshua W. Busby at the University of Texas at Austin, in their 2013 book *AIDS Drugs for All*, documented Magaziner's strategy.[36] Magaziner suggested Ranbaxy "could put the developing countries together to form a sort of 'buying club' that could "ramp up economies of scale and lower cost." This, Magaziner argued, would allow the Third World nations to benefit from the economies of "pooled procurement," while Ranbaxy would welcome the additional demand, buttressed by the economies of scale that would justify the company to operate with "a very low mark-up" and still make a profit. A Kaiser Health News "Morning Briefing" November 21, 2003, reported that Bill Clinton "visited Indian generic drug Ranbaxy Laboratories' pharmaceutical plant in Gurgaon, India, to show support for Indian companies that have agreed to manufacture low-cost generic antiretroviral drugs for nationwide HIV/AIDS treatment plans in four African and more than 12 Caribbean countries."[37]

Kapstein and Busby went on to document that Magaziner's logic also appealed to Stavros Nicolaou, a senior executive at South Africa's Aspen Parmacare. "In late 2000 and early 2001, South Africa was coming to terms with the magnitude of its HIV pandemic," Kapstein and Busby wrote. "Faced with an unprecedented pandemic, Aspen decided that as the largest pharma in South Africa, it had to play a role in meeting the crisis." By introducing generic licenses in 2001 and 2002, along with its first generic ARV in 2003, Aspen was able to bring prices down in the South African market. At the same time, Kapstein and Busby noted, CHAI started to increase its HIV/AIDS efforts and was making progress lowering the price of the generic drugs. When the Clinton team approached Aspen, Nicolaou decided to take "a leap of faith" because the communal procurement process was "unprecedented." Nicolaou bought into the idea of relying on Bill Clinton to coordinate volumes in a highly fragmented market, deciding to believe that by coordinating demand, discounts in generic ARV drugs would be justified in Third World countries working together under CHAI.

The CHAI story, Kapstein and Busby noted, raises the question of whether generic entry into the HIV/AIDS market in the Third World would have happened "on its own," without intervention by the Clinton Foundation or other advocates aimed at organizing the market. To this, Kapstein and Busby said Magaziner responded that it may have happened eventually, but it "sure would have taken a lot longer," with many thousands of lives lost in the process. Magaziner contended that a "fair number of people are alive because we were able to get that done." He also commented that the United Nations World Health Organization had earlier debated internally for a year and a half the idea of organizing demand but did not pursue it in the end. He emphasized that despite discussions in 2002 and 2003, the World Health Organization had not moved forward with pooled procurement. Kapstein and Busby suggested that CHAI "accelerated the development of the generic markets for HIV/AIDS drugs and the price reductions that come with scale."[38]

CLINTON HOOKS UP WITH UNITAID AND WHO

The next breakthrough occurred in 2006, when Bill Clinton decided to reach out to UNITAID, an international fund established by Brazil, Chile, France, Norway, and the United Kingdom, to raise money to prevent, treat, and diagnose HIV/AIDS, tuberculosis, and malaria. The majority of funds raised by UNITAID, estimated by some as up to 90 percent, has come from France through levies imposed by the French government on airline tickets purchased by French air travelers, beginning in July 2006.[39]

In the UNITAID–CHAI joint venture deal proposed by Bill Clinton in 2006, UNITAID would entrust to the Clinton Foundation the millions of dollars raised, largely through the ticket levies, so the Clinton Foundation could further leverage generic HIV/AIDS drugs manufacturers. The UNITAID–CHAI joint venture thus extended the logic Magaziner first introduced with Ranbaxy. By relying on Bill Clinton's status as former U.S. president, the UNITAID–CHAI joint venture could increase demand to further the success CHAI had experienced up until 2008 in getting international pharmaceutical companies to produce ARV drugs throughout the developed world at prices discounted because of the massive scale of the market.

By 2006, UNITAID had reached a deal with the United Nations World Health Organization to send UNITAID funds for HIV/AIDS drugs to the WHO in Geneva for administration. With the implementation of the UNITAID–CHAI joint venture, the Clinton Foundation stepped in as middleman to work with the WHO to help administer the UNITAID funds. By the end of 2008, UNITAID had committed more than $300 million for the purchase of HIV/AIDS drugs and diagnostics. In 2009, the UNITAID board of directors approved an additional $140 million for the purchase of HIV/AIDS drugs, now to be administered and implemented by CHAI.[40]

Again, Ortel was highly critical of the Clinton Foundation's legal status in forming this partnership with UNITAID. "During 2006, the Clinton Foundation secured a valuable strategic partnership with UNITAID under false and materially misleading pretenses, since they were not authorized to pursue the thrust of the partnership," Ortel wrote in the executive summary to his second interim report. "Between November 2006 and December 2013, the Clinton Foundation fraudulently obtained $566 million in donations from UNITAID that were, in turn, sourced via foreign governments and from the Bill and Melinda Gates Foundation."[41] The prestigious Gates Foundation has heavily supported UNITAID, providing 3.2 percent of all contributions to UNITAID from 2006 to 2012, as acknowledged by a statement on the UNITAID web page stating the organization is "supported by 29 countries and by the Bill & Melinda Gates Foundation."[42]

Here, Ortel began to address the issue of the Clinton Foundation diverting funds from UNITAID. "Starting in 2007, the Clinton Foundation and those in position to exercise significant influence over the Clinton Foundation and constituent elements attempted to hide the fact that they had illegally diverted more than $75 million in UNITAID donations from their intended purposes," Ortel charged. "Beginning in November 2008, Clinton Foundation Trustees misled the Obama Transition Team concerning the legal status, accomplishments and prospects of the Clinton Foundation and its constituent elements. Starting the same time, Hillary Clinton misled the Obama Transition Team and the U.S. Senate while securing her role as U.S. Secretary of State between November 2008 and 21 January 2009."[43]

The 2006 deal with UNITAID positioned the Clinton Foundation to have access to hundreds of millions of dollars, starting in 2008, from what amounted to a tax imposed by the French government on millions of average airline passengers and administered through the United Nations World Health Organization. As we shall see at the end of this chapter, the Clinton Foundation financial reporting strongly suggests, after careful analysis, that the CHAI scheme had a hidden objective, over and above the reduction of prices for generic HIV/AIDS drugs. Given how the Clinton Foundation has organized, managed, and reported CHAI, the Clintons have been able to skim off for their personal use tens of millions of dollars from the funds WHO sent to CHAI from UNITAID levies.

In UNITAID's financial statements, the Clinton Foundation and CHAI are described as "implementers," organizations that help ensure essential health products reach intended beneficiaries. The scam was nearly perfected until Ranbaxy in India began enhancing its profit by selling to CHAI HIV/AIDS drugs the company knew to be drastically substandard. In the final analysis, as we shall see in the next section, aside from the public relations statements of the various players involved, including CHAI, UNITAID, and the United Nations, it is difficult to prove that the substandard Ranbaxy ARV drugs had any chance of curing HIV/AIDS patients.

Ortel has argued the story of the CHAI–UNITAID scam is one of the most poignant alleged Clinton Foundation abuses demonstrating how the Clintons used their tax-exempt foundation to conduct a "reverse Robin Hood,"[44] robbing the average air traveler in France to benefit the rich, namely themselves, at the expense of AIDS/HIV patients.

To get an idea of the magnitude of the fraud possible, consider that the levy imposed on airline tickets by the French government alone, according to records published by the French Civil Aviation Authority, was more than 1 billion euros in the approximately six years since the UNITAID program was launched in 2006 through January 23, 2013. "The air ticket levy, a predictable and robust source of revenue, contributes to the fight against HIV/AIDS, tuberculosis and malaria, diseases that cause more than 4 million deaths every year," UNITAID said in January 2013, when congratulating France "for its pivotal role and leadership in innovative financing for development. UNITAID documents that 60.8 percent of all UNITAID contributions from 2006 to 2012 have come from France.[45]

IT'S JUST BLACKS DYING

On May 15, 2013, investigative reporter Katherine Eban published an important article in *Fortune* magazine titled "Dirty Medicine," in which she detailed the criminal fraud in which Ranbaxy manufactured for CHAI substandard and otherwise defective HIV/AIDS medicines.[46] On May 13, 2013, in what developed as a global pharmaceutical scandal, Ranbaxy pleaded guilty to seven federal criminal counts of selling adulterated drugs with an intent to defraud, failing to report that its drugs didn't meet specifications, and making intentionally false statements to the government.[47] In pleading guilty, Ranbaxy also agreed to pay $500 million in fines, forfeitures, and penalties, the most ever levied against a generic-drug company.[48]

The *Fortune* article perhaps best captured the moral bankruptcy of Ranbaxy by relating a conference call Dr. Kathy Spreen, Ranbaxy's executive director of clinical medicine, had with a dozen company executives in which one dismissed the concern that the company was producing defective ARV drugs for HIV/AIDS patients in Africa by saying, "Who cares? It's just blacks dying."[49]

On November 9, 2004, Ranbaxy informed the World Health Organization that it had decided to withdraw voluntarily all seven of its ARVs tested by Vimta Labs. "This action was taken after the company found discrepancies in the documentation relating to proof of the products' bioequivalence with originator medicines," the WHO press release made clear.[50] What was less obvious was that Ranbaxy and the United Nations had decided to shift the blame. Read carefully: the WHO announcement made clear the United Nations was letting Ranbaxy off the hook by accepting the excuse that the defective HIV/AIDS drugs were withdrawn from the market once Ranbaxy realized a rogue contractor had run fraudulent tests.

Less than a year later, on August 16, 2005, the World Health Organization decided to reinstate to the WHO prequalification list the seven Ranbaxy HIV/AIDS ARV drugs. Ranbaxy management had evidently solved the problem by replacing the rogue lab with "globally recognized contract research organizations" assigned to conduct independent tests of the ARV drugs Ranbaxy had produced in its "WHO-approved plants."[51]

CHAI AND UNITAID DECLARE SUCCESS

A UNITAID press release May 17, 2011, announced that since 2008, the CHAI partnership with UNITAID had "achieved price reductions that will generate global savings of at least $600 million over the next three years, making HIV treatment more widely available."

Bill Clinton bragged in the UNITAID press release, "With more than nine million people worldwide in need of HIV/AIDS treatment, we must see rapid action to increase people's access to treatment.

"Over 70 countries and 70% of the HIV-infected population have access to the prices my Foundation negotiated; so these new price reductions, which have been agreed to by a wide range of suppliers, will provide millions of people with increased access to better, cheaper and more convenient first and second-line drug regimens," Clinton continued. "We have helped almost four million people gain access to life-saving medicine, and I'm proud that we can now reach millions more."[52]

What Clinton neglected to mention was that since the formation of the CHAI partnership with UNITAID in 2008 through the date of the 2011 press release, Ranbaxy ARV drugs were on the list of CHAI-provided HIV/AIDS drugs available for distribution in Third World countries. The *Fortune* exposé made clear Ranbaxy never stopped the subterfuge until forced to do so by a Department of Justice settlement in 2013. *Fortune* reported that Ranbaxy "manipulated almost every aspect of its manufacturing process to quickly produce impressive-looking data," including forging standard operating procedures to hide from health inspectors the truth that Ranbaxy never stopped substituting "cheaper, lower-quality ingredients in place of better ingredients, to manipulate test parameters to accommodate higher impurities, and even to substitute brand-name drugs in lieu of their own generics in bioequivalence tests to produce better results."

Fortune further exposed "systemic fraud in Ranbaxy's worldwide regulatory filings" designed to hide that "the majority of products filed in Brazil, Mexico, Middle East, Russia, Romania, Myanmar, Thailand, Vietnam, Malaysia, African Nations, have data submitted which did not exist or data from different products and from different countries." Writer Katherine Eban was not willing to let Ranbaxy off the hook so easily. "The company [Ranbaxy] not only invented data but also fraudulently mixed and matched data, taking the best results from manufacturing in one market and presenting it to regulators elsewhere as data unique to drugs in their markets," she wrote. Referring specifically to Ranbaxy's HIV/AIDS drugs, Eban concluded, "Ranbaxy had used ingredients that failed purity tests and blended them with good ingredients until the resulting mix met requirements," such that "a mélange could degrade or become toxic far more quickly than drugs made from the high-quality materials required."[53]

The UNITAID press release May 15, 2013, cited earlier, specifically mentioned in the last paragraph that Ranbaxy was included among the CHAI/UNITAID "key suppliers of ARVs. A CHAI-produced "Antiretroviral (ARV) Price List" in May 2011 that includes Ranbaxy on the list of approved drugs boasted the following: "The Clinton Health Access Initiative (CHAI) supports national governments to expand high-quality care and treatment to people living with HIV/AIDS. CHAI offers reduced prices for antiretrovirals (ARVs) to members of its Procurement Consortium."

Yet, when visiting Mumbai on April 11, 2013, Bill Clinton praised Ranbaxy for its role in assisting his Clinton Foundation in leading efforts to treat AIDS patients by agreeing ten years earlier to cut the price of its ARV drugs sold in developing nations. Clinton said, as reported in Mumbai by the *Economic Times*, "I told myself that never again will I come to India without saying a thank you," drawing applause from the six-hundred-plus-member audience that included "some of India Inc.'s leading CEOs, businessmen, and strategists."[54]

Despite the problems that Ranbaxy was in the process of finalizing in the $500 million settlement with the Department of Justice in May 2013, Clinton's theme visiting India in 2013 had not changed from ten years earlier, when on November 21, 2003, he was in India to announce enthusiastically the Ranbaxy deal.[55] In 2003, Clinton used a Ranbaxy R&D facility in New Delhi to hold a press conference with Prime Minister Atai Bihari Vajpayee and several representatives of the Indian government to announce the Clinton Foundation had just reached an agreement with Ranbaxy to sell to HIV/AIDS patients in the developing world.[56] In that speech, Clinton bragged that the Clinton Foundation, in conjunction with Ranbaxy, aimed to make low-cost ARV drugs in the countries of South Africa, Rwanda, Mozambique, Tanzania, Haiti, the Bahamas, the Dominican Republic, and the Eastern Caribbean States, with the goal of making ARVs available to "some two million people around the world in the next four to five years."[57]

THE CHAI-UNITAID SCAM QUANTIFIED

To quantify the CHAI–UNITAID scam, Ortel constructed the following table by taking the amount UNITAID contributed to the Clinton Foundation from the information presented in the UNITAID Financial Report for 2013 and comparing those sums to the amounts the Clinton Foundation receipts reported receiving from UNITAID, as disclosed by the Clinton Foundation on IRS Form 990 Schedule B reports for 2006 through 2010.[58]

What table 2 makes clear is that assuming UNITAID reported disbursement figures to CHAI and the CHAI receipts from UNITAID are correct, some $12,691,354 was diverted from UNITAID to be held by CHAI, shown in the final column as a "Potential Cumulative Diversion" of UNITAID funds by CHAI.

	UNITAID REPORTED DISBURSEMENTS TO CHAI	CHAI FOUNDATION RECEIPTS	POTENTIAL ANNUAL "DIVERSION"	POTENTIAL CUMULATIVE "DIVERSION"
2006	$9,100,000	$9,289,897	$(189,897)	$(189,897)
2007	62,700,000	34,743,141	27,956,859	27,766,962
2008	140,352,889	82,740,318	57,612,571	85,379,533
2009	84,973,897	115,397,489	(30,603,592)	54,775,941
2010	129,348,206	108,868,409	20,479,797	75,255,738
2011	56,432,000	105,665,622	(49,233,622)	26,022,116
2012	61,569,200	67,861,583	(6,292,383)	19,729,733
2013	21,609,400	28,647,779	(7,038,379)	12,691,354

Table 2: Estimates of CHAI Diversion of UNITAID Funds

The amount shown as a UNITAID disbursement to the Clinton Foundation in 2006 is derived from a UNITAID Board Resolution, November 29–30, 2006, that indicates UNITAID may have disbursed $9.1 million toward the Clinton Foundation on December 1, 2006.[59] In a WND article on June 16, 2015, Ortel stated the data shown in table 2 document "a long-standing illegal practice dating to 2006, when substantial sums were diverted by persons unknown and for reasons unknown from amounts UNITAID documents were disbursed into the care of the Clinton Foundation."[60]

Except for 2010, all amounts received by the Clinton Foundation from UNITAID are estimates, Ortel pointed out, as the Clinton Foundation does not specifically identify donors in information it has submitted in the public domain. For 2011 through 2013, amounts shown are taken from audits conducted by Mayer Hoffman McCann, PC, a U.S.-based firm with limited international capabilities, of what Ortel calls "New CHAI."

In no year from 2006 through 2013 do the numbers agree. These discrepancies would not have been possible had the independent auditors of the Clinton Foundation, including PricewaterhouseCoopers, conducted a thorough financial audit that reconciled all CHAI-recorded receipt of funds with the UNITAID audited financial records detailing the amount of funds UNITAID sent to CHAI.

These results indicate no Clinton Foundation independent auditor, dating back to 2006, ever bothered to check actual disbursement of funds from UNITAID to determine how the funds were transferred to and deposited at the Clinton Foundation, or even to reconcile Clinton Foundation receipts from UNITAID as reported in Clinton Foundation IRS Form 990 tax filings with audited annual financial statements reported by UNITAID. Nor is there any way to know from reading Clinton Foundation audited financial statements and IRS Form 990 tax filings how the funds are transferred from UNITAID to the Clinton Foundation. The possibility remains that UNITAID could deposit into an undisclosed offshore account maintained for the benefit of the Clinton Foundation. That arrangement would allow the Clinton Foundation to divert funds by drawing off to the Clinton Foundation accounts in the United States some, but not all, of the funds UNITAID deposited. Answering these questions would have demanded an international auditing firm such as PricewaterhouseCoopers (PWC) to have taken the time and expended the effort to trace all wire transfers or other payment mechanisms UNITAID used to transfer funds, checking the amounts and destinations of the funds transferred.

The key problem, Ortel has argued, is that financial results for New CHAI, as reported in Clinton Foundation consolidated financial statements, were never properly verified by any of the Clinton Foundation auditors: BKD, MHM, and PWC.[61]

CHAI AN IMPLEMENTER, AN AGENT, NOT A PURCHASER

There is confusion in various Clinton Foundation published documents regarding whether or not CHAI's role has been simply to negotiate worldwide with generic drug manufacturers to create a market in which HIV/AIDS pharmaceuticals would be available worldwide at discounted prices, or whether CHAI actually used UNITAID funds to purchase generic HIV/AIDS pharmaceuticals to distribute in various Third World countries.

WND reported Ortel's discovery that unlike BKD, MHM concluded by May 23, 2013 that CHAI had been acting all along only as an agent in performing work in conjunction with UNITAID.[62]

As a consequence, CHAI's consolidated revenues and expenses were much smaller than originally reported in BKD's 2011 audit. For 2011, BKD's audit (completed June 27, 2012, but listed as having been updated November 22, 2013) confirmed consolidated revenues of $171.3 million for CHAI, consolidated program costs of $164.5 million, consolidated total costs of $172.7 million, and a consolidated decrease in net assets of $1.4 million.

MHM explained in its report how it understood CHAI was performing work with UNITAID: "CHAI acts as an agent acting on behalf of UNITAID overseeing the various business aspects of enabling the efficient and effective administration of the program. As an agent, CHAI does not record revenue or expenses associated with UNITAID funds." So, in contrast to BKD, when MHM looked at CHAI's 2011 results, it confirmed that revenues were 61.7 percent lower, at $65.6 million; program costs were 64.2 percent lower, at $58.9 million; total costs were 61.2 percent lower, at $67 million; and there was an identical decline in net assets of $1.4 million.

The Clinton Foundation's role as an "implementer" in the UNITAID program suggests CHAI acts primarily as an intermediary finding and negotiating with discount drug companies to connect with UNITAID. But the funds UNITAID pays to CHAI are not allocated by UNITAID to include payment for the discount drugs.

With this complex UNITAID history, Ortel asks, "How much work did the PWC audit team perform to investigate the long pattern of misconduct that is apparent conducting an elementary comparison of amounts UNITAID claims, in publicly available filings, that it disbursed to the Clinton Foundation, with amounts revealed in Clinton Foundation IRS Forms 990 concerning its significant donors from 2006 through 2013?"

Ortel concluded, "PWC did not uncover and reveal the apparent, massive diversions of funds donated by UNITAID toward the Clinton Foundation between 2006 and 2013." He also pointed out that consistent UNITAID claims that the organization donated to "Clinton Foundation HIV/AIDS" or CHAI are problematic. It is unclear such an entity was constituted properly under applicable U.S. laws or that CHAI ever obtained an IRS determination letter authorizing the foundation to accept tax-exempt donations to combat HIV/AIDS globally.

"The Clinton Foundation has never had effective internal controls over the integrity of its financial reporting systems, which makes it impossible for them to provide reliable information to any government authorities, donors, or the general public," Ortel wrote in the executive summary to his second interim report. "Though management is engaged in numerous far-flung and disparate initiatives, the Trustees of the Clinton Foundation have never seen fit to insist that robust and effective financial controls be installed without which it is impossible to make reliable informational returns to government authorities, to donors, and to the general public."[63]

Like the glossy Clinton Foundation annual reports, the MHM audits bragged about CHAI's accomplishments. "As a trusted partner to governments, CHAI's programs have helped more than 8.2 million people in more than 70 countries have access to CHAI-negotiated prices for HIV/AIDS medicines," the MHM 2013 audit reads in note 1. "CHAI negotiated antiretroviral drugs price reductions will generate over $1 billion in savings between 2011 and 2015. In addition to retaining its initial focus on HIV/AIDS care and treatment, CHAI implements programs on vaccines, malaria, health systems strengthening and maternal and child health in more than 25 countries."[64]

Typically, CHAI statistics such as these come with no explanation of the statistical methodology that generated the results. The estimate that CHAI helped 8.2 million people in more than 70 countries appears, then, to be only an estimate based on general population numbers in the countries receiving CHAI/UNITAID generic HIV/AIDS drugs. In other words, it was an estimate of the number of people who could have been helped, not a statistically valid account of the doses of HIV/AIDS generic drugs actually administered in the seventy countries involved in the program.

MASSACHUSETTS SHUTS DOWN CLINTON FOUNDATION IN 2008

The Clinton Health Access Initiative, Inc., registered as an Arkansas nonprofit corporation, continues to list its principal business address in Massachusetts. Although not widely discussed by the Clinton supporters, the state of Massachusetts, on March 31, 2008, involuntarily revoked the registration for what was then legally named the Clinton Foundation HIV/AIDS Initiative, effectively shutting down CHAI's operation.[65]

The first filing to incorporate the Clinton Foundation HIV/AIDS

Initiative, as it was then known, occurred in 2004, in Arkansas, at least two years after the Clinton Foundation began soliciting and potentially receiving donations and grants in the United States and from foreign countries for HIV/AIDS charitable work. The documentation for this can be found in a registration for a foreign corporation certificate that the Clinton Foundation HIV/AIDS Initiative filed with Massachusetts on March 25, 2004, noting that the corporation was organized under the laws of Arkansas, two days earlier, on March 23, 2004. The foreign corporation registration noted the resident Massachusetts agent for the Clinton Foundation HIV/AIDS Initiative was Ira Magaziner, listed as the corporation's chairman, with his residence at 200 Dudley Lane in Milton, Massachusetts, and the corporation's office at 225 Water Street in Quincy, Massachusetts.

The address in Quincy that Magaziner used as the principal business address of the Clinton HIV/AIDS Initiative is the same address he used as the principal office of his Massachusetts-registered consulting firm, SJS Privacy, Inc. SJS Privacy was registered in Massachusetts as a foreign corporation on November 15, 2000. Magaziner named his consulting firms "SJS," using the initials of the first names of his three children—Seth, Jonathan, and Sarah. While Magaziner did not take a salary from the Clinton Foundation until 2008, he earned $308,000 in compensation managing CHAI in 2014, a year in which the Clinton Foundation also paid his SJS advisors $114,565 for unspecified consulting services.[66]

What this proves is that the Clinton Foundation did not establish a separate corporate structure, CHAI, to solicit tax-exempt donations to combat HIV/AIDS until 2004, some two years after the Clinton Foundation launched the HIV/AIDS initiative. Then, registered as a foreign corporation in Massachusetts, CHAI, then known as the Clinton HIV/AIDS Initiative, opened shop in the same South Boston address used by Magaziner for the consulting firm he operated independent of the Clinton Foundation. SJS, Inc., as Magaziner's consulting firm was typically called, continued the corporate strategy consulting Magaziner had been conducting before joining the Clinton White House.[67]

On the same day, March 31, 2008, Massachusetts issued an "involuntary revocation" of both the Clinton Foundation HIV/AIDS Initiative and Magaziner's SJS Privacy, Inc., effectively shutting down both corporations from doing business in Massachusetts. The Massachusetts filing documentation explaining why the involuntary revocations were put in place is not available for download on the Massachusetts Corporation Division Registry website.

Further proof that the original Clinton HIV/AIDS charity was shut down by Massachusetts can be found on an undated renewal United Registration Statement, URS, for Charitable Organizations that the William J. Clinton Foundation filed on a standard form for the year ending December 31, 2005.[68] There, in answer to question 7A on whether the organization, or any of its officers, directors, employees, or fund raisers have ever been enjoined or otherwise prohibited by a government agency/court from soliciting, the Clinton Foundation says yes. But then, in response to 7B, "whether the organization, or any of its officers, directors, employees, or fund raisers had its registration denied or revoked," the Clinton Foundation answers no, a response that appears to be untruthful given the documentation on the Massachusetts Secretary of State website. Ortel characterized this response "a blatant lie."

In subsequent answers to questions on the United Registration Statement, the Clinton Foundation goes on to admit the charity has been "the subject of a proceeding regarding any solicitation or registry" and that it has "entered into a voluntary agreement of compliance with any government agency or in a case before a court or administrative agency." Exhibit A, a form designed to explain affirmative answers to any of the questions from 7A through 7E, is missing from the relevant Clinton Foundation–filed URS, despite the fact the Clinton Foundation admitted it had encountered various unspecified legal problems that included revocation of operating licenses and suspensions of state authority to solicit donations. The URS document references an IRS determination letter May 21, 2002, that appears to be the initial IRS approval to raise money for the Clinton Foundation, not for HIV/AIDS charitable purposes. Strangely, the URS for the Clinton Foundation filed for the year ending December 31, 2005, does not evidence the required notary public seal or signature, casting doubt on the acceptability of the document as a legal statement sworn to be true under penalty of perjury, as the printed form demands.

Despite the involuntary revocation of the Clinton Foundation HIV/AIDS Initiative, Inc., registration implemented by the state of Massachusetts on March 31, 2008, CHAI operates out of 383 Dorchester Avenue in the warehouse section of South Boston, occupying the second floor of a brick street-front building that bears a sign identifying it as the "Addison Wellesley Building." Clinton Foundation and CHAI audited financial reports and IRS Tax Form 990 filings fail to identify the number of people working out of the CHAI offices in South Boston or to specify what their precise duties and activities on behalf of the foundation might be.

There is virtually no detail to be found in any published Clinton Foundation reports of how many, if any, overseas CHAI employees stationed in foreign countries are trained to work with local and international medical professionals to administer generic ARV drugs. This is despite the fact CHAI is the Clinton Foundation entity responsible for administering the Clinton Foundation HIV/AIDS program worldwide. Likewise, the Clinton Foundation–published reports provide no detail on how many foreign employees are responsible for distributing HIV/AIDS generic drugs to the local population, how these employees are managed, and how they are compensated. CHAI reports are devoid of discussions regarding the intricacies of the transportation mechanics involved to get the HIV/AIDS generic drugs into the Third World or how the HIV/AIDS generic drugs are distributed to local areas once they have arrived. Where is the program CHAI implements to train CHAI employees in the Third World to interface with groups like Doctors Without Borders?

HILLARY TOUTS CHAI SUCCESS IN AFRICA

In her 2014 book *Hard Choices*, Hillary Clinton repeats the often-quoted statistics that CHAI publishes to tout the foundation's success in Africa. "Starting in 2002, Bill and a team at CHAI led by Ira Magaziner worked with pharmaceutical makers to reduce the cost of HIV/AIDS drugs and help millions of people afford the medicine they need," Hillary wrote. "By 2014 more than 8 million patients around the world have access to HIV/AIDS medicine at much lower cost in no small part because of CHAI's efforts. And not just a little cheaper—up to 90 percent cheaper." Still, Hillary is even more interested in boasting of the success she had as secretary of state in the Obama administration in providing U.S. taxpayer dollars to buy generic HIV/AIDS drugs in Africa. A few sentences later, Hillary added, "The Obama Administration invested $120 million in 2009 and 2010 to help South Africa buy the less costly medicine. As a result more than double the number of people have been treated."[69]

The Clinton Foundation regularly publishes cumulative statistics claiming CHAI in its partnership with UNITAID is distributing millions of dollars of lower-cost generic HIV/AIDS drugs to millions of disease victims in dozens of Third World countries, with an emphasis on Africa. The Clinton Foundation is also good at public relations efforts touting the success of CHAI. Clinton Foundation annual reports frequently have full-color photos showing African villages, often featuring visits by Bill Clinton. CGI annual meetings regularly feature high-profile panels discussing CHAI efforts to combat HIV/AIDS. Perhaps most surprising is that investigative journalists around the world appear to take CHAI and Clinton Foundation self-reported accounts of success at face value, devoting virtually no time or effort finding out if the generic drugs actually reached patients.

Yet, the CHAI claim to fame, justifying evidently the continued flow of millions of UNITAID dollars into the CHAI coffers, hinges not on the ability to distribute low-cost generic ARV drugs, but strategies to create consortiums to buy discounted HIV/AIDS medications. That was the emphasis published in a paper in 2008. Consider the following paragraph touting the accomplishments of third-party consultation and price negotiation introduced by CHAI in 2003:

> In practice, CHAI attempts to make ARVs more affordable by nego-tiating price ceilings that reflect suppliers' costs plus reasonable and sustainable profit margins. Moreover, CHAI furthers this strategy by providing direct technical assistance to some suppliers to help lower their production costs. The resulting ceiling prices are made available to all members of the CHAI procurement consortium. Countries that wish to become part of the consortium sign a memorandum of understanding with CHAI and manufacturers are required to offer ARVs to these countries at prices equal to or less than CHAI-negotiated ceiling prices.[70]

A more current World Health Organization report published in July 2014, *Global Update on the Health Sector Response to HIV, 2014*, attributed continued reduction in the prices of generic antiretroviral medicines not to the Clinton Foundation or CHAI, but to market forces. "Economies of scale and greater competition between drug manufacturers have reduced the prices of antiretroviral medicines, while adjustments to tender specifications and reductions in transport and logistical expenses, as well as lower tariffs and duties, have contrib-uted to the savings," the WHO report noted in section 9.3.3 on page 106 of the report.[71] Where are the scientific studies that validate what percentage in the lowered price of generic ARV drugs is due to CHAI and what percentage is due to market forces that would operate today if CHAI ceased to exist?

Current World Health Organization Global Health Observatory (GHO) data indicates that since the beginning of the epidemic until 2013, almost 78 million people have been infected with the HIV virus, with some 39 million people dying of the disease. United Nations Sustainable Development goals to eradicate the AIDS epidemic by 2030 seem ambitious, especially with WHO statistics indicating that in 2014 there were 36.9 million people living with HIV, with 2 million people being newly infected in 2014, and 1.2 million dying from AIDS that year.[72] The WHO always seems to single out Africa as the continent most severely affected by HIV/AIDS, noting an estimated 35 million people globally were living with HIV at the end of 2013. "Sub-Saharan Africa remains most severely affected, with nearly 1 in every 20 adults living with HIV and accounting for nearly 71% of the people living with HIV worldwide."[73]

Clearly, an argument can be made that statistics in sub-Saharan Africa could have been worse had CHAI and UNITAID not provided its funding since 2002. Yet, for CHAI to claim great success against a disease of this magnitude and complexity is questionable. Under WHO 2013 guidelines, 79 percent of people living with HIV in Western and Central Africa and 59 percent of people living with HIV in Eastern and Southern Africa eligible for treatment are not accessing antiretroviral therapy (ART). Moreover, 75 percent of adults with HIV in sub-Saharan Africa who are accessing ART have not achieved viral suppression.[74] WHO technical reports on HIV/AIDS include CHAI projections estimating future trends in the HIV/AIDS epidemic worldwide, but none of these publications credit CHAI as being the change agent responsible for increased access to ART in the Third World.

A close reading of current World Trade Organization reports strongly suggests the battle against HIV/AIDS has moved away from the need to jawbone generic ART pharmaceutical companies, the core of the CHAI strategy since the partnership began, to the need to find efficient ways to distribute the drugs through medical professionals in the Third World. The WHO reports that in the last fifteen years, scale-up of ART has been most dramatic in Africa, where now more than 11 million people are receiving HIV treatment, up from 11,000 at the turn of the century. "People living with HIV in Africa are now more likely to receive treatment than people living in most other parts of the world," noted a World Health Organization news statement dated November 30, 2015. "Globally, in June 2015 close to 16 million people out of a total of 37 million people living with HIV were taking ART."[75] The report made no mention of CHAI as being a player when it comes to distributing ART drugs through medical professionals to HIV victims in the Third World.

The WHO has concluded that changes in sexual behavior, "including increased condom use and reductions in high-risk sex, have been important factors in the declines in the number of people newly infected with HIV in the past fifteen years, especially in the African Region," according to a 2015 HIV progress report.[76] But when it comes to educating Third World citizens on behavioral changes needed to prevent HIV infection, CHAI does not appear to be a major player.

6

THE STATE DEPARTMENT SCAM

It [the Clinton Foundation] has the potential to be the Mother of all Clinton Scandals.

—KERRY JACKSON, EDITORIAL WRITER AT *INVESTOR'S BUSINESS DAILY*

This chapter begins with an analysis of how the organizational changes in Clinton Foundation structure and the promises about likely conflicts of interest that Hillary Clinton was forced to make before the Obama transition team would allow her to be nominated for secretary of state.

The chapter will argue that Bill and Hillary Clinton made sure the Memorandum of Understanding (MOU) that the Obama transition team negotiated with Hillary before her nomination was not legally binding. It will further argue that Bill and Hillary used the MOU to create the public impression that the Clinton Foundation and its various entities would take steps to avoid conflicts of interest while Hillary was secretary of state, but the reality is that Hillary used the office for Clinton family profit, continuing throughout her term to actively coordinate with Clinton Foundation principals. The record strongly suggests all parties involved, including Bill and Hillary Clinton, the Clinton

Foundation and its various subgroups, and the Obama administration, disregarded the MOU once Hillary was sworn into office.

The evidence indicated the Clintons used the MOU as a smoke screen behind which they could continue to divert millions of dollars from the charity to their personal use, despite Hillary's sworn testimony before the Senate Foreign Relations Committee to the contrary. The e-mails Hillary received and sent on her private e-mail server while secretary of state demonstrate how she and her top State Department aides, including Cheryl Mills and Huma Abedin, maintained open lines of communication with the Clinton Foundation from the start. The e-mails that have been made public make clear Hillary shared with the Clinton Foundation what appears to be even classified information.

The chapter will further demonstrate that the reorganization the Clinton Foundation engineered after Hillary was secretary of state was utilized as an opportunity by those in charge of the foundation to steal more money, most likely to the benefit of the Clinton family and their top long-term aides. Finally, the chapter ends documenting that the Clinton Foundation never stopped accepting foreign contributions as well as six-figure speaking fees for Bill Clinton from foreign sources. This was despite Hillary's pledge to the Obama transition team and to the Senate Foreign Relations Committee at her confirmation hearing that the foundation would discontinue accepting foreign contributions should she be confirmed as secretary of state.

BARACK PICKS HILLARY

When Barack Obama took office as president in 2009, Hillary Clinton was his choice to become secretary of state. But the problem arose of possible conflicts of interest because of her continued involvement with the Clinton Foundation. Conceivably, speaking fees directed to Bill Clinton, as well as sizable donations by foreign governments to the Clinton Foundation, could compromise Hillary's independence as secretary of state. The concern was that wealthy individuals, including foreigners and foreign governments, could seek to influence State

Department policy by donating large sums to the Clinton Foundation as speaking fees for Bill or simply as grants to advance various Clinton Foundation programs.

As Hillary related during an interview on ABC's *Good Morning America*, president-elect Obama offered her the job as secretary of state by phone. "It was, you know, about . . . five, six days after the election. And my husband and I were out for a walk, actually, in a, sort of, preserve near where we live in New York. And he had his cell phone in his pocket. It started ringing in the middle of this, you know, big nature preserve," Hillary recalled. "Instead of turning it off, he answered it. And it was president-elect Obama wanting to talk to him about some people he was considering for positions."

Hillary concluded the narrative, explaining that she picked up the phone thinking Obama wanted to talk to her generally about Cabinet picks, and that she was surprised when he offered her the job. "He said I want you to be my secretary of state. And I said, 'Oh, no, you don't,'" Clinton recalled. "I said, 'Oh, please, there's so many other people who could do this.'" Hillary decided to accept, thinking that if she had won and called him, she would have wanted Obama to accept. "And, you know, I'm pretty old-fashioned, and it's just who I am," she said. "So at the end of the day, when your president asks you to serve, you say yes, if you can."[1]

On November 18, 2008, the *New York Times* reported that the Clinton camp sought to rebut reports that Bill Clinton's finances and his business dealings since leaving the White House could block Hillary's path to an appointment as secretary of state. "Mr. Obama's aides this week have been reviewing Mr. Clinton's business dealings, focusing on the array of his post-presidential activities, some details of which have not been made public," *Times* reporters Raymond Hernandez and Michael Luo wrote. "That includes the identity of most of the donors to his foundation, the source of some of his speaking fees—he has earned as much as $425,000 for a one-hour speech—and his work for the billionaire investor Ronald W. Burkle."[2] Later in the chapter we will return to examine more closely Bill Clinton's continuing saga with supermarket billionaire Ron Burkle, including questionable business dealings as well as more Clinton sexual escapades.[3]

"SWEEPING GLOBAL ACTIVITIES"

At a press conference in Chicago on December 1, 2008, Obama announced his nomination of Hillary as his secretary of state. On January 13, 2009, at the Senate Foreign Relations Committee confirmation hearings, Hillary was questioned about conflicts of interest that might arise with the Clinton Foundation.

Republican senator Richard Lugar, the ranking member of the Senate Foreign Relations Committee, instead of questioning Hillary closely on potential conflicts of interest, announced a deal had been reached. "The main issue related to Senator Clinton's nomination that has occupied the committee has been the review of how her service as secretary of state can be reconciled with the sweeping global activities of President Bill Clinton and the Clinton Foundation," Lugar said. "To this end, the Obama Transition and the Clinton Foundation completed a memorandum of understanding [MOU] outlining steps designed to minimize potential conflicts of interest."[4] On December 18, 2008, NBC News made public a copy of the MOU as Sen. John Kerry, the chairman of the Senate Foreign Relations Committee, and Lugar's office circulated the agreement to all committee members in advance of Clinton's confirmation hearings.[5]

Throughout his statement, Lugar appears to have assumed Bill and Hillary Clinton would abide by the MOU. "I share the President-elect's view that the activities of the Clinton Foundation, and President Clinton himself, should not be a barrier to Senator Clinton's service, but I also share the view implicitly recognized by the memorandum of understanding that the work of the Clinton Foundation is a unique complication that will have to be managed with great care and transparency," he continued.

"The core of the problem is that foreign governments and entities may perceive the Clinton Foundation as a means to gain favor with the Secretary of State," Lugar properly noted. But he quickly dismissed the concern by once again assuming Bill and Hillary were operating the Clinton Foundation honestly, as a legitimate charity. "Although neither Senator Clinton nor President Clinton has a personal financial stake in the Foundation, obviously its work benefits their legacy and their public service priorities," he posited. "There is nothing wrong with this, and President Clinton is deservedly proud of the Clinton Foundation's good work in addressing HIV/AIDS, global poverty, climate change, and other pressing problems.

"But the Clinton Foundation exists as a temptation for any foreign entity or government that believes it could curry favor through a donation," Lugar continued, posing a problem he believed the MOU had solved. "It also sets up potential perception problems with any action taken by the Secretary of State in relation to foreign givers or their countries." Lugar noted that as secretary of state, Hillary would be unable to recuse herself from specific policy decisions in which there might be a conflict of interest. But this, he clarified, was more a public relations problem than a real concern. "Every new foreign donation that is accepted by the Foundation comes with the risk it will be connected in the global media to a proximate State Department policy or decision," Lugar continued. "Foreign perceptions are incredibly important to United States foreign policy, and mistaken impressions or suspicions can deeply affect the actions of foreign governments toward the United States. Moreover, we do not want our own government's deliberations distracted by avoidable controversies played out in the media."

Lugar's conclusion was that the only way Hillary could avoid any perceived conflicts of interest was for the Clinton Foundation to agree to forgo all foreign donations while she served as secretary of state.

Then, presenting the MOU as a solution to the conflict-of-interest problem, Lugar raised the Obama transition team's effort to craft a workable solution. "Alternatively, the Clinton Foundation and the Obama Transition have worked in good faith to construct a more complex approach based on disclosure and ethics reviews that would allow the Foundation the prospect of continuing to accept foreign donations deemed not to have the appearance of a conflict of interest," he said. "The agreement requires, among other measures, the disclosure of all Foundation donors up to this point; an annual disclosure of donations going forward; and a State Department ethics review process that would evaluate proposed donations from foreign governments and governmental entities." He emphasized that he was counting on Hillary and Bill's integrity for the MOU to succeed. "All of these are positive steps, but we should be clear that this agreement is a beginning and not an end," Lugar noted. "It is not a guarantee against conflict of interest or its appearance. And for the agreement to succeed, the parties must make the integrity of United States foreign policy their first principle of implementation."[6]

Lugar then entered into the record an "Attachment A," which listed additional requirements, beyond those specified in the MOU, that he hoped the Clinton Foundation would follow in an effort to eliminate potential conflicts of interest. The list of additional pledges in Attachment A suggested that all donations to the Clinton Foundation of $50,000 or more in a given year from any source, domestic as well as foreign, should be disclosed immediately upon receipt, rather than waiting twelve months to list them in an annual disclosure. Lugar observed that contributions from foreign governments or corporations controlled by foreign governments often blur the line between government and private citizens. In this spirit, Attachment A noted that individuals with close connections to foreign governments or governing families often act as surrogates for those governments. So, he recommended that all large foreign donations be vetted by the State Department to discover connections between the giver and a foreign government or other potential conflicts of interest.[7] None of these additional conditions were included in the MOU, and neither Hillary Clinton nor the Clinton Foundation made a pledge to go beyond the conditions specified in the MOU.

In his time for questioning, Sen. Bob Menendez, D-NJ, made clear that Clinton had agreed "even pledges and proposed contributions to the Clinton Foundation will be eligible for review by the deputy legal adviser and designated agency ethics official at the State Department."[8]

Sen. David Vitter, R-LA, asked Clinton if she would extend the terms and conditions of her memorandum of understanding to include the Clinton Global Initiative as well as the Clinton Foundation. In reply, Hillary began, "I am very proud of what my husband and the Clinton Foundation and the associated efforts he's undertaken have accomplished." Then she pointed out that the Office of Government Ethics and the career ethics officers at the State Department, having looked at the rules, had concluded there was "no inherent conflict of interest" in Bill Clinton's work with the Clinton Foundation and her future duties at the State Department should she be confirmed as secretary of state. "However," she continued, "the foundation and the president-elect decided to go beyond what the law and the ethics rules call for to address even the appearance of conflict and that is why they signed a memorandum of understanding, which outlines the voluntary steps that the foundation is taking to address potential concerns that might come up down the road."[9]

In an appendix to the Senate Foreign Relations Committee transcript, the committee listed the written responses Hillary Clinton had given to questions submitted for the record. The first question asked regarding the MOU was, "What compensation, if any does President Clinton personally derive from the William J. Clinton Foundation?" Hillary's response created the erroneous impression that her husband's involvement with the foundation was completely philanthropic: "President Clinton receives no compensation from the Clinton Foundation, which is a 501(c)3 charitable foundation." In response to a subsequent question, Hillary stated, "The Foundation is a 501(c)3— neither my husband nor I has any financial interest."[10]

When asked if she had ever been involved personally in soliciting contributions to the Clinton Foundation, Hillary denied any involvement: "While I have participated in events that celebrate the charitable

Foundation and raise funds such as the President's 60th Birthday Celebration, which raised funds for initiatives that provide medicine to those living with HIV/AIDS, combat the threat of global climate change, and address the barriers to sustainable economic development in America, Africa, and Latin America, I have not personally solicited contributions for the Foundation."[11]

NO BINDING LEGAL VALUE

On November 16, 2008, Bruce Lindsey, CEO of the William J. Clinton Foundation, and Valerie Jarrett, cochair of the Obama-Biden Transition Team, signed the MOU.[12] According to its terms, the Clinton Foundation agreed to publish annually the names of all contributors while Hillary served as secretary of state. There was no agreement to publish the names of contributors as the contributions were made.

The MOU also called for the Clinton Foundation to incorporate the Clinton Global Initiative as a separate entity from the foundation. "President Clinton will continue in his role as principal host and be identified as CGI's Founding Chairman, but he will not serve as an officer or director of the newly established entity or otherwise serve as a fiduciary on behalf of CGI," the MOU specified. It continued:

> President Clinton personally will not solicit funds. President Clinton will continue to send invitation letters to potential attendees and guests of CGI; however, he will no longer send sponsorship letters (which seek contributions to CGI). Apart for attendance fees for CGI, CGI will not accept contributions from foreign governments. CGI also will suspend plans for CGI-International events outside the United States during any service by Senator Clinton at the State Department.[13]

The MOU did not require that the Clinton HIV/AIDS Initiative be incorporated into a separate corporate structure, as was required for the Clinton Global Initiative. "Should Senator Clinton be confirmed as Secretary of State, the Foundation will continue to perform its HIV/AIDS support activities on behalf of existing foreign country contributors and in fulfillment of existing and on-going commitments," the MOU specified. Should an existing contributing foreign country elect to increase materially its contribution, or should a new contributor country elect to support CHAI, the Clinton Foundation agreed to share the circumstances of the anticipated contribution with the State Department–designated agency ethics officials for review, and, as appropriate, with the White House Counsel's Office. "In the event the State Department or White House has concerns about a proposed contribution that are related to Senator Clinton's service as Secretary of State, those concerns will be conveyed to her and to the Clinton Foundation for appropriate action," the MOU read.[14]

Through these protocols, the MOU specifically allowed the Clinton Foundation to accept foreign contributions made to the Clinton Foundation, as long as those contributions were made to CHAI. The document was silent on whether or not the Clinton Foundation could accept foreign contributions, either from governments or individuals that were not earmarked for CHAI.

The document, at best, was a preliminary agreement. A MOU is interpreted legally to be an agreement to agree, and as such it is an agreement in principle. The terms used in the Clinton memorandum remained vaguely defined, and the protocols were nonspecific. Only Bruce Lindsey signed the document for the Clinton Foundation.[15] Bill and Hillary did not sign it though it made repeated reference to what activities both would and would not conduct with regard to the Clinton Foundation. The document was also silent on whether or not Hillary as secretary of state could be a Clinton Foundation officer or a member of the board.

At the time the MOU was negotiated and signed with Obama's transition team, Barack Obama had not yet nominated her to be secretary of state. It appears to be an agreement the Obama transition team demanded to be in place as a precondition of Hillary being nominated. That no effort was made to produce a final, legally binding definitive agreement signals that the MOU was a preliminary agreement neither the Obama team nor Clinton Foundation family ever expected would be honored. Clearly, the MOU was not written to be a final, legally binding agreement, nor is there any evidence the Obama transition team or Hillary Clinton regarded the MOU as a binding contract capable of being enforced in a court of law.

Two additional documents bear on the understandings between the Clintons and the Obama transition team regarding how the Clinton Foundation would be operated while Hillary served as secretary of state. One was a letter that Hillary's Washington attorney wrote to the State Department ethics officer, and the other was a letter Hillary wrote on the same day to the same individual. Again, both letters appear to have been motivated by legal concerns, but like the MOU, neither letter conforms to the requirements expected for a genuine contractual agreement enforceable in a court of law.

On January 5, 2009, Bill Clinton's attorney in Washington, DC, David E. Kendall of the law firm Williams & Connolly, wrote to James Thessin, the deputy legal adviser and designated agency ethics official at the State Department, to specify some additional agreements made by Bill Clinton relative to his wife's appointment as secretary of state. Via this letter, Bill voluntarily agreed that, should his wife be confirmed as secretary of state, he would provide to the State Department ethics office the identities of hosts proposing paid speeches as well as the identity of entities offering consulting agreements, so that the State Department in conjunction with the White House could conduct a review for any real or apparent conflicts of interest. The letter stressed that while Bill Clinton had founded the William J. Clinton Foundation, neither he nor Senator Clinton had any financial interest in or fiduciary role with the foundation. Judicial Watch made the letter public for the first time on December 3, 2013, obtained in the same FOIA request that had produced the MOU.[16]

On January 5, 2009, Hillary also wrote a letter to Thessin at the State Department. She pledged to "not participate personally or substantially in any particular matter that has a direct and predictable effect on my financial interests," unless first obtaining a government waiver. Regarding her husband, Hillary pledged to "not participate personally or substantially in any particular matter that has a direct and predictable effect upon his compensation" or participate in any matter "in which a client of my spouse is a party or represents a party," unless first obtaining a waiver. Finally, Hillary pledged to recuse herself from any "matter in which, in my judgment, I determine that a reasonable person with knowledge of the relevant facts would question my impartiality."[17]

In an article posted on the organization's website on April 16, 2015, Judicial Watch noted that as far as the watchdog group could determine, the State Department did not object to a single Bill Clinton speech and that the former president gave at least 215 speeches while Hillary was secretary of state, earning an estimated $48 million. There is not a single discussion in the 240-page Senate Foreign Relations Committee confirmation hearing record that makes any reference to Clinton Foundation speaker fees.

SPEAKING FEE DISCLOSURES

Clearly, if Bill Clinton received $48 million in speaking fees while Hillary Clinton was secretary of state, he did not need direct compensation from the Clinton Foundation. Yet, the $48 million in speaking fees should belie Hillary's hypocritical assertion that neither she nor Bill could possibly have a financial interest in the foundation.

The Clinton Foundation had received as much as $26.4 million in previously undisclosed payments from major corporations, universities, foreign sources, and other sources, paid as fees for speeches given by Bill, Hillary, and Chelsea Clinton, the *Washington Post* reported on May 21, 2015.[18] The excuse given by Clinton Foundation officials was that the speaker fees were tallied internally as "revenue" rather than donations. This disclosure, in addition to raising serious concerns over the now documented accounting irregularity, made clear the Clintons had failed to live up to the obligations specified in the MOU.

Robert W. Wood, writing in *Forbes*, asked why the Clintons had not reported the $24.6 million in speech fees on their federal income tax filings.[19] Typically, the Clinton Foundation attributed the failure to having made a "mistake," "as many organizations of our size do," admitted acting CEO Maura Pally, "but we are acting quickly to remedy them, and have taken steps to ensure they don't happen in the future."[20] The last section of this chapter will examine the serious accounting issues raised by the Clintons' continuing need to restate audited financial statements and IRS Tax Form 990s with regulators in the wake of continuing "new disclosures" such as this.

The public record also indicates that while Hillary was secretary of state, she and Bill simply ignored all the protocols designed and specified in the MOU to make sure foreign contributions accepted by the Clinton Foundation would not cause conflicts of interest. Judicial Watch commented on April 16, 2015, that despite the MOU and the letters written by Kendall and Hillary, there are no records to indicate that the State Department reviewed any foreign contributions made to the foundation while Hillary was secretary of state.[21] A case in point arose on February 26, 2015, when the *Washington Post* reported that the Clinton Foundation had acknowledged that it had accepted in 2010 a $500,000 donation from the government of Algeria to assist in earthquake relief in Haiti, without submitting it for a State Department ethics review, as required by the 2008 MOU.[22]

". . . EXTRAORDINARILY PROUD"

The disclosure of the speaking fees produced a heated exchange at the White House press briefing on April 20, 2015. "Okay, one other quick topic. I'm sure you've seen there are allegations regarding donations to the Clinton Foundation and speaking fees given to President Bill Clinton while Hillary Clinton was Secretary of State," noted ABC correspondent Jonathan Karl. "The allegations that are being made are that there was preferential treatment given to donors to the Clinton Foundation and to those who gave big speaking fees to former President Bill Clinton. Can you say categorically that no donors to the Clinton

Foundation, nobody paying any honoraria to former President Bill Clinton received any favorable treatment from this administration or from the State Department, including from the State Department while Hillary Clinton was Secretary of State?"

White House press secretary Josh Earnest, instead of answering the question directly, made reference to the MOU, suggesting the agreements Hillary made with the Obama transition team should settle the question.

Not satisfied with the response, Karl pushed forward with another attempt. "But I just asked what I thought was a pretty simple question: Can you assure us that there was absolutely no favorable treatment given to donors of the Clinton Foundation?"

This time, Earnest played the "Clintons are victims" card. "Again, Jon, what I'm saying is that there are a lot of accusations like this."

Not giving up, Jonathan Karl asked for an assurance that Hillary had not used her position as secretary of state to leverage contributions to the Clinton Foundation in return for foreign policy decisions favorable to the donors.

"Well, again, I'm not sure there's anybody that has any tangible evidence to indicate that it did," Earnest said. "So I'm not going to be in a position here where every time somebody raises a spurious claim that I'm going to be the one to sit down here and say that that's not true."

Evidently not sure he had yet made his case, Earnest added, "What I can do is I can say clearly what happened, which is that there was a memorandum of understanding that was put in place that went above and beyond the ethical guidelines that the federal government previously had in place. And the President continues to be extraordinarily proud of the work that Secretary Clinton did as a Secretary of State. But for these specific accusations that are presented without any evidence, I'd refer you to the political types that are more well-versed in those kinds of things."[23]

REORGANIZATION IRREGULARITIES
The public record is silent on why the Obama transition team insisted

that the Clinton Global Initiative, CGI, had to be separated out from the Clinton Foundation as a precondition for Hillary Clinton to become secretary of state, but no similar requirement was made for the Clinton HIV/AIDS Initiative. One possibility is that the Obama transition team realized the principal activity of CGI was to hold an annual meeting, typically scheduled for New York, coincident with the opening of the United Nations General Assembly to attract heads of state. Yet, the extent to which CGI was involved with foreign nations should not have been a truly distinguishing characteristic, especially given that CHAI was created to buy and distribute generic HIV/AIDS drugs to foreign nations in the Third World.

Another reason the Obama transition team may have demanded that CGI be separated from the Clinton Foundation but made no similar requirement for CHAI is that the CGI's annual meeting attracted foreign leaders and corporate sponsors, including multinational corporations that the Clinton Foundation was attempting to solicit for charitable pledges. Consider the CGI 2009 annual meeting description posted on the Clinton Foundation website:

> CGI's Annual Meetings have brought together more than 150 heads of state, 20 Nobel Prize laureates, and hundreds of leading CEOs, heads of foundations and NGOs, major philanthropists, and members of the media. Meeting participants analyze pressing global challenges, discuss the most effective solutions, and build lasting partnerships that enable them to create positive social change. To date CGI members have made more than 2,300 commitments, which have improved the lives of over 400 million people in more than 180 countries. When fully funded and implemented, these commitments will be valued at more than $73.1 billion.[24]

From this statement, it remains unclear whether the charitable pledges were meant to be spent independently of the Clinton Foundation or to fund foundation activities. The reporting on the Clinton Foundation audited annual reports and IRS Tax Form 990 regulatory filings never give enough detail to discern the connection, if any, between pledges made at CGI and contributions received by the Clinton Foundation. Yet, the CGI description of the 2009 annual meeting is nearly identical to the one the Clinton Foundation gives of every other CGI annual meeting, including the most current. Over time, the Clinton Foundation descriptions of CGI annual meetings have varied only on the particulars of the philanthropic boasts made regarding (1) the number of foreign heads of state and other notable attendees; (2) how pledges to make charitable donations in the future are reported as "commitments" by the participants; and (3) the number of lives the Clinton Foundation claims were improved and the number of countries by which the pledges were made.

As noted in chapter 4, what has been lacking in every CGI annual meeting since the first one in 2005 is any substantiation that pledges committed were actually satisfied. Addressing this issue, the Clinton Global Initiative tenth annual meeting in 2014 issued a press release reporting on the 2,872 "Commitments to Action" that were made by the "CGI Community" through 2013. The press release claimed the following success rate:

> Out of all commitments made from 2005 through 2013, more than 80% have been completed or are ongoing. 1,202 have been completed, 1,145 are still working toward meeting their initial goals, only 46 of commitments are stalled, and only 139 of all commitments made have been unsuccessful. True to its model, CGI asks each commitment-maker to report progress on their work annually. When a commitment has not reported back in two years, CGI removes its impact metrics and value from the CGI portfolio. Those commitments can be "reactivated" at any time. Currently 11.8% of commitments since 2005 are in this category.[25]

While the results reported are obviously meant to be impressive, the measuring of those results lacks independent verification. No scientific methodology was specified, other than an implied self-reporting that would permit reliable identification of pledge goals and the extent to which the pledges had been fulfilled. An obvious fault is that no criteria are established to verify the "commitments completed." Does this mean the amount of money pledged was actually spent? Or, does this mean the money pledged was spent and the results promised were also achieved? Examined objectively, the assertion that 80 percent of all commitments made by the CGI community have been fulfilled or are ongoing is nothing more than a public relations effort to boast of achievement without rigorous proof of measurable results.

In 2010, the Clinton Foundation separated CGI and the Clinton HIV/AIDS operations as corporate structures, with a renamed Clinton Health Access Initiative creating the basis for what Wall Street analyst Charles Ortel has termed "Old CHAI," as distinguished from the "New CHAI," resulting from the reorganization. Examining how the reorganization was accomplished shows that the Clinton Foundation's explanation for dividing it into three, legally separate tax-exempt organizations—the Clinton Foundation, CGI as described in the previous chapter, and New CHAI—was designed to be misleading. The reorganization was never a straightforward implementation of the MOU, in that the memo never demanded a reorganization of CHAI. The public record confirms that after the reorganization, CGI and New CHAI's financial statements continued to be consolidated into the Clinton Foundation's foundation statement, reported as if the three entities were still just one big happy family, not three distinct corporate entities, each with its own articles of incorporation, by-laws, and board of directors.

Regarding CGI, the Clinton Foundation description of the reorganization is complex, but a careful reading suggests the Clinton Foundation after the reorganization remained an affiliated entity providing support services to CGI. As noted in the previous chapter, the Clinton Foundation website specifies the following about CGI after the reorganization:

> From 2005 to 2009 the Clinton Global Initiative was an initiative of the Foundation. From 2010 to 2013, CGI operated as a separate but

affiliated non-profit organization as part of an agreement between the Foundation and the Obama Administration. During this period, the Foundation continued to consolidate CGI's finances into its annual financial reporting.[26]

The Clinton Foundation description of New CHAI after the reorganization is similar:

> The Clinton Health Access Initiative (formerly the Clinton HIV/AIDS Initiative) became a separately incorporated entity in fiscal year 2010 and remains so today. Under FASB and GAAP rules, the Clinton Foundation is required to consolidate CHAI's finances into its audited financial report given the relationship between the two entities.[27]

Ortel has summarized the various statements drawn from the Clinton Foundation website about the 2009–2010 reorganization, concluding that they suggest the following:[28]

- The Clinton Foundation was originally constituted as one corporate structure that included both CGI and CHAI as program initiatives.

- In 2010, after Hillary was sworn in as secretary of state, the Clinton Foundation supposedly was broken into three distinct tax-exempt organizations, each with its own separate corporate structure and each with its own separate financial reporting regulatory requirements to file three distinct IRS Form 990s.

- This structure, in which CGI and CHAI were separate corporate entities from the Clinton Foundation, remained in place from 2010 through February 1, 2013, when Hillary Clinton submitted to President Obama her letter of resignation as secretary of state.

- The last sentence in each of the previous explanations drawn from the Clinton Foundation are confusing in that they suggest that while CGI and CHAI were supposedly broken into separate corporate entities, with each required to submit its own IRS Form 990, the financial reports of CGI and CHAI from 2010 through 2013 appear to be lumped together into the Clinton Foundation's consolidated financial statements, as if the three were still one entity.

- Just to be clear, the public record includes CGI IRS Form 990s for the years 2009 through 2010, as well as New CHAI IRS Form 990s for the years 2010 through 2013, and separate Clinton Foundation IRS Form 990s for the years 2009–2010. But for the years 2009–2013, CGI and New CHAI do not have a separate audited financial statement. Instead, the Clinton Foundation audited financial statement consolidates the finances of CGI and New CHAI together with the finances of the Clinton Foundation.

- Then, after February 1, 2013, the "Clinton Foundation" collapsed supposedly into two corporate structures: the Clinton Foundation plus CGI, and New CHAI. The confusion is that after February 1, 2013, CGI and New CHAI quit filing their own separate IRS Form 990. After February 1, 2013, the Clinton Foundation, CGI, and New CHAI were consolidated into one Clinton Foundation audited financial statement, as before, as if the three entities had never been separately incorporated.

If that were not confusing enough, consider that the IRS Tax Form 990 filed for CGI in 2010 listed no contributions, no expenditures, and no board of directors. A note at the end of the 2000 IRS Tax Form 990 read: "This is the initial return for this entity. The directors were not determined until 2010; therefore, there were no directors to report for 2009." Remember, attentive regulators and law enforcement authorities should recognize as a red flag charitable foundations that maintain over time confusing corporate structures and complicated financial reporting.

What is clear from a study of the corporate filings of both CGI and CHAI is that when Hillary Clinton was sworn in as secretary of state on January 22, 2009, CGI and CHAI were not broken out as separate corporate structures until months later. The CGI articles of incorporation were not filed with the secretary of state in Arkansas until September

4, 2009. The IRS Tax Forms 990 show the total contributions to CGI in 2011 amounted to $26 million, totaled $28 million in 2012, and $28 million in 2013, making it clear the contributions to CGI were far lower than the amount of pledges made at the CGI annual meeting. This reinforces the conclusion that rather than functioning as a charity, the main business of CGI was to hold the CGI meeting as a four-day, celebrity-packed event.

As noted in the previous chapter, on August 9, 2010, CGI finally submitted to the IRS a Form 1023, applying for a tax-exempt determination letter some one year and eight months after Hillary Clinton became secretary of state. On October 6, 2010, the IRS issued the CGI determination letter. Also as noted in the previous chapter, on December 11, 2009, CHAI in Massachusetts filed an IRS application for tax-exempt status. On March 15, 2010, the IRS issued CHAI in Massachusetts a determination letter. The Form 1023 application and the IRS determination letter are found only through the New York State Charity Bureau. Neither was archived on the Clinton Foundation website as of March 2016. The 2010 IRS determination letter to CHAI was also open-ended, failing to specify any particular charitable purpose for which the corporation was allowed to solicit tax-deductible contributions.[29]

Ortel has argued that the reason for this may be that the CHAI Form 1023 application, together with all supporting details available through correspondence, can be shown to be false and materially misleading. The Clinton Foundation may be keeping these two documents off the Clinton website because their analysis is material to any informed, professional assessment of the legal status of the Clinton Foundation and of its single largest constituent element, New CHAI. What Ortel's analysis shows, for instance, is that the IRS Form 1023 filed by CHAI incorrectly claims that the New CHAI is not a "successor" to any organization, when clearly New CHAI is a successor organization to Old CHAI.

Ortel has stressed that the entity described as "CHAI" in the 2009 filings found at the New York State Charity Bureau website is an outgrowth of illegal operations begun after July 12, 2002, by Bill

Clinton and Magaziner, neither of whom were originally officers or directors of the Clinton Foundation in 2002. These operations, carried out in the name of the Clinton Foundation, were never properly documented or specifically approved by the IRS as valid "tax-exempt purposes." Ortel has also stressed that since the 2010 financial statements for the Clinton Foundation and for New CHAI are false and materially misleading, so are all subsequent financial statements that built on CHAI financial data from 2010.

THE MISSING $17 MILLION: A TALE OF TWO CHAIS

The New CHAI articles of incorporation were filed with the secretary of state in Arkansas on September 4, 2009, the same day the articles of incorporation were filed for CGI. As noted in the previous chapter, CHAI's principal address was listed as 383 Dorchester Avenue, Suite 400, in South Boston, and the principal officer was listed as Ira Magaziner.

The transition from Old CHAI to New Chai permitted the Clintons to take cash off the table, presumably to put it in their pockets and the pockets of their close associates. A careful analysis of Clinton Foundation audit reports prepared by CPA firm BKD as Old CHAI transformed into New CHAI reveals $17 million went missing between the audited balance sheet for Old CHAI at year-end December 31, 2010, and the opening balance for New CHAI at year start January 1, 2010.

Since auditor BKD omitted an opening balance sheet for New CHAI at the start of the year, the year-start balance sheet for 2010 had to be derived from the BKD-provided balance sheet for year-end December 31, 2010, and the BKD-provided Statement of Activities for 2010, from which can be derived a Cash Flow Statement for 2010.[30]

Table 3 shows the calculations required to derive the New CHAI opening balance for the start of the year on January 1, 2010. The total net assets calculation seen in the bottom line shows $17,475,076 went missing when Old CHAI became New Chai.

	BKD-AUDITED CLOSING BALANCE SHEET AT YEAR-END DECEMBER 31, 2010	BKD-AUDITED CASH FLOW STATEMENT, 2010	DERIVED OPENING BALANCE SHEET AT YEAR-START JANUARY 1, 2010
UNRESTRICTED CASH AND EQUIVALENTS	$ 5,757,920	$ (5,757,920)	—
CASH LIMITED AS TO USE	86,304,698	(18,735,855)	67,568,843
TOTAL CASH	92,062,6218	(24,493,775)	67,568,843
ACCOUNTS RECEIVABLE	8,318,466	(1,241,985)	7,076,481
INVENTORY AND PREPAID EXPENSES	439,200	11,619	450,819
NET PROPERTIES	1,092,842	19,351	1,111,909
CORE ASSETS	101,912,842	(25,704,790)	76,208,052
ACCOUNTS PAYABLE/ ACCRUED EXPENSES	8,625,614	(1,828,343)	6,797,271
DEFERRED REVENUE	82,881,932	(15,261,169)	67,620,763
CORE LIABILITIES	91,507,546	(17,089,512)	74,418,034
CORE NET ASSETS	10,405,296	(8,615,278)	1,790,018
ASSETS HELD BY AFFILIATE	11,511,474		
DUE TO AFFILIATE	6,694,455		
NET ASSETS/ LIABILITIES WITH AFFILIATE	4,817,019	(8,859,076)	- 4,042,779
TOTAL NET ASSETS	15,222,315	(7,475,076)	- 2,252,761

Table 3: Closing Balance Sheet and Derived Opening Balance Sheet for New CHAI, 2010

Then, as shown in table 4, comparing the BKD-produced year-end balance sheet for December 31, 2009, and the derived balance sheet for January 1, 2010, it is clear as shown in the bottom line of the right hand column that nearly $16.9 million in cash that had been within

	BKD-AUDITED CLOSING BALANCE SHEET AT YEAR-END DECEMBER 31, 2009	DERIVED OPENING BALANCE SHEET AT YEAR-START JANUARY 1, 2010	DIVERSION
UNRESTRICTED CASH AND EQUIVALENTS	$16,886,755	—	$16,886,755
CASH LIMITED AS TO USE	$67,568,843	$67,568,843	—
TOTAL CASH	$84,455,598	$67,568,843	$16,886,755
ACCOUNTS RECEIVABLE	$4,438,243	—	—
CONTRIBUTIONS RECEIVABLE	$2,638238	—	—
"ACCOUNTS RECEIVABLE"	$7,076,481	$7,076,481	—
INVENTORY AND PREPAID EXPENSES	$450,819	$450,819	—
NET PROPERTIES	$1,111,909	$1,111,909	—
CORE ASSETS	$93,094,807	$76,208,052	$16,886,755
ACCOUNTS PAYABLE/ ACCRUED EXPENSES	$6,439,719	—	—
AGENCY FUNDS	$357,552	—	—
SUBTOTAL	$6,797,271	$6,797,271	—
DEFERRED REVENUE	$67,620,763	$67,620,763	—
CORE LIABILITIES	$74,418,034	$74,418,034	—
CORE NET ASSETS	$18,676,773	$1,790,018	$16,886,755
ASSETS HELD BY AFFILIATE	—	—	—
DUE TO AFFILIATE	—	—	—
NET ASSETS/ LIABILITIES WITH AFFILIATE	- $4,042,779	- $4,042,779	—
TOTAL NET ASSETS	$14,633,994	- $2,252,761	$16,886,755

Table 4: Diversion of Nearly $17 Million in Cash at Formation of New Chai, 2010

Old CHAI was removed before the opening balance sheet for New Chai was struck as of January 1, 2010.

Table 5 is a quick summary of these results that highlights how the nearly $17 million in cash removed from Old CHAI was detected.

	OLD CHAI BKD-AUDITED CLOSING BALANCE SHEET DECEMBER 31, 2009	NEW CHAI ORTEL—DERIVED OPENING BALANCE SHEET JANUARY 1, 2010	DIVERSION AMOUNT REMOVED FROM OLD CHAI BALANCE SHEET AT FORMATION OF NEW CHAI
UNRESTRICTED CASH AND EQUIVALENTS	$16,886,755	—	$16,886,755
CASH LIMITED AS TO USE	$67,568,843	$67,568,843	—
TOTAL CASH	$84,455,598	$67,568,843	$16,886,755

Table 5: Closing Balance Sheet for Old CHAI 2009 and Derived Opening Balance Sheet for New CHAI 2010

This analysis suggests the officers and board of directors ran the Clinton Foundation as "an elaborate criminal scheme" aimed at enriching the Clintons and their close associates that was accomplished by filing inaccurate, incomplete, and intentionally deceptive financial reports.

Ortel stated in his second interim report:

On the specific date between December 31, 2009, and January 1, 2010, approximately $17 million appears to have been diverted out of Old CHAI at a time when New CHAI allegedly had not yet opened a bank account and before New CHAI received its state and federal authorization to operate as a tax-exempt entity, an event that appears to have occurred in March 2010, when New CHAI appears to have received an IRS tax-exempt authorization letter.

Ortel stressed that this is only one of the "several instances where I believe we can document that substantial sums of money, measured in the millions and tens of millions of dollars, were diverted."

"The crime," he said, "is an untold number of donors in the United States and around the world, typically giving relatively small sums, placed the money they gifted to the Clinton Foundation into the fiduciary care of the Clintons, only to have their charitable donations be diverted from the charitable purpose for which the funds were given."

Ortel emphasized the pattern in the $17 million that went missing in the transition from the Old CHAI to the New CHAI "seems consistent with the assumption the Clintons were operating the Clinton Foundation and its subgroups in a fraudulent manner in order to mask inurement, the diversion of the funds to the personal benefit of themselves and their associates."

PUBLIC RESPONSIBILITY

Ortel explained in his second interim report that unlike individual taxpayers, "who stand a small chance of being audited by the IRS after they volunteer information concerning their income and expenses on relevant tax forms, all public charities of the size the Clinton Foundation has been since its original authorization as a tax-exempt organization must procure an independent audit of their financial statements by a competent and empowered firm of accounting professionals who have access to all relevant supporting details and independently confirm material amounts directly with third parties."

From this, Ortel emphasizes the public responsibility that falls on independent auditors when dealing with tax-exempt charities. "After this extensive confirmatory work is completed in all relevant domestic and foreign jurisdictions, an independent audit must be attached to the tax-exempt organization's IRS filing, as elements of the IRS Form 990 and supporting schedules call for reconciliation of numerous financial figures with information contained in the independent audit, prepared by certified accounting professionals," he stressed.

Ortel based his second interim report on the Clinton Foundation on the understanding that directors, executives, and employees for any kind of enterprise bear this public responsibility to ensure in delivering financial reports that reliable control systems are in place and functioning effectively. Otherwise, there is no reasonable assurance reported financial statements are accurate or that the reported measures supposedly used in audits designed to assess performance are valid.

"For activities such as the Clinton Foundation, including the Clinton Global Initiative and the Clinton Health Access Initiative, Inc., having effective internal financial controls in place should have been a top priority, to the board of directors as well as the Clintons themselves," Ortel wrote. Instead, his analysis reveals, "the crucial control function required for responsible financial management was neutered, perhaps by devious design."

Ortel further argued that without effective financial controls in place and responsible operations, the revenues reported by the Clinton Foundation as a whole, as well as its various components, such as CGI and CHAI, are likely to be recorded incorrectly, missed, or diverted.

"SCHEME TO MASK INUREMENT"

In his second interim report, Ortel argued that the Clintons used the organization of the Clinton Foundation and its various subcomponent "initiatives" to manipulate financial statements in "audit reviews" to cover up a criminal inurement scheme aimed at adding tens of millions of dollars to the Clintons' net worth after they left the White House.

Ortel charged the irregularities, inconsistencies, errors, and other omissions he has documented in operational management and financial reporting of the Clinton Foundations in general and CHAI in particular uncover "an elaborate shell game," manipulating the largest constituent element of the Clinton Foundation for personal gain.

Ortel buttressed his conclusion with a detailed analysis of the Clinton Foundation financial regulatory reporting in the years 2009–2011, as Old CHAI morphed into New CHAI. "Absent effective controls, it should not be surprising the Clinton administration's financial reporting of direct and indirect program expenditures, fund-raising charges, and overheads have been repeatedly misallocated, misstated, and misreported since inception," Ortel reported.

CHAI: THE SINGLE LARGEST PART OF THE CLINTON FOUNDATION

As seen in table 6, New CHAI in 2009 was the single largest operating unit within the Clinton Foundation in financial terms.

	CHAI	OTHER	TOTAL CHAI PLUS OTHER	CHAI (AS A PERCENT OF TOTAL CHAI PLUS OTHER)
MAJOR EXTERNAL INFLOWS				
GRANTS	$159,744,957	$2,993,149	$162,738,106	98%
CONTRIBUTIONS	$15,527,078	$67,402,859	$82,929,937	19%
TOTAL INFLOWS	**$175,272,035**	**$70,396,008**	**$245,668,043**	**71%**
MAJOR EXPENDITURE OUTFLOWS				
DIRECT PROGRAMS	$89,301,632	$5,887,117	$95,188,749	94%
OTHER	$34,940,554	$5,392,701	$40,333,264	87%
SALARIES & BENEFITS	$19,332,905	$18,856,225	$38,189,130	51%
PROFESSIONAL/ CONSULTING	$22,782,232	$7,944,113	$30,726,245	74%
TRAVEL	$6,923,401	$3,891,098	$10,814,499	64%
EVENTS	$154,664	$6,771,543	$6,926,207	2%
OCCUPANCY	$2,982,554	$2,893,074	$5,875,628	51%
TOTAL OUTFLOWS	**$176,417,942**	**$51,635,871**	**$228,053,722**	**77%**

Table 6: Summary Breakdown of Information for Old CHAI, Other Activities, and the Clinton Foundation, Derived from Combined Financial Data for 2009

As seen in table 7, in 2010, New CHAI was still the single most significant element within the Clinton Foundation in financial and in operating terms.

Ortel noted that by June 27, 2012, BKD prepared financial statements for New CHAI for 2011 "that subsequently and continuously since then have been held out as being independently audited financial

	NEW CHAI	NEW CHAI OTHER CLINTON FOUNDATION PROGRAMS	TOTAL	NEW CHAI PERCENTAGE OF TOTAL
MAJOR EXTERNAL INFLOWS				
GRANTS	$142,382,522	$6,217,343	$148,599,865	96%
CONTRIBUTIONS	$31,130,891	$135,184,384	$166,315,275	19%
TOTAL INFLOWS	**$173,513,413**	**$141,401,727**	**$314,915,140**	**55%**
MAJOR EXPENDITURE OUTFLOWS				
UNITAID	$110,640,089	—	$110,640,089	100%
DIRECT PROGRAMS	$16,448,474	$58,260,236	$74,708,710	22%
UNITAID/DIRECT	$127,088,563	$58,260,236	$185,348,799	69%
OTHER	$234,762	$14,040,700	$14,275,462	2%
SALARIES & BENEFITS	$29,961,992	$20,108,913	$50,070,905	60%
PROFESSIONAL/ CONSULTING	$3,4775,049	$8,104,607	$11,579,656	30%
TRAVEL	$7,489,920	$4,636,259	$12,126,179	62%
EVENTS	—	$8,902,017	$8,902,017	—

Table 7: Summary Breakdown of Information for New CHAI, Other Activities, and the Clinton Foundation, Derived from Combined Financial Data for 2010

information, free from material misstatements and not omitting to state material facts."

He continued: "Such characterizations have been made by New CHAI, by the Clinton Foundation, and by directors, officers, executives, agents, and those in position to exercise significant influence over each tax-exempt organization. Because these statements start using an incorrect and materially misleading opening position at year-end 2010 . . . they are in essence wholly incorrect, and also misleading."

The BKD reliance letters submitted with the Clinton Foundation financial statements for the years 2005–2009 are characterized by BKD as "audit reviews," suggesting BKD limited the audit to reviewing financial statements produced by the Clinton Foundation without attempting to reconstruct or validate the Clinton Foundation–produced financial statements independently by starting with an examination of item-by-item receipt and expenditure records.

"MINIMAL RESOURCES TO ACCOUNTING AND LEGAL"

As seen in table 8, from 2007 through 2013 the Clinton Foundation allocated what Ortel considered minimal financial resources to discharge financial reporting requirements, compared to resources spent for travel and conference expenses for the Clintons and other unspecified foundation staff and/or related persons.

	LEGAL	ACCOUNTING	TRAVEL	CONFERENCES
2007	$18,437	$193,399	$10,545,743	$8,223,801
2008	$259,491	$230,240	$13,990,039	$12,606,979
2009	$685,227	$407,903	$11,311,615	$8,702,904
2010	$477,145	$410,777	$12,998,034	$11,035,845
2011	$202,787	$437,798	$12,931,692	$10,953,523
2012	$293,174	$700,525	$13,554,476	$14,861,734
2013	$593,058	$524,495	$19,120,401	$16,649,905

Table 8: Clinton Foundation Expenses for Legal and Accounting versus Travel and Conferences, 2007–2013

Ortel emphasized that the allocation of such minimal resources to legal and accounting is another red flag for investigators looking for fraud, suggesting the Clinton Foundation failed to exercise proper care in operating a sprawling multinational organization prudently to serve valid public interests.

HILLARY'S E-MAIL SCANDAL

One of the many dimensions to Hillary Clinton's e-mail scandal that developed in the run-up to the 2016 presidential election was that she used a private e-mail server to transmit classified information in apparent contravention of U.S. national security laws. A second dimension of the FBI's criminal investigation involved what is known as "official acts violations." Here, the allegation is that Hillary Clinton's official acts in her capacity as secretary of state may have been directed to result to Clinton family financial benefit by encouraging donations to the Clinton Foundation. The "official acts" investigation gained momentum when various Freedom of Information Act (FOIA] requests by watchdog groups like the Washington-based Judicial Watch forced the public disclosure of Hillary Clinton State Department e-mails made clear that Hillary and her top associates copied principals at the Clinton Foundation and Teneo on e-mails dealing with State Department business involving the disclosure of classified information.

State Department e-mails sent or copied to Clinton Foundation and Teneo officials, in addition to involving possibly criminal acts, also clearly violate the spirit of the MOU negotiated before Hillary was nominated as secretary of state. The e-mails in question make a mockery of her testimony at her Senate confirmation hearings that she would create a wall of separation between her State Department job and her role as a named principal in the Clinton Foundation, so as to avoid real and perceived conflicts of interest.

On December 3, 2015, Judicial Watch made public a Hillary Clinton e-mail that the State Department was forced to release as a result of a FOIA request Judicial Watch filed in its ongoing litigation.[31] The e-mail in question, dated February 11, 2009, was sent by Hillary Clinton in the first month she served as secretary of state, asking a State Department assistant to put Jonathan Mantz on her call list. Judicial Watch noted the e-mail was a "vignette that speaks volumes about how Mrs. Clinton mixed money and politics at State."

Judicial Watch went on to note that Mantz was "a familiar figure in Clintonworld," identifying him as a "money man" who had worked up through the Clinton ranks and, in 2009, was a lobbyist for the BGR Group. BGR is a well-known, Washington-based public relations firm founded by Haley Barbour, the former two-term Republican governor of Mississippi. Mantz's biography on the BGR website noted that he had served as the national finance director for Hillary Clinton's first presidential campaign throughout 2007–2008, for which he raised more than $235 million in an eighteen-month period. The bio also noted that Mantz served as a principal of BGR Government Affairs, joining the firm in 2009 to lead its Democratic Party outreach efforts.[32]

Judicial Watch noted that Mantz had contacted Secretary of State Clinton at her nongovernmental e-mail address to inquire about Walter Shorenstein,[33] whose *New York Times* obituary June 26, 2010, credited him with being "a real estate investor who was the largest landlord in San Francisco, a top Democratic donor and fundraiser, and an advisor to several presidents." Judicial Watch noted further that Shorenstein was a longtime Clintons supporter who had donated millions to the Clinton Foundation and was a partner in a Clinton Global Initiative project in New Orleans.[34]

A Clinton Foundation press release issued in conjunction with the Clinton Global Initiative's Second Annual Meeting in September 2006 acknowledged Shorenstein's role in the New Orleans project. "Building on the Leadership Dialogues sponsored by Walter H. Shorenstein and others in their 2005 Clinton Global Initiative commitment, Walter Shorenstein, Douglas Ahlers and Walter Isaacson are now committing to work with a number of local partners to revitalize the Broadmoor neighborhood in New Orleans," the press release announced. "The project will promote a redevelopment plan approved by local residents in a neighborhood that was eight feet under water following Hurricane Katrina."[35] A biography on the website of the Belfer Center at Harvard's John F. Kennedy School of Government commented that Ahlers, an entrepreneur who had helped pioneer e-commerce and online advertising with Modern Media, Inc., a company he founded to create Internet strategies for Fortune 500 companies, was the instigator behind the Kennedy School Broadmoor Project.[36] Walter Isaacson is the American author and journalist who has served as the president and CEO of the Aspen Institute.[37]

The Hillary Clinton e-mail that prompted her to get Mantz put on her State Department call list referenced a "great news" message that Mantz wanted to communicate to Clinton concerning Shorenstein. What specifically that "great news" might have been is impossible to know at this point because the FOIA fragment released to Judicial Watch ends inconclusively, with Clinton asking her State Department subordinates to put Mantz on her State Department call list, without any further discussion of what might have been going on at that time with Shorenstein. The e-mail fragment, however, makes clear that right from the start, Hillary Clinton saw no conflict in interest using her private e-mail server to receive information from a top Clinton Foundation donor whom she wanted on her State Department call list, despite the possible criminal "official acts" violations involved, and despite agreements she had made with the Obama transition team as a precondition of her nomination to be secretary of state.

On September 28, 2015, Citizens United published three FOIA e-mail caches that yielded dozens of Hillary Clinton e-mails documenting that Cheryl Mills and Huma Abedin, two of Hillary's longtime aides who were now assisting her as State Department employees, had been in regular contact with both officials at the Clinton Foundation via their Clinton Foundation e-mails and with Doug Band via his e-mail at his consulting firm Teneo.[38] The decision by Citizens United to publish these e-mails in their entirety triggered a firestorm of criticism in the political media. David Bossie, founder of Citizens United, said the e-mails show the "tangled web that is the State Department, Teneo, and the Clinton Foundation."[39]

"The Clinton Foundation had a direct line to Hillary Clinton's former chief of staff at the State Department, Cheryl Mills, seeking her advice on lucrative speaking invitations for former President Bill

Clinton outside of the department's normal ethics process, according to emails that surfaced in a federal lawsuit," reporter Rachael Bade wrote for Politico on September 30, 2015.

"Foundation officials sought guidance from Cheryl Mills, a longtime Clinton lawyer and friend, on whether the former president should accept paid speaking gigs in countries that could have presented public relations problems, including a North Korea appearance that the non-profit said Hillary Clinton's brother was pushing, the emails show," Bade continued.

Noting that Mills sat on the Clinton Foundation board before becoming the State Department's number two employee, Bade commented that "Mills' involvement with some of the most sensitive speaking requests shows that top foundation officials felt comfortable seeking advice directly from Hillary Clinton's closest adviser and consulted her privately on speaking requests involving hundreds of thousands of dollars."

Bade also reported that the attorney for Mills, Beth Wilkinson, a partner at Paul, Weiss, Rifkind, Wharton & Garrison LLP, argued that her client simply gave advice and did not officially approve the arrangements, insisting no State Department rules had been broken.[40]

"A member of Hillary Clinton's staff at the Department of State emailed classified information about the government in Congo to a staffer at the Clinton Foundation in 2012," wrote Alana Goodman in a *Free Beacon* article September 28, 2015, commenting on one of the e-mails Citizens United had published. Goodman reported that Mills sent the e-mail to the Clinton Foundation foreign policy director, Amitabh Desai, on July 12, 2012, noting that the FOIA-released e-mail had been partially redacted because it included "foreign government information" that has been classified as "Confidential" by the State Department.

"The message could add to concerns from congressional and FBI investigators about whether former Secretary Clinton and her aides mishandled classified information while at the State Department," Goodman reported. "The email, which discussed the relationship between the governments in

Rwanda and the Democratic Republic of Congo, was originally drafted by Johnnie Carson, the State Department's assistant secretary for African affairs, who sent it to Mills' State Department e-mail address." Goodman further reported that Mills later forwarded the full message to Desai along with "talking points" for Bill Clinton shortly before he was scheduled to visit the region.[41]

CONFLICT OF INTEREST OVER BILL'S $8 MILLION IN SPEAKING FEES

On December 30, 2015, James V. Grimaldi and Rebecca Ballhaus reported in the *Wall Street Journal* that more than two dozen companies and groups, plus one foreign government, paid Bill Clinton a total of $8 million to give speeches when they had matters before Hillary Clinton's State Department. Fifteen of these also donated a total of between $5 million and $15 million to the Clinton Foundation, according to financial disclosures. Grimaldi and Ballhaus further reported that in several instances, State Department actions "benefited those that paid Mr. Clinton." Yet the reporters, clearly wanting to sidestep an implied allegation of bribery, cautiously added, "The *Journal* found no evidence that speaking fees were paid to the former president in exchange for any action by Mrs. Clinton, now the front-runner for the Democratic presidential nomination."[42]

The *Wall Street Journal* noted that the $1 million that Bill Clinton collected for two appearances sponsored by the Abu Dhabi government while Hillary was secretary of state came during and after the State Department and the Department of Homeland Security were involved in discussions about a plan to open a U.S. facility in the Abu Dhabi airport to ease visa processing for travel to the United States. The State Department supported the facility in the face of substantial opposition from unions, members of Congress, and others. But Clinton campaign spokesman Brian Fallon insisted "no evidence exists" to link any actions taken by Mrs. Clinton's State Department to organizations hosting Mr. Clinton's speeches and that all of her actions were in line with Obama administration policies and priorities.[43]

On October 7, 2015, Judicial Watch released 789 pages of State Department ethics review documents concerning Hillary Clinton, revealing that at least one speech by Bill Clinton appeared to take place without the required State Department ethics approval. Specifically, Judicial Watch reported the documents included heavily redacted e-mails from 2009 about the review of a speech Bill Clinton was set to give to the Institute of Scrap Recycling Industries (ISRI).

Judicial Watch reported that an April 1, 2009, e-mail from then State Department senior ethics counsel Waldo W. "Chip" Brooks notes that the ethics review approval of the speech "was in the hands of Jim [Thessin] and Cheryl Mills. They were to discuss with Counsel to the former President. I do not know if either ever did."

A follow-up September 1, 2009, e-mail to Brooks from a colleague asks: "[W]as there ever a decision on the Clinton request involving scrap recycling? Below is the last e-mail I have on it—I assume it just died since I don't have an outgoing memo approving the event . . ."

Brooks apparently responded two minutes later:

> I think the decision was a soft call to Clinton's attorney and the talk did not take place. You might want to send an email to [Clinton Foundation Director of Scheduling and Advance] Terry [Krinvic] and tell her that you have a gap in your records because you were gone and wanted to know if the President ever did talk before ISRI?

Judicial Watch concluded that Bill Clinton did speak to the scrap-recycling group on April 30, 2009, for a reported fee of $250,000.[44]

DOUG BAND, TENEO, WJC, AND STATE DEPARTMENT REVIEW

The Judicial Watch–released documents also included a request from Doug Band of the Clinton Foundation for an ethics review of Hillary Clinton's proposed consulting arrangement, through WJC with Laureate Education, Inc. Judicial Watch noted that the Obama State Department redacted key terms of the attached May 1, 2010, draft agreement, including Hillary Clinton's fees and the nature of her services. As discussed in detail in chapter 4, WJC is a "shell corporation" that Bill Clinton established to keep consulting and other payments to him off the books of the Clinton Foundation.

Laureate Education, often billed as one of the world's largest for-profit universities, reportedly with eight hundred thousand students and revenues of $4 billion in 2014, hired Bill Clinton in 2004 to be its "honorary chancellor," the appointment that sent Clinton to make appearances at Laureate campuses in countries as diverse as Malaysia, Peru, and Spain.[45] Attracting notable investors, including George Soros, Henry Kravis of Wall Street investment banking firm KKR, and Paul Allen of Microsoft fame, Laureate Education was taken private in 2007 in a $3.8 billion buy-out. The company started struggling in 2010 when the Obama administration began cracking down on recruiting abuses and mounting student debt in the previously booming for-profit "university" market that attracted students many consider "subprime."[46]

Since 2010, Bill Clinton has been paid more than $16 million to serve as "honorary chancellor" of Laureate Education.[47] On October 2, 2015, Bloomberg Business reported that Baltimore-based Laureate Education had filed with the SEC for an initial public offering (IPO) under the new designation of being a public-benefit corporation, a legally incorporated company committed to doing social good.[48] Laureate had begun interviewing investment banks for a $1 billion offering in the United States that would value the company at about $5 billion.

The *Baltimore Sun* reported that when Laureate Education filed for an IPO, it disclosed a massive $4.7 billion in debt, with hundreds of millions of dollars over the past several years.[49] Stephen Davidoff Solomon, known as the "Deal Professor," published in the *New York Times*'s "Deal Book" column in October 2015 a warning that Laureate Education had lost about $227 million in the previous two years, "mainly because of high interest payments on its debt."[50] On May 30, 2014, Moody's Investor Services downgraded the outlook for Laureate Education from "stable" to "negative," largely over concerns over the company's "rising debt levels associated with acquisitions," resulting from Laureate's strategy of expanding through debt-financed acquisitions.[51]

Laureate's founder and CEO, Douglas L. Becker, claims he was accepted at Harvard but declined, preferring to continue working in a local computer store over getting a college degree at the prestigious Ivy League university.[52] An article published in the *New York Times* in 1985 noted that Becker had also declined to attend the University of Pennsylvania, where supposedly he had been accepted as a premedical undergraduate student.[53] Despite the claims of being accepted at Harvard and Penn, biographies written on Becker typically note he did not attend college.

In 2014, while the Clintons were still trying to keep secret how much Bill Clinton was being paid by Laureate Education, Eric Owens, education editor at the *Daily Caller*, took Clinton to task for the assignment with Becker in an article titled "Why Are the Clintons Hawking a Seedy, Soros-Backed For-Profit College Corporation?" Noting that Laureate was "ensnarled in controversy all over the globe," Owens speculated the secret sum Becker was paying Bill Clinton had to be a lot to get him to "hawk" the company worldwide. Hillary Clinton "helped legitimize Laureate in the eyes of the world by making the for-profit education behemoth part of her State Department Global Partnership," Owens wrote.[54]

Clinton openly welcomed Becker into CGI meetings. A Laureate Educational press release in 2013 announced that Laureate International Universities were scheduled to begin live broadcasts of the CGI annual meeting, with more than forty-five thousand Laureate students scheduled to hear presentations by President Obama, rock star Bono, and Archbishop Desmond Tutu. "Four Laureate students from Brazil, Malaysia and Mexico will be granted private, one-on-one interviews with several CGI attendees," the press release noted. "The students are scheduled to interview such CGI attendees as Sheryl Sandberg, Facebook's Chief Operating Officer and author of the *New York Times* best-selling book 'Lean In,' as well as Chelsea Clinton, a member of the Clinton Foundation's board of directors. The conversations will be broadcast in English, Spanish and

Portuguese. This is the second consecutive year Laureate has broadcast CGI's annual meeting." In 2012, when Bill Clinton was in his fifth year running his own CGI University, "CGI U," Doug Becker predictably was a sponsor.[55]

Jennifer Epstein, writing in Bloomberg Politics, noted that Bill Clinton decided to leave his five-year position as Laureate Education's "honorary chancellor," but not before he had visited nineteen of Laureate's eighty-eight campuses around the world and spoken to tens of thousands of its students. Epstein reported Clinton's departure was precipitated by his wife's 2016 presidential campaign, in which she joined Massachusetts Democratic senator Elizabeth Warren in blasting the federal government "for currently subsidizing a for-profit (education) industry that is ripping off young people." Epstein noted that these concerns evidently had not surfaced in 2008 when Hillary accepted a contribution of $4,600 to her presidential campaign from Becker, his second to her. He also gave her $2,000 for her 2000 Senate campaign.[56]

"The fact that Bill recently left behind his role as 'Chancellor' having earned millions, does not actually lessen his and the family's potential exposures for failing to disclose properly on Clinton Foundation and CGI 990s the nature and full extent of ties with Laureate," Charles Ortel observed, noting the WJC "pass-through" arrangement leaves Clinton vulnerable.[57] Ortel has also pointed out that PricewaterhouseCoopers is also vulnerable should the IPO fail to mature to bail Becker out, causing Laureate to collapse in a mountain of debt. Ortel asks, "How could PwC have failed to ferret out Bill's undisclosed inurement?"[58]

Stephen Braun's article that broke the news about Bill Clinton's shell company WJC made clear that Band at Teneo made ready use of the "pass-through" secret bank account to get Bill Clinton paid on the side for lucrative business dealings the Clintons wanted to keep out of audited financial statements and IRS Form 990s prepared for the Clinton Foundation. Braun, writing for the Associated Press, reported that in February 2009, Band asked State Department ethics officials to clear Bill Clinton's consulting work for three companies owned by influential Democratic Party donors. The AP report, published on Yahoo! News, noted that Band's memos proposed that Bill Clinton would provide "consulting services regarding geopolitical, economic and social trends affecting the entity and philanthropic opportunities" through the WJC entity.

According to Braun, State Department officials approved Bill Clinton's consulting work for longtime friend Steve Bing's Shangri-La Industries and another with Wasserman Investments, GP, a firm run by entertainment executive and Democratic Party donor Casey Wasserman. "The ethics officials turned down Bill Clinton's proposed work with a firm run by entertainment magnate and Democratic donor Haim Saban because of Saban's active role in Mideast political affairs," Braun wrote.

"WJC, LLC was also cited by Band in a June 2011 memo sent to State Department ethics officials asking for clearance to allow Bill Clinton to advise Band's international consulting company. . . . State Department officials approved the three-year contract between the two companies." The AP writer also noted that one of Band's Teneo proposals detailed how much Bill Clinton would be paid.[59]

The ability to hide from regulators, possibly including the IRS, the amount of Bill Clinton's direct compensation was an apparent reason WJC was incorporated in Delaware in 2008 and in New York in 2013. What Band's requests demonstrate is that the WJC account's existence allowed Bill Clinton to continue receiving compensation directly, including most likely speaking fees, bypassing the foundation, where forced disclosure was possible, as long as the State Department ethics review was consulted. Evidently, the disclosure requirement did not extend to revealing the amount of the compensation, only the fact that Bill Clinton had been offered a contract. After 2013, when Hillary was no longer secretary of state, there was no way to know how much unreported compensation the Clintons have pumped through WJC.

CLINTON FOUNDATION REFILES TAX RETURNS

In April 2015, Jonathan Allen reported for Reuters that the Clinton Foundation had agreed to refiling at least five annual IRS tax returns after a Reuters review found errors in how the foundation reported donations from foreign governments. The Reuters article explained that for three years in a row, beginning in 2010, the Clinton Foundation reported to the IRS that it received zero in funds from foreign governments, "a dramatic fall-off from the tens of millions in dollars in foreign government contributions" previously reported. PricewaterhouseCoopers, the current Clinton Foundation auditor, would be required to refile amended audited financial statements, providing the data required for the Clinton Foundation to file audited IRS Tax Form 990s for the years in question. "We are prioritizing an external review to ensure the accuracy of the 990s from 2010, 2011 and 2012 and expect to refile when the review is completed," Craig Minassian, a foundation spokesman, said in an e-mail to Reuters. Separately, the Clinton Health Access Initiative (CHAI) planned to refile IRS Tax Forms 990s for at least two years, 2012 and 2013, CHAI spokeswoman Maura Daley explained to Reuters, describing the incorrect government grant breakouts for those two years as typographical errors.[60]

In a statement posted on the Clinton Foundation website on April 26, 2015, titled "A Commitment to Honesty, Transparency, and Accountability," Clinton Foundation acting CEO Maura Pally admitted that publicly available filings submitted in connection with one or more historical fiscal years contain errors and that any material errors found as part of a renewed and ongoing self-examination will be corrected. "I also want to address questions regarding our 990 tax forms," Pally admitted in the statement. She continued:

> We have said that after a voluntary external review is completed we will likely re-file forms for some years. While some have suggested that this indicates a failure to accurately report our total revenue that is not the case. Our total revenue was accurately reported on each year's form—our error was that government grants were mistakenly

combined with other donations. Those same grants have always been properly listed and broken out and available for anyone to see on our audited financial statements, posted on our website.

So yes, we made mistakes, as many organizations of our size do, but we are acting quickly to remedy them, and have taken steps to ensure they don't happen in the future. We are committed to operating the Foundation responsibly and effectively to continue the life-changing work that this philanthropy is doing every day. I encourage you to read more about that good work at www.clinton-foundation.org.[61]

Pally's comments suggest the Clinton Foundation, despite admitting new reports needed to be filed, was still trying to mislead the public by suggesting the irregularities, errors, and omissions in filing financial reports required by state and federal regulators of charities, including the IRS, were minor technical mistakes of no material nature, not major problems of a material nature designed, as Ortel alleges, to cover up a scheme through which the Clintons enriched themselves.

TO REFILE OR NOT TO REFILE

A firestorm of criticism was ignited on November 2, 2015, when Josh Gerstein reported for Politico that the Clinton Foundation had changed its mind and had no plans to refile its tax returns due to mistakes in prior years, contradicting the earlier Reuters report. "Contrary to what was reported, CHAI has consistently stated that they would conduct a review process to determine whether the transposition errors required a refiling," Clinton Health Access Initiative spokesperson Maura Daley told Politico. "After conducting the review, the transpositional errors made had no material impact, and we do not believe a refiling is required." Politico also reported that Clinton Foundation spokesman Craig Minassian indicated that the foundation planned to file its Form 990 by the then rapidly approaching November 16, 2015 deadline.[62] Two days after Gerstein's post, on November 4, 2015, Jonathan Allen reported that the Clinton Foundation, under pressure, had changed its mind yet again on the matter of its erroneous tax returns, saying CHAI had made the decision to refile its 2012 and 2013 IRS Tax Form 990s in response to "recent media interest."[63]

Finally, on November 16, 2015, Allen reported in Reuters that the Clinton Foundation had refiled IRS Tax Form 990s for 2010, 2011, 2012, and 2013, while the Clinton Health Access Initiative was refiled for 2012 and 2013 after Reuters had caught the errors. Reuters further reported that the Clinton Foundation refiled financials admitted receiving nearly $20 million from governments, mostly foreign, between 2010 and 2013. The Clinton Foundation had previously neglected to separately state its government funding as required by IRS Tax Form 990. Clinton Foundation president Donna Shalala attempted to argue it was a technical error. "There is no change in our bottom line numbers: assets, liabilities, and net assets," she wrote in a letter addressed to Clinton Foundation supporters. "There is nothing to suggest that the Foundation intended to conceal the receipt of government grants, which we report on our website."[64]

Josh Gerstein and Kenneth P. Vogel at Politico reported that Shalala announced the refiling as if it were a voluntary act prompted by a Clinton Foundation desire for transparency. "Although the exhaustive review found several additional errors, our external tax reviewers informed us that the errors did not require us to amend our returns; [t]here is no change in our bottom line numbers: assets, liabilities, and net assets; and we do not owe any taxes," Shalala wrote in a letter posted on the foundation's website. "Our reviewers advised us the Foundation has no legal obligation to file amended returns, but that if we did file an amended return it would be important for us to correct errors found in the review." Politico added that the Clinton Health Access Initiative said in a statement, "The refiling of documents was completed in the name of greater transparency and had no impact on the bottom line."[65]

The Clinton Foundation said the review of its tax returns was conducted by a former assistant attorney general for the Justice Department's Tax Division, Kathy Keneally, who was then employed as the chair of the civil and criminal tax litigation group at DLA Piper, according to Politico.[66] Almost immediately, the *Daily Caller* noted that DLA Piper had contributed $171,000 to Hillary Clinton's 2016 presidential campaign, making the New York–based global law firm the fifth-largest corporate donor to Hillary's campaign. The *Daily Caller* further reported that DLA Piper employees gave $700,530 to Hillary Clinton's two Senate campaigns, in addition to the $496,700 the firms' employees gave Hillary Clinton during her 2008 White House bid. Finally, DLA Piper donated between $50,001 and $100,000 to the Clinton Foundation.[67]

In press statements, Keneally joined Shalala in spinning the decision to refile tax returns as voluntary, done in the spirit of transparency, correcting only minor errors that amounted to nothing substantive. "The Foundation voluntarily undertook a thorough review of the returns for those years in which the line on the return concerning government grants was left blank," said Keneally, as reported by the *Washington Free Beacon*. "Foremost, we found nothing to suggest that the Foundation intended to conceal the receipt of government grants, which the Foundation reports on its website." As the *Free Beacon* reported, Keneally praised the foundation for its decision to file amended returns, saying it "reflects an extraordinary commitment to disclosure and thoroughness."[68] In their statements, Shalala and Keneally totally ignored the fact that the refiling was forced on the Clinton Foundation by Reuters, noting irregularities in the reporting of foreign contributions.

What the incident proved was that trustees of the Clinton Foundation had once again released federal tax filings, based on accounting work falsely characterized as "independent certified audits," that were inaccurate and materially misleading, while failing to make important disclosures that are material omissions. Instead of investigating and attempting to correct the false and misleading information, Clinton Foundation trustees, along with professional experts, including PricewaterhouseCoopers (PWC), merely compounded previous errors with misleading, if not illegal, tax and regulatory reporting that trace back to the foundation's creation.

Also apparent was that Clinton Foundation auditors, including BKD, followed by Little Rock–based auditor MHM, and now PWC, either failed to investigate how New CHAI was constituted in each of the many foreign countries where it has operated since December 31, 2009, or they investigated and elected to withhold from government authorities and from the general public the negative, disqualifying conclusions they should have found with due diligence. As noted earlier, the entity described as CHAI in the 2009 filings found at the New York State Charity Bureau website is an outgrowth of illegal operations begun without the benefit of an IRS determination letter after July 12, 2002, by Bill Clinton and Magaziner, neither of whom was originally an officer or director of the Clinton Foundation in 2002. These operations, carried out in the name of the Clinton Foundation, "were never properly documented or specifically approved by the IRS as valid 'tax-exempt purposes,' for which donors might claim tax deductions," Ortel concludes. Since the 2010 financial statements for the Clinton Foundation and for New CHAI are false and materially misleading, all subsequent financial statements are false and materially misleading, including the amendments filed by PWC on November 16, 2015.

"If the Justice Department and law enforcement agencies do their jobs, the foundation will be closed and its current and past trustees, who include Bill, Hillary, and Chelsea Clinton, will be indicted," wrote left-leaning journalist Ken Silverstein on *Harper's Magazine*'s blog in the wake of the refiled financials.

> That's because their so-called charitable enterprise has served as a vehicle to launder money and to enrich Clinton family friends. It is beyond dispute that former President Clinton has been directly involved in helping foundation donors and his personal cronies get rich. Even worse, it is beyond dispute that these very same donors and the Clintons' political allies have won the focused attention of presidential candidate Hillary Clinton when she served as Secretary of State.

"Democrats and Clinton apologists will write these accusations off as conspiracy mongering and right-wing propaganda, but it's an open secret to anyone remotely familiar with accounting and regulatory requirements for charities that the financial records are deliberately misleading," Silverstein concluded. "And not coincidentally, those records were long filed by a Little Rock–based accounting firm called BKD, a regional auditor with little international experience."[69]

7

THE HAITI SCAM

In the aftermath of the January 2010 earthquake, while Hillary Clinton was secretary of state, the Obama administration and Congress gave Bill Clinton carte blanche in handling hundreds of millions of U.S. taxpayer dollars flowing to Haiti for recovery and reconstruction. This translated into enormous political power for the former president in the poorest country in the hemisphere.

—MARY ANASTASIA O'GRADY, *WALL STREET JOURNAL*

On Tuesday, January 12, 2010, a 7.0 magnitude earthquake hit Haiti some fifteen miles southwest of Port-au-Prince, causing massive damage in the capital city and much of the southern part of the island. According to U.S. Geological Service official estimates, 316,000 people were killed, while another 300,000 were injured, and 1.3 million displaced. Property damage was equally severe, with an estimated 97,294 houses destroyed, plus another 188,383 damaged.[1]

"The earthquake, the worst in the region in more than 200 years, left the country in a shambles," the *New York Times* reported. "As night fell in Port-au-Prince, Haiti's capital, fires burned near the shoreline downtown, but otherwise the city fell into darkness. The electricity was out, telephones were not working and relief workers struggled to make their way through streets blocked by rubble."[2]

CLINTONS RUSH TO HAITI DISASTER SCENE

On January 16, 2010, Reuters reported that Secretary of State Hillary Clinton had left Washington for Haiti, accompanied by U.S. Agency for International Development director Rajiv Shah, on an airplane carrying relief supplies. Clinton had planned to meet with Haiti president René Préval and U.S. relief workers on a one-day trip. Reuters reported that Clinton, who cut short a trip to the Asia-Pacific region because of the earthquake, said her trip to Haiti was aimed at getting an up-close look at both the damage and the unfolding relief effort. "We will also be conveying very directly and personally to the Haitian people our long-term unwavering support, solidarity and sympathies," Clinton told a news briefing.[3]

Separately, Mark Landler of the *New York Times* reported from Port-au-Prince on that same Saturday that Cheryl Mills, Clinton's chief of staff, also accompanied Clinton and USAID director Shah to Haiti, noting that Mills oversaw Haiti issues at the State Department. Clinton told Haitian journalists that she was in Haiti at the invitation of the Haitian government to help the people. "I know of the great resilience and strength of the Haitian people," said Clinton, who commented that she had visited Haiti with her husband when they were newlyweds. "You have been severely tested, but I believe that Haiti can come back even stronger and better in the future."[4] Mills conducted two State Department briefings with Shah, one on January 13, 2010,[5] and the second two days later,[6] during which she made clear she was the State Department person in charge when it came to directing the USAID efforts in Haiti.

Six days after the earthquake, Bill Clinton arrived in Haiti, just as citizens of Port-au-Prince were in an exodus from the capital "by boat, bus, car and truck, in uncertain quest for shelter, fresh water and stability in the countryside." The *New York Times* noted that Obama administration defense secretary Robert Gates announced the United States expected by that day to have some five thousand troops arriving in Haiti. Bill Clinton was there as United Nations special envoy to

Haiti,[7] a position to which he had been appointed in 2009, just a few weeks after his wife became Obama's secretary of state.[8]

"It is astonishing what they're accomplishing," said Mr. Clinton, emerging from a tour of Haiti's general hospital, which had been overwhelmed with patients. They filled its rooms and hallways, and even open areas in the yard outside. Mr. Clinton said he heard of vodka being used to sterilize and of operations performed without lights.

One of the patients outside, Vladamir Tanget, 24, lay on a mattress with a broken leg.

"The government is not doing anything," he complained. "We need outsiders to come."

The *New York Times* noted that help was on the way as more United Nations peacekeepers were visible on the streets of the capital after reports of a rash of lootings and shootings the day before.[9]

"In the news from Haiti over the past two weeks, images of a grieving Bill Clinton have been almost as constant as the pictures of the earthquake victims themselves," commented reporter Mary Anastasia O'Grady in a *Wall Street Journal* article titled "Clinton for Haiti Czar?" published January 24, 2010. "Everywhere you look, the former president seems to appear—expressing his sorrow and pledging to make his foundation the cornerstone of a vast rebuilding effort.

"When Mr. Clinton toured the devastation last week, the Miami Herald described him as 'teary eyed,'" O'Grady continued. "But teary eyed is a more apt description of how Haitians could end up if Mr. Clinton takes charge of Haiti's recovery, as it now appears he would like to do.

"According to sources familiar with the issue, word has already gone out that Mr. Clinton has been unofficially designated by the multilateral aid community as the conduit through which anyone who wants to participate in the country's reconstruction will have to go," she continued. "'That means,' one individual told me, "if you don't have Clinton connections, you won't be in the game.'"[10]

However, the United Nations did not heed O'Grady's advice. On February 9, 2010, one month after the earthquake, UN Secretary General Ban Ki-moon asked Clinton to expand his responsibilities as UN special envoy to Haiti, assuming "a leadership role in coordinating international aid efforts from emergency response to recovery and reconstruction in Haiti."[11]

GEORGE W. BUSH JOINS BILL CLINTON IN HAITI

Bill Clinton and George W. Bush joined President Barack Obama in the Rose Garden at the White House on January 16, 2010, to announce the formation of the Clinton Bush Haiti Fund. "At this moment, we're moving forward with one of the largest relief efforts in our history—to save lives and to deliver relief that averts an even larger catastrophe," Obama stated. "The two leaders with me today will ensure that this is matched by a historic effort that extends beyond our government, because America has no greater resource than the strength and the compassion of the American people."[12]

In the aftermath of the Haiti earthquake, George W. Bush replaced his father in creating the Clinton Bush Haiti Fund, modeling their effort after the relief and recovery funds Clinton and George H. W. Bush had established in December 2005 in the aftermath of Hurricane Katrina.[13] George H. W. Bush had also partnered with Bill Clinton in creating the Bush–Clinton Tsunami Relief Fund, in January 2005, in the wake of the tsunami in Indonesia[14] and the Bush–Clinton Coastal Recovery Fund in September 2008 to assist relief and recovery efforts along the Gulf Coast after Hurricane Ike.[15]

Obama clearly endorsed the Bush Clinton fund-raising effort. "This is a model that works," Obama said. "After the terrible tsunami in Asia, President Bush turned to President Clinton and the first President Bush to lead a similar fund. That effort raised substantial resources for the victims of that disaster—money that helped save lives, deliver aid, and rebuild communities. And that's exactly what the people of Haiti desperately need right now."[16]

In his Rose Garden remarks, Clinton recalled the Indonesia effort. "Right now all we need to do is get food and medicine and water and a secure place for them [the people of Haiti] to be," Clinton said. "But when we start the rebuilding effort, we want to do what I did with the President's father in the tsunami area. We want to be a place where people can know their money will be well spent; where we will ensure the ongoing integrity of the process." Clinton also addressed the potential conflict with his assignment as UN special envoy to Haiti. "My job with the U.N. basically is not at all in conflict with this because I'm sort of the outside guy," he stressed. "My job is to work with the donor nations, the international agencies, the business people around the world to try to get them to invest there, the nongovernmental organizations, the Haitian diaspora community."[17]

George W. Bush emphasized that the "most effective way for Americans to help the people of Haiti is to contribute money. That money will go to organizations on the ground and will be—who will be able to effectively spend it. I know a lot of people want to send blankets or water—just send your cash. One of the things that the President and I will do is to make sure your money is spent wisely."[18]

The words spoken in the Rose Garden on the creation of the Bush Clinton Haiti Fund rang of philanthropic intent, as if the histories of the former presidents with the poorest nation in the Caribbean were entirely benign.

Jean-Bertrand Aristide, a Haitian Catholic priest defrocked for preaching Marxist liberation theology, came to political prominence in 1986 as the military ousted corrupt dictator Jean-Claude "Baby Doc" Duvalier. In 1991, Aristide became Haiti's first democratically elected president, winning the Haitian 1990–1991 general election with some 67 percent of the vote, before the military deposed him in a September 1991 coup. David Keene, a *Washington Times* opinion editor, judged harshly Aristide's exile, noting the deposed Haitian former president was "forced to decamp to Georgetown to be wined and dined by Washington's Democratic elite." There, "he became quickly addicted to the finer things in life," as "Washington Democrats, led by members of the Congressional Black Caucus and eventually Bill Clinton, adopted him." Then, in September 1994, President Clinton used twenty thousand U.S. troops in Operation Uphold Democracy to restore Aristide to power in Port-au-Prince, where Aristide "emulated his predecessors by eliminating opponents, outlawing rival political parties, cowing the press, doing business with drug cartels and creating the sort of crony capitalist economy that allowed him to reward his friends and supporters in Haiti and the United States."[19]

On March 22, 2010, some ten weeks after the earthquake, Bill Clinton and George W. Bush made a joint visit to Haiti, where they toured a tent city in a park opposite the presidential palace that housed some sixty thousand people, only to encounter protestors dissatisfied with the pace of the relief effort. "Our fund was established to do what we could in the short run, but to concentrate on Haiti's long-term economic development," Bill Clinton told the people of Haiti, as recorded in a video clip. Clinton was signaling that the funds raised by the Clinton Bush Haiti Fund could end up in the hands of corporations seeking to benefit themselves from long-range development projects with substantial potential for commercial profit, not for meeting the immediate needs of the earthquake victims for food, clothing, medical care, food, and shelter, along with sanitation facilities and electricity. NBC News and the BBC reported that the Clinton Bush Haiti Fund at the time of the visit had already collected $37 million from some two hundred thousand donors.[20] The BBC noted that Haiti officials estimated at the time it would take $11.5 billion to rebuild the country after the earthquake.[21]

THE "CLINTONISTA" BACKSTORY IN HAITI

Wall Street Journal reporter Mary Anastasia O'Grady tells a more complete story of Aristide's maneuvering Democrats in Washington for money during his 1994 exile. "After his ouster, Mr. Aristide needed money," O'Grady wrote. "He got it when President George H. W. Bush released to him Haitian assets held in the U.S. on the grounds that he was the government in exile." O'Grady continued to note the main source of those funds was the payments that U.S. telecom companies were making to the state telephone monopoly, Teleco, to terminate calls to Haiti. "From his exile perch in Georgetown, Mr. Aristide proceeded to draw on those government revenues—by some estimates $50 million—to lobby for his return to power," O'Grady reported. "Among his most important contacts was Michael Barnes, a former Democratic congressman whose law firm at one point was raking in $55,000 a month from his Haitian client."

O'Grady noted that in Clinton's Democratic Party–controlled Washington, money was all Aristide needed to get back into power. "A couple of years of spreading Haitian money around Washington did the trick: In 1994 Mr. Clinton called up the U.S. military to restore Mr. Aristide to the presidency," O'Grady wrote. "When his term was up in 1996 and René Préval took over as president, Mr. Aristide remained the power behind the throne."[22]

Peter Schweizer in *Clinton Cash* lends another story to the Aristide Teleco swindle. When he was restored to power as Haiti's president in 1994, Aristide granted a special deal to a small U.S.-based telecommunications company called Fusion Communications. Schweizer noted that Teleco granted Fusion long distance minutes from the United States to Haiti at deeply discounted prices. It was a big market, Schweizer noted, due to the large number of Haitians in the United States calling back home. "Fusion was a relatively small player in the long-distance telephone market," Schweizer wrote. "But it was top-heavy with operatives and politicians closely aligned with Bill and Hillary." The Fusion board of directors included Tom "Mack" McLarty, Bill Clinton's former chief of staff. Marvin Rosen, the Democratic National Committee's finance chairman for Clinton's 1996 presidential reelection campaign, headed Fusion's board. Schweizer observed that it was under Rosen's tenure "that the notorious White House fundraising coffees, rental of the Lincoln Bedroom to large contributors, and foreign donations from

China and Asia had occurred." He concluded by noting that also on the Fusion board was Ray Mabus, a former Mississippi governor that Bill Clinton had appointed ambassador to Saudi Arabia.[23]

After Clinton's "Operation Uphold Democracy" restored Aristide to power in Haiti, he remained president until 1996 and then again from 2001 to 2004. At that time the military again tired of Aristide's corruption, deposing him a second time in a military coup that Aristide and the political left in the United States blamed on George W. Bush. In a *Los Angeles Times* editorial, Jeffrey D. Sachs, the leftist director of the Earth Institute at Columbia University, also credited with being a former economic adviser to governments in Latin America, agreed. "In point of fact, this U.S. administration froze all multilateral development assistance to Haiti from the day that George W. Bush came into office, squeezing Haiti's economy dry and causing untold suffering for its citizens," Sachs wrote. "U.S. officials surely knew that the aid embargo would mean a balance-of-payments crisis, a rise in inflation and a collapse of living standards, all of which fed the rebellion."[24]

Granted, the Marxist defrocked priest Aristide, turned island mob ruler and corrupt dictator in the poorest nation in the Caribbean, may have appealed more to Bill Clinton than he did to the more conservative former Republican president. In 2001, the George W. Bush administration intervened to block $148 million the Inter-American Development Bank had allocated to Haiti for improving roads, education, and the public health system, as well as increasing the supplies of potable water. The political left in the United States interpreted the move as Bush administration retaliation for the large majorities in both houses in parliament won by candidates in Aristide's Lavalas political party in May 2000. Opposition parties in Haiti, favored by the Bush administration, charged the election had been stolen in fraudulent voting.[25] Eric Michael Johnson of the Department of History at Canada's University of British Columbia summed up the complex policies toward Haiti of the administrations of Bill Clinton and George W. Bush: "The U.S. role towards Haiti can best be understood as a kind of abusive paternalism, at times condescending and at others domineering depending on how fully Haitian governments obey the patriarch's dictates."[26]

There is yet one more chapter to the Aristide story. O'Grady picks up the thread that Aristide was thrown out of Haiti again in 2004. "In February 2001 Mr. Aristide claimed to have been re-elected in a process that international observers cited for pervasive fraud, and that the Organization of American States refused to certify," O'Grady wrote. "Haitians were angry, but it took three more years for that discontent to bubble over. Finally, in February 2004, he was run out of the country."

This is where Teleco and Fusion get rewoven into the narrative. Now, ten years after his first exile, Aristide found that in 2004 the Bush family once again had control of the White House. Given that the Bush family were no friends of the leftist Aristide, and the Democrats in Washington, DC, were doing their best to restore their power and influence after John F. Kerry lost his 2004 presidential bid, Aristide had fewer allies in Georgetown to call upon for assistance. "Hoping to retrieve stolen assets, the interim government that took over filed a 2005 civil action in a southern Florida federal court against Mr. Aristide," O'Grady continued. "It alleged that he had rifled the treasury and set up schemes with 'certain' U.S. telecommunications carriers, 'granting them significantly reduced rates for services provided by Teleco in exchange for kickbacks, which further reduced those rates.' It alleged that one of the companies that made payments 'to certain off-shore companies' was Fusion Telecommunications."

O'Grady noted that Fusion's contract should have been public, but Fusion tried to block its release from the Federal Communications Commission when O'Grady asked to see it. "No wonder," she commented. "It revealed that Fusion had a sweetheart deal with Teleco of 12 cents a minute when the official rate was 50 cents."

O'Grady agreed with Schweizer that the U.S.–Haiti telecom route was particularly valuable because it is one of the busiest in the Western Hemisphere, and the Fusion contract with Teleco was remarkably lucrative because it undercut the competition.[27] The problem for the

Haitian people was that Teleco revenues were also a primary source of the foreign currency Haiti urgently needed, especially in the crisis of reduced economic activity in the aftermath of the earthquake.

In a *Wall Street Journal* article in 2012, titled "The Looting of Haiti Teleco," O'Grady brought forward the narrative to demonstrate how a federal bribery case in Miami shed light on the Aristide-engineered Democratic Party scam with Teleco in Haiti.[28] "The slaying of a former director of the Haitian Central Bank in Port-au-Prince last week might at first seem like a random event in a violent country," O'Grady began. "But the shooting of Venel Joseph at the wheel of his car looks more like a hit job." O'Grady pointed out that the shooting came days after the *Miami Herald* reported that Joseph's son, Patrick, was a key witness in a federal bribery case involving kickbacks paid by American telecom companies such as Fusion to Haitian officials, including Aristide.

"It is possible that by getting to the bottom of how Haiti Teleco operated during the Aristide years, investigators will finally uncover the details of the arrangement that Fusion Telecommunications—run by former Democratic Party Finance Chairman Marvin Rosen with Joseph P. Kennedy II and numerous influential Democrats on the board—had in Haiti during the Clinton years," O'Grady continued in her 2012 article. "That would be edifying, given how Bill Clinton inexplicably tolerated Mr. Aristide's despotism even after the U.S. had restored him to power in 1994." O'Grady said she finally had confirmation that Fusion had an office inside Teleco that was key in the kickback scheme in which hard currency in the form of U.S. dollars earned by Teleco from the Fusion contract were slid over to Aristide under the table. Only after Aristide was ousted in the 2004 popular revolt did O'Grady get confirmation from the interim government that the corrupt kickback scheme had "cleaned out" Teleco.

In her earlier 2010 article, O'Grady got to the heart of the issue, revealing the hypocrisy the Clintons pursued presenting themselves as if their interests in Haiti were strictly philanthropic. "The upshot here is that *clintonista* activity in Haiti was not the work of foreigners deeply committed to the well-being of a long-suffering people," she wrote. "Instead, it capitalized on the chance to make money using government power." O'Grady's conclusion was inescapable: Bill Clinton was, at base, a bandit whose prior history with Haiti should have disqualified him from any further involvement with the country after he left the White House. "A person entrusted with this much power should have an impeccable track record," she concluded. "Mr. Clinton's record doesn't come close. Indeed, the last time he offered to 'help' the country, he propped up a corrupt despot [Aristide] who proceeded to go into business with key Democrats and left the country poorer, institutionally bereft and riddled with political violence."[29]

HAITI: "WHERE IS THE MONEY?"

The fact that United Nations members pledged billions of dollars of aid to Haiti does not mean those pledges were ever fulfilled, no more so than pledges made by individuals and corporations at the Clinton Global Initiative. Similarly, when the State Department said the United States was sending more than $1 billion in aid to Haiti, that did not mean USAID was going to send billions of dollars to a bank account to let the government of Haiti do what it wanted with the money.[30] The aid pledged to Haiti, as will be seen in this section, went to a Haitian government special commission, controlled in part by Bill Clinton.

The sad truth is that much of the aid money pledged and donated after the Haitian earthquake in 2010 did not end up at all in humanitarian efforts administered by the Haitian government to help the people of Haiti. Instead, these "charitable donations" ended up in the hands of foreign corporations commissioned to undertake "long-term development projects." This was what Bill Clinton really meant when he explained to the Haitian people on March 22, 2010, that the Bush Clinton Haiti Fund would not be used to meet short-term emergency needs of the Haitian earthquake victims. Americans induced to donate by deductible contributions, as was the case with the Bush Clinton Haiti Fund, may have been duped if they believed their donations would end up being used for charitable purposes. The hard reality is that politicians like Bill and Hillary Clinton, as well as dozens of celebrities, descend on natural catastrophes understanding the sympathy of the average person can help them get rich.

Bill Quigley, an associate legal director at the Institute for Justice and Democracy in Haiti, and his coauthor, Amber Ramanauskas, a lawyer and a human rights researcher, wrote an article titled "Haiti: Where Is the Money?" published by Haiti Action on January 4, 2012. They estimated that international donors had given Haiti some $2 billion in relief aid by that time. "But two years later, over half a million people remain homeless in hundreds of informal camps, a majority of the tons of debris from destroyed buildings still lays where it fell, and cholera, a preventable disease, was introduced into the country and is now an epidemic killing thousands and sickening hundreds of thousands more," they noted. "Haiti today looks like the earthquake happened two months ago, not two years."

Investigating the question in their article's title, Quigley and Ramanauskas concluded that almost none of the aid money that the general public thought was going to Haiti actually went directly to the country. "Only 1 percent of the money went to the Haitian government," they wrote. "Likewise extremely little went to Haitian companies or Haitian non-governmental organizations. Haitians, by and large, were not even consulted about the relief efforts." The writers found that most of the money that was spent went to outside governments, international aid agencies, and big, well-connected nongovernmental organizations. Some went to for-profit companies whose business centers around disasters. A lot of the pledged money was never actually put up, they said; a lot that was put up was never spent.[31]

Freelance journalists Isabel Macdonald and Isabeau Doucet, writing in the *Nation*, accused Dr. Paul Farmer, Clinton's deputy UN special envoy, and Clinton of utilizing Clinton Foundation aid funds to install for earthquake victims twenty imported prefab trailers constructed by Clayton Homes that were beset by "a host of problems, from sweltering heat to shoddy construction." The reporters noted that in the United States a lawsuit against Clayton Homes (owned by Warren Buffett's Berkshire Hathaway) alleged the company had provided the Federal Emergency Management Agency (FEMA) with formaldehyde-laced trailers in the wake of Hurricane Katrina. Air samples collected from twelve Clayton-built trailers in Haiti were laboratory tested, with one of the homes found to contain dangerous levels of the formaldehyde carcinogen in the air.[32]

Variety reported on January 12, 2004, that actor Sean Penn "gathered an impressive group of A-listers and organized a surprise U2 performance for his third annual Help Haiti Home gala, which raised approximately $6 million benefiting J/P Haitian Relief Organization." *Variety* did not report where the $6 million ultimately went, or what humanitarian good the money raised accomplished in Haiti.[33]

According to an article in the *Boston Review*, USAID awarded more money to one Washington-based for-profit corporation, Chemonics International Inc., than to the entire Haitian government since the earthquake.[34] Unfortunately, an Office of the Inspector General audit of the Haiti Recovery Initiative launched by Chemonics revealed that the contractor was "not on track" to meet program objectives, with the program at risk because a lack of community involvement failed to ensure sustainability.[35] One of the projects Chemonics left unfinished was the $2 million reconstruction of a temporary parliament building for the Haitian government.[36]

Chemonics is part of the Council for International Development Companies that hires the Podesta Group, a Washington-based lobbying firm founded by John Podesta, the Democratic Party operative that heads Hillary Clinton's 2016 presidential campaign. Despite its poor record in Haiti, Chemonics went on to win in February 2011, while Hillary Clinton was secretary of state, an $88.5 million USAID-funded contract to boost employment in Afghanistan that by September 2013 resulted in just 2,458 jobs, instead of the 300,000 jobs specified in the contract.[37]

HAITI GOVERNMENT RELINQUISHES CONTROL

Remarkably, the Haitian government created a special organization outside the government structure to make decisions about how international contributions would be utilized to implement Haiti's relief and recovery from the earthquake.

In April 2010, the Haitian parliament voted to form an Interim Haitian Relief Committee, IHRC, as an eighteen-month effort tasked to funnel into the country the government and private charity relief money anticipated, appointing as cochairs Bill Clinton, in his position as UN special envoy to Haiti, and Haitian prime minister Jean-Max Bellerive. From the moment Bellerive presented the Haitian government's recovery plan to the Haitian Senate, members complained that it gave too much power to foreign hands and that the document sounded too "dependent." Bellerive was defensive in response. "I hope you sense the dependency in this document," he said. "If you don't sense it, you should tear it up!" Next, Bellerive argued the government's recovery plan was only temporary. "I am optimistic that in 18 months, yes, we will be autonomous in our decisions," he said. "But right now I have to assume, as prime minister, that we are not."[38]

The fifty-five-page *Action Plan for National Recovery and Development of Haiti*, published by the Haitian government in March 2010, noted that the members of the IHRC with voting rights would include one representative of each donor that contributes to Haiti's reconstruction a total of at least $100 million over a period of two years, or at least $200 million of debt reduction. The big donors were Canada, Brazil, the European Union, France, the United States, Spain, Venezuela, the Inter-American Development Bank, the United Nations, and the World Bank.[39]

Emily Troutman, reporting for AOL News on July 13, 2010, noted projects valued at between $1 million and $10 million were subject to approval only by Clinton and Bellerive. Projects valued at $10 million or more were subject to approval from the entire twenty-six-member board, including the ten major donors. Troutman further noted that all projects would then have to go through a separate approval process led by experts at the World Bank. The only power exercised directly by the Haitian government was a veto power given Haitian president René Préval to block projects he found objectionable. Troutman concluded by observing that while proponents of the Haiti recovery plan wanted to argue that the IHRC was modeled after the Reconstruction and Rehabilitation Agency that led Indonesia's recovery after the 2004 South Asia tsunami, that agency "leaned more heavily on existing government structures."[40]

More pointed criticism strongly suggested that the IHRC was designed to shift control over the Haiti recovery efforts to the Clintons. "Whereas the constitution mandates shared governance by an executive, a parliament, and a judiciary, the IHRC shifted it to the executive and the international community," wrote Deepa Panchang, the education and outreach coordinator for the women-driven Other Worlds organization on the political left, and Beverly Bell, the founder of Other Worlds. "The Parliament voted to give the IHRC the power to do, effectively, whatever it wanted. The only oversight measure left the Haitian government was veto power by the president."[41] Panchang and Bell noted the IHRC's twenty-six board members were elected by no one and accountable to no one, with half being foreign, including other governments, multilateral financial institutions, and nongovernmental organizations.

The coauthors from Other Worlds stressed that McKinsey and Company, the U.S. management-consulting firm with close ties to the Clintons, was hired by the Haitian government to help design and launch the IHRC. "McKinsey & Co. performed its services pro bono," Panchang and Bell wrote. "Whether paid or not, the post was a lucrative one; it well-positioned the firm both to influence future contracts and to shape a climate favorable to business. A 2010 World Economic Forum document explicitly stated that 'McKinsey helps coordinate with partners to channel interest from the private sector and connect would-be donors and investors to opportunities in Haiti.'"

Panchang and Bell argued that McKinsey was a "natural choice for the job" because the consulting firm advances the paradigm of "government as business," and because the firm was known to give disaster recovery advice not adverse to business interests, as evidenced when McKinsey after Hurricane Katrina allegedly "helped major insurance companies develop tactics that stalled court proceedings and delayed payments that, in practice, allowed them to avoid paying out claims to their clients who suffered in natural disasters or accidents." The McKinsey team that handled the "mission, mandate, structure, and operations" of the IHRC included Eric Braverman, who, as seen earlier, went on to become the CEO of the Clinton Foundation before resigning abruptly, apparently when he realized the extent of the disarray of the Clinton Foundation financial reporting and accountability.[42]

On December 30, 2010, the twelve Haitian members of the IHRC published a letter expressing their dissatisfaction to IHRC cochairs Bellerive and Clinton.[43] "The twelve Haitian members present here feel completely disconnected from the activities of the IHRC," the letter read. "There is a critical communication and information shortage at the TIC [Information and Communication Technology] on the part of the Executive Secretary and even more from the Executive Committee. In spite of our role in the governance structure of the institution, we have so far received no follow-up on the IHRC activities." The letter went on to explain that the Haitian members of the IHRC were consulted only one day before board meetings, when there was time neither to read, to analyze, nor to understand proposals the IHRC intended to fund. The Haitians further complained that Haitian board members were not even told the names of the consultants working for the IHRC, nor the nature of their assignments. "In reality, Haitians [sic] members of the board have one role: to endorse the decisions made by the Director and Executive Committee," the letter stressed.

The signatories to the letter cited Haitian professor Jean-Marie Bourjolly, an IHRC member who objected in a memorandum dated October 4, 2010, that the IRC was voting to implement "a variety of ill-assorted projects" that collectively "can neither meet the urgency nor lay the foundation for the rehabilitation of Haiti, and even less its development." The letter concluded by urging a return to "focus more on building a plan that is strategically and tactically consistent" with the principles set forth in the Haitian government's *Action Plan for National Recovery and Development of Haiti.*

Jake Johnston, in the aforementioned *Boston Review* article, titled "Outsourcing Haiti," revealed more about the October 4, 2010, Bourjolly memorandum. In the memo, Bourjolly further cautioned that by "vesting all the powers and authority of the Board in the Executive Committee (Bellerive and Clinton), it is clear that what is expected of us (the rest of the Board) is to act as a rubber-stamping body." Johnston further noted that at Bill Clinton's directive, the Bourjolly memorandum was not included in the official October meetings of the IHRC board.[44]

UNITED NATIONS COMES UP SHORT

On March 31, 2010, at an international conference at the United Nations in New York, fifty-nine donor nations and international organizations pledged $5.3 billion in Haiti relief and reconstruction funds over the next two years, for a total of $9.9 billion for three years or more. At the conference, UN secretary general Ban Ki-moon set the target at $11.5 billion over the next decade. The *New York Times* reported the United States was among the largest single donors, with Secretary Clinton committing to $1.15 billion on top of the more than $900 million already spent. Writing for the *New York Times*, reporter Neil MacFarquhar noted that Haitians were skeptical the pledges made would ever be realized, given that millions of dollars had been pledged to Haiti in the past for hurricane relief, but only a fraction was ever paid. "The money is supposed to be funneled into a multinational fund supervised by the World Bank, and then doled out through projects agreed to by an interim reconstruction commission consisting of Haitians and the largest donors," MacFarquhar reported. "Former President Bill Clinton and the Haitian Prime Minister, Jean-Max Bellerive, are to lead the commission."[45]

As anticipated, the money pledged at the UN for Haiti was slow to develop. By July 2010, only Brazil had produced its entire pledge of $55 million, and only 10 percent of the $5.3 billion pledged had been handed over to the Haitian government. "I can't understand why, in this budget climate, people want to hold onto their money until the end," Clinton complained to reporters. "We are looking at . . . the commission (IHRC) approving projects and raising money for them. A lot of these donors want to know where their money is going to go for."[46]

Bellerive and Clinton, expressing their disappointment, wrote an op-ed for the *New York Times*, July 11, 2010, titled "Finishing Haiti's Unfinished Work."[47] "Without reliable schedules for disbursement, the commission is unable to plan, finance projects or respond quickly to immediate needs," they wrote. "Haiti's government has done everything it's been asked to do by international donors to inspire confidence, maintain transparency and ensure that not one single cent is lost to corruption. We cannot turn our backs on Haiti's government and its people when the time comes to write the check."

Bellerive and Clinton also complained the World Bank was not doing its job collecting the pledges and funneling them to the IHRC. "In addition to these disbursements, we need the partnership and cooperation of the World Bank. As the steward of the multi-donor trust fund, the World Bank has a responsibility to ensure that money pledged by governments and their taxpayers around the world is delivered quickly to the Haitian government or to projects approved by the reconstruction commission." They continued, "We hope the World Bank will work with us to make this happen, by streamlining the process for releasing money and preventing reconstruction funds from being diverted to redundant technical reviews."

They stressed that there was no time to waste, as hurricane season had already begun. "Ultimately, we will measure the success of reconstruction efforts not in the number of days that have passed since the earthquake, nor in the dollar amounts pledged, but in tangible results that improve the lives of the Haitian people, so that in the next six months, and in the six months after that, they will be closer to the future they envision for themselves, their children and generations to come," Bellerive and Clinton wrote. "We hope the World Bank will work with us to make this happen, by streamlining the process for releasing money and preventing reconstruction funds from being diverted to redundant technical reviews," they added, moderating their enthusiasm for World Bank involvement with caution that its management of the relief and reconstruction money could complicate rather than expedite the post-earthquake efforts to rebuild Haiti.

In July 2011, more than a year and a half after the earthquake, the World Bank reported that United Nations countries pledging contributions to Haiti had only come up with $352 million of the $5.3 billion pledged to have been given in the first two years.[48] Of the $352 million actually contributed, the World Bank reported $335 million had been transferred from the United Nations to the Haiti Reconstruction Fund (HRF). The HRF was established in June 2010 by the Haitian government in conjunction with the Inter-American Development Bank, the United Nations, and the World Bank to collect international aid contributions needed to finance the Haitian government's post-earthquake Action Plan for National Recovery and Development of Haiti. The Interim Haiti Reconstruction Commission was responsible for making decisions on disbursements from the HRF to fund IHRC-approved projects.

CHERYL MILLS MOVES TO CENTER STAGE

In July 27, 2010, the U.S. Congress appropriated more than $1.14 billion in supplemental funds for Haitian reconstruction assistance, most of which was provided to USAID and the State Department. The U.S. government announced plans to allocate about $918 million of the $1.14 billion in supplemental Haiti reconstruction funds available through the end of fiscal year 2012 to USAID and the State Department for Haiti relief and reconstruction efforts.[49] On July 10, 2010, some two weeks before Congress voted to approve the supplemental funding, Cheryl Mills, acting in her capacity as counselor to Secretary Clinton and State Department administrator over U.S. government recovery efforts in Haiti, together with USAID administrator Shah, gave an optimistic assessment of the U.S. government relief efforts in Haiti and the need for additional funding.[50]

The State Department assessment came approximately six months after the earthquake. "I think there is a lot that's happened actually in Haiti and there's still an enormous amount that needs to be done, and I think that's one of the challenges that we're going to be confronting now, because we have gotten past the immediate crisis and we are beginning to look towards the long term," Mills began. "And we are in that challenging space between transitioning from the immediate crisis to the long term."

Mills referenced progress, commenting that the "health metrics" in Haiti were actually better than they were before the earthquake. "The IHRC, which is the government's mechanism to . . . coordinate donors, has been stood up, and was stood up in relatively record time, actually, given the set of challenges that are there," she noted. "Since March, [we] have been spending on the order of about $178 million that have really been designed to help us ramp up to the enormous amount of aid that will hopefully be coming through the supplemental once Congress passes that to be able to build to our long-term strategy there," she said.

Mills, in advocating the need for more U.S. funding, was upbeat. "Once the supplemental passes, and hopefully it passes in its consistent form, then we will be on to the long-term investments that we want to see as—in Haiti and to be good partners in both—investing deeply in the areas of agriculture, energy, health, and ensuring that we also are thoughtful about security and rule of law, as well as continuing the programming that we had been doing in Haiti in a way that benefits where they want to be in the future and the set of challenges that are there," she said.

Shah emphasized that the United States did mount an effective early response. "And I would remind us that we were looking at an environment where we were not sure that people in Haiti would have access to food, to water, to shelter," he said. "And the International Humanitarian Community, working in partnership with the Government of Haiti, effectively met the food needs of more than 3.5 million vulnerable Haitians, has effectively conducted vaccination efforts that have reached more than a million Haitians, and as a result, has contained any large-scale epidemics, which we had all been concerned about, and is in the process of both providing emergency shelter to more than a million Haitians, but also, as Cheryl points out, working on transition strategies to get people into real transitional housing and to rehabilitate homes so that when safe and when improved, people can return to their normal homes of living."

CHOLERA BREAKS OUT IN HAITI

Ironically, especially given the upbeat assessments Mills made about "health metrics" in Haiti, a cholera epidemic broke out some ten months after the earthquake, the first in at least a century. One year later, the U.S. Centers for Disease Control and Prevention reported more than 470,000 cases of cholera, with 6,631 deaths attributed to the disease, "the worst cholera outbreak in recent history."[51]

The outbreak produced in the United States an immediate and angry reaction against both the highly touted Bush Clinton Haiti Fund, which had raised a total of $52 million by December 23, 2010,[52] and the State Department, for whom Congress had raised $1.14 billion in supplemental funding for Haiti relief.

"Breaking: North American news outlets 'excited' by Haiti cholera outbreak. They say for them, 'without a crisis, Haiti doesn't exist,'" wrote left-leaning freelance writer Ansel Herz, quoting a tweet by Vanderbilt University historian Peter James Hudson. Herz, who had reported from Haiti for two years for Inter-Press Service and Free Speech Radio News, was venting his rage in an editorial published in the *New York Daily News* on November 1, 2010.

"The cholera outbreak itself is a symptom of failed foreign policies and organizations that have left the Haitian people as poor as ever and disconnected from the mechanisms of their own development," Herz wrote.

Noting that Refugees International had called the UN-led humanitarian efforts at earthquake relief and recovery in Haiti "paralyzed" and finding "appalling" conditions in the makeshift camps amid the rubble of Port-au-Prince, "despite the billions of dollars pledged for earthquake relief," Herz was in no mood to praise the efforts of former presidents Bill Clinton and George W. Bush.

"For example, the Clinton-Bush Haiti fund, inaugurated by President Obama with both former Presidents at his side, is still running Web advertisements that say '100% of donations go directly to relief efforts,'" Herz reported. "That's a cruel lie, considering the quake victims living in flood zones under withered plastic tarps. Only 8% of its $50 million had been spent by this summer, according to The Chronicle of Philanthropy." But Herz did not stop there.

"The fund's website now talks about supporting long-term programs to develop Haiti's business class," he continued. "The Interim Haiti Recovery Commission has approved only one water project: $200 million to expand the public water supply in Port-au-Prince. But it remains only 57% funded, according to the group's website."

Herz attributed the problem to politics-as-usual. "Clinton's much-lauded connections with international donors appear to have come to naught," he charged. "Busy campaigning for Democrats ahead of Tuesday's election, he has not spoken out about Haiti during the cholera outbreak."

Herz's conclusion: "There has been no meaningful recovery or reconstruction since the quake."

The Haiti cholera epidemic should have sounded a warning bell for U.S. regulators and law enforcement on both the state and federal levels that pure philanthropic impulses might not be the sole motivators of those organizing Haiti relief and recovery efforts. "Over half of American households donated their hard-earned money to Haitian earthquake victims," Herz sadly observed. "It's high time we take stock of where that money went and demand some accountability, which our high-profile journalists have failed to do."[53]

But if being UN special envoy to Haiti and being appointed cochair of the IHRC in Haiti, as well as teaming up with former president George W. Bush in a new Bush-Clinton disaster fund, were not enough, Bill Clinton also made sure the Clinton Foundation got fully into the act. The Clinton Global Initiative annual meeting in September 2010, some eight months after the earthquake, conveniently opened the back door to the continued involvement of Secretary of State Hillary Clinton, whose senior aide Cheryl Mills headed the State Department's Haiti relief effort. The arrangement conveniently allowed Clinton to keep in touch with Clinton Foundation top officials via her private e-mail server, informing them of key Haiti developments that might represent profitable business opportunities to help redevelop Haiti, as well as build the Clinton family fortune, provided the State Department, the Clinton Foundation, the Bush Clinton Haiti Fund, and the IHRC worked together in economic development harmony.

On September 23, 2010, at the Clinton Global Initiative's 2010 Annual Meeting in New York City, Bill Clinton hosted a special panel session on recovery in Haiti. At center stage for the webcast event were Haiti president Réne Préval and Clinton's IHRC cochair, Bellerive, along with Klaus Schwab, the founder and executive chairman of the World Economic Forum. Also on the panel was a global entrepreneur from Ireland who, we shall soon see, played a major role in the Haiti aid saga—Denis O'Brien. "Since the Haiti earthquake in January, CGI members have made $224 million in commitments to help Haiti build back better, in addition to the more than $140 million in commitments made before the quake," Bill Clinton bragged during the panel discussion. "Working together alongside the Interim Haiti Reconstruction Commission, CGI members are delivering measurable results in housing, clean energy, infrastructure, health care, and education, among other important sectors, to give the Haitian people the tools to create a better future for their nation."[54]

On October 8, 2013, the *New York Times* reported that the Institute for Justice and Democracy in Haiti, a Boston-based human rights group, had filed a class action lawsuit against the United Nations in federal district court, charging the UN peacekeeping force from Nepal stationed in Haiti was responsible for introducing disease through sewage contamination from its barracks.[55] On January 9, 2015, U.S. District Court judge Paul Oetken in Manhattan threw the case out, ruling the United Nations was immune from such a lawsuit.[56] "The UN cannot deny that it is responsible for Haiti's cholera, or that it has an obligation to its victims," said Brian Concannon Jr., director of the Institute for Justice and Democracy in Haiti and counsel for the plaintiffs. "The UN's only defense is that no one can make it respect the law. We are disappointed that the U.S. government and the Court accepted this position, but more disappointed that the UN would take it. It goes against everything the UN is supposed to stand for."[57]

CLINTON INVITES IRELAND BILLIONAIRE TO HAITI PARTY

On January 6, 2012, Stephanie Strom reported in the *New York Times* on a visit to Haiti by Irish billionaire Denis O'Brien, the owner of Digicel, a telecom operator incorporated in Bermuda providing mobile phone service in Haiti as one of its thirty-three markets across the Caribbean, Central America, and South Pacific.[58] O'Brien was in Port-au-Prince, Haiti, to open the fiftieth school that Digicel had rebuilt since the earthquake struck in 2010 and to pledge that Digicel would build another eighty schools by 2014.

O'Brien, Strom reported, had become the "de facto ambassador for an emerging business-centered approach to the redevelopment of this disaster-prone nation, which has so long relied on the work of nonprofit groups and aid agencies that it is known as the Republic of N.G.O.'s, or nongovernmental organizations." Digicel, then Haiti's largest employer and taxpayer, had invested $600 million in Haiti, "making it by far the country's largest foreign investor ever, and it has democratized communications with its strategy of selling low-price cellphones and services to the masses." The *Times* said O'Brien had "profited extensively" from Haiti, noting it is the company's largest market, accounting for roughly one-third of its 11.1 million subscribers.

Strom went on to report that Digicel had unveiled plans in November 2011 to invest $45 million in a new, 173-room hotel to be run by Marriott in a new industrial park in Caracol, an impoverished fishing village of some six thousand inhabitants on Haiti's north coast, until the Clinton Global Initiative, with funding from USAID and the Inter-American Industrial Bank, decided in October 2012 to transform the area into an industrial park.[59] The *Times* announced that the anchor tenant was planned to be Sae-A, a Korean apparel manufacturer with extensive experience in Latin America. Sae-A planned "to employ 20,000 and, unlike the low-wage apparel manufacturing operations that spawned vast urban slums, incorporate housing developments and other infrastructure." The article also noted that O'Brien was in charge of overseeing commitments made by the approximately sixty members of the Clinton Global Initiative's Haiti Action Network to install solar panels in Haiti, increase energy supplies, refurbish homes, and provide job training.[60]

Those presuming O'Brien's decision to construct schools in post-earthquake Haiti was strictly a philanthropic endeavor funded by Digicel do not yet fully appreciate Haiti's post-earthquake political reality, dominated as it was by the Clintons. On August 25, 2010, USAID announced that the first school built under "an innovative public-private partnership was opened by Digicel Foundation and USAID as the École Louis de Borno in Léogâne, the town at the epicenter of the earthquake. The school planned to welcome six hundred primary students when the school year began on October 4, 2010.

"The school is the first of 50 planned by the Digicel Foundation, providing permanent and transitional schools for up to 30,000 children, at two school shifts per day," the USAID press release read. "Under the USAID partnership, some of these schools will be constructed with U.S. military shipping containers which are being converted into school campuses to replace those destroyed in the earthquake."[61] After the earthquake, 4,800 schools in Haiti were damaged or destroyed.[62]

But where Digicel really made its money was in the idea of a wireless mobile phone money-transfer system for Haiti that the Clintons began promoting in the wake of the earthquake. It would enable friends and relatives in the United States to send money directly to people in the earthquake-ravaged nation. As investigative reporter Peter Schweizer noted in *Clinton Cash*, Digicel was the big winner with its TchoTcho Mobile system (*TchoTcho* means "pocket money" in Creole). "The USAID Food for Peace program, under the direct control of the State Department through Cheryl Mills, chose the TchoTcho system for its money transfers," he wrote. "Haitians were given cell phones and a free TchoTcho account. When Haitians used the system, they paid O'Brien's company millions in fees. They also became users of O'Brien's TchoTcho system." By 2012, Digicel had 77 percent of the Haitian mobile phone market, "a rise fueled in part by the fact that it was a digital bank supplier." From April 2011 to March 2012, Schweizer added, Digicel's revenues increased by 14 percent and its subscriber base by 27 percent. By September 2012, Haiti overtook Jamaica as Digicel's most profitable market, and O'Brien granted himself $300 million in dividends from the company.[63]

DIGICEL GAINS USAID AND GATES FOUNDATION FUNDING
Tracing the money trail, Digicel got its first break with its TchoTcho application when Scotiabank Haiti announced a partnership with Digicel on November 24, 2010, after Digicel received formal approval from the Banque de la Republique d'Haiti as well as the country's telecoms regulator. Although Scotiabank Haiti declined to disclose the terms of the partnership, the deal almost certainly involved financing.[64] A joint press release by Digicel and Scotiabank announced, "TchoTcho Mobile allows Haitians to complete basic banking functions such as cash withdrawals, deposits and transfers safely and securely through their mobile phone and does not require them to have a traditional bank account." The release further pointed out that the "mobile money concept is guaranteed to take off in Haiti, where only 10 percent of the population had used a commercial bank pre-earthquake (according to USAID), but where mobile penetration stands at over 35 percent. This

number is up from a low 5 percent before Digicel's launch in 2006—and continues to grow each year."[65]

The money trail traces to an announcement by USAID in June 2010 that the U.S. agency was "jumpstarting" the delivery of financial services by mobile phone in Haiti with a $10 million fund aimed at the creation of the Haiti Mobile Money Initiative (HMMI), which was formed as a partnership between the Bill & Melinda Gates Foundation and the U.S. government, through USAID.[66] The idea was that HMMI would offer prize money from the USAID fund to encourage mobile money service providers to develop rapidly a mobile money transfer system operating throughout Haiti. The HMMI program was to be implemented by the Haiti Integrated Finance for Value Chains and Enterprise, (HIFIVE), also a USAID-funded project, which offered technical and management assistance to provide financial access for the impoverished majority in Haiti.[67] On January 11, 2011, USAID and the Gates Foundation announced a $2.5 million award to Digicel from the HMMI for being the first to launch a mobile money service in Haiti, TchoTcho Mobile, that met the competition's stringent criteria.[68]

Despite the great hoopla at the start of the "electronic wallet" program in Haiti, *Seattle Times* business reporter Ángel González observed in a 2015 article that the push by USAID and the Gates Foundation to make Haiti an e-cash economy fell far short.[69] Only some sixty thousand people in Haiti actually used mobile phone applications to transfer money to relatives and friends, internationally or within Haiti, or to pay bills and transact business, in a country of 10 million people. "Lots of nonprofits wanted to funnel billions of relief dollars directly to recipients without going through a government they mistrusted," González wrote. "Boosted by a $10 million incentive from the Gates Foundation and the U.S. Agency for International Development (USAID), e-cash here got off to a strong start. The two main cellphone operators scrambled to get their subscribers to open accounts. One of the wireless companies was Voilà, owned by Bellevue-based Trilogy International Partners—which in 2010 was the largest U.S. investor in Haiti." In 2012, Digicel acquired Voilà, eliminating its major competitor in the Haiti mobile phone market.

The aim, González said, was to get 1 million users active in two years, according to Claude Clodomir, who heads HIFIVE, "the project that spearheads the Haitian mobile cash effort with backing from the Gates Foundation and USAID." USAID and the Gates Foundation had hoped Haiti would be another Kenya, where e-cash took off because it helped migrants working in the capital city of Nairobi to send money home to the provinces. In Kenya, González noted, e-cash became a stepping-stone to more advanced financial services, including borrowing for the type of small businesses that development experts see as critical to lifting a country out of poverty. In Kenya, a nation of 44 million people, there are 12.2 million e-cash active users, for a market share of 27.5 percent of the population, as compared to 0.6 percent in Haiti. In Haiti, initial results were favorable as eight hundred thousand initially applied for the e-cash service, but over time the results have been disappointing, both to the U.S. government and to the Gates Foundation.

As with fighting HIV/AIDS, solutions that work must take culture into account. Simply providing cheaper generic pharmaceutical drugs will not alone solve the problem. In Haiti, where Gonzáles reports only 22 percent of those older than fifteen have bank accounts and where as much as half the population is typically unemployed, e-cash has so far failed to take off. Still, the market in Haiti is profitable for Digicel: 6 million Haitians, 60 percent of the population, have cell phones, up fifteenfold in a decade. "People are very attached to cash," a Haiti cash manager told González. "When you tell people that their money is going to be deposited into their telephone, they freak out."

CLINTON FOUNDATION GOES INTO HOTEL BUSINESS

On February 24, 2015, Bill Clinton joined Denis O'Brien for the opening of a 175-room Marriott Hotel in the Turgeau area of Port-au-Prince, just seven miles from the Toussaint L'Ouverture International Airport, with easy access to the capital city's commercial district.[70]

Bill Clinton, representing the Clinton Global Initiative, and Hillary

Clinton, acting in her capacity as secretary of state, engineered the public funding required to construct the hotel. A Marriott Corporation press release on the hotel's opening noted that TDSA, a development company established and owned by Digicel, managed the design and oversaw the building of the hotel, with Digicel owning the hotel after investing $45 million in the project. Marriott International's flagship Marriott Hotels brand was chosen as its operating partner under a long-term management contract.[71]

Bill Clinton and O'Brien, touted as the head of the Clinton Global Initiative Haiti Action Network, attended the hotel's opening ceremony with Haiti president Michel Martelly and Marriott International's president for the Caribbean and Latin America Region, Craig R. Smith.[72] "I know lots of people were asking: What on earth is a telecom company doing getting into the hotel business?" O'Brien said. "The idea of investing in this new Marriott Hotel came from Haiti's great friend, President Clinton. . . . His guiding words to Arne [Sorenson, president and chief executive officer of Marriott International] and myself on this project was, 'Let's do this together for Haiti.'"[73] What was little noticed in the opening ceremony press releases was the funding from the World Bank the Clintons had arranged behind the scenes to help subsidize O'Brien and Digicel in the construction of the project.

On July 3, 2013, the *Caribbean Journal* announced the Washington-headquartered International Finance Corporation of the World Bank Group had agreed to provide $26.5 million in financing for Turgeau Developments SA, a special-purpose operating company fully owned by Digicel and created to construct the Marriott Hotel.[74] *Haiti Business Week* confirmed the IFC had syndicated the loan with FMO (the Netherlands Development Finance Company),[75] a private-sector development bank based in The Hague, the Netherlands, known as the "Dutch Development Bank," operated under the supervision of the Dutch central bank.[76]

Among the State Department e-mails sent through Hillary Clinton's private e-mail server that have become public was one sent by Richard

L. Friedman, a Clinton Foundation donor and Boston hotel developer who reached out to Cheryl Mills on May 17, 2011, to discuss the Marriott project in Haiti. "We had a good meeting with Jean-Louis, Marriott executives, [the Overseas Private Investment Corporation], etc regarding building hotels in Haiti—I am pursuing this vigorously and hope to be able to develop 2 to 3 hotels with Marriott as manager," wrote Friedman, as reported by Alana Goodman in the *Washington Free Beacon* on October 19, 2015. "I am talking with Commerce and Export/Import Bank today."

The *Free Beacon* further reported that Friedman said he had recently had a discussion with Hillary Clinton at the White House, and he asked Mills to forward to her a note for him. Goodman noted that it was unclear what Friedman and Clinton had discussed, since portions of the e-mail were redacted by the State Department due to "personal private interests." Friedman further told Mills in the e-mail, "I will keep you informed about our progress in Haiti—we are going to need all the help we can get." According to Goodman, Mills forwarded Friedman's full e-mail to Clinton and her scheduler, Lona Valmoro, on June 7, 2011, with the note "See highlight—resending."

Friedman contributed between $1,000 and $5,000 to the Clinton Foundation and gave $2,300 to Clinton's presidential campaign in 2008, records show. The *Free Beacon* also reported that Digicel had contributed between $25,000 and $50,000 to the Clinton Foundation and O'Brien had donated between $5 million and $10 million. Unigestion Holdings, a subsidiary of Digicel that was reportedly tasked with managing the hotel project, gave between $10,000 and $25,000. Finally, Goodman reported that Marriott International is also a "hefty donor" to the Clinton Foundation, contributing between $50,000 and $100,000.[77]

Washington Post reporters David A. Fahrenthold, Tom Hamburger, and Rosalind S. Helderman were also onto the connections between donating to the Clinton Foundation and involvement in the Marriott hotel project in Haiti. "After Clinton introduced O'Brien to Marriott, another foundation donor, the company joined O'Brien to build a hotel near the headquarters of O'Brien's company in Port-au-Prince."[78] For O'Brien, being a friend of Clinton has proved profitable. *Institutional Investor* reported that in 2014 he paid himself a $650 million dividend on his 94 percent stake in Digicel, padding a fortune that *Forbes* estimates at $5.6 billion, making him "Ireland's richest son," even though O'Brien declares his residence in Malta to avoid paying taxes in his home country.[79]

But the Clinton Global Initiative was not the only aid organization involved in building luxury hotels in Haiti. On June 27, 2012, Julie Lévesque reported for GlobalResearch that the Bush Clinton Haiti Fund invested $2 million in the Royal Oasis Hotel, in Haiti, a deluxe structure to be built in a poverty-stricken metropolitan area "filled with displaced persons camps housing hundreds of thousands."[80] According to Lévesque, Royal Oasis belongs to SCIOP SA, a Haitian investment group that developed and promoted the project, and that the hotel when completed would be managed by the Spanish hotel chain Occidental Hotels & Resorts. The hotel's construction was already under way before the quake and was resumed after the earthquake once it was determined that the building remained structurally sound. The International Finance Corporation of the World Bank Group provided $7.5 million in financing, with the total cost projected at $29 million.[81]

THE CLINTON INDUSTRIAL PARK BOONDOGGLE

"On the fifth anniversary of the 7.0 magnitude earthquake in Port-au-Prince, Haiti remains a poster child for waste, fraud and corruption in the handling of aid," wrote investigative reporter Mary Anastasia O'Grady in a January 11, 2015, *Wall Street Journal* article titled "Hillary's Half-Baked Haiti Project." "Nowhere is the bureaucratic ineptitude and greed harder to accept than at the 607-acre Caracol Industrial Park, a project launched by former Secretary of State Hillary Clinton with U.S. taxpayer money, under the supervision of her husband Bill and his Clinton Foundation."[82]

USAID provided $170.3 million to construct a 10-megawatt

power plant to provide electricity to the Caracol Industrial Park.[83] On December 12, 2014, the Inter-American Development Bank approved a grant of $55 million plus cofinancing from the United States government in the amount of $15 million, for a total of $70 million, to expand business facilities at Caracol.[84] What attracted the Korean manufacturer anchor-tenant Sae-A Trading to commit a $78 million investment to Caracol was special trade legislation passed by the U.S. Congress in December 2006, allowing Haitian-sewn apparel to enter the United States duty-free, with no restriction on where the manufacturers purchase their fabrics worldwide.

"With lower wages than in many Asian markets and proximity to North America, Haitian-based producers have comparative advantages that might offset the country's low productivity," O'Grady noted. "The State Department initially promised that the park would be able to support 65,000 direct jobs by 2020. The Clinton Foundation has made similar statements. That means constructing 40 10,000 square-meter buildings for garment assembly. It won't happen at the current pace." O'Grady further observed that Sae-A Trading, Ltd., currently hires some 4,500 Haitians, but to hire the 20,000 originally planned, the company would need another dozen buildings. Apparel manufacturers wanting to build their own production space have faced opposition from Hillary Clinton at the State Department and Bill Clinton at the Clinton Foundation, who "wanted to retain that responsibility for reasons that can only be guessed."[85]

Peter Schweizer in *Clinton Cash* suggested one motivation for the Clintons to push the Caracol Industrial Park was that U.S. retailers projected to benefit from the lower-cost products expected to emerge from the Caracol fabric manufacturers, including GAP and Target, both longtime Clinton financial supporters, as well as Wal-Mart. Schweizer reported that members of Wal-Mart's Walton family had begun writing checks to a Clinton super PAC since the Korean factory opened, even though some have not shared the Clintons' politics, dating back to when Bill was governor of Arkansas.[86] Yet, even the Government

Accountability Office, in a June 2013 report, found that USAID projects in Haiti in general, as well as the funding for the Caracol power plant in particular, experienced "mixed results" and faced "sustainability challenges." The GAO estimated that completing the power plant's second phase and constructing the proposed port would require an estimated $117 million to $189 million, in addition to the $170.3 million initially allocated. It was "unclear whether the Haitian government will be able to find a private sector company willing to finance the remainder of the project."[87]

New York Times reporter Randal Archibold noted that the GAO report showed USAID had spent just 31 percent, or $204 million, of the $1.14 billion Congress authorized in 2010 for rebuilding Haiti. In addition to problems already noted here with the USAID funding for Caracol, the GAO report found "management lapses" in a major USAID housing project that included "underestimated or inaccurate cost projections" that have swelled spending on the project—to $97 million from $59 million—while reducing the number of housing units to be built. According to Archibold, USAID once planned to build 15,000 homes for 75,000 to 90,000 people, but its latest target was 2,649 homes for up to 15,900 people. The GAO attributed the shortfall to "the complexity of acquiring land titles in Haiti, a well-known problem there, as well as the difficulty of working with the Haitian government, which demanded that the homes have flush toilets—despite the country's limited sewage treatment."[88]

WHY IS HAITI YET SO POOR?

On December 11, 2014, the World Bank reported that while the percentage of people living in extreme poverty in Haiti, as defined by living on $1 or less a day, dropped from 31 percent to 24 percent between 2000 and 2012, most of the improvement was in Port-au-Prince, where extreme poverty had dropped from 20 percent to 5 percent. Despite this, a high degree of vulnerability threatens these improvements, as 2.5 million Haitians are unable to cover their basic food needs, while 1 million are in danger of falling into poverty. Worse, Haiti continues to exhibit dramatic income inequality, with the richest 20 percent of households earning 64 percent of the country's total income, while the poorest 20 percent earn just 1 percent. "Seeing that foreign aid is starting to slow down after an exceptionally high period following the disaster, social indicators could be easily reversed if efforts stop and if growth does not resume," the World Bank report concluded.[89]

Jonathan Katz, who spent three and a half years covering Haiti for the Associated Press, wrote critically of the Clintons in his article titled "The King and Queen of Haiti" published in *Politico Magazine* on May 4, 2015. "Hillary Clinton once hoped that Haiti would be the shining jewel of her foreign policy," Katz observed. "But far from transforming this poorest of countries, many of the Clintons' grandest plans and promises remain little more than small pilot projects—a new set of basketball hoops and a model elementary school here, a functioning factory there—that have done little to alter radically the trajectory of the country." Familiar with Haiti through the early recovery efforts, Katz had personal experience with which to judge the impact of the Clinton funding on Haiti. "Visiting some of their projects over the course of an April research trip affirmed as much about their tenuousness as about the limited benefits they've provided," he wrote. "Many of the most notable investments the Clintons helped launch, such as the new Marriott in the capital, have primarily benefited wealthy foreigners and island's ruling elite, who needed little help to begin with."[90]

Kept secret until it was revealed in a batch of Hillary Clinton's e-mails released by the State Department in a FOIA request is a seven-page, undated memo from Chelsea, addressed to "Dad" and "Mom," in which she criticized her parents' efforts in Haiti. "There is NO accountability in the UN system or international humanitarian system," she wrote,[91] perhaps unmindful of the fact that her father had been designated UN special envoy for Haiti and was "the top dog" for the UN relief effort.[92]

Katz, in a September 2, 2015, *Politico* story, commented on

Chelsea's e-mail. "First off, there was the secrecy," he wrote. "The memo—by a Clinton, with a master's in public health from Columbia University, pursuing a doctorate in international relations from Oxford and with a prominent role at her family's foundation—would have obliterated the public narrative of helpful outsiders saving grateful earthquake survivors that her mother's State Department was working so hard to promote. Instead," he continued, "like so much of the inner workings of the Clintons' vast network, it was kept secret, released only in an ongoing dump of some 35,000 emails from Hillary's private server, in response to a Freedom of Information Act Lawsuit wrapped up in the politics of the 2016 presidential election."

Katz concluded that Chelsea correctly understood that "disaster survivors are best positioned to take charge of their own recovery, yet often get pushed aside by outside authorities who think, wrongly, that they know better."[93] Included among those pushing the survivors aside were Bill and Hillary Clinton, determined to position themselves center stage in Haiti. Correctly, Denis O'Brien early on credited Bill Clinton with being "the chief development officer in Haiti."[94]

Still, despite her secret criticism, Chelsea stepped to the microphone at the Clinton Global Initiative 2015 Annual Meeting and celebrated O'Brien for "his tireless leadership" in Haiti.[95] In arguing that the Clintons were paid back for their efforts in Haiti, Schweizer noted in *Clinton Cash* that O'Brien arranged for Bill Clinton at least three lucrative speeches in Ireland, for which Clinton was paid $200,000 apiece, plus a speech in Jamaica for which he was paid $225,000. Clinton also made free use of O'Brien's private airplane, a Gulfstream 550 that seats twenty.[96] Consulting Clinton Global Initiative financial reports, it remains uncertain whether the speaking fees were paid to CGI for Clinton's time, or were paid directly to Clinton. Nor is it clear if Clinton tax attorneys evaluated the income tax consequences of accepting transportation without charge on O'Brien's private aircraft.

"In the aftermath of the January 2010 earthquake, people in the U.S., Canada and the EU, who made donations to those humanitarian organizations and NGOs did not realize that their contribution to Haiti's reconstruction would be channeled towards the building of five star hotels to house foreign businessmen," Julie Lévesque wrote for Global Research in 2012. "Their expectation was that the money would be used to provide food and housing for the Haitian people."

"While, Haiti was lacking in hotel rooms in the wake of the earthquake and job creation is a key to poverty reduction, a majority of the population still live in makeshift shelters of cardboard, scrap metal and old bed sheets. People struggle to have water to drink and food on their table—and in many cases they do not have a table," Lévesque continued in her 2012 piece. "Meanwhile, the construction of luxury hotels for foreigners is a number one priority, in comparison to 'housing for the locals.'"[97]

THE PLEDGE TO "BUILD BACK BETTER"

In 2009, when Bill Clinton accepted the honor of being named UN special envoy to Haiti, Jacqueline Charles of the *Miami Herald* reported that Clinton's goal with the disaster-prone Caribbean nation was to "build back better," stressing he not only wanted to repair the damage from the then recent hurricanes that devastated Haiti, but to "lay the foundations for the long-term sustainable development that has eluded [the people of Haiti] for so long."[98] Five years after the quake, in 2015, there remained uncertainty over exactly how much foreign aid was poured into Haiti. Officially, the text of the "Assessing Progress in Haiti Act of 2014" that President Obama signed into law on August 8, 2014—after the Government Accountability Office reported massive inefficiencies in the Haitian relief effort—claims the total spent was $13.5 billion, consisting of $10.4 billion pledged by the United States and the United Nations for humanitarian relief and recovery, supplemented by $3.1 billion in private charitable donations.[99]

In 2011, a four-person independent panel of experts on the cholera outbreak in Haiti issued a thirty-two-page report to the United Nations that left no doubt that the cholera spread from a United Nations camp in the upper Artibonite River valley occupied by UN peacekeepers from

Nepal. Human waste products from the camp polluted waters used by tens of thousands of Haitians for bathing, washing, and drinking.[100] Richard Knox, blogging for NPR on January 13, 2015, three days after the fifth anniversary of the earthquake, reported that the cholera epidemic struck more than 720,000 Haitians, killing almost 9,000. Knox further reported that at current donation levels, the United Nations predicted it will take forty years to eliminate cholera in Haiti.[101]

Granted, there has been some progress. Jacqueline Charles reported in the *Miami Herald* on January 11, 2015, that at the peak of the disaster, 1.5 million Haitians lived in more than 1,500 camps, while today that number has dropped 94 percent, with only 79,397 people registered in 105 sites.[102] Even here the numbers are deceptive. NBC News reported that of the 1.5 million Haitians that were in camps in 2010, the vast majority had been moved, but many were not yet in permanent housing. "At least 200,000 people are in new hillside slums, known as Canaan-Jerusalem, where there are wooden and tin homes, but no running water, electricity or sanitation yet," NBC reported on January 12, 2015.[103] Add to that the sad reality that five years after the earthquake, nearly 80,000 Haitians remained in camps.

Jake Johnston, a research associate at the Washington-based Center for Economic and Policy Research, and a leading author on Haiti, wrote a scathing article titled "Is USAID Helping Haiti to Recover, or U.S. Contractors to Make Millions?" published in the *Nation* on January 21, 2015.[104] The article's subtitle suggested that while the international community pledged enough aid to give every Haitian a check for $1,000, the money went elsewhere. "For every $1 that USAID has spent, less than one penny went directly to Haitian organizations, be it the Haitian government or in Haiti's private sector," Johnston wrote. "More than 50 cents went to Beltway firms—handling everything from housing construction, rubble removal, health services, security and more—located in DC, Maryland and Virginia. As a jobs creator back home, USAID's Haiti reconstruction has been an astounding success." Johnston pointed out that the largest recipient of USAID funding in Haiti was the Democratic

Party–connected, for-profit firm Chemonics International, contracted through the USAID's Office of Transition Initiatives.

When he submitted a FOIA request for more specific information about Chemonic's work in Haiti, every document he received was heavily redacted. The USAID explained that to release the information on Chemonics "could willfully stir up false allegations . . . and cause strife within the target communities," adding that "the release of the information . . . would instigate demonstrations and create an unsafe environment" to work in. "But business was good for Chemonics," Johnston reported, good enough for the CEO of Chemonics at the time to receive a $2.5 million bonus.

Johnston was equally critical of the Caracol Industrial Park, a project that had received "high-level support" from Bill and Hillary Clinton. "While the plan had been to build 15,000 houses, only 900" had been built, with a reliance on foreign contractors and imported materials, ballooning costs from $55 million to $90 million. "In October 2014, barely a year after the first families moved into homes in Caracol, USAID awarded $4.5 million to yet another American firm to oversee massive repairs needed to fix the faulty work of the first contractor," Johnston wrote.

Yet even today, the pages of the Clinton Foundation annual reports and website remain peppered with photographs of Clinton family members, often in the company of Denis O'Brien, mixing with the Haitian people. The Clinton Global Initiative prose waxes eloquent with praise for the philanthropic good Bill and Hillary Clinton have accomplished in Haiti. The Clinton Foundation 2013–2014 annual report mentions Haiti forty-eight times. One section, titled "Clinton Foundation in Haiti: Investing in Sustainable Economic Growth," contains a two-page spread of full-page, color photographs showing smiling Haitian children at their desks in a schoolroom, being instructed by a smiling teacher at the chalkboard at the front of the class. The accompanying text reads, "After the 2010 earthquake, President Clinton formed the Clinton Foundation Haiti Fund and raised $16.4 million from individual efforts for immediate relief efforts."[105] Yet on the Clinton Foundation website, there is no indication that an IRS Form 1023 application to establish the Clinton Foundation Haiti Fund had ever been filed, nor is there any documentation of an IRS determination letter granting the Clinton Foundation Haiti Fund tax-exempt status.

The text continues: "Since 2010, the Clinton Foundation has raised a total of $36 million for Haiti, including relief funds as well as funds for projects focused on restoring Haiti's communities, sustainable development, education, and capacity building." The text, undoubtedly crafted by a professional public relations firm, belies the reality that it would take a dedicated law enforcement effort to uncover whether or not the Clintons ever received personal benefit from their Haiti fundraising, including the possibility of minority shares or other financial benefits received from the likes of Denis O'Brien, whose Digicel has been able to pay him hundreds of millions of dollars in dividends since the Clintons paved the way for his mobile phone company to dominate the Haiti market.

8

THE INDIA SCAM

The story begins with Bill Clinton's relationship to shady Indian-American restaurateur Sant Chatwal, who in 2001 became a trustee of the Clinton Foundation. In addition to raising millions for the foundation, Chatwal never missed a chance to donate to a Clinton political campaign.

—MICHAEL HOWARD, FREELANCE JOURNALIST

Chapter 2 addressed the first part of the India scam, focusing on Bill Clinton and the Clinton Foundation's role in creating and raising millions of dollars for the fraudulent American India Fund (AIF), created supposedly to help victims of the disastrous earthquake that hit Gujarat, India, on January 26, 2001. Chapter 2 also brought the story of the Clinton Foundation forward to discuss the role of Rajat Gupta, the senior partner of McKinsey and Company, a close associate of Bill Clinton in the formation of the AIF who was convicted of criminal insider trading and ordered by a federal district court to report to prison on December 11, 2012, to begin a two-year sentence and to pay $5 million in fines.

Peter Schweizer in his book *Clinton Cash* details how prominent Indians in the United States contributed to the Clinton Foundation and paid Bill Clinton six-figure speaker's fees to influence his wife, as senator and, later, as secretary of state, to support India's efforts to develop nuclear weapons. This chapter examines the evidence not to argue a bribery allegation against the Clintons, as does Schweizer, but to raise the key question of inurement: Did the Clintons use the Clinton Foundation to enrich themselves and/or their close associates through cash payments made by prominent Indians in the United States who wanted to see U.S. foreign policy accept a nuclear-armed India?

INTRODUCING SANT SINGH CHATWAL?

Sant Singh Chatwal, born in Punjab, India, in 1946, came to the United States in 1975 and became a U.S. citizen in 1994. "Mr. Chatwal, now 64 years old, stands out in crowd at 6 feet, 1 inch, always wearing a red turban and full beard," noted reporter Kris Hudson in a *Wall Street Journal* profile. "He was born in India as the third of eight children of a cantina owner and a homemaker. He spent three years as a pilot in the Indian navy before moving in the 1970s to Ethiopia, where he managed a friend's restaurants and opened his own. He then moved to Montreal and, in 1979, to New York as he built Bombay Palace into a chain of Indian restaurants.

"In the 1980s, Mr. Chatwal started buying hotels on the cheap in the then-depressed Times Square area," the *Journal* continued, "which started its renaissance in 1982 when Marriott International Inc. committed to build the massive Times Square Marriott."[1]

Chatwal's star property, the Bombay Palace, just off Fifth Avenue on Fifty-Second Street in Midtown Manhattan, has a history of serving a sophisticated northern Indian spicy cuisine in an elegant environment. The website for the Bombay Palace advertises, "The lavish dining room is decorated with spacious banquettes, a three-tier Czech chandelier and plush Scottish wool carpeting," plus brass fixtures imported from Moradabad, the brass capital of India, along with glass etchings featuring places, temples, and mosques, in what is billed as a "regal atmosphere."[2] Chatwal, as president and CEO of Hampshire Hotels & Resorts, owns hotels in the United States, the United Kingdom, and Thailand. "New York hotelier Sant Singh Chatwal, founder-president of the $750 million Manhattan-based Hampshire Hotels and Resorts, is setting up a series of high-end boutique hotels in India," the editor of eHotelier wrote in a 2005 piece highlighting Chatwal's success in the hotel business internationally.

"The hotels, first in Mumbai, will be opened under the brand 'Dream' conceived by Chatwal's son Vikram, a New York socialite and lead actor in crossover film 'One Dollar Curry' who is better known as the 'Turban Cowboy,'" the post continued.

The editor went on to note, "Chatwal, whose Bombay Palace restaurant is a landmark in Manhattan and boasts of hosting high-profile guests like the Clintons, was tight-lipped about the investments he intends to make in the hotel projects in India."[3]

BANKRUPTCIES, UNPAID TAXES, LAWSUITS, AND ARRESTS

One reason that Chatwal might have been tight-lipped about his investments is that his history is strewn with financial train wrecks.

In 2000, Chatwal was the subject of "a massive bankruptcy case with debts estimated at more than $100 million—including more than $30 million in taxes owed to the IRS, New York City, and several states, including New York," Russ Buettner and Bob Port wrote in the *New York Daily News*.[4] Yet, this did not slow Chatwal down in his enthusiasm to court the Clintons.

"An immigrant businessman who funneled hundreds of thousands of dollars in soft money to Hillary Rodham Clinton was accused by the federal government of stiffing a New York bank out of millions of dollars in improper loans," Buettner and Port stated. "In fact, in September, when the President and First Lady dined on chicken tandoori at a fund-raiser in Chatwal's luxury Upper East Side penthouse, they were visiting an apartment their own government had considered to be an ill-gotten gain."

According to the *Daily News* writers, the Clintons "raked in" a reported $500,000 in donations for Hillary's Senate campaign from the private party. "At least $210,000 of it came from at least 14 businesses controlled by Chatwal, making him one of the First Lady's most prominent financial backers."

"Chatwal, who accompanied President Clinton and his daughter, Chelsea, on their trip to India in March, has also mobilized Indian-Americans to give hundreds of thousands of dollars in donations to Clinton's Senate bid," Buettner and Port continued, adding that despite Chatwal's "checkered history," Bill and Hillary "have accepted large soft-money campaign donations from him since at least the 1996 election, according to sources in the Democratic Party."

The *Daily News* went on to say that in 1996, the Federal Deposit Insurance Corporation (FDIC) "went to bankruptcy court and accused Chatwal of obtaining improper loans from the failed First New York Bank for Business—a small bank formerly known as First Women's Bank—causing the bank to lose more than $25 million.

> Chatwal, a bank director, arranged more than $14 million in loans to himself and his businesses, often with no collateral, then failed to repay most of the loans on time, the FDIC said in court documents. Chatwal's bad loans to himself alone cost the bank more than $12 million, according to the FDIC.
>
> Chatwal's bank also had loaned his wife, Pardaman Chatwal, $1.8 million in 1987, which she used to buy their seven-thousand-square-foot rooftop mansion at 300 E. 93rd St., according to the FDIC. Years later, ownership of the penthouse mysteriously shifted to a real estate company held in name by Chatwal's brother, the FDIC said.
>
> Chatwal claimed his wife, not he, held a lease on the apartment—an "oral lease" for $5,000 a month in rent—creating an obstacle for creditors wanting to claim the property.
>
> It was unclear last week how much was ever recovered by the FDIC, a government agency that bails out banks to protect the public's cash. During the legal fight, Chatwal said he made only $1,500 a week as a hotel consultant.

"ONE OF THE BIGGEST FUNDRAISERS FOR THE DEMOCRATS"

In May 2001, in one of his many trips to India with Bill Clinton, Chatwal, who then reportedly owed $22 million to three banks owned by the government of India, was arrested by authorities and charged with defrauding the New York City branch of the Bank of India out of $9 million he borrowed in 1994. But the Clintons always seemed to weather Chatwal's troubles with the law. The *New York Daily News* reported that Chatwal posted bail equivalent to $32,000, then fled to India, boarding a flight to Vienna despite an attempt by authorities to detain him.[5] The year before, after Chatwal paid a $125,000 federal government fine to settle the charges in 2000 that he owed governments, banks, and creditors tens of millions of dollars, the Clintons attended the wedding of Chatwal's youngest son, Vivek, at the posh Tavern on the Green in New York City's Central Park.

Nor did Chatwal's arrest in India deter the Clintons from traveling there with him. On February 27, 2005, the *Financial Express* in India reported that Chatwal had accompanied then senator Hillary Clinton to India, where he introduced her to political notables, including then Congress president Sonia Ghandi.

"Senator Clinton's visit is not for any personal purpose," Chatwal told the *Financial Express*. "I wanted her to see the changes India was undergoing. Anyway, it's not a secret that the Clintons feel much for India and are emotionally attached to this country. My only selfish motive is to see India grow stronger, as it will give us a better image." Then, calling Chatwal "one of the biggest fundraisers for the Democrats," the *Financial Express* reported that in New York, before starting out on the trip to India, Chatwal had treated Hillary to dinner in his home.[6]

In Chatwal's world, even the Bombay Palace has seen days of financial trouble. Kris Hudson in the *Wall Street Journal* noted that Chatwal's restaurant chain sought bankruptcy protection in 1989 to block the IRS from seizing its restaurants for unpaid taxes. "The next year, the U.S. Securities and Exchange Commission simultaneously filed and settled a case against Bombay Palace, its former finance chief and Mr.

Chatwal as its chairman, court records show. The lawsuit alleged that Bombay took $2 million from recently acquired Lifestyle Restaurants Inc. to bolster its own financial results." The lawsuit was settled without a financial penalty, the newspaper noted. "Instead, Bombay Palace, Mr. Chatwal and the chief financial officer agreed not to violate securities laws again. Bombay exited bankruptcy court in 1991," Hudson added. "Mr. Chatwal also settled lawsuits brought against him by lenders seeking to recoup losses from his earlier bankruptcies, court records show."[7]

THE BIG, FAT SIKH WEDDING

In 2006, *New York Magazine* described the wedding Chatwal threw for his then thirty-four-year-old son, Vikram, noting, "When one of New York's most-eligible, hard-living, jet-setting, model-dating, turban-wearing bachelors decides (or, more generously, when his dad decides) the time has come for him to get married, it's bound to be quite a party."[8]

The keynote speaker at the wedding in India—described as lasting a week, with ten parties spread out over three cities and a thousand guests, transported by three chartered 737s and "a small air force of private jets"—was none other than Bill Clinton.

FIRMLY IN THE CLINTONS' INNER CIRCLE

Beginning on page 62 of his book *Clinton Cash*, Peter Schweizer detailed the relationship between Sant Singh Chatwal and the Clintons. The relationship began when Chatwal first raised money for the Clintons, starting with Bill Clinton's 1998 presidential run and continuing through Hillary's run for the Senate in 2000. "By the time Bill left the Oval Office in 2001, Chatwal was firmly in the Clintons' inner circle," Schweizer wrote. "Bill appointed him a trustee for the Clinton Foundation, an appointment reserved only for long-time friends and large financial benefactors. Chatwal had lavished money on the Clintons, including hundreds of thousands in soft-money donations and millions in campaign funds raised, and he continued his largesse once Bill was a private citizen."

Schweizer pointed out that Chatwal helped arrange for millions of dollars in lucrative speaking fees for the former president, while he steered additional millions to the Clinton Foundation. "When Hillary ran for the Democratic presidential nomination in 2007, [Chatwal] was cochair of her presidential exploratory committee. He even received that most prized of gifts in the Clinton universe: an invitation to attend Chelsea's wedding."[9]

In 2007 and 2008, Chatwal raised about $100,000 for Hillary Clinton's first presidential campaign.[10] The problem was that Chatwal raised money by engineering a massive and blatant violation of federal election laws, in which he illegally reimbursed donors for their contributions in an elaborate straw donor scheme.

CHATWAL PLEADS GUILTY TO VIOLATING CAMPAIGN FINANCE LAWS

In 2014, the *New York Times* reported that Chatwal had pleaded guilty in federal court in Brooklyn to violations of campaign contribution laws.[11] In court, Chatwal admitted he had funneled more than $180,000 in illegal contributions between 2007 and 2011 for three Democratic Party candidates, Hillary Clinton, for her 2008 presidential campaign; Sen. Christopher J. Dodd of Connecticut; and Rep. Kendrick B. Meek of Florida.

Noting that Chatwal, in addition to his other legal problems in the United States and India, had filed for bankruptcy twice and owed back taxes to the IRS and the state of New York estimated at $30 million, the *New York Times* observed that Chatwal was a "regular" at the Clinton Global Initiative. In April 2007, he had formed "Indian Americans for Hillary 2008" and pledged to raise $5 million for her presidential campaign. "One of the straw donor schemes that prosecutors sketched out in court records started that year [2007]. Mr. Chatwal asked an associate, who owed him $2.5 million, to help him raise money for a candidate, prosecutors said," the *Times* reported. "The court records say that the associate distributed $90,000 and kept a 'minimal sum' as a 'commission,' and that Mr. Chatwal reduced the total the associate owed him by $100,000."

The *Times* further reported that Chatwal was on the record, making statements to the effect that political donations to candidates were necessary to buy influence once they were elected.

> Mr. Chatwal could be frank about the power of money in politics. In the fall of 2010, according to court documents, Mr. Chatwal and a business owner who is now cooperating with prosecutors decided that they should raise money, using straw donors, for another candidate so the candidate might intervene with a federal regulatory agency that had issued an "adverse ruling" regarding the other person's business. "That's the only way to buy them, get into the system," Mr. Chatwal was recorded as saying to the person, who by then was cooperating with prosecutors.

The article concluded that "it was not hard to discern Chatwal's motivation" for his straw donor contribution, given that in a recorded conversation with a government informant, Chatwal once described the importance of campaign contributions: "Without that nobody will even talk to you. When they are in need of money, the money you give, then they are always there for you. That's how you buy them."

By 2012, both the IRS and the FBI were looking into Chatwal's activities. "He was recorded multiple times telling an associate to lie about the donations, according to court records," the *Times* said.

In December 2014, federal Judge I. Leo Glasser sentenced Chatwal to three years of probation, a fine of $500,000, and one thousand hours of community service.[12] It was a remarkably lenient sentence given that the plea agreement prosecutors reached with Chatwal initially called for a sentence of forty-six to fifty-seven months, based on federal guidelines.

The *New York Times* reported that Judge Glasser had described Chatwal's crimes as an "aberrance" and seemed swayed by the 272 letters written on his behalf, as well as by the argument that his grown sons needed his help at home. The judge also determined that Chatwal did not seem to personally benefit from his campaign contributions. The

Times article suggested Glasser was influenced by his left-leaning political sentiments to go light on Chatwal in sentencing.

"NOT A GOVERNMENT PENNY USED TO HOST THE CLINTONS"

Another prominent Indian was included on the donor list posted on the Clinton Foundation website as Hillary Clinton was being considered by the Obama transition team as a possible nominee for secretary of state, reported Peter Baker in the *New York Times*. "The potential for foreign donors to the Clinton foundation to create the appearance of conflicts of interest for Hillary Clinton as she handles foreign policy matters was illustrated by Amar Singh, listed as giving between $1 million and $5 million. Singh is apparently a prominent Indian politician of that same name," the *Times* said. "In September, Singh visited Washington to lobby Congress to support a deal allowing India to obtain civilian nuclear fuel and technology from the United States. The deal was controversial because India has developed nuclear weapons but is not a party to the Nuclear Non-Proliferation Treaty. Singh met and posed for photographs with Bill Clinton, afterwards telling Indian reporters that Clinton had assured him that Democrats would not block the deal. Congress approved the nuclear cooperation deal with India a few days later."[13]

Bill Clinton's ties to Amar Singh can be traced to 2005. On September 9, 2005, Rediff *India Abroad*'s Sharat Pradhan reported that Singh had hosted Clinton in a fifteen-hour stay in Lucknow, the capital of the state of Uttar Pradesh, India. The report stated that Singh was the general secretary of the Samajwadi Party, a recognized, left-leaning, state-authorized political party in Uttar Pradesh. Clinton's chartered airplane arrived from Uzbekistan at 7:15 a.m. and took off at 10:00 p.m. local time, heading for China. Pradhan noted that "Clinton's entourage included well-known expatriate hotel magnate Sant Chatwal," and that among the delegation from the Clinton Foundation accompanying Clinton on the India stopover was Doug Band.[14]

"While everyone wondered who was footing the bill for the truly extravagant reception accorded to the former U.S. president, Amar

Singh took the opportunity to clarify that the government was not involved in the show at all," Pradhan noted. The newspaper went on to quote Singh's denial. "Not a penny of the government has been used in hosting the Clinton visit to Lucknow," Singh told the gathering at an earlier function meant to mark the launching of the Rural Health Mission in the state. Instead, he claimed, "the Uttar Pradesh Development Council is footing the entire bill for the program." Still, Pradhan noted that where the Uttar Pradesh Development Council got the money to fund Clinton's visit "is a mystery."[15]

The stopover in India in September 2005 was only nine months after the airplane trip to Davos, Switzerland, in January 2005 in which Band proposed that Bill Clinton could form his own Davos World Economic Forum, the idea that led to the formation of the Clinton Global Initiative, as discussed in chapter 1. According to a *New York Post* report by Deroy Murdock on June 12, 2015, Singh sat at the head table at the first annual meeting of the Clinton Global Initiative in 2005 and dined privately with the Clintons at their home.[16] A separate *Post* article reported that Clinton "first met Singh in 2005 through Sant Chatwal, an Indian-American businessman who generated millions of dollars for the foundation, in speaking fees for the ex-president, and for Hillary's 2008 presidential campaign."[17]

"Chatwal is the key player who sets-up the meetings between Bill Clinton and the Indian officials, principally, Amar Singh in 2005; donations followed from other Indian industrialists," *Asia Times* reported on May 9, 2015. "After the Bush administration signed a MOU (Memorandum of Understanding) with the then Prime Minister Manmohan Singh's government, allowing India access to nuclear technology which generated heated debate in the U.S. Congress, Indians were concerned that the deal might be stalled. Amar Singh was an Indian politician from the state of Utter Pradesh, one of the leaders of the Samajwadi Party, and a member of the upper house of the Indian parliament. His party provided coalition support to the Congress Party (UPA) during the nuclear negotiations."[18]

The *Indian Express* reported from New Delhi on January 7, 2010, that Singh had resigned from all posts he held in his party, citing health reasons related to a recent kidney transplant,[19] not the election defeats the previous November.[20] On February 2, 2010, the leadership of the Samajwadi Party expelled Singh from the party on grounds of "indulging in anti-party activities and denting its socialist image."[21] In 2011, Singh was jailed in New Delhi on suspicion of his involvement in a criminal "cash for votes" scheme.[22] Then, on October 25, 2011, the *Hindu* reported that the Delhi High Court had granted bail to Singh on health grounds.[23]

When Schweizer's *Clinton Cash* was published in 2015, Singh predictably denied donating $5 million to the Clinton Foundation, claiming that amount would have amounted to his entire net worth.[24] As far back as 2008, Singh denied making the donation, telling reporters the "payment could have been made by someone else on his behalf." On December 19, 2008, the *Times of India* reported that Singh refused to be drawn out on that remark. "When asked about the huge donation, a seemingly unperturbed Singh told reporters, 'I have nothing to say. I won't deny anything.'"[25]

OBAMA 2008 ATTACKS CLINTONS: "IT'S ALL ABOUT THE MONEY"

To argue that the Clintons have personally benefited financially from their many associations with India, including those detailed with the American India Fund in chapter 1, we need look no farther than Barack Obama's 2008 presidential campaign. In June 2007, Obama's presidential campaign leaked an opposition research piece titled "Hillary Clinton (D-Punjab)'s Personal Financial and Political Ties to India." The three-page, undated document is a scathing attack on the Clintons, arguing that Bill as former president and Hillary Clinton as a sitting senator had utilized their political positions to enrich themselves personally and to raise money for Hillary's 2008 presidential campaign. The first paragraph of the preamble to the document states the Obama campaign's indictment of the Clintons' exploitation of India:

The Clintons have reaped significant financial rewards from their relationship with the Indian community, both in their personal finances and Hillary's campaign fundraising. Hillary Clinton, who is the co-chair of the Senate India Caucus, has drawn criticism from anti-offshoring groups for her vocal support of Indian business and unwillingness to protect American jobs. Bill Clinton has invested tens of thousands of dollars in an Indian bill payment company, while Hillary Clinton has taken tens of thousands from companies that outsource jobs to India. Workers who have been laid off in upstate New York might not think that her recent joke that she could be elected to the Senate seat in Punjab is that funny.[26]

The existence of the document was picked up immediately in India. On June 15, 2007, *India Abroad* published an article titled "Obama Camp Attacks Hillary's Indian Links."[27] The article began with a dig at Obama, noting that his campaign apparently was not listening to his message when Obama entered the 2008 presidential race calling for a new kind of politics, devoid of personal attack.

> Members of the Senator's campaign staff have been circulating a document that, in its title, slightingly refers to Democratic rival Senator Hillary Clinton as the Democrat from Punjab—a seeming slur on Clinton's ties with India and Indian Americans.
>
> The three page "opposition research paper," titled Hillary Clinton (D-Punjab)'s Personal Financial and Political Ties, which has begun circulating in the blogosphere, criticizes the Clintons' links to India in an effort and attacks her record on outsourcing, and on protecting American jobs.

HILLARY: "THE SENATOR FROM PUNJAB"

India Abroad further reported that the "D-Punjab" reference apparently refers to a joke Clinton made at a fund-raiser hosted by Chatwal in which she claimed she could easily have been elected a senator in Punjab, India, if that were possible. A March 17, 2006, *India Abroad* story noted that more than eighty prominent Sikh professionals and entrepreneurs from the Washington metropolitan area had raised $50,000 for Clinton's senate reelection campaign by paying $500 to $2,000 apiece to attend a fund-raising dinner chaired by Chatwal at the Potomac, Maryland, home of Dr. Rajwant Singh. At the fund-raiser, Hillary promised to address the concerns and issues of the Sikh community, "especially the continuing racial profiling and hate crimes against the community that first manifested itself in the aftermath of 9/11 when Sikhs with their turbans and flowing beards were mistakenly thought to be followers of al Qaeda chief Osama bin Laden." The report said Clinton began her comments by joking, "I can certainly run for the Senate seat in Punjab and win easily, after being introduced by Dr. Rajwant Singh as the Senator not only from New York, but also Punjab."[28]

The Obama campaign opposition piece referenced Hillary Clinton's then recently released disclosure forms, noting that Bill Clinton had accepted $300,000 for speeches from Cisco, a company that the document noted has "shifted hundreds of jobs from America to India." The document further claimed that Hillary had accepted almost $60,000 from employees of Cisco systems, "which laid off American workers to hire Indian techies." It also hit Hillary hard for her role in 2004 in cofounding and cochairing of the Senate India Caucus that the document claimed was coordinated with the U.S. India Political Action Committee (USINPAC). This was coupled with the claim that Hillary, on a trip to India in 2005, had done everything possible to allay apprehensions in India that legislation in the U.S. Congress would end the outsourcing of jobs to India.[29]

One of the most damaging allegations in the Obama 2008 campaign opposition research document was that Bill Clinton had used a previously unknown corporation in 2006, WJC Investments, LP, LLC, to hold between $15,001 and $50,000 worth of stock in Easy Bill Limited, an India-based company. The document quoted Easy Bill's website as saying: "Functioning as a one-stop bill payment shop, Easy Bill facilitates payment of utility bills as well as recharging of pre-paid mobile connections at a place the consumer is already familiar and comfortable with the neighborhood store." It also noted that in addition to providing terminals throughout India where customers can pay their bills, the company also maintains a call center described as "a dedicated response center for efficient customer service."[30]

Until the Obama 2008 presidential campaign opposition research became public, the Clintons had managed to keep the existence of WJC Investments completely secret. On May 27, 2015, following the Associated Press's discovery that Bill Clinton used WJC, LLC, as a shell company, Jennifer Epstein of Bloomberg Politics stressed that he also owns WJC International Investments GP, LLC, as well as WJC International Investments LP, LLC.[31] The mainstream media, generally hyperprotective of all things Clinton, has neglected to investigate his "WJC" limited liability corporate holdings, even after the *Washington Post* in 2014 reported the general partnership WJC International Investments GP, LLC, was created by Bill Clinton in 2006.[32]

While there are many legitimate reasons to create and operate LLC structures, including tax planning, an additional benefit to the Clintons is secrecy. Unlike public corporations, the filing and disclosure requirements for an LLC benefits those, like the Clintons, who want to maximize privacy by avoiding public disclosure requirements. How many investments have the Clintons derived from connections established with donors to the Clinton Foundation and/or members of the Clinton Global Initiative? The American public may never know. The likelihood is WJC, LLC, as well as WJC International Investments, GP, LLC, and WJC Investments, LP, LLC, were created and maintained as limited liability corporations—with WJC, LLC, being nothing more than a shell corporation—precisely so that question could never be answered.

CLINTON FORTUNE "AN EMBARRASSMENT"

On June 15, 2007, Patrick Healy in the *New York Times* reported that after the release of the Obama campaign opposition research hit piece on India, the Clintons decided to liquidate holdings in their blind trust, valued at the time at somewhere between $5 million and $25 million.[33] According to the *Times*, the Clintons had determined to sell investments, including oil and pharmaceutical companies, military contractors, and Wal-Mart shares, worried that their personal finances could become an issue in Hillary's 2008 bid for the White House. By disposing of all their stocks and going into cash, the Clintons hoped to position their blind trust favorably, "in an effort to eliminate any chance of ethical problems or political embarrassment from their holdings as Mrs. Clinton runs for 2008 Democratic presidential nomination, their advisers said." Healy reported that according to financial disclosure documents, the couple's net worth was between $10 million and $50 million, with Bill Clinton earning $10 million in paid speeches in 2006, and Hillary Clinton earning $320,025 in royalties for her autobiography, *Living History*.

Healy further reported that according to their 1993 financial disclosure form, the Clintons had a net worth in 1993 at the time the blind trust was created, valued at between $633,015 and $1.62 million, with Bill Clinton's share of the blind trust valued from $15,001 to $50,000, and Hillary's share at $500,001 to $1 million. This invites a comparison to today, with the Clintons having amassed an enormous fortune since leaving the White House in 2000.

"THE CLINTON $3 BILLION MONEY MACHINE"

As noted in chapter 1, the *Washington Post* in 2015 documented that the Clinton Foundation had become a $2 billion global empire, operating eleven major initiatives focused on issues as divergent as crop yields in Africa, earthquake relief in Haiti, and the cost of drugs worldwide. "In all, the Clintons' constellation of related charities has raised $2 billion, employs more than 2,000 people and has a combined annual budget of more than $223 million," the *Washington Post* story continued. The *Post* reported further that adding the money the Clintons had raised in the Clinton Foundation to that raised in political campaigns and causes, the "Clinton money machine" had generated a total of $3 billion since Bill Clinton first decided to run for public office, with $2 billion going to the Clinton Foundation and $1 billion to support the Clintons' political races and legal defense fund.[34]

A central argument of this book is that the Clintons have used their foundation as an intentionally complex structure to divert hundreds of millions of dollars, accomplished largely through fraudulent accounting, to benefit themselves and close associates, including Doug Band, Ira Magaziner, Cheryl Mills, and Huma Abedin. The Clinton get-rich-quick formula has been simple: a complex charity structure with multiple subdivisions and separate corporations, haphazard IRS applications, virtually incomprehensible financial reporting in which six-figure speaking fees are comfortably mixed with CGI pledges that may or may not materialize and that may or may not be run through one of the various Clinton Foundation subgroups, with ample opportunities to participate in foundation-related business ventures through a largely secret investment structure, as was created in WJC Investments LP, LLC, with a shell-company pass-through account cleverly arranged in WJC to hide money even from IRS auditors. Today, most estimates put the Clintons' combined net worth at between $100 million and $200 million.[35]

Yet, as noted in chapter 1, the Clintons constantly cry poor, with Bill Clinton still complaining to host David Gregory in a June 29, 2014, interview on NBC's Meet the Press, "I had the lowest net worth of any American president in the 20th century when I took office."[36] But even left-leaning PunditFact, on its famous "Truth-O-Meter," labeled the claim at best as "half true." PunditFact noted that today Clinton "is considered the wealthiest living president and among the top-10 all-time wealthiest, with the Clintons' combined net worth at about $55 million, according to the website 24/7 Wall Street, which started evaluating the net worth of presidents in 2010."[37]

In 2010, the Clintons were sufficiently wealthy that tax advisers created for them residence trusts to hold ownership of their house in Chappaqua, New York, to prevent the IRS from collecting estate taxes on the property upon the Clintons' deaths. The financial planning tax strategy is commonly considered of benefit to only the top 1 percent of U.S. households in wealth. Pointing out the hypocrisy, tax policy reporter Richard Rubin, writing for Bloomberg Business, noted in 2014, "Bill and Hillary Clinton have long supported an estate tax to prevent the U.S. from being dominated by inherited wealth. That doesn't mean they want to pay it."[38]

INDIAN "FRIENDS OF BILL AND HILL" GO TO PRISON TOGETHER

No discussion of India-related scams is complete without a final mention of how India-born Rajat Gupta and Sri Lanka–born Raj Rajaratnam—both contributors to the Clinton Foundation, both participants in the Clinton Global Initiative participant, and both top-dollar contributors to Hillary's political campaigns—have ended up in the same federal prison.

Rajaratnam, like his fellow AIF cofounders Gupta and Chatwal, wanted Hillary and Bill back in the White House. Federal Election Commission records show Rajaratnam contributed to Hillary Clinton's Senate campaign in 2005 and began contributing to her 2008 presidential campaign in 2007. ABC News reported in 2009 that Rajaratnam and his wife gave a total of $118,000 to Democratic Party candidates, including Sen. Chuck Schumer and Barack Obama, as well as to Hillary Clinton. After Hillary dropped out of the 2008 presidential campaign, Rajaratnam appears to have switched over to contributing to Obama.[39] If Rajaratnam were out of prison, he would probably still be looking for a way to elect Hillary president, so Bill could be "first husband."

In 2011, Rajaratnam was sentenced to federal prison for eleven years after being convicted in Wall Street's biggest insider trading scandal,[40] which ABC News claimed made him one of the wealthiest men in America, with an estimated net worth of $3.5 billion.[41] In 2012, Gupta, the former head of McKinsey & Co. who was also on the board of the Clinton Foundation and Goldman Sachs, was convicted of insider trading in the Galleon hedge fund debacle and sentenced to two years in federal prison and fined $5 million. As we saw earlier in this chapter, Chatwal was convicted of violating campaign finance laws but avoided prison because a left-leaning judge had sympathy with the donations he'd made to Democratic Party candidates, including Hillary Clinton.

As noted in chapter 1, investigative journalist Alana Goodman has reported that Rajaratnam, Gupta, and Chatwal joined a long list of felons associated with Bill Clinton as cofounders and directors of the American India Fund.[42]

"In their heyday, Raj Rajaratnam and Rajat K. Gupta were business partners who lent each other a helping hand," wrote Anita Raghavan in the *New York Times* on August 2, 2015. "The two men were very different. Mr. Rajaratnam was a high-rolling hedge fund manager who loved to take risks, while Mr. Gupta was a consultant educated at Harvard Business School who worked all his life at one firm, McKinsey & Company."

Yet today, Raghavan noted, Gupta and Rajaratnam find themselves at the same prison, Federal Medical Center Devens, in Ayer, Massachusetts, northwest of Boston, with one thousand other inmates. "The two lead parallel lives that sometimes intersect," she wrote. "They occasionally run into each other in the common areas at Devens and exchange pleasantries. Although both men are in prison for the same crime, their friendship is irrevocably broken."[43]

Gupta and Rajaratnam were both close to Bill Clinton. "When Gupta was raising money on behalf of AIF for earthquake relief in Gujarat, in step with his new friend Bill Clinton, he approached Rajaratnam directly," Anita Raghavan noted in her 2013 book, *The Billionaire's Apprentice*, devoted to an examination of the $20 million insider trader ring that built Galleon to its fraudulent heights. "Again, the Galleon hedge fund manager gave generously."[44]

WHY DID RAJAT GUPTA GO ROGUE?
Duff McDonald, in his 2013 book-length treatment of McKinsey & Co., *The Firm*, asks an important question: Why did Rajat Gupta go criminal?[45] McDonald noted Gupta's sterling résumé on leaving the firm.[46] As McKinsey managing partner, he had earned in the range of

$5 million a year. After becoming managing director, Gupta and his family moved into an $8 million mansion near Long Island Sound in Westport, Connecticut. His winter retreat was a $4 million oceanfront house on Palm Island, a private resort at Florida's Gulf coast. One estimate in 2012 pegged Gupta's net worth at $130 million.[47] But it was not enough. Seeing the great wealth that fund managers were accumulating on Wall Street, Gupta evidently aspired to be a billionaire.

In the final analysis, there was no doubt Gupta was guilty of passing insider information to Rajaratnam. According to testimony and wiretaps, prosecutors established that Gupta was negotiating with Rajaratnam for a 10 to 15 percent stake in the Galleon International Fund and a possible role as the fund's chairman at the time he was sharing inside tips with Rajaratnam that earned Rajaratnam $18.5 million in trading profits.[48] After leaving McKinsey, Gupta joined the board of Wall Street investment banking firm Goldman Sachs. Perhaps the most damaging indictment against Gupta was feeding Rajaratnam information from Goldman board meetings in 2008 while he was still working out of McKinsey's New York offices. Gupta had given up his McKinsey partnership in 2007, but he still retained an office at the firm.[49]

The Enron debacle also happened during Gupta's ten-year watch as McKinsey managing director. Malcolm Gladwell, writing in the *New Yorker* in 2002, noted that McKinsey, at the height of its consulting arrangement with Enron, was conducting some twenty separate projects for Enron, billing more than $10 million a year. "The Enron scandal is now almost a year old," Gladwell wrote. "The reputations of Jeffrey Skilling and Kenneth Lay, the company's two top executives, have been destroyed. Arthur Andersen, Enron's auditor, has been driven out of business, and now investigators have turned their attention to Enron's investment bankers. The one Enron partner that has escaped largely unscathed is McKinsey, which is odd, given that it essentially created the blueprint for the Enron culture. Enron was the ultimate 'talent' company."

Gladwell credited McKinsey with setting the "talent mind-set" as "the new orthodoxy of American management. But the Enron scandal caused Gladwell to reevaluate this formula. "The management of Enron, in other words, did exactly what the consultants at McKinsey said that companies ought to do in order to succeed in the modern economy," Gladwell noted. "It hired and rewarded the very best and the very brightest—and it is now in bankruptcy. The reasons for its collapse are complex, needless to say. But what if Enron failed not in spite of its talent mind-set but because of it? What if smart people are overrated?"[50]

Enron failed because the $13 billion the firm's accountant Arthur Anderson showed on the company books was dwarfed by the off-balance-sheet liabilities that tripled Enron's real debt to more like $38 billion. "The collapse of the firm [Enron] was the largest bankruptcy in U.S. history at the time," McDonald wrote in *The Firm*. "And McKinsey's Houston office saw its revenues fall off a cliff."[51] McDonald in large part faulted Gupta for the debacle, noting that while McKinsey would never admit as much, "under Gupta, McKinsey began working for just about anyone with a fat bank account and a checkbook."[52] John Byrne reported on Bloomberg, July 7, 2002, that while Gupta did not do anything illegal at McKinsey, the firm "turned a blind eye to signs of trouble to preserve a lucrative relationship."

Byrne pointed out that on becoming managing partner, Gupta rejected the idea that McKinsey should be kept small to safeguard its consulting culture and quality. Instead, he aggressively expanded the consultancy worldwide, opening branches in Asia and eastern Europe. "Gupta was of another mind," Byrne noted in 2002. "In all, he expanded McKinsey's network to 84 worldwide locations from 58, boosted the consulting staff to 7,700 from 2,900, and lifted revenues to $3.4 billion from $1.2 billion in 1993. Meanwhile, the number of partners grew from 427 to 891." Nancy Killefer, a senior McKinsey partner in Washington, DC, told Bloomberg, "It's a less personal place than it used to be. In the old days, you knew everybody. That's not possible anymore."[53] Gupta's orientation was commercial, making money and then making more money, even if McKinsey's commitment to excellence was tainted in the process.

Adil Rustomjee, writing in an Indian publication in 2014, phrased his question about Gupta this way: "And so in the end the How and What and When all got answered. The Why was not answered. Why? Why? Why?" In the final analysis, Rustomjee could not explain to his satisfaction why Gupta threw away his career when he could have played the role of the *éminence grise* in retirement. "Did he do it for the money?" Rustomjee asked. "Someone who was worth a hundred mill moving around in the company of billionaires and not feeling up to the mark." Rustomjee's conclusion, "Perhaps."[54]

The same question can be asked about Bill and Hillary Clinton. The ultimate answer for the Clintons may turn out to be as unsatisfying as it is for Gupta, especially if the Clintons' luck is no better than Gupta's, and they, too, finally end up getting caught and brought to justice for creating and operating the "vast criminal enterprise" masquerading under their names as a philanthropic charity.

Then, too, there is this: the White House press release dated November 24, 2009, listing the "Expected Attendees at Tonight's State Dinner" held in honor of "Dr. Manmohan Singh, Prime Minister, India."[55] Among the guests listed are Mr. Rajat Gupta and his wife, Mrs. Anita Gupta.

And finally, there is this: in *The Billionaire's Apprentice,* Anita Raghavan quoted Bala Balachandran, a neighbor of Gupta in Winnetka, Illinois, who went on to become dean of the Great Lakes Institute of Management in Chenai, India. On one side, Gupta was "very humble, accessible, and open," Balachandran told Raghavan. On the other side, Gupta was "enamored with prestige, power, and the finer aspects of life." According to Balachandran, Gupta also liked to name-drop. "He was very proud of saying 'I hired Chelsea Clinton—I hired Hillary Clinton's daughter,'" Balachandran explained to Raghavan.[56]

In the final analysis, however, it may just all come down to greed. In summing up the contradictions of Gupta's career at McKinsey, McDonald in *The Firm* reflects finally on Marvin Bower, a major leadership guiding force in the creation of the modern McKinsey, who served as managing director of the firm from 1950 through 1967, and then as director and partner until 1992. "Still, there was no question that McKinsey was left to wonder how, just nine years after his death [in 2003], the spirit of Marvin Bower had been so desecrated in such a short period of time," McDonald wrote reflecting on Gupta and his federal criminal conviction for insider trading in 2012. "'Marvin Bower said they were greedy f**ks at the end,' said one client who knew the man. 'He was old but lively.' And at least in this case [Rajat Gupta], it seems [Bower] was right."[57]

PART THREE

CRIMINAL PHILANTHROPY— ENDGAME

No one should be too big to jail.

—HILLARY RODHAM CLINTON, *NEW YORK TIMES*

art 3 consists of one chapter and a conclusion, describing the "endgame," to bring the Clinton family and their top associates to justice. In chapter 9, the "Hillary for President 2016" scam is presented as a scheme to advance Hillary from secretary of state to the White House. With free access to Air Force One and all the accoutrements of White House power, there should be no limit to the level of corruption President Hillary Clinton and first spouse Bill Clinton could accomplish.

In the wings is Chelsea Clinton, being groomed for her first run for public office, apparently ready and willing to follow in her parents' footsteps.

The book concludes with a systematic plan the reader can implement to help bring the Clinton crime family to justice. All that is required is to begin writing to the attorney general in the state where you live, demanding that a criminal investigation of the Clinton Foundation be undertaken immediately.

9

THE "HILLARY FOR PRESIDENT 2016" SCAM

A source at NBC, where Chelsea was paid $600,000 a year, said, "If someone wanted to talk to Chelsea about something, they had to go through a producer."
—RICHARD JOHNSON, *PAGE SIX*

Hillary Clinton's run for the White House a second time, after her 2008 campaign as the Democrat's "presumed nominee" failed, is certainly her last chance to capture the prize she has desired her entire adult life. For the Clinton family, getting Hillary in the White House would return Bill Clinton as "first spouse." But for this most political of married couples, the real opportunity of a Hillary presidency would be not only to wield the power of the U.S. government as chief executive but to position the Clinton Foundation for another round of criminal philanthropy that could well dwarf all previous efforts.

Not satisfied with the historic possibility of being the first husband-wife team to be elected each as president, the Clinton family has positioned Chelsea Clinton as head of the Clinton Foundation, where she can be groomed, conceivably, to take the Clinton charity crime enterprise into a second generation. As Clinton Foundation head, she would be positioned to leverage a Hillary Clinton presidency into inurement riches and "pay-to-play" dollars that could increase Clinton wealth exponentially.

WHO IS ED MEZVINSKY?

On July 31, 2010, Chelsea Clinton, then thirty, married New York hedge fund manager Marc Mezvinsky, son of a Nixon-era congressman who served a five-year term in federal prison for cheating investors out of millions of dollars.

Ed Mezvinsky grew up in Ames, Iowa, the son of a Jewish grocery store owner. There, he went from being the "golden boy" of Ames local high school sports, the former all-state football player and member of the Ames High School state championship basketball and track teams of 1955, to privately being dubbed by lawyers as "Fast Talking Eddie" in the 1970s. In 1974, Rep. Ed Mezvinsky, a Democrat who represented Iowa's First Congressional District in the House of Representatives for two terms, 1973–1977, was one of the thirty-eight members of the House Judiciary Committee who voted to submit three articles of impeachment against sitting Republican president Richard Nixon to the full House.[1]

In a profile of Mezvinsky written in 2003, the *Des Moines Register* described his investment schemes in Africa. "Mezvinsky's most common fraud was telling victims that he needed money to deposit in a trust account that would not be moved. He needed it, he would say, to show he had the financial wherewithal to make an investment," the newspaper noted. "He promised a hefty return." But instead of investment returns, those who trusted Mezvinsky found themselves defrauded. "He then spent the money on African schemes, used it to cover debts, or paid off those who complained the loudest about not being paid back from previous bogus deals."[2] Prosecutors said Mezvinsky, in advancing what amounted to a massive Ponzi scheme, habitually dropped the names of

Bill and Hillary Clinton and boasted of his friendship with them, as he bilked family, friends, and institutions out of $10 million in the 1990s.[3]

WHAT DOES MARC MEZVINSKY DO?

Rob Copeland of the *Wall Street Journal* reported on February 3, 2015, that Eaglevale Partners, LP, the hedge fund Marc Mezvinsky cofounded with two former colleagues from Goldman Sachs, had suffered a loss of 3.6 percent in 2014, largely because of ill-timed bets on the Greek economy, far trailing the 5.7 percent rise for similar hedge funds, as tracked by a respected rating agency. A smaller Eaglevale hedge fund focused solely on Greece lost a stunning 48 percent in 2014. "Our recent predictions regarding Greek politics have proved incorrect," Marc Mezvinsky and the other Eaglevale founders wrote to investors after a radical leftist party won national elections in an upset of Europe's political order. "We are reticent to render decisive predictions at this time." According to Copeland, Eaglevale is a "relatively small player in the hedge-fund world," managing approximately $400 million, pursuing a "so-called macro strategy that looks to profit from macroeconomic trends." The *Journal* also reported that Eaglevale since its founding has spent twenty-seven of its thirty-four months in operation below its "high-water mark," a term that describes whether a Day One investor is in the black. Eaglevale's annualized rate of return from inception is 0.87 percent, according to investor documents examined by the newspaper.[4]

Andrew Stiles, in a *Washington Free Beacon* article titled "Don't Give Your Money to Clinton Son-in-Law Marc Mezvinsky," had a slightly different take on the value of an investment in Eaglevale. "This is not to say that giving your money to Eaglevale is a bad investment," Stiles wrote. "Of course, if your primary concern is short-term profit, you should probably look elsewhere. But if you are a wealthy Democratic donor who places a high value on long-term political access to one of America's most powerful families, Eaglevale is the fund for you. Not surprisingly, the fund's early group sessions for prospective investors attracted 'standing-room-only crowds.'" Stiles noted that prominent investors in Mezvinsky's hedge fund included Lloyd Blankfein, chairman and CEO of Goldman Sachs, where Mezvinsky used to work. "Blankfein has contributed generously to Democrats over the years, and has hosted fundraisers for Hillary Clinton," he wrote. Another Democratic supporter, Marc Lasry, the billionaire hedge fund manager who co-owns the Milwaukee Bucks NBA team, is also an investor in Mezvinsky's hedge fund. "Lasry, who used to employ Chelsea Clinton at his $13.3 billion hedge fund, Avenue Capital Group, is a longtime Democratic donor and figures to be one of Hillary Clinton's top fundraisers in 2016," Stiles commented. "Lasry had been President Obama's choice to serve as U.S. ambassador to France, but was forced to withdraw his name over his ties to an alleged poker ring run by the Russian mob."[5]

MARC MEZVINSKY LEARNS TO PLAY THE CLINTON FAMILY GAME

On December 7, 2015, Chuck Ross reported in the Daily Caller that Secretary of State Hillary Clinton had sought to help "her wealthy hedge fund son-in-law," who was seeking a meeting with the State Department and Clinton herself to discuss a deep-sea mining company in which he had invested. Ross noted that an investor named Harry Siklas e-mailed Marc Mezvinsky on May 25, 2015, to see if a meeting could be set up with someone at the State Department to discuss Neptune Minerals, a sea-floor sulfide mining company founded in 2011. "Both Siklas and Mezvinsky had worked at Goldman Sachs, which itself has been cozy with Clinton. The Wall Street behemoth was the fourth largest corporate donor to Clinton's 2008 presidential campaign." Ross said it was unclear what came of the request for a State Department meeting. Neptune Minerals did not respond to a request for comment, Ross reported, nor did the Clinton campaign. An e-mail the Daily Caller sent to an address listed for Siklas was returned undeliverable.[6]

In December 2015, the conservative watchdog group Foundation for Accountability and Civic Trust (FACT) filed a complaint with the U.S. Office of Government Ethics, accusing Clinton of giving special government access to Harry Silas, an investor in Neptune Minerals because of his connections to Clinton's son-in-law, Marc Mezvinsky.[7]

In May 2012, as *Time* magazine reported, Siklas had asked Mezvinsky to connect him with officials at the State Department to discuss mining regulations affecting his investments. Siklas noted that he was lobbying for access on behalf of a friend who had founded the deep-sea mining firm. "Hey bud," Siklas wrote in his note to Mezvinsky. "I need a contact in Hillary's office: someone my friend Josh (and I perhaps) can reach out via email or phone to discuss mining and the current legal issues and regulations." *Time* further reported that three months later, State Department e-mails show that Clinton forwarded the message to another department official, Deputy Secretary of State Thomas Nides, asking, "Could you have someone follow up on this request which was forwarded to me?" Nides replied, "I'll get on it." This e-mail exchange was made public by the State Department's release of Clinton's e-mails and was first reported by the Associated Press. "Clinton's email usage is already the subject of federal probes in her and her aides' handling of classified information on the private server she maintained in her Westchester, N.Y., home," the *Time* article noted.[8]

Fox News, reporting the backstory of the Neptune Minerals affair, noted that at the time Clinton was advocating for an Obama administration push to win Senate approval for a sweeping law-of-the-sea treaty. "The pact would have aided U.S. mining companies scouring for minerals in international waters, but the Republican-dominated Senate blocked it." In the e-mail, Siklas also said that his then employer, Goldman Sachs, was representing Neptune. "Before joining Eaglevale, Mezvinsky also had worked for eight years at Goldman, partly during Siklas' tenure there between 2004 and 2007," Fox News reported. "Members of the influential New York firm were one of Clinton's top funders in her 2008 presidential race, giving more than $225,000 that cycle. The firm has also been a major donor to the Clinton Foundation, giving between $1 million and $5 million."[9]

CHELSEA GROWS UP TO BECOME JUST ANOTHER CLINTON

On May 18, 2015, Richard Johnson triggered a controversy when he reported at PageSix.com that "Chelsea Clinton is so unpleasant to colleagues, she's causing high turnover." Johnson said several top staffers had left the Clinton Foundation since Chelsea became vice chair in 2011. Johnson noted that former Clinton Foundation CEO Bruce Lindsey was "pushed upstairs" to be board chair in 2013, so Chelsea could bring in her McKinsey colleague Eric Braverman, who, as previously noted, appeared to have quit in a dispute over what he considered to be failures in Clinton Foundation financial audits and regulatory reporting. Johnson's source told him that Braverman was "Chelsea's boy," but he was pushed out because he tried to hire his own communications professionals and "actually tried to run the place." Rather than side with Chelsea, Johnson's report ended up being critical of the Clinton family's overall management of the Clinton Foundation, noting that Chelsea was now as culpable as her parents. "Instead of being something Hillary can point to with pride," Johnson's report concluded, "the foundation has become a bloated slush fund that some critics say deserves an official investigation. And Chelsea's fingerprints are all over it."[10]

But Chelsea's reported abrasive personality has not prevented her from campaign fund-raising for her mother, while continuing her pursuit of charitable donations in her role as Clinton Foundation vice chair. On January 19, 2016, CNN reported that Chelsea was heading to London to headline a February 23 Clinton campaign fund-raiser to be attended by *Vogue* editor-in-chief Anna Wintour and hosted by Natalie Sara Massenet, the founder of the fashion website Net-a-Porter, with tickets between $1,000 and $2,700, the maximum an individual can contribute to Hillary Clinton's presidential campaign.[11] Chelsea was also scheduled to cohost fund-raisers for her mother in California, Florida, and New York City.[12]

With the Clinton Foundation rolling along in 2015 donations, Chelsea appeared to be fitting right in to the family business, undistracted by any possible conflicts of interest her campaigning for her mother in

2016 might entail as Clinton Foundation vice chair. The *Washington Post* reported on October 29, 2015, that Clinton Foundation donations are on the rise, measured both in dollars and in the number of contributions to the charity, after Hillary emerged early in the 2016 presidential campaign as, once again, the "presumptive nominee of the Democratic Party." According to the *Post*, the Clinton Foundation announced that it had raised more money since the start of 2015 than it had during the same period in 2014, "pushing back against suggestions that the family's global charity has been adversely affected by scrutiny associated with Hillary Clinton's presidential run."[13] Quite the contrary appeared obvious. Calculating that Hillary might be president on this second try, donors and prospective donors apparently began to realize it was time to make their contributions before the proverbial train left the station.

Hillary Clinton opened her office to dozens of influential Democratic Party fund-raisers, former Clinton administration and campaign loyalists, and corporate donors to her family's global charity, according to State Department calendars obtained by the Associated Press.[14] Clinton spoke by phone with nearly one hundred corporate executives and longtime Clinton Foundation charity donors during her four years at the State Department between 2009 and 2013, according to her calendar records. The AP further reported these formally scheduled meetings involved heads of companies and organizations that pursued business interests with the Obama administration, including with the State Department while Clinton was in charge. While it's unlikely Chelsea could be White House chief of staff during her mother's presidency and still keep her title as vice chair of the Clinton Foundation, it remains highly probable Clinton Foundation donors and campaign contributors would have no less access to the Oval Office in a Hillary presidency than they had to the secretary of state's office.

NO LUXURY DENIED

Increased involvement in her mother's presidential campaign did not stop Chelsea from vacationing at one of the world's most exclusive resorts,

Morgan Chalfant reported on January 19, 2016, in the *Washington Free Beacon*. She and her husband, and their daughter, Charlotte, were spotted at the Amanyara Resort on Providenciales Island in Turks and Caicos. Chalfant reported that Chelsea, "who is pregnant, appeared to be taking a break from campaigning for her mother." Chalfant calculated that rooms at the resort, rated as one of the world's most expensive, begin at $1,500 per night during the slow season, with Amanyara's most exclusive accommodations, its six-bedroom villa, cost $34,000 per night during the resort's busy season. One night in the top villa easily costs more than the average American worker makes in a year, Chalfant added, taking the latest measure of per capita income over twelve months at $28,555, according to the U.S. Census Bureau.[15] The *Daily Mail* in London reported that back in Iowa, Chelsea gave a speech casting her mother in glowing terms when telling a crowd of five thousand, "I can't imagine a better role model for me as a woman, as a Democrat, as a progressive, and as a working mom."[16]

Chelsea's attacks on the Democratic Party's admittedly socialist candidate for president, Bernie Sanders, over his health care reforms drew instant pushback from political pundits shocked to see Chelsea grow up to act just like another Clinton political attack dog. Michelle Cottle, writing in the *Atlantic* on January 19, 2016, noted how disturbing it was to realize Chelsea was just another "political hack," as some critics immediately charged. Cottle quoted Chelsea saying in a 2014 interview, "It is frustrating, because who wants to grow up and follow their parents? I've tried really hard to care about things that were very different from my parents." But Cottle had to concede that "the Clinton gravitational pull" is strong. "And, her many talents notwithstanding, there is arguably no job for which Chelsea is more qualified—or, for now, more needed—than professional daughter," Cottle wrote. "But woe be unto her mom's campaign if she behaves like your typical political veteran and picks any more fights."[17] In her new adult roles, Chelsea might have to shed the softening touch she gave her mother's political campaigns by playing the role of "first daughter." But if the money continued to flow, both to the foundation and the campaign, a bit of adverse press from Democrats displeased to see Chelsea on the attack might end up being a small price the Clinton family would be more than willing to pay.

HILLARY: "NO ONE IS TOO BIG TO JAIL"

In the fourth Democratic presidential debate with Sanders, in response to being challenged over her extensive financial ties to Wall Street, Hillary Clinton made a statement that could haunt her in the future. "There's no daylight on the basic premise that there should be no bank too big to fail," she said, "and no individual too powerful to jail. We agree on that."[18] The remark, tweeted out by the Clinton camp to Hillary's five-million-plus Twitter followers, caught the Clinton campaign by surprise. Dozens on Twitter responded within seconds that the remark applied to Hillary herself.[19] Responders on Twitter brought up the FBI investigation of Clinton's private e-mail server, as well as political corruption allegations regarding the Clinton Foundation. Thomas Lifson, editor and publisher of the *American Thinker*, attributed the remark to a guilty conscience. "There may still be a reasonable debate on whether or not Hillary Clinton has a conscience, but Sunday night's Democratic presidential debate proves that she does have a subconscious," Lifson wrote. "That part of her mind put words into her mouth that her conscious mind would rather not admit."[20]

On August 27, 2015, Quinnipiac University released a poll that showed Americans overwhelmingly think Hillary Clinton is a habitual liar. In fact, "liar" is "the first word that comes to mind" more than others in an open-ended question when voters think of Hillary Clinton. The poll further reported that 61 percent of voters say Hillary is not honest and trustworthy.[21] A Fox News poll released August 14, 2015, showed 58 percent of responders believe Hillary Clinton knowingly lied when denying her private e-mail system at the State Department contained no classified information. Only 2 percent of the respondents believed she had told the truth about her private e-mail server.[22] The results have held consistent through polling conducted by Quinnipiac at the end of 2015.[23] The inevitable conclusion: the majority of Americans have seen through the Hillary Clinton façade, judging that she will lie—presumably either through her own misrepresentations or through the "spin" of her surrogates—whenever it's politically advantageous.

BILL CLINTON VIEWED AS "SERIAL RAPIST," HILLARY AS "ABUSER" OF HIS VICTIMS

In the 1990s, Bill Clinton skated by accusations of serial rape and numerous other sexual infidelities simply by having Hillary Clinton "stand by her man," while the cute and devoted child Chelsea held their hands. Meanwhile, Bill Cosby, once a television comedian loved by millions of Americans, is facing accusations by nearly sixty women of sexual assault since the mid-1960s, and criminal charges have been filed in one case.

A 2015 book by Roger Stone and Robert Morrow, *The Clintons' War on Women*, has spotlighted the documentation dating back to the earliest days of the Clintons' relationship, detailing woman by woman the sordid accusations against Bill and Hillary's cover-up campaign to demonize and terrorize the accusers.[24] In 2016, however, the Clintons' ability to cover up this disgrace appears to be coming to a rapid end. In what might be termed the "Cosby Effect," sexual assaults by a male politician appear no longer excusable, despite the efforts of a calculating wife with the skills of an attorney and the power of a family fortune.[25]

Stone has openly charged that Hillary Clinton promoting herself as an advocate for women and children is hypocrisy, calling her "an enabler of rape. She has been the person to enable the serial rape and sexual assaults by her husband Bill Clinton. Some of which are known publicly: Paula Jones, Juanita Broaddrick, and Kathleen Willey."

But Stone has charged there are "many, many who are not publically known." He accused Bill Clinton of violating the women physically, followed by Hillary coming to his aid by hiring detectives to gather information that could be used to silence the victims. Stone has charged that Hillary has gone to great lengths to do "horrific things" to the victims, including killing their pets—as Willey claimed was done to her cat, slashing tires, smashing windshields, leaving bullets in the front seat of their cars, and late-night, anonymous phone calls.[26]

"Far from her public image, Hillary Clinton is a violent, scheming, ambitious, foul-mouthed woman with an insatiable appetite for luxury, money, and power," Stone and Morrow wrote. "Hillary is also a physically violent person, famous for hitting, scratching, and throwing things at her cheating husband. She is a classic abuser of anyone who gets in the way of her drive for power."[27]

Increasingly, Hillary and Bill are being confronted at campaign rallies about the allegations against Bill and Hillary's role in attacking his accusers. On December 3, 2015, at a campaign event in New Hampshire, a woman in the audience asked Hillary Clinton, "You say that all rape victims should be believed, but would you say that about Juanita Broaddrick, Kathleen Willey, and Paula Jones? Should we believe them as well?" Clinton, taken aback, responded awkwardly, "Well, I would say everybody should be believed until they are disbelieved based on evidence."[28]

Then in Derry, New Hampshire, at Hillary's first town hall meeting in 2016, Katherine Prudhomme-O'Brien, a state representative, confronted the candidate about claims that her husband had sexually assaulted Broaddrick and Willey. "I was a Democrat, but I became a Republican because of this, because of this stuff. Because of what I saw happen in the Clinton years, the hypocrisy of so-called women who fight for women," said Prudhomme-O'Brien, interrupting Clinton's town hall meeting.[29]

GOP presidential candidate Donald Trump has charged that Bill Clinton's sexual history is fair game in the 2016 presidential campaign. "Hillary is an enabler," Trump alleged. "She is married to an abuser," he charged in another context. "If Hillary is going to play the woman's card, it's all fair game."[30]

SHE IS OFTEN CONFUSED

On November 16, 2015, Judicial Watch released more than thirty-five pages of e-mails from Secretary of State Hillary Clinton's aide Huma Abedin revealing that Abedin had advised Clinton aide and frequent companion Monica Hanley that it was "very important" to go over phone calls with Clinton because the former secretary of state was "often confused."[31]

In May 2014, responding to former George W. Bush adviser Karl Rove's assertion that Hillary had suffered brain damage after falling in December 2012, Bill Clinton revealed that his wife's injury "required six months of very serious work to get over."

Clinton was frank in discussing the extent of his wife's injury. "They went to all this trouble to say she had staged what was a terrible concussion that required six months of very serious work to get over," he said. "It's something she never low-balled with the American people, never tried to pretend it didn't happen."[32]

On December 15, 2012, the *New York Times* revealed Clinton had fainted and suffered a concussion after striking her head falling, when she was alone at her home in Washington. The report said the incident was precipitated when Clinton became dehydrated because of a stomach virus she contracted during a trip to Europe.[33] The State Department confirmed that the concussion was not diagnosed until several days after the fall but was serious enough to postpone Clinton's scheduled testimony before the Senate Foreign Relations Committee and the House Foreign Relations Committee investigating the September 11, 2012, attack on the American diplomatic outpost in Benghazi that took the life of U.S. Ambassador Christopher Stevens. When Clinton finally did testify to Congress, a spokesperson confirmed the thick glasses she had been wearing since her fall and concussion were prescribed to deal with the lingering effects of her health problems, including a blood clot that supposedly had developed.[34] Investigating further, the *New York Daily News* reported on January 24, 2013, that a Fresnel prism taped to Clinton's eyeglasses was designed to treat the double vision resulting from the concussion and blood clot.[35]

Investigative reporter Ed Klein, in an article published by Newsmax on December 15, 2015, revealed that concerns about Hillary Clinton's health problems had not diminished. Hillary continued to suffer from blinding headaches, exhaustion, insomnia, and a tremor in her hands. "As a precaution against the spectacle of fainting in public, which could easily doom her candidacy, Hillary now travels with a personal physician on all her major campaign trips," Klein wrote. "There have been several incidents in which she has nearly collapsed. For example, after her 11-hour testimony before the Trey Gowdy Benghazi committee, Hillary swooned as she walked to a waiting car. She had to be supported in the arms of her aides and helped into the back seat." Klein also noted that tension headaches continued to plague Hillary and often make it hard for her to maintain her grueling schedule. "Huma Abedin, deputy chief of staff and her closest adviser, frequently orders campaign aides to alter Hillary's schedule at the last moment so the candidate can catch her breath and take out time for naps," he wrote. "This may explain why Hillary is often as much as two hours late for a campaign appearance."[36]

$1 BILLION GOAL AND THE "LAST HURRAH"

The Last Hurrah, a 1956 best-selling novel, tells the story of an aging former governor named Frank Skeffington, generally taken for a fictionalized version of former Boston mayor and Massachusetts governor James Michael Curley, who suffers a massive heart attack and dies shortly after losing a tough battle to be elected mayor of an unnamed Eastern city.[37] Hillary Clinton, born October 26, 1947, would be sixty-nine if she were to be inaugurated president on January 20, 2017, and Bill Clinton, born August 19, 1946, would be seventy. It would make her the second-oldest president at the time of her inauguration, with the oldest being Ronald Reagan.[38]

While age is no disqualification to being elected president of the United States, for the Clintons this is clearly their "last hurrah." With Chelsea positioned at the helm of the Clinton Foundation, there is nothing to indicate the Clinton family has any intention of closing down the foundation should Hillary be elected president. Given the increase in donations to the Clinton Foundation as Hillary's 2016 presidential campaign kicks into high gear, there is no reason to presume the game the Clintons tested while Hillary was secretary of state would not be perfected should Hillary win the White House.

The history of the Clinton Foundation may not predict the future, but it's a good way to bet. While a donation to the Clinton Foundation might not be a precondition of obtaining an Oval Office audience or getting a favorable policy determination from the administration of Hillary Clinton, the odds are it would be well received, to say the least. Aging dictators in Third World countries pad their coffers to die in style and position their progeny to enjoy in luxury an anticipated generational succession of power. Would a Hillary Clinton presidency reduce the United States of America to the level of a Third World banana republic? Will we be documenting in 2020 the next round of "Clinton scams," which we predict that the crime partnership President Hillary Clinton and "first spouse" Bill Clinton will be happy to sponsor, should the Clintons regain the White House?

10

THE PLAN TO SHUT DOWN
THE CLINTON FOUNDATION

But how much good has the Clinton Foundation actually done?

—PETER SCHWEIZER, *CLINTON CASH*

A s noted in the preface, the purpose of this book is not specifically to cause Hillary Clinton to withdraw from the 2016 election. Even if she were to shut down her 2016 presidential campaign, the Clinton Foundation would remain in place. There is abundant evidence that the Clinton family has defrauded charitable donors to enrich themselves and their close associates while trading favorable State Department policy decisions for generous donations to the Clinton Foundation and to Hillary's 2016 presidential campaign.

This concluding chapter begins with the realization that the Clintons will do anything possible to recapture the White House in 2016, not only because it is their last chance to do so, but moreover because they believe they have devised a strategy to win. The conclusion explains why Attorney General Loretta Lynch is unlikely to recommend Hillary

Clinton be prosecuted for her use of a private e-mail server while she was secretary of state if the FBI recommends it. This final chapter ends by laying out a strategy that readers can use to close down the Clinton Foundation, whether or not Hillary wins the presidential election in 2016. The point of this book is that the foundation is a vast criminal enterprise—exactly as Charles Ortel has alleged—and it needs to be shut down before permanent and irreparable damage is done to genuine charities that rely on the trust of donors.

WHY THE CLINTONS BELIEVE HILLARY WILL WIN IN 2016

As the 2016 election cycle unfolds, voters appear tired of dynasties, with Democrats reacting much more negatively to Hillary Clinton's 2016 campaign than they did in her losing effort eight years earlier, and Republicans rejecting the candidacy of former Florida governor Jeb Bush as perhaps one Bush too many. The core base of the Democratic Party has moved far left, embracing in the early stages aging Vermont senator Bernie Sanders, an admitted socialist.

The Clintons, acknowledging these disadvantages, still calculate that as the primary season proceeds and the Democratic National Convention draws near, the party regulars will gravitate to a more centrist candidate like Hillary. The argument will be that Hillary has the best chance to keep together the Democratic Party coalition that propelled Barack Obama into office in 2008. Hillary advisers and donors clearly recognize the greatest hurdle for her will be to win the nomination. Once the nomination is secure, Hillary's top advisers, including Bill Clinton and her top campaign contributors, believe her experience will win her the general election against any candidate the Republicans nominate, including Donald Trump.

As in 2008 and 2012, the Democratic Party begins each presidential general election campaign with a huge advantage in electoral votes. The reality of the Electoral College mathematics presents the GOP a daunting hill to climb. As most students of politics know, presidential elections are settled on Electoral College votes, not popular votes.

Currently, there are 538 electors, based on there being 435 members of the House of Representatives, 100 U.S. senators, and three electors from the District of Columbia. An absolute majority of 270 electoral votes is required to win the presidency.

In recent presidential election cycles, the Democrats have started with an enormous advantage, with California's 55 electoral votes and New York's 29 virtual locks, meaning only an additional 186 electoral votes are needed to win. For all practical purposes, the presidential election of 2012 was reduced to the nine "swing states" of Nevada, Colorado, Iowa, Ohio, Virginia, North Carolina, and Florida.[1]

Obama entered the 2012 presidential campaign calculating he had locked up as many as 251 electoral votes and needed only to pick up just twenty from the swing states while Romney needed 79, approximately four times as many.

While the mathematics of the 2016 presidential election are beyond the scope of this book, the point is the Democratic Party has reason to believe its electoral advantages can be mobilized to win the White House, regardless who the Democrats nominate is. Barring a wild card, such as a split in the Democratic vote by an independent such as former New York mayor Michael Bloomberg, the Clintons can reasonably calculate their chances in 2016 are good.

THE CLINTONS CALCULATE BEYOND CRIMINAL INDICTMENT

The Clintons realize the FBI investigation into Hillary's private e-mail server could result in a recommendation for a criminal indictment. The hurdle is that Attorney General Loretta Lynch would make the decision. As a Democrat, Lynch could calculate politically, deciding to decline prosecution. Or, if she were concerned that the political backlash might be too severe, she could recommend the appointment of a special prosecutor. The time required for a special prosecutor to establish an office and conduct an independent investigation could drag the possibility of a criminal indictment past the November 2016 election date.

Even if the Obama Department of Justice were to indict Hillary, that alone might not be sufficient to force her to withdraw from the 2016 presidential race.

Conceivably, a criminal indictment might allow her to gain votes by evoking the typical Clinton counterattack of claiming the charges were a politically motivated "witch hunt" undertaken by the "vast right-wing conspiracy" that has always opposed the Clintons politically. The Constitution is silent over whether a person convicted of federal crimes or even serving a prison term would be ineligible.

If Hillary Clinton's presidential campaign could survive a Department of Justice criminal indictment over use of a private e-mail server while secretary of state, her candidacy could also survive an attempt to close down the Clinton Foundation and/or to prosecute the Clintons for civil and/or criminal offenses regarding their operation and management of the foundation. Just to be clear, this book is not recommending an attempt to shut down the Clinton Foundation as a strategy to force Hillary Clinton to withdraw from the 2016 presidential campaign or as a tactic to increase the chances she might lose the 2016 presidential campaign. The point of this book is that the Clinton Foundation needs to be shut down because it is a vast criminal conspiracy, regardless of whether or not Hillary Clinton withdraws from the 2016 presidential campaign.

What the Clintons should fear is that a national campaign to shut down their foundation might just work, provided the right tactics are employed.

THE PLAN TO SHUT DOWN THE BILL, HILLARY, AND CHELSEA CLINTON FOUNDATION

The Clinton Foundation; the Clinton Health Access Initiative, Inc.; and the Clinton Global Initiative, Inc.; are registered as corporations in the state of Arkansas. But under state law, the Clinton Foundation is required to register as a 501(c)(3) charity in each state where it accepts donations. Clearly, this today means the Clinton Foundation and its various subsidiary organizations must be registered in all fifty states to accept charitable donations nationwide.

Following this logic forward, any person in the United States who has contributed to the Clinton Foundation, or to one of its various subgroups, should have standing to appeal to the state attorney general to request an investigation of whether or not the Clinton Foundation, and its various subgroups, are acting lawfully according to the requirements under state law for the operation of organizations claiming IRS 501(c)(3) tax-exempt status.

Under state law, a state attorney general ought to be able to go to a state court to obtain a temporary restraining order under state law, placing the Clinton Foundation and its various subgroups into receivership, until the state investigation is concluded.

In his first interim report, April 20, 2015, concerning public disclosures of the Clinton Foundation titled "False Philanthropy?" Charles Ortel asked a series of important questions: "Did the directors take reasonable care, as fiduciaries, under applicable state, federal, and foreign laws to operate this charity serving, at all times, a public interest? Are all business arrangements with material 'related' parties fully and adequately disclosed in annual, publicly available filings that comparable charities regularly complete on time? Or, do the Clintons, and others who operate the Clinton Foundation, function as Robin Hood in reverse—do they dupe small, modest income donors to enrich themselves and cronies?"[2]

Ortel noted, "Rather than discharging clear-cut legal duties to use donated funds solely for authorized tax-exempt purposes, Clinton Foundation Trustees, certain individuals in position to exercise significant influence over the Clinton Foundation, and certain donors have, instead, engaged and continue to engage in a vast criminal conspiracy to defraud the general public, enrich themselves, and entrench their political influence."[3]

Ortel listed the following as elements of the criminal conspiracy.

1. Grossly reckless, negligent, and illegal operation of public charities inside and outside the United States;

2. Repeated false and materially misleading statements under penalties of perjury to government authorities and to the general public;

3. Solicitation using the mail to obtain donations on the basis of false and materially misleading information;

4. Solicitation using digital media to obtain documents on the basis of false and materially misleading information;

5. Creation of billions of dollars in private gain through operation of a public charity; and

6. Appropriation of private gain by certain Clinton Foundation Trustees, executives and connected insiders.

Ortel notes the geographic extent of the criminal conspiracy "extends far beyond the Little Rock, Arkansas, headquarters campus, to each of the additional 49 U.S. states, and to more than 75 foreign countries, where the Clinton Foundation solicits donations and/or operates." He also argues that victims of this ongoing criminal conspiracy number in the millions of persons and include financially unsophisticated donors reached through illegal mass-marketing campaigns, governments that suffered reductions in their tax revenues, governments that contributed to the Clinton Foundation in good faith, and tax-exempt organizations "whose contributions to an illegally constituted charity create significant exposure."

Ortel takes to task both independent auditors, including PricewaterhouseCoopers, and state law enforcement authorities, as well as the IRS and foreign governments for failure to investigate Clinton Foundation criminal behavior.

"To date, independent auditors and certain other advisors engaged by the Clinton Foundation have failed to exercise due inquiry into the true activities of the Clinton Foundation and its constituent parts," Ortel wrote in his second interim report. "Moreover, though the ongoing criminal conspiracy involves felony crimes, no state, federal, or foreign government authority has chosen to investigate and, as appropriate, hold those persons accountable, fully responsible."

Ortel, confident that concerted action by the public can produce results, made ten predictions about the Clinton Foundation, posted on his website on January 4, 2016.[4]

- Prediction #1: Intense focus on Clinton Foundation public disclosures will lead prime money sources to abandon support for Hillary Clinton's candidacy.

- Prediction #2: Filings submitted on 16 November 2015 by the Clinton Foundation compound legal problems for trustees, for major donors, and for other insiders.

- Prediction #3: Clinton Foundation trustees and insiders will grow to understand why they face legal exposure for creating "public gain" and "inurement."

- Prediction #4: Creation, operation, and attempted refinancing of Laureate Education, Inc. will attract focus for many reasons.

- Prediction #5: Voters will question whether any legal agreement will effectively restrain the Clinton Foundation, if Hillary Clinton is elected president.

- Prediction #6: Investigators will re-examine the creation of the Clinton Foundation, starting in 1997.

- Prediction #7: Bill Clinton's ongoing role with the American India Foundation and Clinton Foundation ties with McKinsey will receive focus.

- Prediction #8: Bill Clinton's work with International Aids Trust and his early work fighting HIV/AIDS internationally will be re-examined.

- Prediction #9: Bill Clinton's work with other presidential foundations and accounting treatment for this work will be compared and contrasted.

- Prediction #10: The evolving history of the Clinton Foundation will affect how President Obama shapes and ultimately directs his foundation.

The remedy requires you, the reader, to contact the attorney general in your state to demand the Clinton Foundation be shut down until a competent law enforcement agency in the state can investigate these important criminal allegations.

The appendix at the end of this book lists each state attorney general, along with each office location, mailing address, and telephone number.

We recommend filing complaints with state attorneys general because federal authorities in the Obama Department of Justice and IRS may, for political reasons, decline to investigate rigorously and prosecute the Clintons and the foundation trustees, along with officers and other key operatives in the foundation for their criminal offenses. A sample letter is provided in the appendix that you can individualize in making an appeal to the attorney general in each state to initiate a criminal investigation of the Clinton Foundation.

The Clintons anticipate no law enforcement authority in the United States will dare undertake a serious investigation of the Clinton Foundation, given the family's power and wealth. This book is written and published in the contrary conviction that no family is above the law, not even the Clintons. State attorneys general will not be able to ignore hundreds and hopefully thousands of letters, e-mails, and phone calls.

Granted, the Obama administration IRS and Department of Justice have imposed a political standard of allowing liberal Democrats to violate federal laws with impunity. Please note in the appendix that not all state attorneys general are Democrats. But we also anticipate that Democrats in the states may not yet be lost to a radical left concept of justice that presumes laws should be applied ideologically, with a partisan determination to punish conservatives.

This book was dedicated to Dinesh D'Souza in large part because he sets an example of how one person, selectively prosecuted by a partisan justice system, can rise above that injustice to pursue the dream of America. In this instance, that dream remains alive in the hope that not even a political family as wealthy and powerful as the Clintons should ever be permitted to sacrifice genuine philanthropy on their altar of limitless greed and unbridled disrespect for those yet desiring to uphold the hopes and dreams embodied in the principles of genuine charitable giving.

One state alone, as well as any combination of states, determined to uphold the laws of charitable giving as written, is all we need to end the criminal conspiracy embodied at the heart of the Clinton Foundation, hopefully establishing in the process a strong deterrent against any future ex-president who thinks he can follow the example of the Clinton family with impunity.

LIST OF STATE ATTORNEYS GENERAL

Source: National Association of Attorneys General, NAAG,
www.naag.org/naag/attorneys-general/whos-my-ag/alabama/luther-strange.php

ALABAMA
Luther Strange (R)
Elected: 2010, 2014
501 Washington Ave.
P.O. Box 300152
Montgomery, AL 36130-0152
(334) 242-7300
www.ago.state.al.us/

ALASKA
Craig W. Richards (R)
Appointed: December 2014
P.O. Box 110300
Juneau, AK 99811-0300
(907) 465-2133
www.law.state.ak.us/

ARIZONA
Mark Brnovich (R)
Elected: 2014
1275 W. Washington St.
Phoenix, AZ 85007
(602) 542-4266
www.azag.gov/

ARKANSAS
Leslie Rutledge (R)
Elected: 2014
323 Center St., Suite 200
Little Rock, AR 72201-2610
(800) 482-8982
www.ag.arkansas.gov/

CALIFORNIA
Kamala D. Harris (D)
Elected: 2010, 2014
1300 I St., Ste. 1740
Sacramento, CA 95814
(916) 445-9555
http://ag.ca.gov/

COLORADO
Cynthia Coffman (R)
Elected: 2014
Ralph L. Carr Colorado Judicial Center
1300 Broadway, 10th Floor
Denver, CO 80203
(720) 508-6000
www.coloradoattorneygeneral.gov/

CONNECTICUT
George Jepsen (D)
Elected: 2010, 2014
55 Elm St.
Hartford, CT 06106
(860) 808-5318
www.ct.gov/ag/

DELAWARE
Matthew Denn (D)
Elected: 2014
Carvel State Office Bldg.
820 N. French St.
Wilmington, DE 19801
(302) 577-8338
http://attorneygeneral.delaware.gov/

DISTRICT OF COLUMBIA
Karl A. Racine (D)
Elected: 2014
441 4th Street, NW, Suite 1100S
Washington, DC 20001
(202) 727-3400
http://oag.dc.gov/

FLORIDA
Pam Bondi (R)
Elected: 2010, 2014
The Capitol, PL 01
Tallahassee, FL 32399-1050
(850) 414-3300
http://myfloridalegal.com/

GEORGIA
Sam Olens (R)
Elected: 2010, 2014
40 Capitol Square, SW
Atlanta, GA 30334-1300
(404) 656-3300
http://law.ga.gov/

HAWAII
Douglas S. Chin (D)
Appointed: 2015
425 Queen St.
Honolulu, HI 96813
(808) 586-1500
http://ag.hawaii.gov/

IDAHO
Lawrence Wasden (R)
Elected: 2002, 2006, 2010, 2014
Statehouse
Boise, ID 83720-1000
(208) 334-2400
www.ag.idaho.gov/

ILLINOIS
Lisa Madigan (D)
Elected: 2002, 2006, 2010, 2014
James R. Thompson Ctr.
100 W. Randolph St.
Chicago, IL 60601
(312) 814-3000
http://illinoisattorneygeneral.gov/

INDIANA
Greg Zoeller (R)
Elected: 2008, 2012, 2014
Indiana Government Center South, 5th Floor
302 West Washington St.
Indianapolis, IN 46204
(317) 232-6201
www.in.gov/attorneygeneral/

IOWA
Tom Miller (D)
Elected: 1978, 1982, 1986, 1994, 1998, 2002,
        2006, 2010, 2014
Hoover State Office Bldg.
1305 E. Walnut
Des Moines, IA 50319
(515) 281-5164
www.iowaattorneygeneral.gov

KANSAS

Derek Schmidt (R)
Elected: 2010, 2014
120 S.W. 10th Ave., 2nd Fl.
Topeka, KS 66612-1597
(785) 296-2215
www.ag.ks.gov/

KENTUCKY

Andy Beshear (D)
Elected: 2015
700 Capitol Avenue
Capitol Building, Suite 118
Frankfort, KY 40601
http://ag.ky.gov/

LOUISIANA

Jeff Landry (R)
Elected: 2015
P.O. Box 94095
Baton Rouge, LA 70804-4095
225-326-6000
www.ag.state.la.us/

MAINE

Janet T. Mills (D)
Appointed: 2008, 2012, 2014
State House Station 6
Augusta, ME 04333
(207) 626-8800
www.maine.gov/ag/

MARYLAND

Brian Frosh (D)
Elected: 2014
200 St. Paul Place
Baltimore, MD 21202-2202
(410) 576-6300
www.oag.state.md.us

MASSACHUSETTS

Maura Healey (D)
Elected: 2014
1 Ashburton Place
Boston, MA 02108-1698
(617) 727-2200
www.mass.gov/ago/

MICHIGAN

Bill Schuette (R)
Elected: 2010, 2014
P.O. Box 30212
525 W. Ottawa St.
Lansing, MI 48909-0212
(517) 373-1110
www.michigan.gov/ag

MINNESOTA

Lori Swanson (D)
Elected: 2006, 2010, 2014
State Capitol, Ste. 102
St. Paul, MN 55155
(651) 296-3353
http://www.ag.state.mn.us

MISSISSIPPI

Jim Hood (D)
Elected: 2003, 2007, 2011
Department of Justice
P.O. Box 220
Jackson, MS 39205
(601) 359-3680
www.ago.state.ms.us/

MISSOURI

Chris Koster (D)
Elected: 2008, 2012
Supreme Ct. Bldg., 207
W. High St.
Jefferson City, MO 65101
(573) 751-3321
http://ago.mo.gov/

MONTANA

Tim Fox (R)
Elected: 2012
Justice Bldg.
215 N. Sanders
Helena, MT 59620-1401
(406) 444-2026
https://doj.mt.gov/

NEBRASKA
Doug Peterson (R)
Elected: 2014
State Capitol
P.O. Box 98920
Lincoln, NE 68509-8920
(402) 471-2682
www.ago.ne.gov/

NEVADA
Adam Paul Laxalt (R)
Elected: 2014
Old Supreme Ct. Bldg.
100 N. Carson St.
Carson City, NV 89701
(775) 684-1100
www.ag.nv.gov

NEW HAMPSHIRE
Joseph A. Foster (D)
Appointed: May 2013
33 Capitol St.
Concord, NH 03301
(603) 271-3658
http://doj.nh.gov/

NEW JERSEY
John Jay Hoffman (R), Acting AG
Appointed: May 2013
Richard J. Hughes Justice Complex
25 Market Street
P.O. Box 080
Trenton, NJ 08625
(609) 292-8740
www.state.nj.us/lps/

NEW MEXICO
Hector Balderas (D)
Elected: 2014
P.O. Drawer 1508
Santa Fe, NM 87504-1508
(505) 827-6000
www.nmag.gov

NEW YORK
Eric Schneiderman (D)
Elected: 2010, 2014
Dept. of Law—The Capitol
2nd floor, Albany, NY 12224
(518) 474-7330
www.ag.ny.gov/

NORTH CAROLINA
Roy Cooper (D)
Elected: 2000, 2004, 2008, 2012
Dept. of Justice
P.O. Box 629
Raleigh, NC 27602-0629
(919) 716-6400
www.ncdoj.gov/

NORTH DAKOTA
Wayne Stenehjem (R)
Elected: 2000, 2004, 2006, 2010, 2014
State Capitol
600 E. Boulevard Ave.
Bismarck, ND 58505-0040
(701) 328-2210
www.ag.state.nd.us

OHIO
Mike DeWine (R)
Elected: 2010, 2014
State Office Tower
30 E. Broad St.
Columbus, OH 43266-0410
(614) 466-4320
www.ohioattorneygeneral.gov/

OKLAHOMA
Scott Pruitt (R)
Elected: 2010, 2014
313 NE 21st St.
Oklahoma City, OK 73105
(405) 521-3921
www.oag.state.ok.us/

OREGON
Ellen F. Rosenblum (D)
Appointed June 2012, Elected: November 2012
Justice Bldg.
1162 Court St., NE
Salem, OR 97301
503-378-6002
www.doj.state.or.us/

PENNSYLVANIA
Kathleen Kane (D)
Elected: 2012
1600 Strawberry Square
Harrisburg, PA 17120
(717) 787-3391
www.attorneygeneral.gov/

RHODE ISLAND
Peter Kilmartin (D)
Elected: 2010, 2014
150 S. Main St.
Providence, RI 02903
(401) 274-4400
www.riag.ri.gov

SOUTH CAROLINA
Alan Wilson (R)
Elected: 2010, 2014
Rembert C. Dennis Office Bldg.
P.O. Box 11549
Columbia, SC 29211-1549
(803) 734-3970
www.scattorneygeneral.org

SOUTH DAKOTA
Marty J. Jackley (R)
Appointed: 2009, Elected: 2010, 2014
1302 East Highway 14, Suite 1
Pierre, SD 57501-8501
(605) 773-3215
http://atg.sd.gov/

TENESSEE
Herbert H. Slatery, III (R)
Appointed: October 1, 2014
425 5th Avenue North
Nashville, TN 37243
615-741-3491
www.tn.gov/attorneygeneral

TEXAS
Ken Paxton (R)
Elected: 2014
Capitol Station
P.O. Box 12548
Austin, TX 78711-2548
(512) 463-2100
www.texasattorneygeneral.gov/

UTAH
Sean Reyes (R)
Appointed: 2013, 2014
State Capitol, Rm. 236
Salt Lake City, UT 84114-0810
(801) 538-9600
http://attorneygeneral.utah.gov/

VERMONT
William H. Sorrell (D)
Appointed: 1997 Elected: 1998, 2000, 2002, 2004, 2006, 2008, 2010, 2012, 2014
109 State St.
Montpelier, VT 05609-1001
(802) 828-3173
www.atg.state.vt.us/

VIRGINIA
Mark Herring (D)
Elected: 2013
900 East Main St.
Richmond, VA 23219
(804) 786-2071
www.oag.state.va.us/

WASHINGTON
Bob Ferguson (D)
Elected: 2012
1125 Washington St. SE
PO Box 40100
Olympia, WA 98504-0100
(360) 753-6200
www.atg.wa.gov

WEST VIRGINIA
Patrick Morrisey (R)
Elected: 2012
State Capitol, 1900
Kanawha Blvd. E.
Charleston, WV 25305
(304) 558-2021
www.wvago.gov/

WISCONSIN
Brad Schimel (R)
Elected: 2014
Wisconsin Department of Justice
State Capitol, Room 114 East
PO Box 7857
Madison, WI 53707-7857
(608) 266-1221
www.doj.state.wi.us

WYOMING
Peter K. Michael (R)
Appointed: July 2013
State Capitol Bldg., Cheyenne, WY 82002
(307) 777-7841
http://attorneygeneral.state.wy.us

APPENDIX B

SAMPLE COMPLAINT FORMS

Each state may have a complaint form on the Attorney General website devoted to regulating charities. Samples of the complaint form are included here. To establish lending, the reader may have to contribute $1.00 to the Clinton Foundation. This $1.00 donation will make you a contributor to the Clinton Foundation. Legal standing to file a criminal complaint will be identical if the reader contributes $1.00, or $1 million dollars.

The point of "legal standing" is that you have a basis in law as a donor to the Clinton Foundation to allege you were defrauded, provided it can be established the Clinton Foundation under the laws of the state in which you reside is a criminal enterprise, not operated as a legitimate charity. Look up on your state's attorney general's website for the charity complaint form. Most states offer a form that can be filled out online and mailed or faxed to the appropriate regulatory office. See the next page for the sample complaint form for the New York State Charity Complaint/Inquiry Form.

NEW YORK STATE DEPARTMENT OF LAW
CHARITIES BUREAU

120 Broadway - 3rd Floor
New York, NY 10271
http://www.charitiesnys.com

ERIC T. SCHNEIDERMAN
Attorney General

COMPLAINT/INQUIRY FORM

The Charities Bureau has jurisdiction to investigate complaints that involve 1) wrongdoing by charitable corporations, trusts or other nonprofit organizations; 2) fraudulent or misleading solicitation and improper expenditure of money for charitable purposes; and 3) improper activities of executors, administrators, trustees and personal representatives responsible for honoring pledges or bequests to a charity. This Bureau generally does not become involved in governance disputes within nonprofit organizations. The Bureau also responds to general inquiries concerning matters within its jurisdiction.

INSTRUCTIONS: 1. Please TYPE or PRINT clearly.
2. Please complete the entire form.
3. Please enclose copies of any documents relating to this complaint or inquiry.

1. Your Contact Information:

Name: _____

Address: _____

Home phone number: _____ Business phone number: _____

Fax number: _____ Email address: _____

2. Give the following information, if available, for the organization and/or individuals about whom you are complaining or inquiring:

Organization Name: _____

Organization Address: _____

Organization phone number _____: Organization email address: _____

Individual Name	Individual Title/Position	Individual Address	Individual Phone No.
_____	_____	_____	_____
_____	_____	_____	_____
_____	_____	_____	_____

3. Details of your complaint or inquiry (Please include as much specific detail as possible- continue on additional sheets if necessary).

4. If you have any documents in your possession that relate to your complaint or inquiry, please attach copies of them.

5. Have you submitted your complaint or inquiry to the organization? yes ☐ no ☐
If "yes," what was its response?

6. Have you submitted your complaint or inquiry to any other government agency? yes ☐ no ☐

If "yes," please list the name of the agency, address, telephone number and name of any person contacted.

Agency	Contact Person	Address	Phone No.
_____	_____	_____	_____
_____	_____	_____	_____

7. Is a court action pending? yes ☐ no ☐
If "yes," please provide the name, title and index number of the proceeding and the name and location of the court, if available.

8. List the names, addresses and telephone numbers of any other individuals who may have knowledge of the contents of this complaint or inquiry.

Name Address Phone No.

_____	_____	_____	_____
_____	_____	_____	_____

9. Do you have any objection to the contents of this complaint or inquiry being forwarded to or discussed with another government agency? yes ☐ no ☐

10. Do you have any objection to your name and/or address being forwarded to or discussed with the organization or person who is the subject of this complaint or inquiry?

Objection to Name and Address: yes ☐ no ☐
Objection to Name only: yes ☐ no ☐

The Attorney General is not your private attorney but represents the public by enforcing laws designed to protect the public and charities from misleading or unlawful practices. If you have any questions concerning your personal legal rights or responsibilities, you should contact a private attorney.

_____   _____   _____
Signature   Print Name   Date

CHAR030 (rev. 12/10)

NOTES

ACKNOWLEDGMENTS

1. Wall Street Transcript, "Investing in Volatility in a Tense Geopolitical Environment—Charles Ortel—Newport Value Partners, L.L.C.," Yahoo Finance, January 11, 2012, http://finance.yahoo. com/news/investing-volatility-tense-geopolitical-environment-185800664.html.

2. Dan Fisher, "Accounting Tricks Catch Up with GE," *Forbes*, August 4, 2009, http://www.forbes. com/2009/08/04/ge-immelt-sec-earnings-business-beltway-ge.html.

3. Jerome R. Corsi, "Wall Street Analyst Uncovers Clinton Foundation Fraud," WND, August 4, 2015, http://www.wnd.com/2015/04/wall-street-analyst-uncovers-clinton-foundation-fraud/.

4. Jerome R. Corsi, "Wall Street Expert: Clinton Foundation 'a Vast Criminal Conspiracy,'" WND, September 9, 2015, http://www.wnd.com/2015/09/wall-street-expert-clinton-foundation-a-vast-criminal-conspiracy/.

5. Peter Schweizer, *Clinton Cash: The Untold Story of How and Why Foreign Governments and Businesses Helped Make Bill and Hillary Rich* (New York: HarperCollins, 2015).

6. Edward Klein, *Blood Feud: The Clintons vs. the Obamas* (Washington, DC: Regnery, 2014).

7. Edward Klein, *Unlikeable: The Problem with Hillary*" (Washington, DC: Regnery, 2015).

8. John E. O'Neill and Jerome R. Corsi, *Unfit for Command: Swift Boat Veterans Speak Out Against John Kerry* (Washington, DC: Regnery, 2004).

9. Roger Stone and Robert Morrow, *The Clintons' War on Women* (New York: Skyhorse, 2015).

PREFACE

1. Jerome R. Corsi, "Wall Street Expert: Clinton Foundation 'a Vast Criminal Conspiracy,'" WND, September 9, 2015, http://www.wnd.com/2015/09/wall-street-expert-clinton-foundation-a-vast-criminal-conspiracy/.

2. Roger Stone and Robert Morrow, *The Clintons' War on Women* (New York: Skyhorse, 2015).

CHAPTER 1: CRYING POOR

1. "Hillary Clinton: 'We Came Out of the White House Dead Broke,'" Real Clear Politics Video (transcript), posted on June 9, 2014, http://www.realclearpolitics.com/video/2014/06/09/hillary_clinton_we_came_out_of_the_white_house_dead_broke.html.

2. Neil A. Lewis, "Exiting Job, Clinton Accepts Immunity Deal," *New York Times*, Jan. 20, 2001, http://www.nytimes.com/2001/01/20/politics/20CLIN.html.

3. Pete Yost, Associated Press, "Clinton Accepts 5-Year Law Suspension," *Washington Post*, January 19, 2001, http://www.washingtonpost.com/wp-srv/aponline/20010119/aponline132649_000.htm.

4. Michael Kirkland, "Final Lewinsky report: No One above law," UPI, March 6, 2002, http://www.upi.com/Top_News/2002/03/06/Final-Lewinsky-report-No-one-above-law/49691015442173/.

5. Peter Baker, "Clinton Settles Paula Jones Lawsuit for $850,000," *Washington Post*, November 14, 1998, http://www.washingtonpost.com/wp-srv/politics/special/clinton/stories/jones111498.htm.

6. Kathleen Willey, *Target: Caught in the Crosshairs of Bill and Hillary Clinton* (Los Angeles: World Ahead Publishing, 2007).

7. Laura Collins, "Hillary Clinton's Camp Fears a new 'Bimbo-Eruption' Will Put the Kibosh on Candidacy," *Daily Mail* (UK), July 31, 2015, http://www.dailymail.co.uk/news/article-3180398/Hillary-Clinton-s-camp-fears-new-bimbo-eruption-kibosh-candidacy-especially-Gennifer-Flowers-claimed-Bill-liked-blindfolded-tied-silk-scarves-called-wife-Hilla-Hun.html.

8. Associated Press in Washington, "Hillary Clinton Memoir: We 'Were Broke' after Presidency," *Guardian* (UK), June 10, 2014, http://www.theguardian.com/world/2014/jun/10/hillary-clinton-memoir-broke-after-presidency.

9. David D. Kirkpatrick, "Hillary Clinton Book Advance, $8 Million, Is Near Record," *New York Times*, December 16, 2000, http://www.nytimes.com/2000/12/16/nyregion/hillary-clinton-book-advance-8-million-is-near-record.html.

10. Jon Greenberg, "Hillary Clinton Says She and Bill Were 'Dead Broke,'" PolitiFact, June 10, 2014, http://www.politifact.com/truth-o-meter/statements/2014/jun/10/hillary-clinton/hillary-clinton-says-she-and-bill-were-dead-broke/.

11. Michael Falcone and Shushannah Walshe, "Hillary Clinton on Post-White House Debt: We Had to 'Keep Working Really Hard,'" ABC News, June 10, 2014, http://abcnews.go.com/Politics/hillary-clinton-post-white-house-debt-working-hard/story?id=24064204.

12. Katie Sanders, "Bill Clinton: 'I Had the Lowest Net Worth of Any American President in the 20th Century,'" PunditFact, June 29, 2014, http://www.politifact.com/punditfact/statements/2014/jun/29/bill-clinton/bill-clinton-i-had-lowest-net-worth-any-american-p/. See also "Harry S. Truman—President & Haberdasher," *Gentleman's Gazette*, October 18, 2012, http://www.gentlemansgazette.com/harry-s-truman-suits-haberdasher/.

13. Agustino Fontevecchia, "The Richest and Poorest Presidential Candidates: From Hillary's Millions to Marco Rubio's Debts," *Forbes*, September 29, 2015, http://www.forbes.com/sites/afontevecchia/2015/09/29/the-richest-and-poorest-presidential-candidates-from-hillarys-millions-to-marco-rubios-debts/.

14. Dan Alexander, "The Mystery of Hillary's Missing Millions," *Forbes*, October 19, 2015, http://www.forbes.com/sites/danalexander/2015/09/29/the-mystery-of-hillarys-missing-millions/.

15. Mark Sherman, "Clintons Got $75,000 in Home Furniture," Associated Press, February 12, 2002.

16. George Lardner Jr., "Clintons Say They'll Return Disputed Gifts," *Washington Post*, February 6, 2001, https://www.washingtonpost.com/archive/politics/2001/02/06/clintons-say-theyll-return-disputed-gifts/accd07f5-3cd2-4ebf-ba49-b3ac30a35a7d/.

17. Sherman, "Clintons Got $75,000 in Home Furniture."

18. Ibid.

19. "Bruce Lindsey, Chairman of the Board, Clinton Foundation," biography posted on the Clinton Foundation blog, accessed March 23, 2016, https://www.clintonfoundation.org/blog/authors/bruce-lindsey.

20. "Attorneys," the website of Wright Lindsey Jennings, accessed March 23, 2016, http://wlj.com/attorneys; http://wlj.com/attorneys/bruce-r-lindsey.

21. Daniel Halper, *Clinton, Inc.: The Audacious Rebuilding of a Political Machine* (New York: HarperCollins, 2014), xv.

22. Cynthia McFadden, Jake Whitman, and NBC News, "Bill Clinton Defends His Foundation's Foreign Money," NBC News, May 4, 2015, http://www.nbcnews.com/news/us-news/bill-clinton-defends-his-foundations-foreign-money-n352981.

23. Al Weaver, "'I Can't Understand the Things He Said': Halperin Rips Bill Clinton's 'Pay the Bills' Remark," *Daily Caller*, May 4, 2015, http://dailycaller.com/2015/05/04/i-cant-understand-the-things-he-said-halperin-rips-bill-clintons-pay-the-bills-remark-video/.

24. Jennifer Rubin, "Bill Clinton: 'I gotta pay our bills,'" *Right Turn* (blog), May 4, 2015, https://www.washingtonpost.com/blogs/right-turn/wp/2015/05/04/bill-clinton-i-gotta-pay-our-bills/.

CHAPTER 2: PROFITING IN INDIA

1. Anu James, "2001 Gujarat Earthquake: When India Faced One of Its Worst Disasters 14 Years Ago," *International Business Times*, January 25, 2015, http://www.ibtimes.co.in/2001-gujarat-earthquake-when-india-faced-one-its-worst-disasters-14-years-ago-photos-621365.

2. Jake Miller, "15 years ago: Bill Clinton's historic denial," CBS News, January 26, 2013, http://www.cbsnews.com/news/15-years-ago-bill-clintons-historic-denial/.

3. "Vajpayee, Musharraf Talk over Gujarat Quake Calamity," ZeeNews, India, February 2, 2001, http://zeenews.india.com/home/vajpayee-musharraf-talk-over-gujarat-quake-calamity_7847.html.

4. Monica Whatley and Jeanne Batalova, "Indian Immigrants in the United States," Migration Policy Institute, August 21, 2013, http://www.migrationpolicy.org/article/indian-immigrants-united-states-0.

5. Bill Clinton, *Giving: How Each of Us Can Change the World* (New York: Alfred A. Knopf, 2007), 133–34.

6. James V. Grimaldi, "Denise Rich Gave Clinton Library $450,000," *Washington Post*, February 10, 2001, https://www.washingtonpost.com/archive/business/2001/02/10/denise-rich-gave-clinton-library-450000/e0e10291-841a-4e38-893e-d500ee4a5b30/.

7. Josh Gerstein, "Secrets of the Clinton Library," Politico, August 25, 2014, http://www.politico.com/story/2014/08/secrets-of-the-clinton-library-110289. See also Jeffrey St. Clair, "Bill Clinton and the Rich Women," *CounterPunch*, May 29, 2008, http://www.counterpunch.org/2008/05/29/bill-clinton-and-the-rich-women/.

8. Steven T. Miller, Internal Revenue Service, to William J. Clinton Presidential Foundation, letter 1045 dated January 29, 1998, https://www.clintonfoundation.org/sites/default/files/clinton_foundation_irs_determination_letters_1998_and_2002.pdf.

9. William J. Clinton Presidential Foundation, IRS Form 1023, "Application for Recognition of Exemption under Section 501(c)(3) of the Internal Revenue Code," dated December 23, 1997, https://www.clintonfoundation.org/sites/default/files/clinton_foundation_form_1023_application_for_tax_exemption.pdf.

10. "About Us: The American India Foundation Is Dedicated to Catalyzing Social and Economic Change in India and Building a Lasting Bridge Between the United States and India," AIF website, accessed March 23, 2016, http://aif.org/about/about-aif/.

11. Celia W. Dugger, "Whatever Happened to Bill Clinton? He's Playing India," *New York Times*, April 5, 2001, http://www.nytimes.com/2001/04/05/world/whatever-happened-to-bill-clinton-he-s-playing-india.html.

12. TNN, "Clinton's India Connection," *Times of India*, August 24, 2003, http://timesofindia.indiatimes.com/home/sunday-times/Clintons-India-connection/articleshow/144077.cms.

13. Specifically, the website reads, "Hon. William J. Clinton (Honorary Chair): 42nd President of the United States of America." See "Council of Trustees," AIF, accessed March 23, 2016, http://aif.org/about/people/trustees/.

14. Dugger, "Whatever Happened to Bill Clinton?"

15. K. G. Suresh, "Clinton Promises Focused Action Plan to Help Kutchis," rediff.com, April 4, 2001, http://www.rediff.com/news/2001/apr/04bill1.htm.

16. Suman Guha Mozumder, "Clinton's Foundation Raises $800,000 for Quake Relief," rediff.com, May 23, 2001, http://www.rediff.com/news/2001/may/23us9.htm.

17. Geeta Anand, "Bill Clinton Returns to India to Promote Health and Food Projects," *India Real Time* (blog), July 15, 2014, http://blogs.wsj.com/indiarealtime/2014/07/15/bill-clinton-returns-to-india-to-promote-health-and-food-projects/.

18. This phrase was taken from Charles K. Ortel, *Second Interim Report on the Clinton Foundation*, September 8, 2015, available online at the website of Charles Ortel, http://charlesortel.com/second-interim-report-on-the-clinton-foundation. See pages 15, 17, 22–23. The previous two paragraphs are also drawn from this Charles Ortel source.

19. Andrew Tangel, "Ex-Goldman Director Gets Two Years in Jail for Insider Trading," *Los Angeles Times*, October 24, 2012, http://articles.latimes.com/2012/oct/24/business/la-fi-mo-gupta-sentenced-20121024.

20. Alana Goodman, "String of Felons Worked with Nonprofit Cofounded by Bill Clinton," *Washington Free Beacon*, November 16, 2015, http://freebeacon.com/politics/string-of-felons-worked-with-nonprofit-cofounded-by-bill-clinton/.

21. Clinton, *Giving*, 133.

22. Michael Rothfeld, "The Rise and Fall of Rajat Gupta," *Wall Street Journal*, October 24, 2012, http://www.wsj.com/articles/SB10001424052970203400604578075291193560764.

23. Press Release, "SEC Charges Former Executives in Illegal Scheme to Enrich CEO with Perks," Securities and Exchange Commission, March 15, 2010, https://www.sec.gov/news/press/2010/2010-39.htm.

24. Shannon Henson, "InfoGroup Ex-CEO to Pay $7.3M to Settle SEC Claims," Law360, March 16, 2010, http://www.law360.com/articles/155700/infogroup-ex-ceo-to-pay-7-3m-to-settle-sec-claims.

25. Jonathan Allen, "Hillary Clinton Faces Scrutiny for Use of Private Jets," Bloomberg Business, January 29, 2015, http://www.bloomberg.com/news/articles/2015-01-29/hillary-clinton-flew-jets-on-taxpayer-funds-in-senate.

26. Bill McMorris, "Clintons' Wall Street Pal to Serve Out Prison Term," *Washington Free Beacon*, April 21, 2015, http://freebeacon.com/politics/clintons-wall-street-pal-to-serve-out-prison-term/.

27. John Helyar, Carol Hymowitz, and Mehul Srivastava, "Gupta Secretly Defied McKinsey Before SEC Tip Accusation," Bloomberg Business, May 17, 2011, http://www.bloomberg.com/news/articles/2011-05-17/gupta-secretly-defied-mckinsey-before-sec-s-tipster-accusation.

28. McMorris, "Clintons' Wall Street Pal to Serve Out Prison Term."

29. Stipulation of Settlement in Re: InfoUSA, Inc., Shareholders Litigation, in the Court of Chancery of the State of Delaware, August 20, 2008, http://www.sec.gov/Archives/edgar/data/879437/000095013408015652/d59811exv10w1.htm.

30. McMorris, "Clintons' Wall Street Pal to Serve Out Prison Term."

31. Sunita Sohrabji, "Rajat Gupta Headed Many India-Related Charities," *India West*, November 1, 2011, http://www.indiawest.com/news/global_indian/rajat-gupta-headed-many-india-related-charities/article_e91c28f8-51e5-595a-999d-693836816353.html.

32. Jerome R. Corsi, "Clinton Foundation 'Fraud Began with Exploiting Earthquake,'" WND, October 28, 2015, http://www.wnd.com/2015/10/clinton-foundation-fraud-began-with-exploiting-earthquake/.

33. The Office of the Secretary of State, "Search the Maryland Charities Database," Maryland.gov, accessed March 23, 2016, http://www.sos.state.md.us/Charity/SearchCharity.aspx.

34. "Charities," website of the Attorney General of Georgia Sam Olens, accessed March 23, 2016, http://law.ga.gov/charities.

CHAPTER 3: REINVENTING DAVOS

1. Alec MacGillis, "Scandal at Clinton Inc.: How Doug Band Drove a Wedge through a Political Dynasty," *New Republic*, September 22, 2013, https://newrepublic.com/article/114790/how-doug-band-drove-wedge-through-clinton-dynasty.

2. David A. Fahrenthold, Tom Hamburger, and Rosalind S. Helderman, "The Inside Story of How the Clintons Built a $2 Billion Global Empire," *Washington Post*, June 2, 2015, https://www.washingtonpost.com/politics/the-inside-story-of-how-the-clintons-built-a-2-billion-global-empire/2015/06/02/b6eab638-0957-11e5-a7ad-b430fc1d3f5c_story.html.

3. MacGillis, "Scandal at Clinton Inc."

4. Peter Schweizer, *Clinton Cash: The Untold Story of How and Why Foreign Governments and Businesses Helped Make Bill and Hillary Rich* (New York: HarperCollins, 2015).

5. MacGillis, "Scandal at Clinton Inc."

6. See "Ted Malloch: Senior Fellow in Management Practice," on the website of Said Business School, University of Oxford, accessed March 23, 2016, http://www.sbs.ox.ac.uk/community/people/ted-malloch.

7. Theodore Roosevelt Malloch, *Davos, Aspen & Yale: My Life Behind the Elite Curtain as a Global Sherpa* (Washington, DC: WND Books, 2016).

8. See, for instance, Theodore Roosevelt Malloch, with Jordan D. Mamorsky, *The End of Ethics and a Way Back: How to Fix a Fundamentally Broken Global Financial System* (New York: Wiley, 2013).

9. "Curriculum Vitae: Klaus Schwab, Founder and CEO," World Economic Forum website, accessed March 23, 2016, http://www.weforum.org/professor-klaus-schwab-founder-and-executive-chairman.

10. Malloch, *Davos, Aspen & Yale*, chap. 9.

11. Matthew Miller, "The Rise of Ron Burkle," *Forbes*, November 24, 2006, http://www.forbes.com/forbes/2006/1211/104.html.

12. Clinton Global Initiative, "Press Release: Second Annual Meeting of Clinton Global Initiative—3 Days, 215 Commitments, $7.3 Billion," ClintonFoundation.org, September 22, 2006, https://www.clintonfoundation.org/main/news-and-media/press-releases-and-statements/press-release-second-annual-meeting-of-clinton-global-initiative-3-days-215-comm.html.

13. *Los Angeles Times*, accessed March 24, 2016, http://www.latimes.com/nation/la-clinton2a_j8fkkfnc-photo.html.

14. Mike McIntire, "Clinton's Efforts on Ethanol Overlap Her Husband's Interests," *New York Times*, February 28, 2008, http://www.nytimes.com/2008/02/28/us/politics/28ethanol.html?_r=0&pagewanted=all.

15. Thomas B. Edsall, What Did Clinton Do to Get $15 Million from Ron Burkle?" *HuffPost Politics*, April 12, 2008, http://www.huffingtonpost.com/2008/04/04/what-did-bill-do-to-get-1_n_95189.html.

16. John R. Emshwiller, "Bill Clinton May Get Payout of $20 Million," *Wall Street Journal*, January

22, 2008, http://www.wsj.com/articles/SB120097424021905843.

17. Todd Purdum, "The Comeback Id," *Vanity Fair*, June 30, 2008, http://www.vanityfair.com/news/2008/07/clinton200807.

18. Evan Harper, "Ron Burkle Raised $10 Million for the Clintons. Now, He Has Almost Nothing to Do with Them." *Los Angeles Times*, January 7, 2016, http://www.latimes.com/nation/politics/la-na-ron-burkle-clintons-20160107-story.html.

19. Kim Masters, "Bill Clinton's $20 Million Breakup," *Daily Beast*, March 29, 2010, http://www.thedailybeast.com/articles/2010/03/29/bill-clintons-20-million-breakup.html.

20. Emshwiller, "Bill Clinton May Get Payout of $20 Million."

21. John R. Emshwiller and Gabriel Kahn, "How Bill Clinton's Aide Facilitated a Messy Deal," *Wall Street Journal*, September 26, 2007, http://www.wsj.com/articles/SB119076741770539360.

22. Alec MacGillis, "Scandal at Clinton Inc.," *New Republic*, September 22, 2013, https://newrepublic.com/article/114790/how-doug-band-drove-wedge-through-clinton-dynasty.

23. Emshwiller and Kahn, "How Bill Clinton's Aide Facilitated a Messy Deal."

24. Getty Images, "Clinton Global Initiative Holds Reception at Museum of Modern Art," September 20, 2006, http://www.gettyimages.com/detail/news-photo/actress-anne-hathaway-and-boyfriend-raffaello-follieri-news-photo/71954768.

25. Clinton Global Initiative, "Press Release: Clinton Global Initiative Two Day Total—139 Commitments, Almost $6 billion," ClintonFoundation.org, September 21, 2006, https://www.clintonfoundation.org/main/news-and-media/press-releases-and-statements/press-release-clinton-global-initiative-day-two-total-139-commitments-almost-6-b.html.

26. Michael Shnayerson, "The Follieri Charade," *Vanity Fair*, September 30, 2008, http://www.vanityfair.com/news/2008/10/follieri200810.

27. John R. Emshwiller, "Burkle v. Follieri Offers a Window on Ugly Breakup," *Wall Street Journal*, June 14, 2007, http://www.wsj.com/articles/SB118178401183834708.

28. Jose Martinez and Bill Hutchinson, "Anne Hathaway's Ex-Boyfriend, Raffaello Follieri, Arrested on Fraud Charge," *New York Daily News*, June 24, 2008, http://www.nydailynews.com/entertainment/gossip/anne-hathaway-ex-boyfriend-raffaello-follieri-arrested-fraud-charge-article-1.293454.

29. Lama Hasan and Katie Hinman, "Anne Hathaway's Ex Raffaello Follieri 'Happy' for Actress, Ready to 'Live My Life' after Prison," ABC News, June 27, 2012, http://abcnews.go.com/Entertainment/anne-hathaways-raffaello-follieri-happy-actress-ready-live/story?id=16656717.

30. Glenn Thrush, Maggie Haberman, and John Bresnahan, "Abedin repped clients while at State," Politico, May 16, 2013, http://www.politico.com/story/2013/05/huma-abedin-consultant-state-091503.

31. S.A. Miller, "State Dept. Sued over Huma Abedin *pay deal*," *New York Post*, September 25, 2013, http://nypost.com/2013/09/25/state-dept-sued-over-huma-abedin-pay-deal/.

32. Rosalind S. Helderman and Tom Hamburger, "How Huma Abedin Operated at the Center of the Clinton Universe," *Washington Post*, August 27, 2015, https://www.washingtonpost.com/politics/how-huma-abedin-operated-at-the-center-of-the-clinton-universe/2015/08/27/cd099eee-4b32-11e5-902f-39e9219e574b_story.html.

33. Aaron Klein, "The Explosive Secret Huma Is Hiding," WND, July 25, 2013, http://www.wnd.com/2013/07/the-explosive-secret-huma-is-hiding/.

34. Tierney McAfee, "Hillary Clinton's Top Aide Huma Abedin Describes the 'Amazing' Moment They first met: I Thought, 'Oh My God, She's So Beautiful,'" People, April 4, 2016, http://www.people.com/article/huma-abedin-hillary-clinton-first-meeting.

35. Rachael Bade, "Hillary Email Probe Turns to Huma," Politico, August 13, 2015, http://www.politico.com/story/2015/08/hillary-clinton-email-probe-turns-to-huma-121314.

36. Rachael Bade, "Emails Show Huma Abedin's Ties to Private Consulting Firm," Politico, September 23, 2015, http://www.politico.com/story/2015/09/huma-abedin-teneo-clinton-foundation-email-213965.

37. Rachael Bade, "Sen. Grassley Asks FBI for Clarification on Huma Abedin Probe," Politico, August 5, 2015, http://www.politico.com/story/2015/08/sen-chuck-grassley-asks-fbi-for-clarification-on-huma-abedin-probe-121072.

38. Patrick Howley, "Exclusive: Senator Grassley Slams Clinton Aide as 'Unresponsive,'" Breitbart, August 24, 2015, http://www.breitbart.com/big-government/2015/08/24/exclusive-senator-grassley-slams-clinton-aide-as-unresponsive/.

39. Isabel Vincent and Melissa Klein, "Clinton Confidant Cuts Ties with Formidable Family," *New York Post*, June 21, 2015, http://nypost.com/2015/06/21/clinton-confidant-cuts-ties-with-the-formidable-family/.

40. Caroline Howe, "Exclusive: Power-Hungry Chelsea Clinton Pushed the Man Who Was Bill's 'Surrogate Son' out of the Clinton Foundation and Now She's Even Jealous of Her Husband Marc, Who's Grown Closer to Her Father, Says New Book," *Daily Mail* (UK), September 30, 2015, http://www.dailymail.co.uk/news/article-3255198/Power-hungry-Chelsea-Clinton-pushed-man-Bill-s-surrogate-son-Clinton-Foundation-s-jealous-husband-Marc-s-getting-closer-father.html.

41. Edward Klein, *Unlikeable: The Problem with Hillary* (Washington, DC: Regnery, 2015), 93–95.

42. Ibid., 93.

43. Nicholas Confessore and Amy Chozick, "Unease at Clinton Foundation over Finances and Ambitions," *New York Times*, August 13, 2013, http://www.nytimes.com/2013/08/14/us/politics/unease-at-clinton-foundation-over-finances-and-ambitions.html?_r=0.

44. Clinton Foundation, "Eric Braverman Named Chief Executive Officer of the Clinton Foundation," press release, July 2, 2013, https://www.clintonfoundation.org/main/news-and-media/press-releases-and-statements/eric-braverman-named-chief-executive-officer-of-the-clinton-foundation.html.

45. Stuart Jeffries, "The Firm," *Guardian* (UK), February 21, 2003, http://www.theguardian.com/education/2003/feb/21/mbas.highereducation.

46. Evgenia Peretz, "How Chelsea Clinton Took Charge of Clintonworld," *Vanity Fair*, August 31, 2015, http://www.vanityfair.com/news/2015/08/chelsea-clinton-foundation-nbc-first-daughter.

47. Confessore and Chozick, "Unease at Clinton Foundation over Finances and Ambitions."

48. Maggie Haberman, "Bill Clinton Changes Relationship with Teneo," *Burns & Haberman Blog*, February 19, 2012, http://www.politico.com/blogs/burns-haberman/2012/02/bill-clinton-changes-relationship-with-teneo-114956.

49. Steven Shepard, "Clinton Foundation CEO Steps Down," Politico, January 9, 2015, http://www.politico.com/story/2015/01/clinton-foundation-replaces-ceo-114113.

50. Kenneth P. Vogel, "Eric Braverman Tried to Change the Clinton Foundation. Then He Quit," *Politico Magazine*, March 1, 2015, http://www.politico.com/magazine/story/2015/03/clinton-foundation-eric-braverman-115598.

51. Rosalind S. Helderman, "Shalala Formally Named New Head of the Clinton Foundation," *Washington Post*, March 11, 2015, https://www.washingtonpost.com/news/post-politics/wp/2015/03/11/shalala-formally-named-new-head-of-the-clinton-foundation/.

CHAPTER 4: THE CANADA SCAM

1. Jo Becker and Don Van Natta Jr., "After Mining Deal, Financier Donated to Clinton," *New York*

Times, January 31, 2008, http://www.nytimes.com/2008/01/31/us/politics/31donor.html?_r=0.

2. Douglas Todd, "Frank Giustra: Rescuing Global Capitalism from Itself," *The Search* (blog), September 13, 2008, http://blogs.vancouversun.com/2008/09/13/frank-giustra-rescuing-global-capitalism-from-itself/.

3. Lisa Wright, "Clintons' Canadian Buddy," *Toronto Star*, February 3, 2008, http://www.thestar.com/business/2008/02/03/clintons_canadian_buddy.html.

4. *Vancouver Sun*, "Media-Shy Giustra a Friend of Former President," November 13, 2005, Canada.com, http://www.canada.com/story_print.html?id=4a72b62c-ed7d-42c6-9a4d-bb36cc6eb3b3&sponsor=.

5. Margaret Wente, "It Pays to Be a Friend of Bill," *Toronto Globe and Mail*, March 4, 2008, http://www.theglobeandmail.com/globe-debate/it-pays-to-be-a-friend-of-bill/article1052354/.

6. Robert Lenzner, "Clinton Commits No Foul in Kazakhstan Uranium Deal," January 12, 2009, http://www.forbes.com/2009/01/12/giustra-clinton-kazakhstan-pf-ii-in_rl_0912croesus_inl.html.

7. Peter Schweizer, *Clinton Cash: The Untold Story of How and Why Foreign Governments and Businesses Helped Make Bill and Hillary Rich* (New York: HarperCollins, 2015), chap. 2, "The Transfer: Bill's Excellent Kazakh Adventure" (21–37); and chap. 3, "Hillary's Reset: The Russian Uranium Deal," (39–57).

8. Ibid., 27.

9. Ibid., 21.

10. Ibid., 29.

11. Transcript, "Chris Wallace Grills Lanny Davis on Clinton Cash: Except 'For a Few Inadvertent Errors,' The Clintons Have Been Transparent," *RealClearPolitics*, April 26, 2015, http://www.realclearpolitics.com/video/2015/04/26/chris_wallace_grills_lanny_davis_on_clinton_cash_except_for_a_few_inadvertent_errors_the_clintons_have_been_transparent.html.

12. Becker and Van Natta, "After Mining Deal, Financier Donated to Clinton."

13. Wilson Andrews, "Donations to the Clinton Foundation, and a Russian Uranium Takeover," *New York Times*, April 22, 2015, http://www.nytimes.com/interactive/2015/04/23/us/clinton-foundation-donations-uranium-investors.html.

14. Transcript, "Chris Wallace Grills Lanny Davis on Clinton Cash."

15. U.S. Department of the Treasury, "The Committed on Foreign Investment in the United States (CIFUS)," Resource Center, last updated December 20, 2012, https://www.treasury.gov/resource-center/international/Pages/Committee-on-Foreign-Investment-in-US.aspx.

16. Schweizer, *Clinton Cash*, 54.

17. Michael Patrick Leahy, "Clinton Cash Uranium Deal Approved by Foreign Investment Committee 52 Days after Shareholders Finalized Takeover," Breitbart News, May 4, 2005, http://www.breitbart.com/big-government/2015/05/04/clinton-cash-uranium-deal-approved-by-foreign-investment-committee-52-days-after-shareholders-finalized-takeover/.

18. Michael Patrick Leahy, "Sen. Grassley Demands DOJ Answers about Hillary's 'Clinton Cash' Uranium Transfer to Russia," Breitbart News, July 2, 2015, http://www.breitbart.com/big-government/2015/07/02/senate-judiciary-committee-chairman-demands-doj-answer-questions-about-hillarys-role-in-uranium-deal/.

19. Transcript, "Chris Wallace Grills Lanny Davis on Clinton Cash."

20. *Vancouver Sun*, "Archived Profile: Frank Giustra," June 21, 2007, http://www.canada.com/vancouversun/story.html?id=1227e085-a744-4f9e-aef8-cf646d92f72f.

21. Patrick Brethour, Andy Hoffman, and Sinclair Stewart, "The Pursuit of Wealth for the Greater Good," *Globe and Mail*, June 22, 2007, last updated March 13, 2009, http://www.theglobeandmail.

com/news/national/the-pursuit-of-wealth-for-the-greater-good/article688229/.

22. "Lionsgate Entertainment Corporation History," Funding Universe, accessed March 24, 2016, http://www.fundinguniverse.com/company-histories/lions-gate-entertainment-corporation-history/. See also Encyclopedia.com, s.v. "Lionsgate Entertainment Corporation," accessed March 24, 2016, http://www.encyclopedia.com/doc/1G2-2843900080.html.

23. "Lionsgate Entertainment Corp/CN/—Form 10-K/A," getfilings.com, July 29, 2010, http://www.getfilings.com/sec-filings/100729/LIONS-GATE-ENTERTAINMENT-CORP-CN-_10-K.A/.

24. Wright, "Clintons' Canadian Buddy."

25. "Executive Profile: Frank Giustra," Bloomberg Business, December 28, 2015, http://www.bloomberg.com/research/stocks/private/person.asp?personId=230079&privcapId=58101798.

26. Brian Hutchinson, "Furious B.C. Magnate Says He's Caught Up in 'Vicious' Smear Campaign against Clinton Charities," *National Post*, May 6, 2015, http://news.nationalpost.com/news/canada/furious-b-c-magnate-says-hes-caught-up-in-vicious-smear-campaign-against-clinton-charities.

27. Paul Bond, "Lionsgate to Distribute Dinesh D'Souza's 'America,'" *Hollywood Reporter*, May 6, 2014, http://www.hollywoodreporter.com/news/lionsgate-distribute-dinesh-dsouzas-america-701693.

28. Lionsgate Entertainment Corporation, Yahoo! Finance, accessed March 24, 2016, http://finance.yahoo.com/q/pr?s=LGF+Profile.

29. Anu Narayanswamy, "Travels with Bill and Frank: A Look at the Clinton-Giustra Friendship," *Washington Post*, May 3, 2015, https://www.washingtonpost.com/news/post-politics/wp/2015/05/03/travels-with-bill-and-frank-a-look-at-the-clinton-giustra-friendship/.

30. Tom Hamburger, Rosalind S. Helderman, and Anu Narayanswamy, "The Clintons, a Luxury Jet and Their $100 Million Donor from Canada," *Washington Post*, May 3, 2015, https://www.washingtonpost.com/politics/the-clintons-a-luxury-jet-and-their-100-million-donor/2015/05/03/688051d0-ecef-11e4-8abc-d6aa3bad79dd_story.html.

31. Narayanswamy, "Travels with Bill and Frank."

32. David Remnick, "The Wanderer: Bill Clinton's Quest to Save the World, Reclaim His Legacy—and Elect His Wife," *New Yorker*, September 18, 2006, http://www.newyorker.com/magazine/2006/09/18/the-wanderer-3.

33. Andrew Jack, "Charm offensive," *Financial Times*, August 19, 2006, http://www.ft.com/intl/cms/s/0/6f1b8566-2f1e-11db-a973-0000779e2340.html#axzz3vdpnULee.

34. Schweizer, *Clinton Cash*, 44.

35. Ibid., 45.

36. Siobhan Hughes and James V. Grimaldi, "Clinton Foundation Provides Details on Canadian Donation," *Wall Street Journal*, April 26, 2015, http://www.wsj.com/articles/clinton-foundation-provides-details-on-canadian-donation-1430092540.

37. "Frank Giustra, Fiore Financial Corporation," Cambridge House, accessed March 24, 2016, https://cambridgehouse.com/u/20882/frank-giustra.

38. The 2007 IRS Form 990 for the Clinton Foundation is included with the BKD "Independent Accountants' Report and Financial Statements," dated December 31, 2007 and 2006, archived on the Clinton Foundation website, https://www.clintonfoundation.org/files/2007_Audit.pdf.

39. Jo Becker and Mike McIntire, "Cash Flowed to Clinton Foundation Amid Russian Uranium Deal," *New York Times*, April 23, 2015, http://www.nytimes.com/2015/04/24/us/cash-flowed-to-clinton-foundation-as-russians-pressed-for-control-of-uranium-company.html?_r=0.

40. Mike McIntire and Jo Becker, "Canadian Partnership Shielded Identities of Donors to Clinton Foundation," *New York Times*, April 29, 2015, http://www.nytimes.com/2015/04/30/us/politics/canadian-partnership-shielded-identities-of-donors-to-clinton-foundation.html.

41. Schweizer, *Clinton Cash*, 45.

42. "Contributor and Grantor Information," Clinton Foundation website, accessed March 24, 2016, https://www.clintonfoundation.org/contributors.

43. McIntire and Becker, "Canadian Partnership Shielded Identities of Donors to Clinton Foundation."

44. Becker Mike McIntire, "Cash Flowed to Clinton Foundation Amid Russian Uranium Deal."

45. Schweizer, *Clinton Cash*, 35–36.

46. John Sexton, "Canadian Charity's Revenue Dropped Substantially the Year Hillary Clinton Resigned as Secretary of State," Breitbart News, April 30, 2013, http://www.breitbart.com/big-government/2015/04/30/canadian-charitys-revenue-dropped-substantially-the-year-hillary-clinton-resigned-as-secretary-of-state/.

47. Schweizer, *Clinton Cash*, 112.

48. Stephen Braun (AP), "Bill Clinton Company Shows Complexity of Family Finances," May 26, 2015, http://news.yahoo.com/bill-clinton-company-shows-complexity-family-finances-180745584--election.html. This AP article was widely published. For international coverage, see Associated Press, "Hillary Clinton's Financial Disclosure Omitted 'Pass-Through' Company Used by Bill Clinton to Collect Consulting Fees—and Nobody Knows How Much," *Daily Mail*, May 26, 2015, http://www.dailymail.co.uk/news/article-3098027/Bill-Clinton-company-shows-complexity-family-finances.html.

49. Ibid.

50. Money Laundering Threat Assessment Working Group, *U.S. Money Laundering Threat Assessment* (December 2005), chap. 8, "Shell Companies and Trusts," 47, https://www.treasury.gov/resource-center/terrorist-illicit-finance/Documents/mlta.pdf. See also: US Department of the Treasury, *National Money Laundering Risk Assessment* (2015), 43–44, https://www.treasury.gov/resource-center/terrorist-illicit-finance/Documents/National%20Money%20Laundering%20Risk%20Assessment%20–%2006-12-2015.pdf.

51. Federal Financial Institutions Examination Council, *Bank Secrecy Act Anti-Money Laundering Examination Manual*, no date, https://www.ffiec.gov/bsa_aml_infobase/pages_manual/OLM_097.htm.

52. Gwen Preston, "Giustra Gives U.S. $100M to Charity," *Northern Miner*, July 2, 2007, http://www.northernminer.com/news/giustra-gives-us-100m-to-charity/1000213489/.

53. Lachlan Markay, "Clinton Foundation Quietly Revises Mexican Billionaire's Donation," *Washington Free Beacon*, August 12, 2015, http://freebeacon.com/politics/clinton-foundation-quietly-revises-mexican-billionaires-donation/.

54. "Contributor Information: Cumulative through 2015," Clinton Foundation website, accessed March 24, 2016, https://www.clintonfoundation.org/contributors?category=%24250%2C001%20to%20%24500%2C000&page=2.

55. "More About the Clinton Giustra Enterprise Program," on the Clinton Giustra Enterprise Partnership at ClintonFoundation.org, accessed March 24, 2016, https://www.clintonfoundation.org/our-work/clinton-giustra-enterprise-partnership.

56. Press Releases, "GGI America Attendees Make 79 New Commitments to Action to Impact Lives of More than 1.6 Million People in the United States," Clinton Global Initiative, June 10, 2015, http://press.clintonglobalinitiative.org/press_releases/cgi-america-attendees-make-79-new-commitments-to-action-to-impact-lives-of-more-than-1-6-million-people-in-the-united-states/.

57. "Press Release: Second Annual Meeting of Clinton Global Initiative—3 Days, 215 Commitments, $7.3 Billion," Clinton Global Initiative, September 22, 2006, https://www.clintonfoundation.org/main/news-and-media/press-releases-and-statements/press-release-second-annual-meeting-of-clinton-global-initiative-3-days-215-comm.html.

58. Priscilla Murphy, "The Only Risk Is Wanting to Stay," Inter-American Development Bank, September 30, 2010, http://www.iadb.org/Micamericas/section/detail.cfm?language=English&id=8083.

59. Alana Goodman, "Clinton Foundation Running Private Equity Fund in Colombia," *Washington Free Beacon*, November 18, 2015, http://freebeacon.com/politics/clinton-foundation-running-private-equity-fund-in-colombia/.

60. Alana Goodman, "Clinton Foundation's Colombian 'Private Equity Fund' Was Unregistered," *Washington Free Beacon*, November 23, 2015, http://freebeacon.com/politics/clinton-foundations-colombian-private-equity-fund-was-unregistered/.

61. Amy Davidson, "Five Questions about the Clintons and a Uranium Company," *New Yorker*, April 24, 2015, http://www.newyorker.com/news/amy-davidson/five-questions-about-the-clintons-and-a-uranium-company.

62. This and the next four paragraphs are quoted directly or otherwise drawn heavily from *Free Republic* comments submitted by "Liz," in response to a posting on May 3, 2015, of an article published by *New York Post* discussing Peter Schweizer's book *Clinton Cash*, http://www.freerepublic.com/focus/f-news/3285741/posts. Despite attempts to establish contact with "Liz," her identity remains unknown. Judging from the content of her various *Free Republic* posts over time, "Liz" appears to have a professional's command of Bank Secrecy Act requirements. She appears to be an expert on the Bank Secrecy Act requirements imposed on financial institutions operating in the United States to detect money laundering and other financial transactions suspicious for criminal activity. The *New York Post* article in question was Kyle Smith, "Hill and Bill Can't Hide from Shady Deals Exposed in 'Clinton Cash,'" *New York Post*, May 3, 2015, http://nypost.com/2015/05/03/clinton-cash-is-a-blistering-indictment-of-hill-and-bills-behavior/.

63. Maura Pally, "A Commitment to Honesty, Transparency, and Accountability," Clinton Foundation, ClintonFoudation.org, April 26, 2015, https://www.clintonfoundation.org/blog/2015/04/26/commitment-honesty-transparency-and-accountability.

CHAPTER 5: THE HIV/AIDS SCAM

1. Bill Clinton, *Giving: How Each One of Us Can Change the World* (New York: Knopf, 2007), 179.

2. "Clinton and Mandela rally AIDS fight," CNN, July 12, 2012, http://www.cnn.com/2002/WORLD/europe/07/12/aids.conference/.

3. "AIDS 2002 Barcelona: Bill Clinton's HIV/AIDS Record of Shame! 'We Cannot Forgive, and Must Never Forget' Act Up New York," posted on the website of actupny.org, accessed March 25, 2016, http://www.actupny.org/reports/bcn/BCNclinton.html.

4. Clinton, *Giving*, 179.

5. Peter Petre and Darienne L. Denis, "A Liberal Gets Rich Yet Keeps the Faith," *Fortune* magazine, August 31, 1987, http://archive.fortune.com/magazines/fortune/fortune_archive/1987/08/31/69480/index.htm. See also "Ira Magaziner—Student Activism," LiquidSearch.com, accessed March 25, 2016, http://www.liquisearch.com/ira_magaziner/student_activism.

6. Roger Stone and Robert Morrow, *The Clintons' War on Women* (New York: Skyhorse, 2015), 40–41.

7. Petre and Denis, "A Liberal Gets Rich Yet Keeps the Faith."

8. Ibid.

9. Nicholas Confessore and Amy Chozick, "Unease at Clinton Foundation over Finances and Ambitions," *New York Times*, August 13, 2013, http://www.nytimes.com/2013/08/14/us/politics/unease-at-clinton-foundation-over-finances-and-ambitions.html?_r=0.

10. Maureen Dowd, "Money, Money, Money, Money, MONEY!" *New York Times*, August 17, 2013, http://www.nytimes.com/2013/08/18/opinion/sunday/dowd-money-money-money-money-money.html?ref=topics.

11. Maggie Haberman, "Review Reveal Divisions Within the Clinton Health Initiative, Starting at the Top," *New York Times*, November 18, 2015, http://www.nytimes.com/2015/11/19/us/politics/reviews-reveal-divisions-within-the-clinton-health-initiative-starting-at-the-top.html?ref=topics.

12. Jonathan Rauch, "This Is Not Charity," *Atlantic*, October 2007, http://www.theatlantic.com/magazine/archive/2007/10/-this-is-not-charity/306197/.

13. Caribbean Community (CARICOM), "Memorandum of Understanding Signed with the William J. Clinton Presidential Foundation," press release, August 22, 2001, http://www.caricom.org/jsp/pressreleases/pres105_02.jsp?null&prnf=1.

14. Clinton, *Giving*, 179–80.

15. "Ahern's €110m Donation to Clinton Makes Ireland Third Largest Buyer of AIDS Drugs," *Irish Examiner*, July 8, 2003; Kaiser Health News, "Ireland, Clinton Foundation Sign $158.2 Million Agreement to Provide AIDS Drugs to Mozambique," KHN Morning Briefing, July 9, 2003, http://khn.org/morning-breakout/dr00018695/.

16. See Development Cooperation Division, Department of Foreign Affairs and Trade, "Irish Aid," Government of Ireland, https://www.irishaid.ie/about-us/.

17. "Irish Aid Annual Report 2004," Development Cooperation Division, Department of Foreign Affairs and Trade, "Irish Aid," Government of Ireland, https://www.irishaid.ie/news-publications/publications/publicationsarchive/2005/september/irish-aid-annual-report-2004/.

18. "Taoiseach and President Clinton sign €70 million agreement to fight HIV/AIDS in Africa," press release, September 23, 2006, http://www.taoiseach.gov.ie/eng/News/Archives/2006/Taoiseach's_Press_Releases_2006/Taoiseach_and_President_Clinton_sign_%E2%82%AC70_million_agreement_to_fight_HIV_AIDS_in_Africa.html#sthash.HdfpK7QY.dpuf; no longer accessible. See Kaiser Health News, "Ireland, Clinton Foundation Sign $158.2 Million Agreement to Provide AIDS Drugs to Mozambique."

19. See "Press Release: Irish Government Announces Agreement with Clinton Foundation to Support HIV/AIDS Work in Lesotho and Mozambique," Clinton Foundation website, September 29, 2006, https://www.clintonfoundation.org/main/news-and-media/press-releases-and-statements/press-release-irish-government-announces-agreement-with-clinton-foundation-to-su.html.

20. James V. Grimaldi and Rebecca Ballhaus, "Clinton Charity Tapped Foreign Friends," *Wall Street Journal*, March 19, 2015, http://www.wsj.com/articles/clinton-charity-tapped-foreign-friends-1426818602.

21. James V. Grimaldi, "Clinton Foundation to Keep Foreign Donors," *Wall Street Journal*, April 15, 2015, http://www.wsj.com/articles/clinton-foundation-to-keep-foreign-donors-1429140593.

22. *Irish Aid Annual Report 2014*, Development Cooperation Division, Department of Foreign Affairs and Trade, "Irish Aid," Government of Ireland, https://www.irishaid.ie/media/irishaid/allwebsitemedia/20newsandpublications/publicationpdfsenglish/Irish-Aid-Annual-Report-2014-final.pdf.

23. Office of the Revenue Commissioners, Charities Section, Government Offices, Nenagh, Co. Tipperary, Ireland, "Frequently Asked Questions—Charities," Irish Tax and Customs, Revenue Law, accessed March 25, 2016, http://www.revenue.ie/en/business/faqs-charities.html#section11.

24. Oonagh B. Breen, Patrick Ford, and Gareth G. Morgan, "Cross-Border Issues in the Regulation of Charities: Experiences from the UK and Ireland," n.d., https://c.ymcdn.com/sites/www.istr.org/resource/resmgr/working_papers_barcelona/breen.ford.morgan.pdf, accessed March 25, 2016.

25. This section draws heavily on the work of Charles Ortel as reported in Jerome R. Corsi, "Drip, Drip, Drip: New Clinton Foundation Scandal!" WND, October 6, 2015, http://www.wnd.com/2015/10/drip-drip-drip-new-clinton-foundation-scandal/. All Ortel quotes in this section are from this article.

26. James O'Brien, "Global Charity Admits €25 'Missing' in Massive Fraud," *Irish Independent*, January 25, 2011, http://www.independent.ie/irish-news/global-charity-admits-25m-missing-in-massive-fraud-26617213.html.

27. This subsection and the next draws heavily on the work of Charles Ortel as reported in Jerome R. Corsi, "Clinton Foundation Illegally Solicited Tax-Exempt Donations," WND, September 13, 2015, http://www.wnd.com/2015/09/clinton-foundation-illegally-solicited-tax-exempt-donations/.

28. Charles Ortel, Executive Summary, "False Philanthropy: Second Interim Report Concerning Public Disclosures of the Bill, Hillary & Chelsea Clinton Foundation," November 24, 2015, http://charlesortel.com. Much of this subsection also draws on material previously published by Charles Ortel in this "Second Interim Report," reprinted in Corsi, "Clinton Foundation Illegally Solicited Tax-Exempt Donations." Again, this subsection and the next draw heavily on Ortel's work as cited in his Second Interim Report and reported in WND as noted here.

29. BKD, "William J. Clinton Presidential Foundation, Inc., Independent Accountants' Report and Financial Statements (Modified Cash Basis) December 31, 2004 and 2003," Found at the website of the Office of the Massachusetts Attorney General, Non-Profits & Charities, under the entry for the "Clinton Foundation HIV/AIDS Initiative, Inc." AG Account Number: 043231. Federal Tax ID (FEIN): 20-092162, http://www.charities.ago.state.ma.us/charities/index.asp?charities_app_ctx=details&charities_sub_ctx=entry&origin=search&did=2834313329&bod=1460126457.

30. Clinton Foundation, "William J. Clinton Foundation Annual Report 2004." Found on the Clinton Foundation website at https://www.clintonfoundation.org/files/2004_AR.pdf.

31. Clinton Foundation HIV/AIDS Initiative, Inc, IRS Form 990, 2004. Found at the website of the Office of the Massachusetts Attorney General, Non-Profits & Charities, under the entry for the "Clinton Foundation HIV/AIDS Initiative, Inc." AG Account Number: 043231. Federal Tax ID (FEIN): 20-092162, http://www.charities.ago.state.ma.us/charities/index.asp?charities_app_ctx=details&charities_sub_ctx=entry&origin=search&did=2834313329&bod=1460126457.

32. Clinton Global Initiative, Inc., IRS FORM 1023, "Application for Recognition of Exemption Under Section 501(c)(3) of the Internal Revenue Code, dated August 9, 2010, https://www.clintonfoundation.org/sites/default/files/cgi_1023.pdf.

33. IRS "Determination Letter," addressed to the Clinton Global Initiative, Inc., Little Rock, AR, October 6, 2010, https://www.clintonfoundation.org/sites/default/files/cgi_irs_determination_letter.pdf.

34. Jeffrey S. Tenenbaum, Venable LLP, "Forming and Operating Subsidiaries and Related Entities: Maximizing the Benefits and Minimizing the Risks," ASAE, June 2002, https://www.venable.com/forming-and-operating-subsidiaries-and-related-entities-maximizing-the-benefits-and-minimizing-the-risks-01-01-1999/.

35. Charles Ortel, Executive Summary, "False Philanthropy: Second Interim Report Concerning Public Disclosures of THE Bill, Hillary & Chelsea Clinton Foundation," September 8, 2015, https://phaven-prod.s3.amazonaws.com/files/document_part/asset/1556725/s4dUYTpsSqmLI_05SWxZJK_CJyg/False_Philanthropy_2.pdf.

36. Ethan B. Busby and Joshua W. Kapstein, *AIDS Drugs for All: Social Movements and Market Transformations* (Oxford, UK: Cambridge University Press, 2013), 164.

37. Kaiser Health News, "Former President Clinton Visits Generic Drug Maker Ranbaxy in India, Shows Support for Lower-Cost AIDS Drugs," KHN Morning Briefing, November 21, 2003, http://khn.org/morning-breakout/dr00020986/.

38. Busby and Kapstein, *AIDS Drugs for* All, 164–65.

39. Lael Brainard, Abigail Jones, and Nigel Purvis (editors), *Climate Change and Global Poverty: A Billion Lives in the Balance?* (Washington, DC: Brookings Institute Press, 2009), 191.

40. "UNITAID and the Clinton HIV/AIDS Initiative Announce New Price Reductions for Key Drugs," Press Release, UNITAID, accessed March 25, 2016, http://www.unitaid.eu/en/resources/news/198-unitaid-and-the-clinton-hivaids-initiative-announce-new-price-reductions-for-key-drugs.

41. Charles Ortel, Executive Summary, "False Philanthropy: Second Interim Report Concerning Public Disclosures of the Bill, Hillary & Chelsea Clinton Foundation," September 8, 2015, op.cit.

42. "How UNITAID Came About," UNITAID, accessed March 25, 2016, http://www.unitaid.eu/en/about/-background-mainmenu-18/159.

43. Ortel, "False Philanthropy."

44. Charles Ortel, "False Philanthropy? First Interim Report Concerning Disclosures of the Bill, Hillary & Chelsea Clinton Foundation," April 20, 2015, https://phaven-prod.s3.amazonaws.com/files/document_part/asset/1415940/urnZzpSpSWlQ3OQRKOXI_UNI-u4/First_Interim_Report_Clinton_Foundation__Charles_Ortel_.pdf. See also Jerome R. Corsi, "'Big 4' Firm 'Let Clintons Skim Millions from Aids Charity,'" WND, June 16, 2015, http://www.wnd.com/2015/06/big-4-firm-let-clintons-skim-millions-from-aids-charity/.

45. E2Pi, the Global Health Group, "Partnership Profile: UNITAID," July 2004, Global Health Sciences, University of California–San Francisco, http://globalhealthsciences.ucsf.edu/sites/default/files/content/ghg/e2pi-unitaid-profile.pdf.

46. Katherine Eban, "Dirty Medicine: The Epic Inside Story of Long-Term Criminal Fraud of Ranbaxy, the Indian Drug Company That Makes Generic Lipitor for Millions of Americans," *Fortune*, May 15, 2013, http://fortune.com/2013/05/15/dirty-medicine/.

47. Katherine Eban, "Maker of Generic Lipitor Pleads Guilty to Selling 'Adulterated Drugs,'" *Fortune*, May 13, 2013, http://fortune.com/2013/05/13/maker-of-generic-lipitor-pleads-guilty-to-selling-adulterated-drugs/.

48. U.S. Department of Justice, "Generic Drug Manufacturer Ranbaxy Pleads Guilty and Agrees to Pay $500 Million to Resolve False Claims Allegations, cGMP Violations and False Statements to the FDA," press release, May 13, 2013, http://www.justice.gov/opa/pr/generic-drug-manufacturer-ranbaxy-pleads-guilty-and-agrees-pay-500-million-resolve-false.

49. Eban, "Dirty Medicine."

50. United Nations World Health Organization, "Ranbaxy Withdraws All Its Antiretroviral Medicines from WHO Prequalification," press release, November 9, 2004, http://www.who.int/mediacentre/news/releases/2004/pr79/en/.

51. Henry J. Kaiser Family Foundation, "Indian Generic Drug Firm Ranbaxy Announces Seven Antiretroviral Drugs Reinstated to WHO-Approved List," TheBody.com, August 16, 2005, http://www.thebody.com/content/art9525.html.

52. UNITAID, "CHAI, UNITAID and DFID Announce Lower Prices for HIV/AIDS Medicines in Developing Countries," press release, May 17, 2011, http://www.unitaid.eu/en/resources/331-clinton-health-access-initiative-unitaid-and-dfid-announce-lower-prices-for-hivaids-medicines-in-developing-countries.

53. Eban, "Dirty Medicine."

54. Economic Times Bureau, "Bill Clinton Praises Pharma Companies Ranbaxy and Cipla for Fight against AIDS," *Economic Times* (India), April 11, 2013, http://articles.economictimes.indiatimes.com/2013-04-11/news/38463484_1_clinton-foundation-india-inc-drug-maker-cipla.

55. Vikas Pota, India, Inc: How India's Top Ten Entrepreneurs Are Winning Globally (Boston: Nicolas Brealey, 2010), 73.

56. Josy Joseph, "Clinton's Plan: Making AIDS Drugs Affordable," rediff.com, November 21, 2003, http://www.rediff.com/money/2003/nov/21clinton.htm; "Ranbaxy Joins Hands with Clinton Foundation on Drugs for HIV/AIDS," India Business Wire, October 27, 2003, http://businesswireindia.com/news/news-details/ranbaxy-joins-hands-with-clinton-foundation-drugs-hivaids/4084.

57. Joseph, "Clinton's Plan."

58. UNITAID, "Financial Reports: 2013 Financial Statements," UNITAID.eu, http://www.unitaid.eu/en/about/budget-mainmenu-130.

59. UNITAID, Resolution Number 8, UNITAID Board Meeting of November 29–30, 2006, "Action name: HIV/AIDS—Pediatric ARV; Partner organizations: Clinton Foundation—HIV/AIDS Initiative (CHAI)," UNITAID.eu, http://www.unitaid.eu/images/governance/eb2en/utd_eb2_res8_en.pdf.

60. This section is drawn heavily from Corsi, "'Big 4' Firm 'Let Clintons Skim Millions from Aids Charity.'" See also Jerome R. Corsi, "Clinton Foundation Scheme 'Defrauds Air Travelers,'" WND, April 23, 2015, http://www.wnd.com/2015/04/clinton-foundation-scheme-defrauds-air-travelers/.

61. Ibid.

62. Ibid.

63. Ortel, Executive Summary, "False Philanthropy: Second Interim Report Concerning Public Disclosures of the Bill, Hillary & Chelsea Clinton Foundation."

64. Consolidated Financial Statements: Clinton Health Access Initiative, Inc. and Subsidiaries, December 31, 2013 and 2012, http://45.55.138.94/content/uploads/2015/05/Clinton-Health-Access-Initiative-Financial-Statements-2013.pdf, 9.

65. This section draws heavily from Jerome R. Corsi, "Clinton AIDS Charity Was Shut Down in Massachusetts," WND, May 20, 2015, http://www.wnd.com/2015/05/clinton-aids-charity-was-shut-down-in-massachusetts/.

66. Maggie Haberman, "Reviews Reveal Divisions Within the Clinton Health Initiative, Starting at the Top," New York Times, November 18, 2015, http://www.nytimes.com/2015/11/19/us/politics/reviews-reveal-divisions-within-the-clinton-health-initiative-starting-at-the-top.html?_r=0.

67. "Meet the Patriotic Speaker for the 227th Fourth of July Celebration—Ira C. Magaziner," Bristol 4th of July 2012, http://www.july4thbristolri.com/2012.patriotic.speaker.htm.

68. Clinton Foundation, Unified Registration Statement (URS) for Charitable Organizations, Form URS v.3.02, NAAG/NASCO Standardized Reporting, Year Ending 31/12/2005, EIN 31-1580204, State: New York, State ID 06-79-83, Organization Name "William J. Clinton Foundation," Renewal/Update, 3 pages, signed by Bruce R. Lindsey, CEO.

69. Hillary Clinton, Hard Choices (New York: Simon & Schuster, 2014), 292.

70. Brenda Waning et al., "Global Strategies to Reduce the Price of Antiretroviral Medicines: Evidence from Transactional Databases," Bulletin of the World Health Organization, 2009, http://www.who.int/bulletin/volumes/87/7/08-058925/en/.

71. World Health Organization, Global Update on the Health Sector Response to HIV, 2014, http://apps.who.int/iris/bitstream/10665/128494/1/9789241507585_eng.pdf?ua=1.

72. "Global Summary of the AIDS Epidemic, 2014," World Health Organization, HIV Department, July 21, 2015, http://www.who.int/hiv/data/epi_core_july2015.png?ua=1.

73. World Health Organization Global Health Observatory, GHO, "HIV/AIDS," http://www.who.int/gho/hiv/en/.

74. "HIV and AIDS in Sub-Saharan Africa, Regional Overview," AVERT, May 1, 2015, http://www.avert.org/professionals/hiv-around-world/sub-saharan-africa/overview.

75. WHO, "Accelerate Expansion of Antiretroviral Therapy to All People Living with HIV," World Health Organization News, November 30, 2015, http://www.who.int/mediacentre/news/statements/2015/antiretroviral-therapy-hiv/en/.

76. World Health Organization, *Progress Report: Global Health Sector Response to HIV, 2000–2015: Focus on Innovations in Africa*, 2015, http://apps.who.int/iris/bitstream/10665/198065/1/9789241509824_eng.pdf.

CHAPTER 6: THE STATE DEPARTMENT SCAM

1. Andy Barr, "Clinton: I'd Have Hired Obama," Politico, October 14, 2009, http://www.politico.com/story/2009/10/clinton-id-have-hired-obama-028278.

2. Raymond Hernandez and Michael Luo, "Clinton Said to Be Unsure about Cabinet Job," *New York Times*, November 18, 2008, http://www.nytimes.com/2008/11/19/us/politics/19clinton.html.

3. Pareene, "Ron Burkle, Billionaire Creep, Owes Bill Clinton Money," Gawker, March 30, 2010, http://gawker.com/5505406/ron-burkle-billionaire-creep-owes-bill-clinton-money.

4. *Nomination of Hillary R. Clinton to Be Secretary of State*, U.S. Senate Committee on Foreign Relations, January 13, 2009 (Washington, DC: US Government Printing Office, 2010), p. 9, https://www.gpo.gov/fdsys/pkg/CHRG-111shrg54615/pdf/CHRG-111shrg54615.pdf.

5. Ken Strickland and Andrea Mitchell, "Clinton, Obama 'Memo of Understanding,'" NBC News, December 18, 2008, http://firstread.nbcnews.com/_news/2008/12/18/4426618-clinton-obama-memo-of-understanding.

6. Nomination of Hillary R. Clinton to Be Secretary of State, 9.

7. Ibid., 10.

8. Ibid., 63.

9. Ibid., 72–73.

10. Ibid., 138, 140.

11. Ibid., 138.

12. "Clinton, Inc., December 3, 2013 Production Pgs. 2–6," Judicial Watch Document Archive, http://www.judicialwatch.org/document-archive/clinton-inc-december-3-2013-production-pg-2-6/.

13. Ibid., http://www.judicialwatch.org/wp-content/uploads/2014/07/Clinton-Inc-December-3-2013-production-pg-2-6.pdf, 4.

14. Ibid., 4–5.

15. Ibid., 5.

16. "Clinton, Inc., December 3, 2013, Pgs. 7–9," Judicial Watch Document Archive, http://www.judicialwatch.org/document-archive/december-3-2013-pg-7-9/.

17. "Hillary R. Clinton Termination EA," Judicial Watch Document Archive, http://www.judicialwatch.org/document-archive/hillary-clinton-termination/.

18. Rosalind S. Helderman and Tom Hamburger, "Clinton Foundation Reveals up to $26 Million in Additional Payments," *Washington Post*, May 21, 2015, https://www.washingtonpost.com/politics/clinton-foundation-reveals-up-to-26million-in-additional-payments/2015/05/21/e49da740-0009-11e5-833c-a2de05b6b2a4_story.html.

19. Robert W. Wood, "Why Aren't Those $26.4 Million Speech Fees Taxable to Bill and Hillary Clinton?" *Forbes*, May 26, 2015, http://www.forbes.com/sites/robertwood/2015/05/26/why-arent-those-26-4m-speech-fees-taxable-to-bill-hillary/.

20. "Clinton Foundation Admits Making Mistakes on Taxes," Reuters, April 26, 2015, http://www.reuters.com/article/us-usa-election-clinton-foundation-idUSKBN0NH0TP20150426.

21. Judicial Watch, "The Hillary File: State Dept. Ethics Agreements," *Investigative Bulletin*, April 16, 2015, http://www.judicialwatch.org/bulletins/the-hillary-file-state-dept-ethics-agreements/.

22. Rosalind S. Helderman, "Obama Officials Defend Clinton Foundation Donation," *Washington Post*, February 26, 2015, https://www.washingtonpost.com/news/post-politics/wp/2015/02/26/obama-officials-defend-clinton-foundation-donation/.

23. "Press Briefing by Press Secretary Josh Earnest, 4/20/2015," White House, Office of the Press Secretary, April 20, 2015, https://www.whitehouse.gov/the-press-office/2015/04/20/press-briefing-press-secretary-josh-earnest-4202015.

24. Clinton Global Initiative, "2009 Annual Meeting," ClintonFoundation.org, https://www.clintonfoundation.org/clinton-global-initiative/meetings/annual-meetings/2009/.

25. Press Release, "Analysis of CGI Commitments Since 2005 Reveals Key Trends, Metrics, and Lessons," CGI, September 23, 2014, http://press.clintonglobalinitiative.org/press_releases/analysis-of-cgi-commitments-since-2005-reveals-key-trends-metrics-and-lessons/.

26. Clinton Foundation, "Annual Reports, Financials & Tax-Exempt Materials," ClintonFoundation.org, accessed March 28, 2016, https://www.clintonfoundation.org/about/annual-financial-reports, "Clinton Global Initiative,"

27. Ibid., "Clinton Health Access Initiative."

28. This section is drawn heavily from Charles Ortel's work, as reported in Jerome R. Corsi, "Clinton Foundation Made Shifty Split When Hillary Joined Obama," WND, May 12, 2015, http://www.wnd.com/2015/05/clinton-foundation-made-shifty-split-when-hillary-joined-obama/.

29. This and the next two paragraphs are drawn from Charles Ortel, "Executive Summary: Key Elements in the Continuing Clinton Foundation Frauds," Draft #9, August 16, 2015, copy e-mailed to the author by Charles Ortel. See: IRS "Determination Letter," addressed to the Clinton Global Initiative, Inc., Little Rock, AR, October 6, 2010, https://www.clintonfoundation.org/sites/default/files/cgi_irs_determination_letter.pdf.

30. This section and the text through table 8 is drawn heavily from Charles Ortel's work, as reported in Jerome R. Corsi, "How Did $17 Million Disappear from Clinton Foundation?" WND, May 17, 2015, http://www.wnd.com/2015/05/how-did-17-million-disappear-from-clinton-foundation/. The primary source for this section is Charles Ortel, "False Philanthropy? Second Interim Report Concerning Public Disclosures of the Bill, Hillary & Chelsea Foundation," Preliminary Analysis, Draft #16, May 11, 2015, copy e-mailed to the author by Charles Ortel.

31. Judicial Watch, "The Hillary File: Mixing Money & Politics at State," *Investigative Bulletin*, December 3, 2015, http://www.judicialwatch.org/bulletins/the-hillary-file-mixing-money-politics-at-state/.

32. "Jonathan Mantz, Principal, BGR Government Affairs," BGR Group website, accessed March 28, 2016, BGRDC.com, http://www.bgrdc.com/x-bios/bgr-mantz.html.

33. Judicial Watch, "The Hillary File."

34. Michael S. Schmidt, "Walter Shorenstein, Democratic Donor, Dies at 95," *New York Times*, June 26, 2010, http://www.nytimes.com/2010/06/27/us/politics/27shorenstein.html.

35. "Press Release, Second Annual Meeting of Clinton Global Initiative—3 Days, 215 Commitments, $7.3 Billion," Clinton Global Initiative, September 22, 2006, https://www.clintonfoundation.org/main/news-and-media/press-releases-and-statements/press-release-second-annual-meeting-of-clinton-global-initiative-3-days-215-comm.html.

36. "Douglas Ahers," a biography posted on the website of the Belfer Center at Harvard's John F. Kennedy School of Government, accessed March 28, 2016, http://belfercenter.ksg.harvard.edu/experts/832/doug_ahlers.html.

37. "Walter Isaacson, President and CEO, Aspen Institute," a biography posted on the website of the Aspen Institute, accessed March 28, 2016, http://www.aspeninstitute.org/about/about-walter-isaacson.

38. "Press Releases: Citizens United Releases Huma Abedin and Cheryl Mills Email Productions in their Entirety," CitizensUnited.org, September 28, 2015, http://www.citizensunited.org/press-releases.aspx?article=10113.

39. Rosalind S. Helderman and Tom Hamburger, "How Huma Abedin Operated at the Clinton Universe," *Washington Post*, August 27, 2015, https://www.washingtonpost.com/politics/how-huma-abedin-operated-at-the-center-of-the-clinton-universe/2015/08/27/cd099eee-4b32-11e5-902f-39e9219e574b_story.html.

40. Rachael Bade, "Clinton's Chief of Staff Gave Advice to Clinton Foundation." Politico, September 30, 2015, http://www.politico.com/story/2015/09/hillary-clinton-emails-cheryl-mills-foundation-214243.

41. Alana Goodman, "Clinton Aide Shared Classified Information with Foundation, Email Shows," *Washington Free Beacon*, July 12, 2012, http://freebeacon.com/politics/clinton-aide-shared-classified-information-with-foundation-email-shows/.

42. James V. Grimaldi and Rebecca Ballhaus, "Speaking Fees Meet Politics for Clintons," *Wall Street Journal*, December 30, 2015, http://www.wsj.com/articles/speaking-fees-meet-politics-for-clintons-1451504098.

43. Ibid.

44. "Judicial Watch: New State Department Documents Raise More Questions on Clinton Conflict of Interest Reviews," Judicial Watch Press Room, October 7, 2015, http://www.judicialwatch.org/press-room/press-releases/judicial-watch-new-state-department-documents-raise-more-questions-on-clinton-conflict-of-interest-reviews/.

45. Ibid.

46. Mina Kimes and Michael Smith, "Laureate, a For-Profit Education Firm, Finds International Success (with Clinton's Help," *Washington Post*, January 18, 2014, https://www.washingtonpost.com/business/laureate-a-for-profit-education-firm-finds-international-success-with-a-clintons-help/2014/01/16/13f8adde-7ca6-11e3-9556-4a4bf7bcbd84_story.html. The term "subprime students" was coined by Charles Ortel in an e-mail copied to the author, dated December 12, 2015.

47. Michael Vasquez and Patricia Mazzei, "Higher-Ed Hustle: For-Profit Colleges Cast Shadow over Presidential Race," *Miami Herald*, August 15, 2015, http://www.miamiherald.com/news/local/education/article31216595.html.

48. Alex Barinka, "Laureate Education Plans IPO as a Public Benefit Company," Bloomberg Business, October 2, 2015, http://www.bloomberg.com/news/articles/2015-10-02/kkr-backed-laureate-education-files-for-initial-public-offering.

49. Carrie Wells, "Laureate Education Files IPO with $4.7 Billion Debt," *Baltimore Sun*, October 5, 2015, http://www.baltimoresun.com/business/bs-bz-laureate-ipo-folo-20151005-story.html.

50. Steven Davidoff Solomon, "Idealism That May Leave Shareholders Wishing for Pragmatism," *New York Times*, "Deal Book," October 13, 2015, http://www.nytimes.com/2015/10/14/business/dealbook/laureate-education-for-profit-school-public-benefit.html?_r=0.

51. Moody's Investors Services, "Rating Action: Moody's Changes Laureate's Outlook to Negative," May 30, 2014, https://www.moodys.com/research/Moodys-changes-Laureates-outlook-to-negative--PR_300256.

52. Joe Cavanaugh, "Sylvan's Fast Learners," *Johns Hopkins Magazine*, September 1998, http://pages.jh.edu/jhumag/0998web/sylvan.html.

53. Irvin Molotsky, "Encyclopedic Medical Card Shows the Worth of Young Ideas," *New York Times*, May 19, 1985, http://www.nytimes.com/1985/05/19/us/encyclopedic-medical-card-shows-the-worth-of-young-ideas.html.

54. Eric Owens, "Why Are the Clintons Hawking a Seedy, Soros-Backed For-Profit College Corporation?" *Daily Caller*, January 13, 2014, http://dailycaller.com/2014/01/13/why-are-the-clintons-hawking-a-seedy-soros-backed-for-profit-college-corporation/.

55. "Laureate International Universities Broadcasts Clinton Global Initiative's Annual Meeting," press release, Laureate International Universities, September 24, 2013, http://www.laureate.net/NewsRoom/PressReleases/2013/09/Laureate-International-Universities-Broadcasts-Clinton-Global-Initiatives-Annual-Meeting. See also Clinton Global Initiative, "President Clinton Announces Program for the Fifth Annual Clinton Global Initiative Meeting," ClintonGlobalInitiative.org, March 8, 2012, http://press.clintonglobalinitiative.org/press_releases/president-clinton-announces-program-for-the-fifth-annual-clinton-global-initiative-university-meeting/.

56. Jennifer Epstein, "Bill Clinton Leaves For-Profit College Position," Bloomberg Politics, April 24, 2015, http://www.bloomberg.com/politics/articles/2015-04-24/bill-clinton-leaves-for-profit-college-position.

57. Charles Ortel in an e-mail copied by Ortel to the author, dated December 11, 2015.

58. Charles Ortel in a second e-mail copied by Ortel to the author, dated December 11, 2015.

59. Stephen Braun, "Bill Clinton Company Shows Complexity of Family Finances," Yahoo! News, May 26, 2015, http://news.yahoo.com/bill-clinton-company-shows-complexity-family-finances-180745584--election.html.

60. Jonathan Allen, "Exclusive: Clinton Charities Will Refile Tax Returns, Audit for Other Errors," Reuters, April 23, 2015, http://www.reuters.com/article/us-usa-election-clinton-taxes-exclusive-idUSKBN0NE0CA20150423.

61. Maura Pally, "A Commitment to Honesty, Transparency, and Accountability," ClintonFoundation.org, April 26, 2015, https://www.clintonfoundation.org/blog/2015/04/26/commitment-honesty-transparency-and-accountability.

62. Josh Gerstein, "Clinton Foundation Spinoff Won't Refile Tax Returns," *Under the Radar* (blog), November 2, 2015, http://www.politico.com/blogs/under-the-radar/2015/11/clinton-foundation-spin-off-wont-refile-tax-returns-215448.

63. Jonathan Allen, "Clinton Charity, under Pressure, Will Amend Tax Return Errors," Reuters, November 4, 2015, http://www.reuters.com/article/us-usa-election-clinton-idUSKCN0ST2GD20151104?feedType=RSS&feedName=everything&virtualBrandChannel=11563.

64. Jonathan Allen, "Clinton Charities Refile Six Years of Tax Returns to Amend Errors," Reuters, November 16, 2015, http://www.reuters.com/article/us-usa-election-clinton-foundation-idUSKCN0T608W20151117.

65. Josh Gerstein and Kenneth P. Vogel, "Clinton Foundation Refiles Tax Returns," Politico, November 16, 2015, http://www.politico.com/story/2015/11/clinton-foundation-refiles-tax-returns-215959.

66. Ibid.

67. Chuck Ross, "Major Hillary Donor Conducted Review of Erroneous Clinton Foundation Tax Returns," *Daily Caller*, November 17, 2015, http://dailycaller.com/2015/11/17/major-hillary-donor-conducted-review-of-erroneous-clinton-foundation-tax-returns/.

68. Brent Scher, "Clinton Foundation Donor Conducted Review of Clinton Foundation Tax Returns," *Washington Free Beacon*, November 17, 2015, http://freebeacon.com/politics/clinton-foundation-donor-conducted-review-of-clinton-foundation-tax-returns/.

69. Ken Silverstein, "Shaky Foundations," *Browsings* (blog), November 17, 2015, http://harpers.org/blog/2015/11/shaky-foundations/.

CHAPTER 7: THE HAITI SCAM

1. USGS, "Magnitude 7.0—Haiti Region," US Geological Service Earthquakes Hazards Program, accessed March 28, 2016, http://earthquake.usgs.gov/earthquakes/eqinthenews/2010/us2010rja6/#details.

2. Simon Romero and Marc Lacey, "Fierce Quake Devastates Haitian Capital," *New York Times*, January 12, 2010, http://www.nytimes.com/2010/01/13/world/americas/13haiti.html?_r=0.

3. Andrew Quinn, "Clinton heads to Haiti with relief supplies," Reuters, January 16, 2010, http://www.reuters.com/article/us-quake-haiti-clinton-idUSTRE60E5NA20100116.

4. Mark Landler, "In Show of Support, Clinton Goes to Haiti," *New York Times*, January 16, 2010, http://www.nytimes.com/2010/01/17/world/americas/17diplo.html.

5. "Briefing by State Department Counselor Cheryl Mills, USAID Administrator Dr. Raj Shah, and US SOUTHCOM Commander General Douglas Fraser on the Situation in Haiti," USAID.gov, January 13, 2010, https://www.usaid.gov/content/briefing-state-department-counselor-cheryl-mills-usaid-administrator-dr-raj-shah-and-us.

6. "Briefing by State Department Counselor Cheryl Mills, USAID Administrator Dr. Raj Shah on the Situation in Haiti," USAID.gov, January 15, 2010, https://www.usaid.gov/news-information/speeches/briefing-state-department-counselor-cheryl-mills-and-usaid-administrator-0.

7. Simon Romero and Marc Lacey, "Escaping the Capital as Help Is Arriving," *New York Times*, January 18, 2010, http://www.nytimes.com/2010/01/19/world/americas/19haiti.html?pagewanted=all.

8. "Former US President Clinton Appointed U.N. Special Envoy for Haiti," United Nations News Center, May 19, 2009, UN.org, http://www.un.org/apps/news/story.asp?NewsID=30843#.Vnh37ITT_XE.

9. Romero and Lacey, "Escaping the Capital as Help Is Arriving."

10. Mary Anastasia O'Grady, "Clinton for Haiti Czar?," *Wall Street Journal*, January 24, 2010, http://www.wsj.com/articles/SB10001424052748704509704575019070435720154.

11. Office of the Spokesman, US Department of State, "Former President Clinton's Role in Haiti," State.gov, February 9, 2010, http://www.state.gov/r/pa/prs/ps/2010/02/136593.htm.

12. "Remarks by President Obama, Former President Bill Clinton, and Former President George W. Bush on the Recovery and Rebuilding Effort in Haiti," White House transcript, WhiteHouse.gov, January 16, 2010, https://www.whitehouse.gov/photos-and-video/video/presidents-obama-bush-clinton-help-haiti#transcript.

13. "Announcement of Major Bush-Clinton Katrina Fund Grants," press release, Clinton Foundation, December 7, 2005, https://www.clintonfoundation.org/main/news-and-media/press-releases-and-statements/press-release-announcement-of-major-bush-clinton-katrina-fund-grants.html.

14. Associated Press, "Clinton to Be U.N.'s Envoy on Tsunami Relief," NBC News, Feb.February 1, 2005, http://www.nbcnews.com/id/6894871/ns/world_news-tsunami_a_year_later/t/clinton-be-uns-envoy-tsunami-relief/.

15. "President Clinton Opens Fourth Annual Clinton Global Initiative Meeting in New York," press release, Clinton Foundation, September 24, 2008, https://www.clintonfoundation.org/main/news-and-media/press-releases-and-statements/press-release-president-clinton-opens-fourth-annual-clinton-global-initiative-me.html. See also Jeannie Kever, "Ike Reunites Ex-Presidents Bush, Clinton for Relief Effort," *Houston Chronicle*, September 23, 2008, http://www.chron.com/news/hurricanes/article/Ike-reunites-ex-Presidents-Bush-Clinton-for-1781620.php.

16. "Remarks by President Obama, Former President Bill Clinton, and Former President George W. Bush on the Recovery and Rebuilding Effort in Haiti."

17. Ibid.

18. Ibid.

19. David Keene, "How Bill Clinton Oversells His Rescue of Haiti," *Washington Times*, September 23, 2014, http://www.washingtontimes.com/news/2014/sep/23/keene-how-bill-clinton-oversells-his-rescue-of-hai/.

20. Nancy Snyderman, "Clinton, Bush Make Joint Visit to Haiti," NBC Nightly News, March 22, 2010, http://www.nbcnews.com/video/nightly-news/35993007#35993007.

21. "Bush and Clinton Visit Haiti in Fund-Raising Effort," BBC News, March 22, 2010, http://news.bbc.co.uk/2/hi/8580641.stm.

22. O'Grady, "Clinton for Haiti Czar?"

23. Peter Schweizer, *Clinton Cash: The Untold Story of How and Why Foreign Governments and Businesses Helped Make Bill and Hillary Rich* (New York: HarperCollins, 2015), 165.

24. Jeffrey D. Sachs, "From His First Day in Office, Bush Was Ousting Aristide," *Los Angeles Times*, March 4, 2004, http://articles.latimes.com/2004/mar/04/opinion/oe-sachs4.

25. Tracy Kidder, "The Trials of Haiti: Why Has the US Government Abandoned a Country It Once Sought to Liberate?" *Nation*, October 9, 2003, http://www.thenation.com/article/trials-haiti/. See also G. Dunkel, "Haiti Tense as US Blocks aid," *Workers World*, September 12, 2002, http://www.workers.org/ww/2002/haiti0912.php.

26. William Fisher, "US-Haiti: The Loan That Wasn't, Part 1," IPS, February 12, 2010, http://ipsnorthamerica.net/print.php?idnews=2854.

27. O'Grady, "Clinton for Haiti Czar?"

28. Mary Anastasia O'Grady, "The Looting of Haiti Teleco," *Wall Street Journal*, March 12, 2012, http://www.wsj.com/articles/SB10001424052970204781804577271812965314018.

29. O'Grady, "Clinton for Haiti Czar?"

30. Tambay A. Obenson "Watch Now: Raoul Peck's 'Fatal Assistance' (Exposé on Haiti's Post-Earthquake Billions)," *Shadow and Act* (blog), April 22, 2013, http://blogs.indiewire.com/shadowandact/watch-now-raoul-pecks-fatal-assistance-expose-on-haitis-post-earthquake-billions.

31. Bill Quigley and Amber Ramanauskas, "Haiti: Where Is the Money?" HaitiAction.net, January 4, 2012, http://www.haitiaction.net/News/BQ/1_4_12/1_4_12.html.

32. Isabel Macdonald and Isabeau Doucet, "The Shelters That Clinton Built," *Nation*, July 11, 2011, http://www.thenation.com/article/shelters-clinton-built/.

33. Andrea Seikaly, "Sean Penn Gathers Celebs to Help Haiti Home, U2 Closes Out the Night," *Variety*, January 12, 2004, http://variety.com/2014/scene/awards/sean-penn-gathers-celebs-to-help-haiti-home-u2-closes-out-the-night-1201048762/.

For the continuing controversy over Sean Penn's effectiveness in Haiti, See: Jonathan M. Katz, "Sean Penn Accuses the Media of Ignoring Haiti's Progress. But He's Ignoring a Few Uncomfortable Facts, Too," New Republic, June 19, 2014, https://newrepublic.com/article/118254/sean-penns-wsj-op-ed-haiti-ignores-few-uncomfortable-facts.

34. Jake Johnston, "Outsourcing Haiti," *Boston Review*, January 16, 2014, http://bostonreview.net/world/jake-johnston-haiti-earthquake-aid-caracol.

35. Jake Johnston and Alexander Main, "Breaking Open the Black Box: Increasing Aid Transparency and Accountability in Haiti," Center for Economic and Policy Research, Washington, DC, April 2013, 4, http://cepr.net/documents/publications/haiti-aid-accountability-2013-04.pdf.

36. Kevin Edmonds, "The People vs. the Pirates: Controversy Abounds in Haitian Reconstruction Investigations," NACLA, April 5, 2012, https://nacla.org/blog/2012/4/5/people-vs-pirates-controversy-abounds-haitian-reconstruction-investigations.

37. Sarah Westwood, "Failed Afghan Project Highlights Clinton's Contractor Ties," *Washington Examiner*, June 26, 2015, http://www.washingtonexaminer.com/failed-afghan-project-highlights-clintons-contractor-ties/article/2567076.

38. Martin Kaste, "After Quake in Haiti, Who's the Boss?" Nashville Public Radio, March 31, 2010, http://www.npr.org/templates/story/story.php?storyId=125328026.

39. The Government of the Republic of Haiti, *Action Plan for National Recovery and Development of Haiti: Immediate Key Initiatives for the Future* (March 2010), 54, https://www.kirkensnodhjelp.no/contentassets/ee77fa84ec654fb2a01ac3ea8f72bd98/haiti_action_plan_eng.pdf.

40. Emily Troutman, "Clintons Will Have a Big Say in Haiti's Future," AOL News, July 13, 2010, archived at *Who We Are/How We Live* (blog), http://emilytroutman.blogspot.com/2010/07/clintons-will-have-big-say-in-haiti_13.html.

41. Deepa Panchang and Beverly Bell, "Business as Government: Capitalizing on Disaster in Post-Earthquake Haiti," Common Dreams, March 1, 2012, http://www.commondreams.org/views/2012/03/01/business-government-capitalizing-disaster-post-earthquake-haiti.

42. Johnston, "Outsourcing Haiti."

43. Text of Protest Letter published in Norman Girvan, "Protest Letter from Haitian IHRC Members to Commission Co-Chairs," trans. Isabeau Doucet, Real News Network, December 30, 2010, http://therealnews.com/t2/about-us/524-protest-letter-from-haitian-ihrc-members-to-commission-co-chairs.

44. Johnston, "Outsourcing Haiti."

45. Neil MacFarquhar, "Skepticism on Pledges for Haiti," *New York Times*, March 31, 2010, http://www.nytimes.com/2010/04/01/world/americas/01haiti.html.

46. Bryan Schaaf, "A Country Should Not Depend on the International Community," *Haiti Innovation* (blog), July 15, 2010, http://haitiinnovation.org/en/2010/06/13/haiti-earthquake-update-6-13-2010.

47. Jean-Max Bellerive and Bill Clinton, "Finishing Haiti's Unfinished Work," *New York Times*, op-ed, July 11, 2010, http://www.nytimes.com/2010/07/12/opinion/12clinton-1.html.

48. World Bank, "HRF Becomes Key Source for Haiti's Reconstruction," ReliefWeb, July 22, 2011, http://reliefweb.int/report/haiti/hrf-becomes-key-source-haiti's-reconstruction.

49. "US Efforts Have Begun, Expanded Oversight Still to Be Implemented," US Government Accountability Office, 11-415, May 19, 2011, http://www.gao.gov/products/GAO-11-415.

50. Cheryl Mills and Rajiv Shah, "Update on Efforts in Haiti: Special Briefing," U.S. Department of State, July 11, 2010, State.gov, http://www.state.gov/r/pa/prs/ps/2010/07/144466.htm.

51. US Centers for Disease Control and Prevention, "Cholera in Haiti: One Year Later," CDC.gov, October 25, 2011, http://www.cdc.gov/haiticholera/haiti_cholera.htm.

52. Give Well, "Clinton Bush Haiti Fund," GiveWell.org, http://www.givewell.org/international/disaster-relief/Clinton-Bush-Haiti-Fund.

53. Ansel Herz, "Insult to Injury: Cholera Has Haiti Reeling, and Bill Clinton & Anderson Cooper Haven't Done Enough," *New York Daily News*, November 1, 2010, http://www.nydailynews.com/opinion/insult-injury-cholera-haiti-reeling-bill-clinton-anderson-cooper-haven-article-1.451973.

54. Clinton Global Initiative, "Press Releases: President Bill Clinton Hosts Special Session on Recovery in Haiti at the Clinton Global Initiative's 2010 Annual Meeting," ClintonGlobalInitiative.org, September 23, 2010, http://press.clintonglobalinitiative.org/press_releases/president-bill-clinton-hosts-special-session-on-recovery-in-haiti-at-the-clinton-global-initiative-s-2010-annual-meeting/.

55. Rick Gladstone, "Rights Advocates Suing U.N. over the Spread of Cholera," *New York Times*, October 8, 2013, http://www.nytimes.com/2013/10/09/world/americas/rights-advocates-suing-un-over-the-spread-of-cholera-in-haiti.html?_r=0.

56. J. Paul Oetken, Opinion and Order, US District Court, Southern District of New York, Delama Georges, et. al., Plaintiffs, v. United Nations, et. al., Defendants, January 9, 2015, http://www.ijdh.org/2015/01/topics/health/united-states-district-court-southern-district-of-new-york/.

57. "Judge Deems U.N. Immune from Lawsuit for Haiti Cholera Disaster," press release, Institute for Justice and Democracy in Haiti, January 9, 2015, http://www.ijdh.org/2015/01/topics/health/judge-deems-un-immune-from-lawsuit-for-haiti-cholera-disaster/.

58. Stephanie Strom, "A Billionaire Lends Haiti a Hand," *New York Times*, January 6, 2012, http://www.nytimes.com/2012/01/07/business/digicels-denis-obrien-helps-rebuild-haiti.html.

59. See Clinton Foundation in Haiti, "Caracol Industrial Park: Creating up to 60,000 Jobs in Northern Haiti," Clinton Foundation, accessed March 29, 2016, https://www.clintonfoundation.org/our-work/clinton-foundation-haiti/programs/caracol-industrial-park.

60. Strom, "A Billionaire Lends Haiti a Hand."

61. USAID Press Office, "Digicel Foundation and the US Government Partner to Provide New Schools in Earthquake-Affected Communities in Haiti," press release, USAID, August 25, 2010, https://www.usaid.gov/news-information/press-releases/digicel-foundation-and-us-government-partner-provide-new-schools.

62. Janice Laurente, "USAID Provides New Schools to Earthquake Affected Communities in Haiti," *Impact Blog*, September 10, 2010, https://blog.usaid.gov/2010/09/usaid-provides-new-schools-to-earthquake-affected-communities-in-haiti/.

63. Schweizer, *Clinton Cash*, 166–67.

64. Mark Titus, "Digicel, Scotiabank Partner on Mobile Banking Product," *Gleaner* (Jamaica), November 24, 2010, http://jamaica-gleaner.com/gleaner/20101124/business/business5.html.

65. Digicel, "Mobile Money Service Comes to Haiti with 'TchoTcho Mobile' from Digicel and Scotiabank," press release, MarketWired, November 22, 2010, http://www.marketwired.com/press-release/mobile-money-service-comes-to-haiti-with-tchotcho-mobile-from-digicel-and-scotiabank-1357676.htm.

66. USAID Fact Sheet, "Haiti Mobile Money Initiative," USAID.gov, last updated December 7, 2012, https://www.usaid.gov/news-information/fact-sheets/haiti-mobile-money-initiative.

67. WOCCU, USAID and Bill & Melinda Gates Foundation, "Gates Foundation and USAID Announce $1.5 Million Award for Second Haiti Mobile Money Launch," press release, Microlinks, https://www.microlinks.org/news/gates-foundation-and-usaid-announce-15-million-award-second-haiti-mobile-money-launch.

68. USAID and Bill & Melinda Gates Foundation, "Foundation and US Government Give $2.5 Million Prize for Transforming Banking Sector in Hawaii," press release, Gates Foundation Press Room, January 11, 2011, http://www.gatesfoundation.org/Media-Center/Press-Releases/2011/01/Foundation-and-US-Government-Give-25-Million-Prize-for-Transforming-Banking-Sector-in-Haiti.

69. Ángel Gonzáles, "Push to Make Haiti an E-Cash Economy Fell Far Short," *Seattle Times*, "Nation & World," December 22, 2015, http://old.seattletimes.com/flatpages/nationworld/haiti-shaky-recovery-part-2-earthquake-five-years-later-annivers.html.

70. Marriott Port-au-Prince Hotel, Marriott.com, accessed March 29, 2016, http://www.marriott.com/hotels/travel/papmc-marriott-port-au-prince-hotel/.

71. "Digicel and Marriott Open Haiti Hotel," PR Newswire, February 25, 2015, http://www.prnewswire.com/news-releases/digicel-and-marriott-open-haiti-hotel-300041208.html.

72. "Digicel and Marriot Open Haiti Hotel," Hotel-Development.Marriott.com, February 25, 2015, https://hotel-development.marriott.com/2015/02/digicel-and-marriott-open-haiti-hotel/.

73. Jacqueline Charles, "Haiti, Bill Clinton Welcome First Marriott hotel," *Miami Herald*, February 24, 2015, http://www.miamiherald.com/news/nation-world/world/americas/haiti/article11107349.html.

74. Caribbean Journal Staff, "Haiti Marriott Project Receiving $26.5 Million in Financing from IFC," *Caribbean Journal*, July 3, 2013, http://caribjournal.com/2013/07/03/haiti-marriott-project-receiving-26-5-million-in-financing-from-ifc/#.

75. Marina Vatav, "Heavy Investments for a Marriott Hotel in Port-au-Prince," Haiti Business Week, July 14, 2013, http://haitibusinessweek.com/business-news/99/heavy-investments-for-a-marriott-hotel-in-port-au-prince.

76. "FMO—Netherland Development Finance Company," EDFI, accessed March 29, 2016, http://www.edfi.be/members/7-netherlands-development-finance-company-.html.

77. Alana Goodman, "Emails: Clinton Foundation Donor Lobbied State Department for Haiti Hotels," *Washington Free Beacon*, October 19, 2015, http://freebeacon.com/issues/emails-clinton-foundation-donor-lobbied-state-department-for-haiti-hotels/.

78. David A. Fahrenthold, Tom Hamburger, and Rosalind S. Helderman, "The Inside Story of How the Clintons Built a $2 Billion Global Empire," *Washington Post*, June 2, 2015, https://www.washingtonpost.com/politics/the-inside-story-of-how-the-clintons-built-a-2-billion-global-empire/2015/06/02/b6eab638-0957-11e5-a7ad-b430fc1d3f5c_story.html.

79. Tom Buerkle, "For Digicel's Denis O'Brien, Mobile + Philanthropy = Real Wealth," *Institutional Investor*, July 23, 2014, http://www.institutionalinvestor.com/article/3364217/banking-and-capital-markets-corporations/for-digicels-denis-obrien-mobile-+-philanthropy-=-real-wealth.html#/.VUu1VtNViko.

80. Julie Lévesque, "HAITI: Humanitarian Aid for Earthquake Victims Used to Build Five Star Hotels," GlobalResearch, June 28, 2012, http://www.globalresearch.ca/haiti-humanitarian-aid-for-earthquake-victims-used-to-build-five-star-hotels/31646.

81. Meg Galloway Pearce, "Clinton Bush Haiti Fund Invests to Complete Construction of Haitian-owned Hotel and Conference Center in Port au Prince," press release, Clinton Bush Haiti Fund, May 9, 2011, http://www.clintonbushhaitifund.org/media/entry/clinton-bush-haiti-fund-invests-to-complete-construction-of-haitian-owned-h/.

82. Mary Anastasia O'Grady, "Hillary's Half-Baked Haiti Project," *Wall Street Journal*, January 11, 2015, http://www.wsj.com/articles/mary-anastasia-ogrady-hillarys-half-baked-haiti-project-1421018329.

83. "Caracol Industrial Park," USAID, last updated December 14, 2015, https://www.usaid.gov/haiti/caracol-industrial-park.

84. "News Releases: Haiti to Expand Business Facilities at Caracol Industrial Park with Support from IDB," Inter-America Development Bank, December 12, 2014, http://www.iadb.org/en/news/news-releases/2014-12-12/caracol-industrial-park-and-haiti,11020.html.

85. O'Grady, "Hillary's Half-Baked Haiti Project."

86. Schweizer, *Clinton Cash*, 175.

87. Government Accountability Office, *Haiti Reconstruction: USAID Infrastructure Projects Have Had Mixed Results and Face Sustainability Challenges* (June 2013), 11–12, http://foreignaffairs.house. gov/sites/republicans.foreignaffairs.house.gov/files/zkVt_d13558._Restricted.pdf.

88. Randal C. Archibold, "Report Finds Lapses in United States Aid Efforts in Haiti," *New York Times*, June 25, 2013, http://www.nytimes.com/2013/06/26/world/americas/report-finds-lapses-in-united-states-aid-efforts-in-haiti.html.

89. "Extreme Poverty Drops in Haiti. Is It Sustainable?" World Bank, December 11, 2014, http://www. worldbank.org/en/news/feature/2014/12/11/haiti-the-day-that-the-news-were-good.

90. Jonathan M. Katz, "The King and Queen of Haiti," *Politico Magazine*, May 4, 2015, http://www. politico.com/magazine/story/2015/05/clinton-foundation-haiti-117368#.VUi6K85Nvdn. See also Jonathan M. Katz, *The Big Truck That Went By: How the World Came to Save Haiti and Left Behind a Disaster* (New York: Palgrave Macmillan, 2013).

91. Kyle Blaine, "Chelsea Clinton Wrote Bill and Hillary about Being 'Profoundly Disturbed' by Haiti Response," BuzzFeed News, September 1, 2015, http://www.buzzfeed.com/kyleblaine/chelsea-clinton-wrote-bill-and-hillary-about-being-profoundl#.jkVV7qYJZ.

92. Brent Scher, "Month After Haiti Criticism Revealed, Chelsea Clinton Praises Relief Effort," *Washington Free Beacon*, October 6, 2015, http://freebeacon.com/politics/chelsea-clinton-praises-haiti-relief-effort/.

93. Jonathan M. Katz, "The Clintons' Haiti Screw-Up, as Told by Hillary's Emails," *Politico Magazine*, September 2, 2015, http://www.politico.com/magazine/story/2015/09/hillary-clinton-email-213110.

94. Klara Glowczewska, "T&C Philanthropy 2015, with Activist-in-Chief Bill Clinton," *Town and Country* magazine, April 7, 2015, http://www.townandcountrymag.com/society/money-and-power/news/a2977/tc-may-cover-star-bill-clinton/.

95. "Chelsea Clinton Thanks Denis O'Brien for His 'Tireless Leadership' in Haiti," YouTube video, 0:36, posted by Dave Jones, September 28, 2015, https://www.youtube.com/watch?v=3g28W7o RMkU&feature=youtu.be.

96. Schweizer, *Clinton Cash*, 167–68.

97. Julie Lévesque, "Haiti: Humanitarian Aid for Earthquake Victims Used to Build Five Star Hotels," Global Research, June 28, 2012, http://www.globalresearch.ca/haiti-humanitarian-aid-for-earthquake-victims-used-to-build-five-star-hotels/31646.

98. Jacqueline Charles, "Bill Clinton Named Special Envoy to Haiti," *Miami Herald*, May 19, 2009, http://www.mcclatchydc.com/news/nation-world/world/article24538804.html.

99. "Text of the Assessing Progress in Haiti Act of 2014," GovTrack.us, signed by President Obama on August 8, 2014, https://www.govtrack.us/congress/bills/113/s1104/text.

100. *Final Report of the Independent Panel of Experts on the Cholera Outbreak in Haiti*, accessed March 29, 2016, http://www.un.org/News/dh/infocus/haiti/UN-cholera-report-final.pdf. See also Richard Knox, "Verdict: Haiti's Cholera Outbreak Originated in U.N. Camp," *Shots* (NPR health blog), May 6, 2011, http://www.npr.org/blogs/health/2011/05/06/136049974/verdict-haitis-cholera-outbreak-originated-in-u-n-camp.

101. Richard Knox, "5 Years After Haiti's Earthquake, Where Did the $13.5 Billion Go?" *Goats and Soda* (NPR blog), January 13, 2015, http://www.npr.org/sections/goatsandsoda/2015/01/12/376138864/5-years-after-haiti-s-earthquake-why-aren-t-things-better.

102. Jacqueline Charles, "Rebuilding Haiti: Still a Work in Progress," *Miami Herald*, January 11, 2015, http://www.miamiherald.com/news/nation-world/world/americas/haiti/article6031617.html.

103. Tracy Connor, Hannah Rappleye, and Erika Angulo, "What Does Haiti Have to Show for $13 Billion in Earthquake Aid?" NBC News, January 12, 2015, http://www.nbcnews.com/news/investigations/what-does-haiti-have-show-13-billion-earthquake-aid-n281661.

104. Jake Johnston, "Is USAID Helping Haiti to Recover, or US Contractors to Make Millions?" *Nation*, January 21, 2015, http://www.thenation.com/article/usaid-helping-haiti-recover-or-us-contractors-make-millions/.

105. *Unlocking Human Potential: Clinton Foundation 2013–2014 Annual Report*, ClintonFoundation.org, https://www.clintonfoundation.org/sites/default/files/clinton_foundation_annual_report_2014.pdf, 38–39.

CHAPTER 8: THE INDIA SCAM

1. Kris Hudson, "Survivor Stands on Verge of a Grand New Expansion," *Wall Street Journal*, August 30, 2010, http://www.wsj.com/news/articles/SB1000142405274870341800457545602369080854.

2. "Bombay Palace, The Culinary Ambassador of India," BombayPalaceNYC.com, http://www.bombaypalacenyc.com/AboutUs.aspx; no longer accessible.

3. Editor, "New York Hotelier Sant Chatwal to Open Boutique Hotels in India," eHotelier.com, May 26, 2005, http://ehotelier.com/news/2005/05/26/new-york-hotelier-sant-chatwal-to-open-boutique-hotels-in-india/.

4. The remaining quotes in this section are from Russ Buettner and Bob Port, "Hillary's Shady Moneyman: Big-Bucks Donor Stiffed Bank–Feds," *New York Daily News*, November 5, 2000, http://www.campaignfinance.org/statehtml/hillarys_shady_moneyman.html.

5. William Sherman, "TAX DEADBEAT IS LIVIN' LARGE: Clinton's Buddy Owes City $2.4 Million," *New York Daily News*, November 24, 2002, http://www.nydailynews.com/archives/news/tax-deadbeat-livin-large-clinton-buddy-owes-city-2-4m-article-1.496489.

6. "Why Is Sant Singh Chatwal Famous?" *Financial Express* (India), February 27, 2005, http://archive.financialexpress.com/news/why-is-sant-singh-chatwal-famous/128020.

7. Kris Hudson, "Survivor Stands on Verge of a Grand New Expansion," *Wall Street Journal*, August 30, 2010.

8. Deborah Schoeneman, "Vikram's Big Fat Sikh Wedding," *New York Magazine*, March 5, 2006, http://nymag.com/relationships/features/16368/.

9. Peter Schweizer, *Clinton Cash: The Untold Story of How and Why Foreign Governments and Businesses Helped Make Bill and Hillary Rich* (New York: HarperCollins, 2015).

10. Megha Bahree, "Sant Chatwal: An Indian American Hotelier's Fall from Grace," *Forbes*, April 22, 2014, http://www.forbes.com/sites/meghabahree/2014/04/22/sant-chatwal-an-indian-american-hoteliers-falls-from-grace/.

11. Stephanie Clifford and Russ Buettner, "Clinton Backer Pleads Guilty in a Straw Donor Scheme," *New York Times*, April 17, 2014, http://www.nytimes.com/2014/04/18/nyregion/clinton-backer-pleads-guilty-in-a-straw-donor-scheme.html?_r=1.

12. Stephanie Clifford, "Hotelier Avoids Prison for Violating Campaign Finance Laws," *New York Times*, December 18, 2014, http://www.nytimes.com/2014/12/19/nyregion/hotelier-avoids-prison-for-violating-campaign-finance-laws.html?_r=0.

13. Peter Baker, "Arab states and business moguls are big donors to Clinton Charity," *New York Times*, December 18, 2008, http://www.nytimes.com/2008/12/18/world/americas/18iht-19clinton.18792562.html?pagewanted=all&_r=1.

14. Sharat Pradhan, "Clinton's Day Out in Lucknow," Rediff *India Abroad*, September 9, 2005, http://www.rediff.com/news/2005/sep/08spec.htm.

15. Ibid.

16. Deroy Murdock, "Clinton's Shady Pals: Not Quite 'Everyday' Americans," *New York Post*, June 12, 2015, http://nypost.com/2015/06/12/clintons-shady-pals-not-quite-everyday-americans/.

17. Geoff Earle and Carl Campanile, "'Clinton Cash' Questions India Politician's $5M Donation," *New York Post*, April 28, 2015, http://nypost.com/2015/04/28/clinton-cash-questions-india-politicians-5m-donation/.

18. Dinesh Sharma, "All Politics Is Global: A Tale of the Turban Cowboy, Amar Singh, Clinton Global Initiative and the Indian Nukes Deal," *Asia Times*, May 9, 2015, http://atimes.com/2015/05/all-politics-is-global-a-tale-of-the-turban-cowboy-amar-singh-clinton-global-initiative-and-the-indian-nukes-deal/.

19. Ghaziabad, "Amar Singh Says Will Retire from Politics after Elections," *Indian Express*, May 11, 2008, http://archive.indianexpress.com/news/amar-singh-says-will-retire-from-politics-after-elections/457565/.

20. Gargi Parsai, "Amar Singh Quits All Party Posts," *Hindu*, January 7, 2010, http://www.thehindu.com/todays-paper/article678974.ece.

21. "Amar, Jaya Expelled from SP," *Times of India*, February 2, 2010, http://timesofindia.indiatimes.com/india/Amar-Jaya-expelled-from-SP/articleshow/5527183.cms.

22. Indrani Basu and Neeraj Chauhan, "Jail No Bar, 'VIP Prisoner' Amar Singh Lives King-Size in Tihar," *Times of India*, September 12, 2011, http://timesofindia.indiatimes.com/india/Jail-no-bar-VIP-prisoner-Amar-Singh-lives-life-king-size-in-Tihar/articleshow/9950688.cms.

23. "Amar Singh Granted Bail by High Court," *Hindu*, October 25, 2011, http://www.thehindu.com/news/national/amar-singh-granted-bail-by-high-court/article2567244.ece.

24. Nistulia Hebbar, "Amar Singh Denies Donating Money to Clinton Foundation," *Economic Times*, April 29, 2015, http://articles.economictimes.indiatimes.com/2015-04-29/news/61652605_1_amar-singh-former-samajwadi-party-donation.

25. "Amar Singh Makes Huge Donation to Clinton Foundation," *Times of India*, December 19, 2008, http://timesofindia.indiatimes.com/india/Amar-Singh-makes-huge-donation-to-Clinton-Foundation/articleshow/3864349.cms.

26. "Hillary Clinton (D-Punjab)'s Personal Financial and Political Ties to India," no author, no date, archived by the *New York Times* at http://graphics8.nytimes.com/packages/pdf/politics/memo1.pdf, 1. Attributed to the 2008 presidential campaign of Sen. Barack Obama.

27. Rediff News Bureau, "Obama Camp Attacks Hillary's Indian Links," *India Abroad*, June 15, 2007, http://www.rediff.com/news/2007/jun/15clinton.htm.

28. Aziz Haniffa, "Sikhs Throw Weight, Wallets behind Sen. Clinton," *India Abroad*, March 17, 2006, https://www.highbeam.com/doc/1P1-122206413.html.

29. "Hillary Clinton (D-Punjab)'s Personal Financial and Political Ties to India," 1–2.

30. Ibid., 1.

31. Jennifer Epstein, "Bill Clinton's Shell (Company) Game," Bloomberg Politics, May 27, 2015, http://www.bloomberg.com/politics/articles/2015-05-27/bill-clinton-s-shell-company-game.

32. Phillip Bump, "'Dead Broke': A Deep Dive into the Clintons' Finances," *Washington Post*, June 12, 2014, https://www.washingtonpost.com/news/the-fix/wp/2014/06/12/dead-broke-a-deep-dive-into-the-clintons-finances/.

33. Patrick Healy, "To Avoid Conflicts, Clintons Liquidate Holdings," *New York Times*, June 15, 2007, http://www.nytimes.com/2007/06/15/us/politics/15clintons.html?pagewanted=2&ei=5088&en=02b5bf8e901baebf&ex=1339560000&partner=rssnyt&emc=rss.

34. Matea Gold, Tom Hamburger, and Anu Narayanswamy, "Two Clintons. 41 Years. $3 Billion," *Washington Post*, November 19, 2015, https://www.washingtonpost.com/graphics/politics/clinton-money/?hpid=hp_hp-top-table-low_clintondonor_blurb8am%3Ahomepage%2Fstory.

35. Bob Fredericks, "How Foreign Cash Made Bill and Hillary 'Filthy Rich,'" *New York Post*, April 20, 2015, http://nypost.com/2015/04/20/book-claims-foreign-cash-made-bill-and-hillary-filthy-rich/.

36. "Meet the Press Transcript—June 29, 2014," NBC News, http://www.nbcnews.com/meet-the-press/meet-press-transcript-june-29-2014-n143826.

37. Katie Sanders, "Bill Clinton: 'I Had the Lowest Net Worth of Any American President in the 20th Century," Punditfact, June 29, 2014, http://www.politifact.com/punditfact/statements/2014/jun/29/bill-clinton/bill-clinton-i-had-lowest-net-worth-any-american-p/. See also "The Net Worth of the American Presidents: Washington to Obama," 24/7 Wall Street, May 17, 2010, http://247wallst.com/banking-finance/2010/05/17/the-net-worth-of-the-american-presidents-washington-to-obama/.

38. Richard Rubin, "Wealthy Clintons Use Trusts to Limit Estate Tax They Back," Bloomberg Business, June 17, 2014, http://www.bloomberg.com/news/articles/2014-06-17/wealthy-clintons-use-trusts-to-limit-estate-tax-they-back.

39. Richard Esposito et al., "Indicted N.Y. Financier Gave Big to Hillary and Terror Charity," ABC News, October 16, 2009, http://abcnews.go.com/Blotter/raj-rajaratnam-indicted-20-million-insider-trading-case/story?id=8845975.

40. "Billionaire Convicted in Wall Street's Biggest Insider Trader Scandal Is Jailed for 11 Years," *Daily Mail*, October 14, 2011, http://www.dailymail.co.uk/news/article-2048914/Raj-Rajaratnam-convicted-Wall-Streets-biggest-insider-trading-scandal-jailed.html.

41. Esposito et al., "Indicted N.Y. Financier Gave Big to Hillary and Terror Charity."

42. Alana Goodman, "String of Felons Worked with Nonprofit Cofounded by Bill Clinton," *Washington Free Beacon*, November 16, 2015, http://freebeacon.com/politics/string-of-felons-worked-with-nonprofit-cofounded-by-bill-clinton/.

43. Anita Raghavan, "Onetime Allies Rajaratnam and Gupta Have Uneasy Prison Reunion After Insider Trader Trials," *New York Times*, August 2, 2015, http://www.nytimes.com/2015/08/03/business/dealbook/onetime-allies-on-wall-streethave-uneasy-prison-reunion-after-insider-trading-trials.html.

44. Anita Raghavan, *The Billionaire's Apprentice: The Rise of the Indian-American Elite and the Fall of the Galleon Hedge Fund* (New York: Business Plus, 2013), 201.

45. Duff McDonald, *The Firm: The Story of McKinsey and Its Secret Influence on American Business* (New York: Simon & Simon, 2013).

46. Ibid., 311.

47. Ibid., 267.

48. Ibid., 315–16.

49. Ibid., 322.

50. Malcolm Gladwell, "The Talent Myth: Are Smart People Overrated?," *New Yorker*, July 22, 2002, http://www.newyorker.com/magazine/2002/07/22/the-talent-myth.

51. McDonald, *The Firm*, 247.

52. Ibid., 266.

53. John A. Byrne, "Inside McKinsey," Bloomberg, July 7, 2002, http://www.bloomberg.com/bw/stories/2002-07-07/inside-mckinsey.

54. Adil Rustomjee, "The Finally Unanswered Question: Why Did Gupta Do It?" *First Post India*, June 25, 2014, http://www.firstpost.com/world/finally-unanswered-question-rajat-gupta-1588683.html.

55. White House, Office of the Press Secretary, "Expected Attendees at Tonight's State Dinner," WhiteHouse.gov, November 24, 2009, https://www.whitehouse.gov/the-press-office/expected-attendees-tonights-state-dinner.

56. Raghavan, The Billionaire's Apprentice, 202. See also "The Evolution of Chelsea Clinton," *New York* magazine, March 3, 2008, http://nymag.com/news/features/44454/index4.html.

57. McDonald, *The Firm*, 320.

CHAPTER 9: THE "HILLARY FOR PRESIDENT 2016" SCAM

1. "Members of the House Judiciary Committee," Watergate.info, accessed March 30, 2016, http://watergate.info/impeachment/members-of-the-house-judiciary-committee.

2. Mike Klein, "Whirlpool of lies swallows Mezvinsky," Des Moines Register, August 3, 2003, http://crab.rutgers.edu/~mchugh/nigeriamezvinsky.html.

3. "TRUE: Father of the Groom," Snopes.com, last updated May 26, 2015, http://www.snopes.com/politics/clintons/mezvinsky.asp.

4. Rob Copeland, "Hedge Fund Co-Founded by Chelsea Clinton's Husband Suffers Losses Tied to Greece," *Wall Street Journal*, February 3, 2015, http://www.wsj.com/articles/hedge-fund-co-founded-by-chelsea-clintons-husband-suffers-losses-tied-to-greece-1423000325.

5. Andrew Stiles, "Don't Give Your Money to Clinton Son-in-Law Marc Mezvinsky," *Washington Free Beacon*, February 4, 2015, http://freebeacon.com/blog/dont-give-your-money-to-clinton-son-in-law-marc-mezvinsky/.

6. Chuck Ross, "Email: Hillary Sought to Help Millionaire Son-in-Law's Friend with State Department Business Meeting," *Daily Caller*, December 7, 2015, http://dailycaller.com/2015/12/07/email-hillary-sought-to-help-millionaire-son-in-laws-friend-with-state-department-business-meeting/.

7. Sam Frizell and Zeke J. Miller, "Exclusive: Conservative Group Calls for Federal Inquiry into Hillary Clinton Son-in-Law Request," *Time*, December 13, 2015, http://time.com/4147115/hillary-clinton-emails-marc-mezvinsky/.

8. Ibid.

9. "Watchdog Group Calls for Probe of Clinton Relationship with Firm Tied to Son-in-Law," Fox News, December 14, 2015, http://www.foxnews.com/politics/2015/12/14/watchdog-group-reportedly-calls-for-probe-clinton-relationship-with-firm-tied-to-son-in-law.html.

10. Richard Johnson, "Staff quit Clinton Foundation over Chelsea," PageSix, May 18, 2015, http://pagesix.com/2015/05/18/chelsea-sends-clinton-foundation-staff-running/.

11. Dan Merica, "Chelsea Clinton Goes Global on Fundraising Trail," CNN, January 19, 2016, http://www.cnn.com/2016/01/19/politics/chelsea-clinton-london-anna-wintour/.

12. Nikki Schwab, "Chelsea Clinton Will Head to London for $2,700-per-Plate Fundraiser with Anna Wintour," *Daily Mail*, January 20, 2016, http://www.dailymail.co.uk/news/article-3408646/Chelsea-Clinton-head-London-2-700-plate-fundraiser-Anna-Wintour.html.

13. Rosalind Helderman, "Clinton Foundation Says Donations Are on the Rise," *Washington Post*, October 29, 2015, https://www.washingtonpost.com/news/post-politics/wp/2015/10/29/clinton-foundation-says-donations-are-on-the-rise/.

14. Associated Press, "Clinton Opened State Department to Dozens of Corporate Donors, Dem Fundraisers," Fox News, November 30, 2015, http://www.foxnews.com/politics/2015/11/30/clinton-opened-state-department-office-to-dozens-corporate-donors-dem-fundraisers.html.

15. Morgan Chalfant, "Chelsea Clinton Vacations at One of the World's Most Expensive Resorts," *Washington Free Beacon*, January 19, 2016, http://freebeacon.com/politics/chelsea-clinton-vacations-at-one-of-the-worlds-most-expensive-resorts/.

16. Snejana Farberov, "Pictured: Pregnant Chelsea Clinton Takes a Break from Campaign Trail for a Stay at One of Turks and Caicos' Priciest Resorts Where Villas Cost up to $34,000 a Night," *Daily Mail*, January 19, 2016, http://www.dailymail.co.uk/news/article-3405230/Pictured-Pregnant-Chelsea-Clinton-takes-break-campaign-trail-stay-one-Turks-Caicos-priciest-resorts-villas-cost-1-500-34-000-night.html.

17. Michelle Cottle, "Chelsea Clinton Grows Up," *Atlantic*, January 19, 2016, http://www.theatlantic.com/politics/archive/2016/01/chelsea-clinton-bernie-sanders/424623/.

18. Tom S. Elliott, "Hillary: 'No One Is Too Big to Jail,'" *National Review*, January 17, 2016, http://www.nationalreview.com/corner/429910/hillary-no-one-too-big-jail.

19. Gabby Morrongiello, "Clinton's 'No Individual Too Big to jail' tweet backfires . . . Hard," *Washington Examiner*, January 17, 2016, http://www.washingtonexaminer.com/clintons-no-individual-too-big-to-jail-tweet-backfires/article/2580775.

20. Thomas Lifson, "Hillary's Subconscious Acts Up in Dem Debate, Provides 6 Words That Will Haunt Her," *American Thinker*, January 18, 2016, http://www.americanthinker.com/blog/2016/01/hillarys_subconscious_acts_up_in_dem_debate_provides_6_words_that_will_haunt_her.html.

21. Tim Malloy and Rubenstein Associates, Inc., "Biden Runs Better than Clinton against Top Republicans, Quinnipiac University National Poll Finds; Trump GOP Lead Grows as Clinton Dem Lead Shrinks," press release, Quinnipiac University, August 27, 2015, http://www.quinnipiac.edu/images/polling/us/us08272015_Ueg38d.pdf.

22. Fox News Poll, interviews conducted August 11–13, 2015, released August 14, 2015, http://www.foxnews.com/politics/interactive/2015/08/14/fox-news-poll-iran-deal-and-clinton-emails/; no longer accessible.

23. Tim Malloy and Rubenstein Associates, Inc., "Half of US Voters Embarrassed with Trump as President, Quinnipiac University National Poll Finds; Trump at Top of GOP Pack, But Cruz Closes In," press release, Quinnipiac University, December 22, 2015, https://www.quinnipiac.edu/images/polling/us/us12222015_Uhkm63g.pdf.

24. Roger Stone and Robert Morrow, *The Clintons' War on Women* (New York: Skyhorse, 2015).

25. Robert Wilde, "Roger Stone: 'Pets Killed, Tires Slashed, Late Night Phone Calls' to Silence Bill Clinton's Sexual Assault Victims," Breitbart, September 27, 2015, http://www.breitbart.com/big-government/2015/09/27/roger-stone-pets-killed-tires-slashed-late-night-phone-calls-to-silence-bill-clintons-sexual-assault-victims/.

26. Ibid.

27. Stone and Morrow, "The Clintons' War on Women," 29.

28. Robert Kraychik, "WATCH: Hillary Asked Whether She Believes Bill's Sexual Assault Accusers," *Daily Wire*, December 3, 2015, http://www.dailywire.com/news/1583/video-clinton-asked-about-her-husbands-rapesexual-robert-kraychik.

29. Gabriel Debenedetti, "Heckler Confronts Hillary Clinton over Bill Clinton's Conduct," Politico, January 3, 2016, http://www.politico.com/story/2016/01/heckler-confronts-hillary-clinton-over-bill-clintons-conduct-217308.

30. Doyle McManus, "Column: Sadly, Trump Is Right in This Case: Bill Clinton Is Fair Game," *Los Angeles Times*, January 13, 2016, http://www.latimes.com/opinion/op-ed/la-oe-0113-mcmanus-bill-clinton-fair-game-20160113-column.html.

31. Press Release, "Judicial Watch: Email Reveals Top Aide Huma Abedin Warning State Department Staffer that Hillary Clinton Is 'Often Confused,'" Judicial Watch, November 16, 2015, http://www.judicialwatch.org/press-room/press-releases/judicial-watch-email-reveals-top-aide-huma-abedin-warning-state-department-staffer-that-hillary-clinton-is-often-confused/.

32. Mary Bruce, "Hillary Clinton Took 6 Months to 'Get Over' Concussion, Bill Says of Timeline," ABC News, May 14, 2014, http://abcnews.go.com/blogs/politics/2014/05/hillary-clinton-took-6-months-to-get-over-concussion-bill-says-of-timeline/.

33. Mark Mazzetti and Michael R. Gordon, "Clinton Is Recovering from a Concussion," *New York Times*, December 15, 2012, http://www.nytimes.com/2012/12/16/us/politics/hillary-clinton-concussion.html.

34. Dana Hughes and Dan Childs, "Hillary Clinton's Glasses Are for Concussion, Not Fashion," ABC News, January 25, 2013, http://abcnews.go.com/Politics/hillary-clintons-glasses-concussion-fashion/story?id=18313426.

35. Tina Moore, "Seeing Double: Clinton Spokesperson Confirms Daily News Analysis That Secretary of State Is Wearing Glasses to Correct Vision Problems after Concussion and Blood Clot," *New York Daily News*, January 24, 2013, http://www.nydailynews.com/news/national/hillary-double-mrs-clinton-specs-hint-impairment-article-1.1247375.

36. Ed Klein, "Hillary Clinton's Health Is an Issue," NewsMax, December 15, 2015, http://www.newsmax.com/Headline/Ed-Klein-Hillary-Clinton-Health-Issue/2015/12/15/id/705847/.

37. Edwin O'Connor, *The Last Hurrah* (New York: Little, Brown, 1956).

38. Philip Bump, "In 2016, We Could Elect the Second-Oldest President—or the Third-Youngest," *Washington Post*, April 22, 2015, https://www.washingtonpost.com/news/the-fix/wp/2015/04/22/in-2016-we-could-elect-the-second-oldest-president-or-the-third-youngest/.

CHAPTER 10: THE PLAN TO SHUT DOWN THE CLINTON FOUNDATION

1. For my more complete analysis of the 2012 presidential election, see: Jerome R. Corsi, *What Went Wrong: The Inside Story of the GOP Debacle of 2012 . . . And How It Can Be Avoided Next Time* (Washington, DC: WND Books, 2013).

2. Charles Ortel, "False Philanthropy?" First Interim Report Concerning Public Disclosures of the Bill, Hillary, and Chelsea Clinton Foundation," CharlesOrtel.com, http://charlesortel.com, April 20, 2015, https://phaven-prod.s3.amazonaws.com/files/document_part/asset/1415940/urnZzpSpSWlQ3OQRKOXI_UNI-u4/First_Interim_Report_Clinton_Foundation__Charles_Ortel_.pdf.

3. Charles Ortel, "False Philanthropy?" Second Interim Report Concerning Public Disclosures of the Bill, Hillary, and Chelsea Clinton Foundation," CharlesOrtel.com, http://charlesortel.com, September 8, 2015, https://phaven-prod.s3.amazonaws.com/files/document_part/asset/1556725/s4dUYTpsSqmLI_05SWxZJK_CJyg/False_Philanthropy_2.pdf.

4. See "10 Predictions For the Clinton Foundation in 2016" on the website of Charles Ortel, accessed March 30, 2016, http://charlesortel.com/10-predictions-for-the-clinton-foundation-in-2016.

INDEX